Celtic Guitar Treasures

El McMeen

The guitar pictured on the cover is the
"El McMeen Signature Model" guitar
built by Nick Kukich of the Franklin Guitar Company.

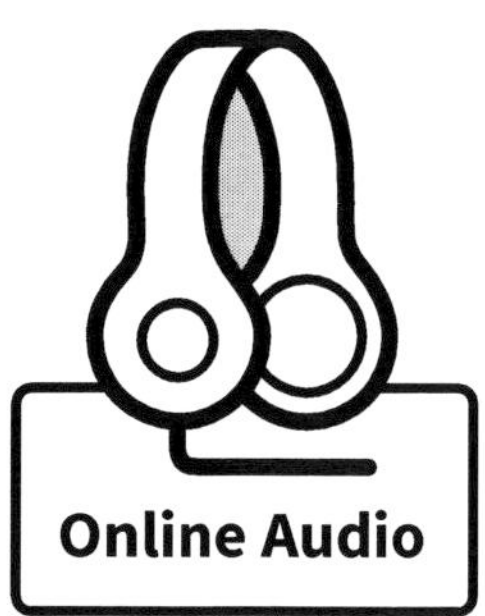

To access the online audio recording go to:

WWW.MELBAY.COM/30765MEB

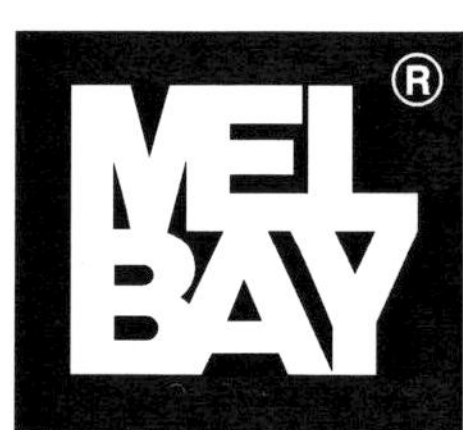

WWW.MELBAY.COM

Preface

Celtic music, broadly defined, changed my life. The songs, dance tunes, and instrumental airs did more than simply engross me; they transported me to another emotional place - in the same way that spiritual music can. In rendering this music, I try to sing through the guitar if not along with it.

The arrangements are in the evocative and accessible tuning of CGDGAD, bass to treble. A chord chart is provided for the convenience of the reader.

While the tab/music thoroughly presents each tune, the recorded versions of these tunes do not match the tab/music note-for-note. Many guitarists tend to learn the pieces, memorize and internalize them, and experiment with capo positions. They proceed to express the music in different ways at different times as felt in the moment. Such was the case for me. (In addition, Castle of Dromore was recorded on a high-strung guitar.)

Thanks to Mel Bay Publications for allowing me to present some of my favorite Celtic tunes to guitar players throughout the world.

El McMeen
Sparta, NJ
www.elmcmeen.com

Contents

The Music

The "Low C" Chord Chart

For Guitars Tuned to CGDGAD

by Jon Elion, Chris Heard, Mark Hanson, and El McMeen

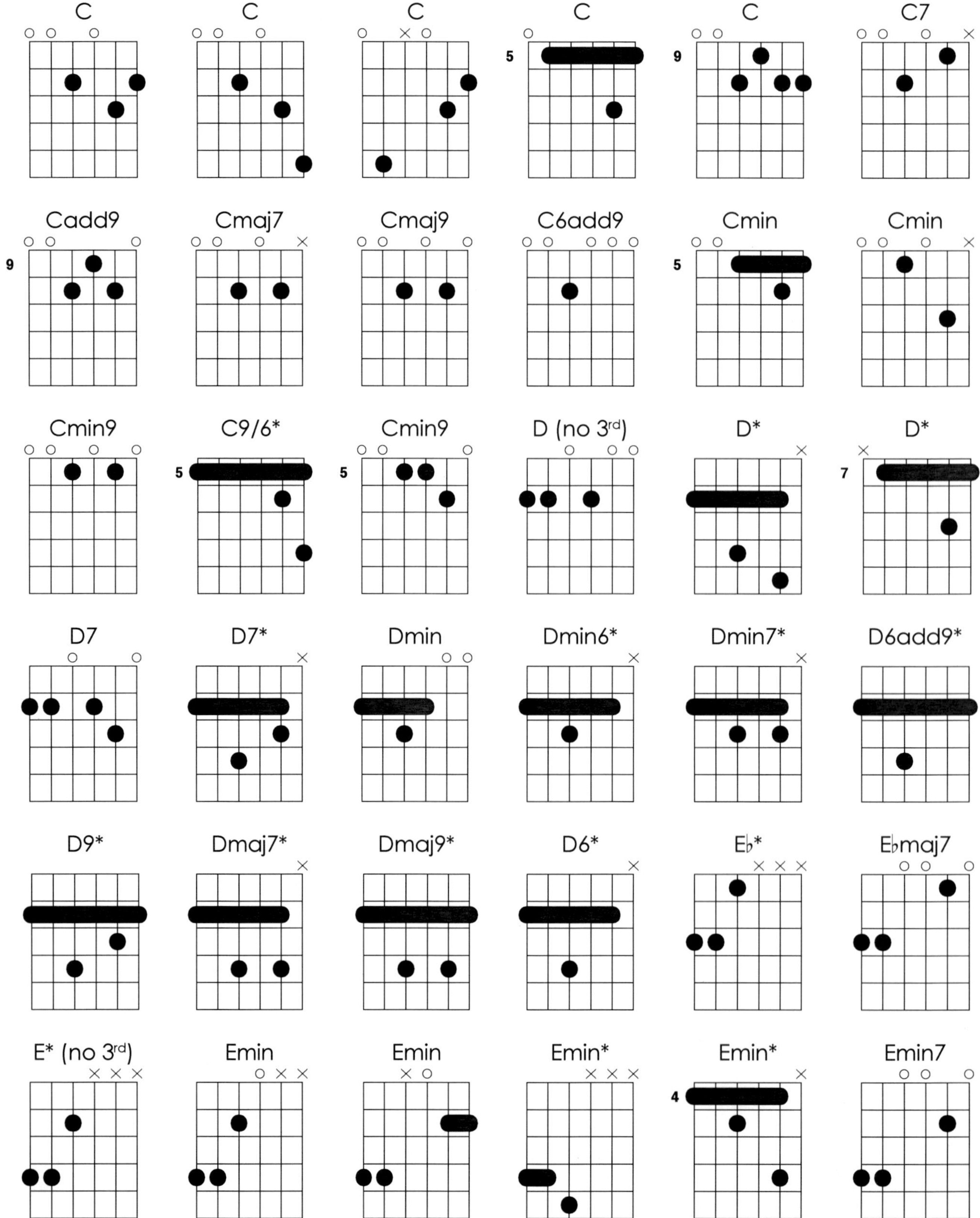

* denotes a chord that can be moved to different positions on the neck

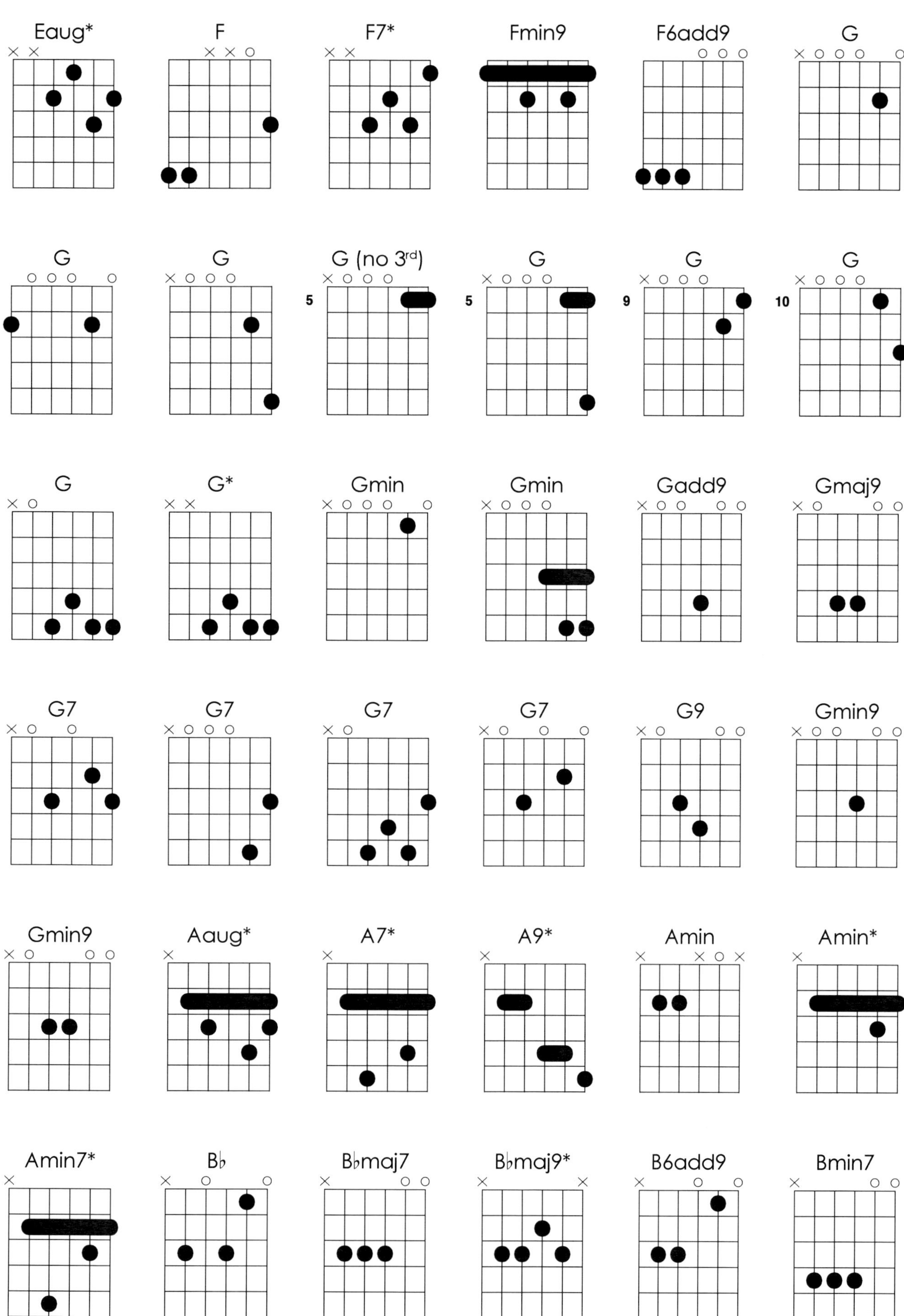

* denotes a chord that can be moved to different positions on the neck

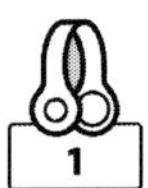

Carolan's Concerto

(T. O'Carolan)

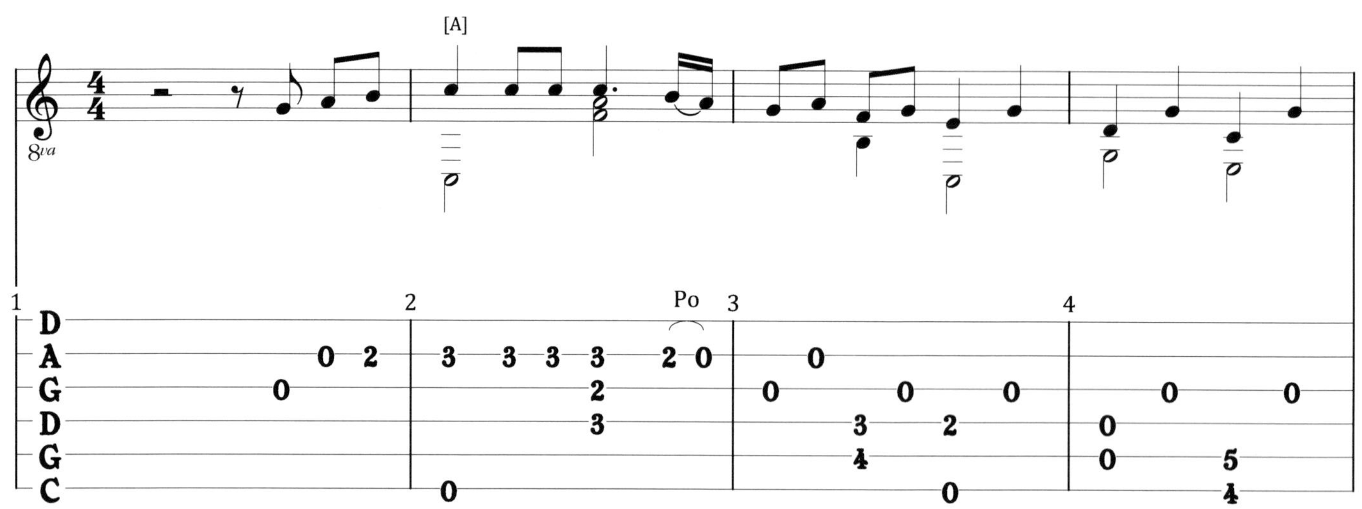

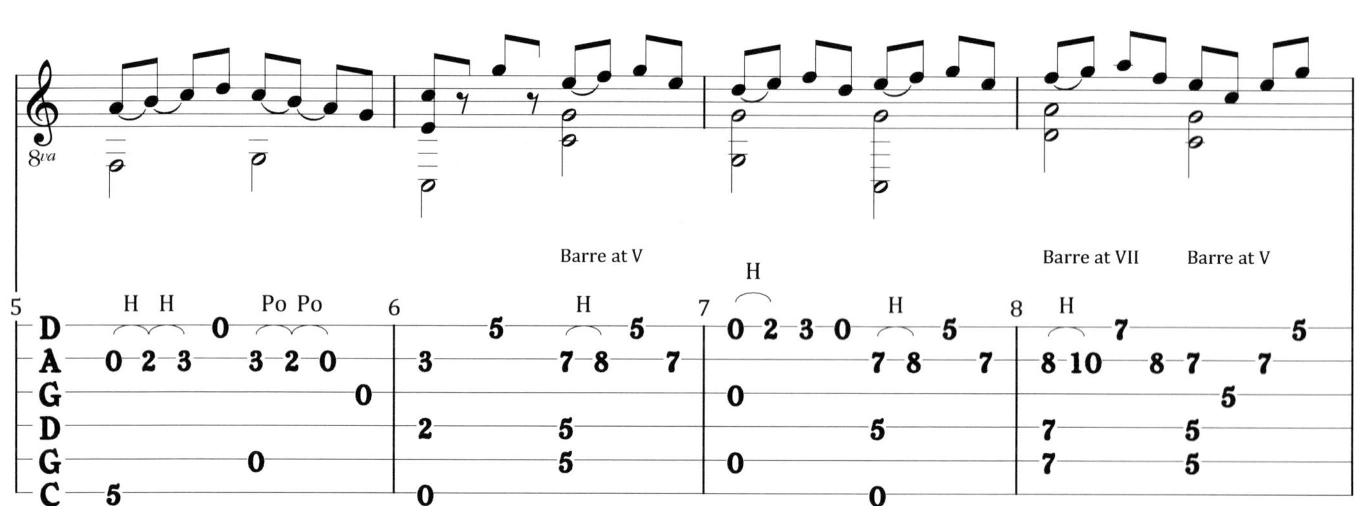

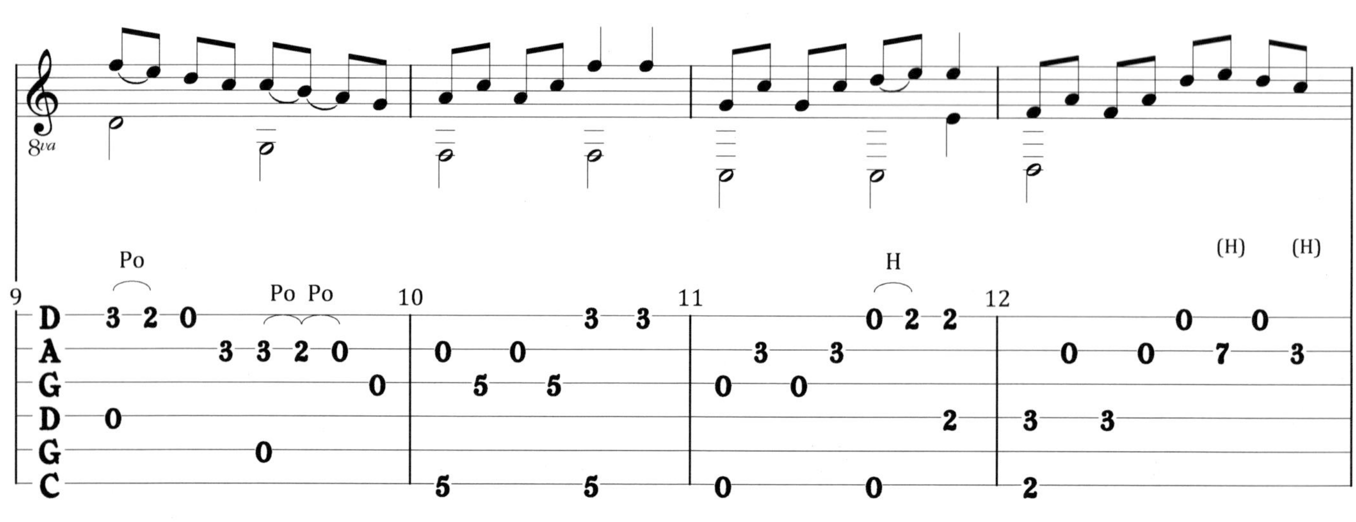

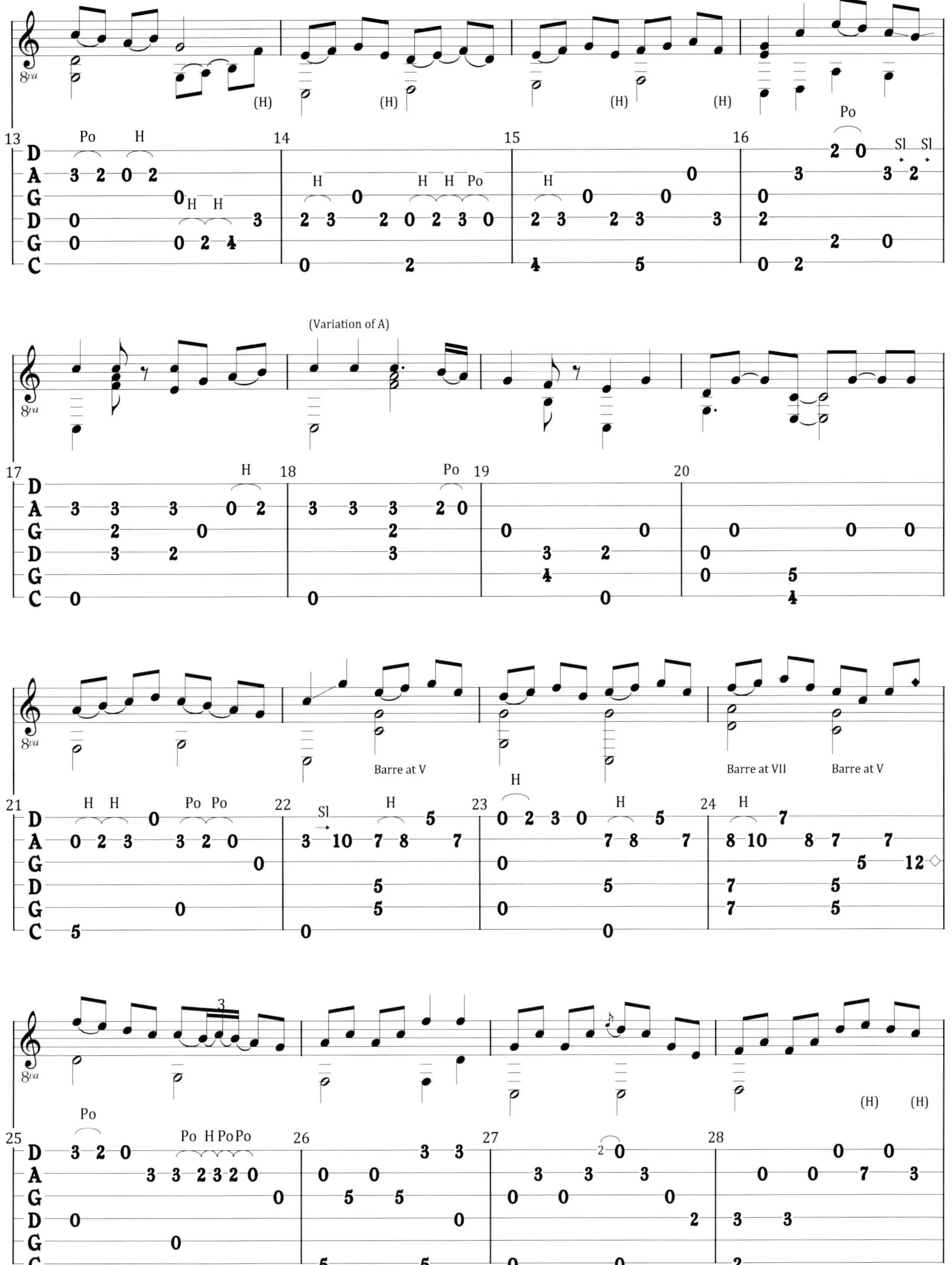
(Variation of A)
Barre at V
Barre at VII
Barre at V

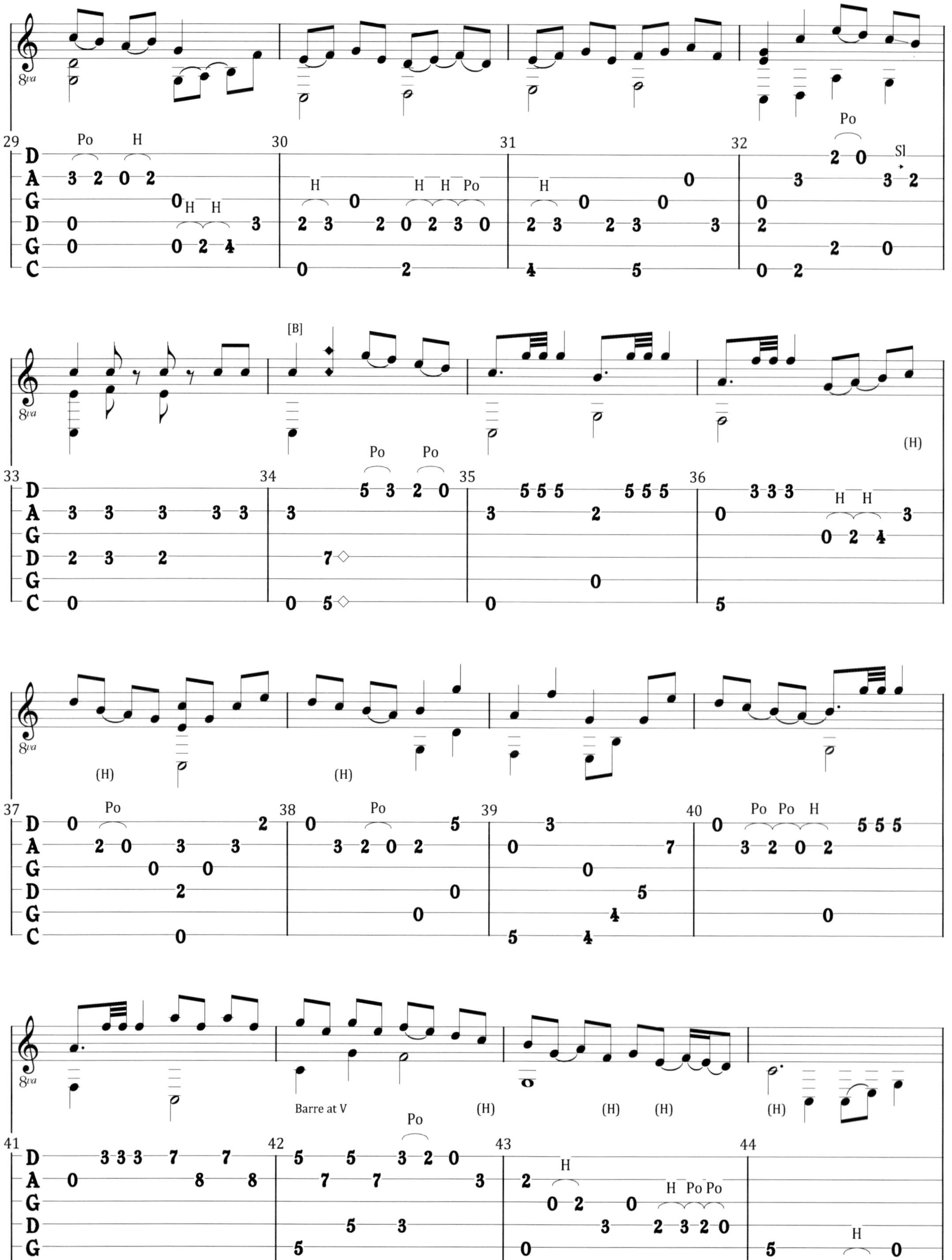

[B]
Barre at V

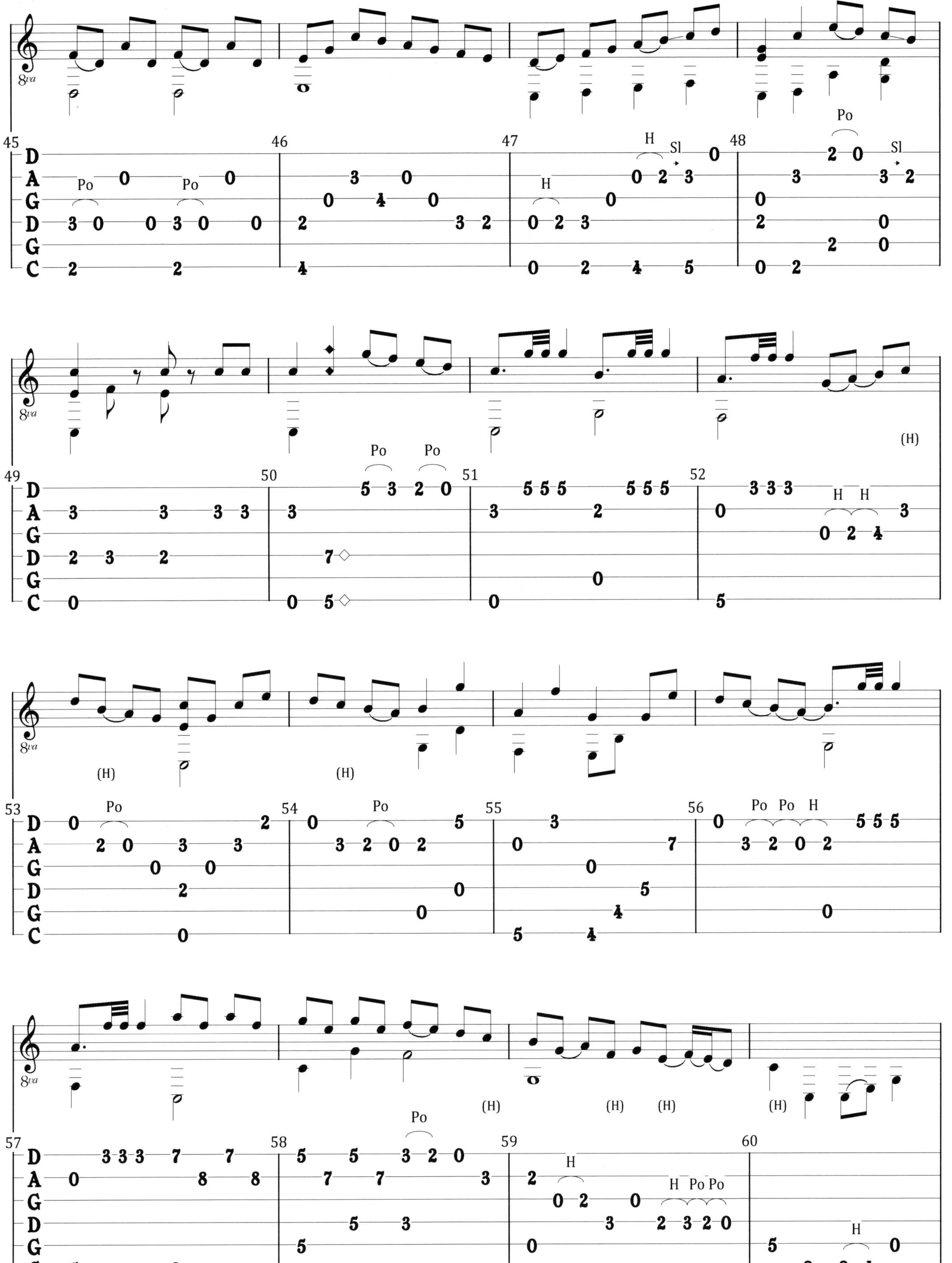

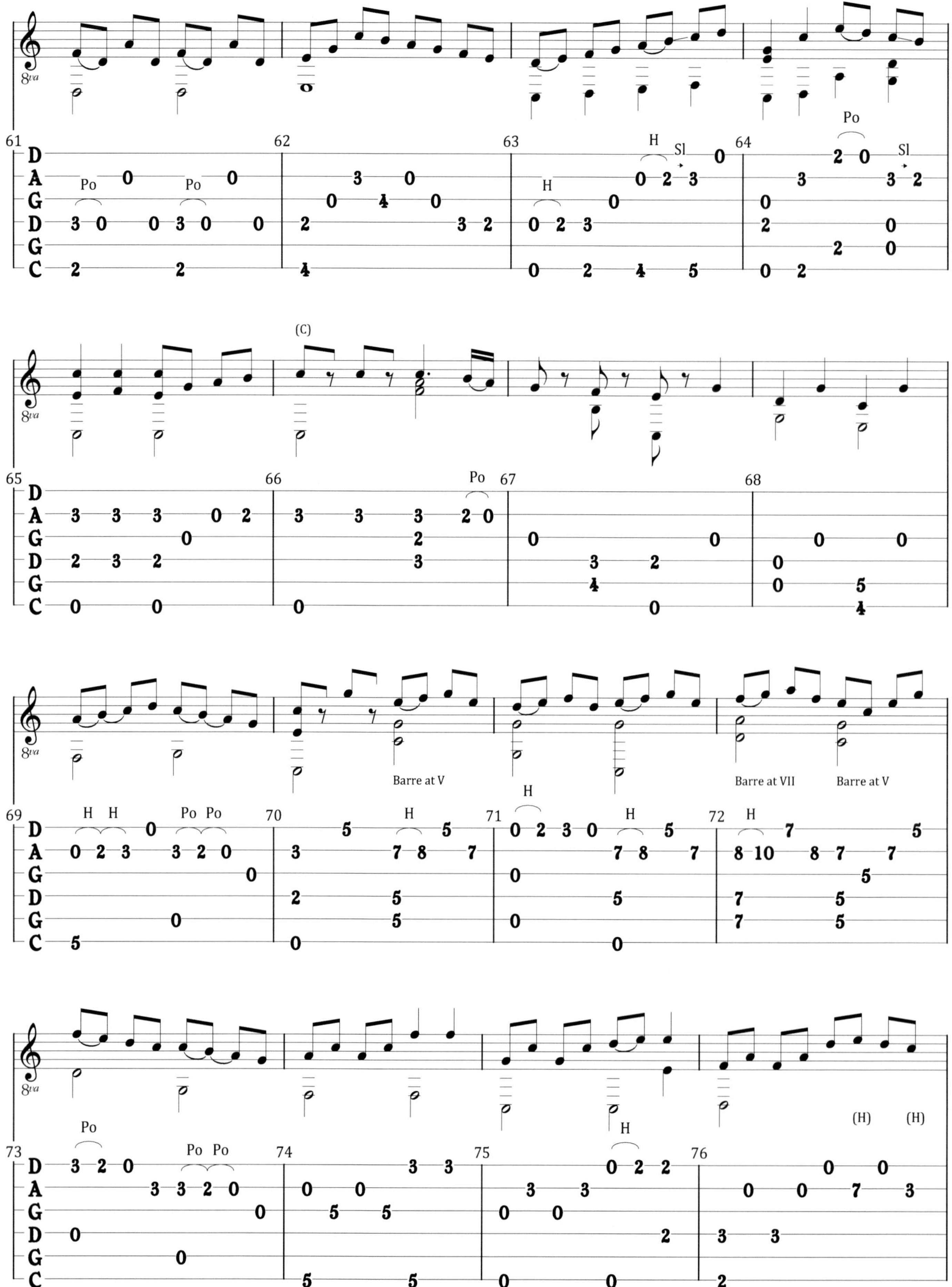

8va
(C)
Barre at V
Barre at VII
Barre at V
Po
H
Sl
(H)
D
A
G
D
G
C

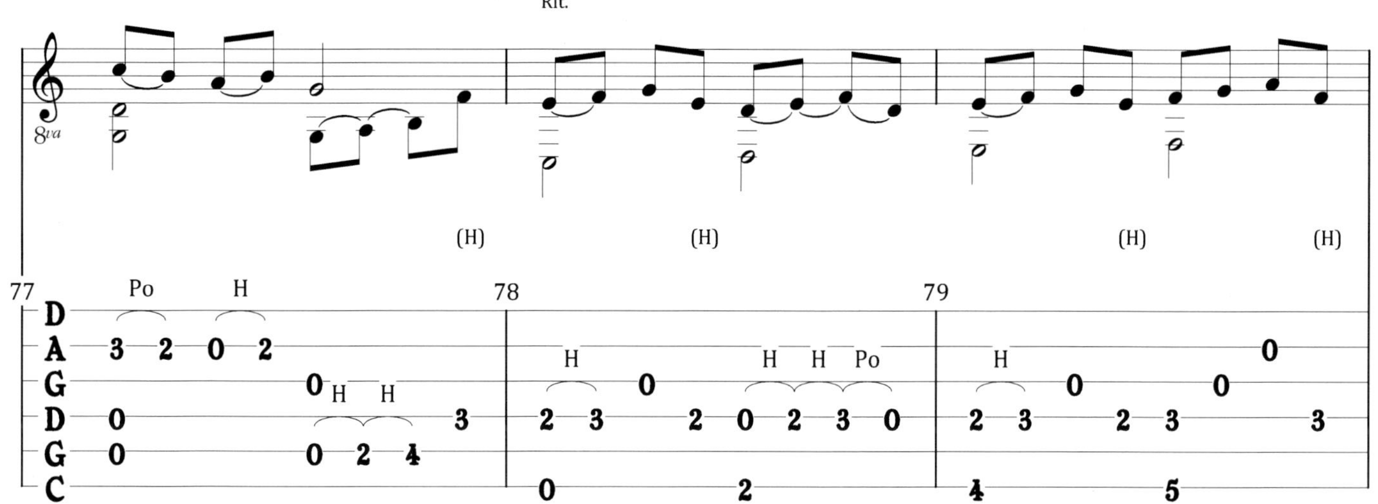
Rit.
8va
(H)
(H)
(H)
(H)
77
Po
H
H
H
78
H
H
H
Po
79
H
D
A
G
D
G
C

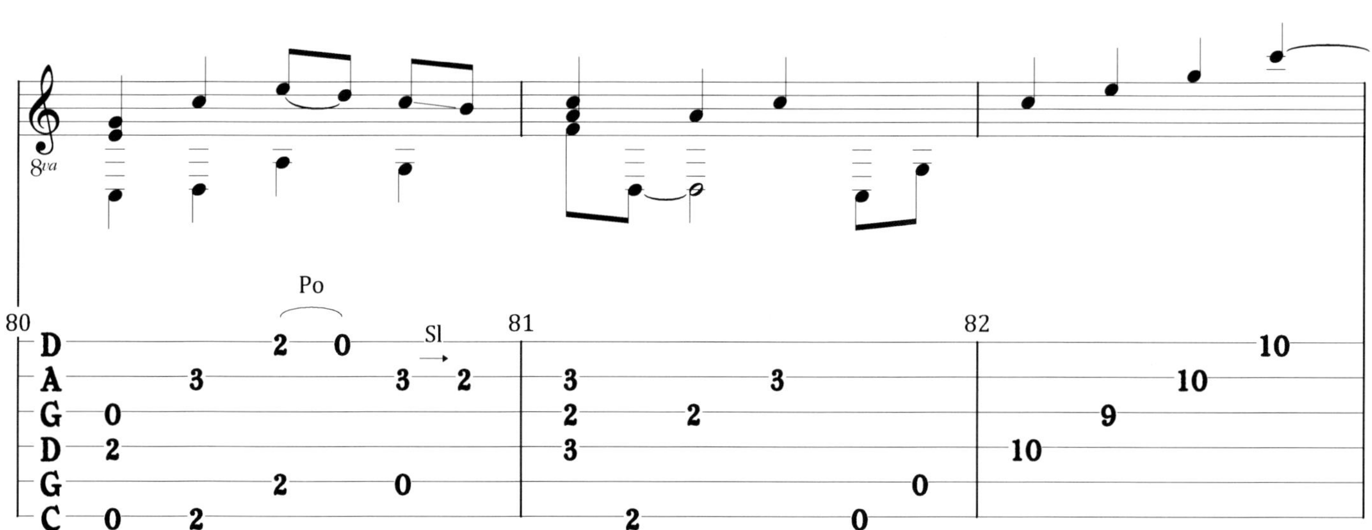
8va
80
Po
Sl
81
82
D
A
G
D
G
C

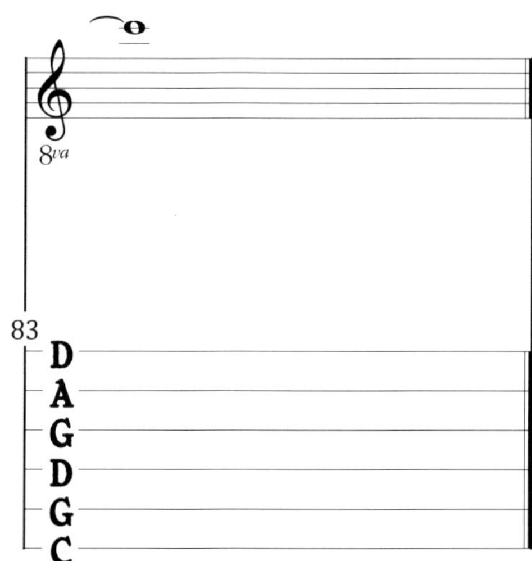
8va
83
D
A
G
D
G
C

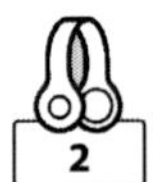

When You and I Were Young, Maggie

(Johnson; Butterfield)

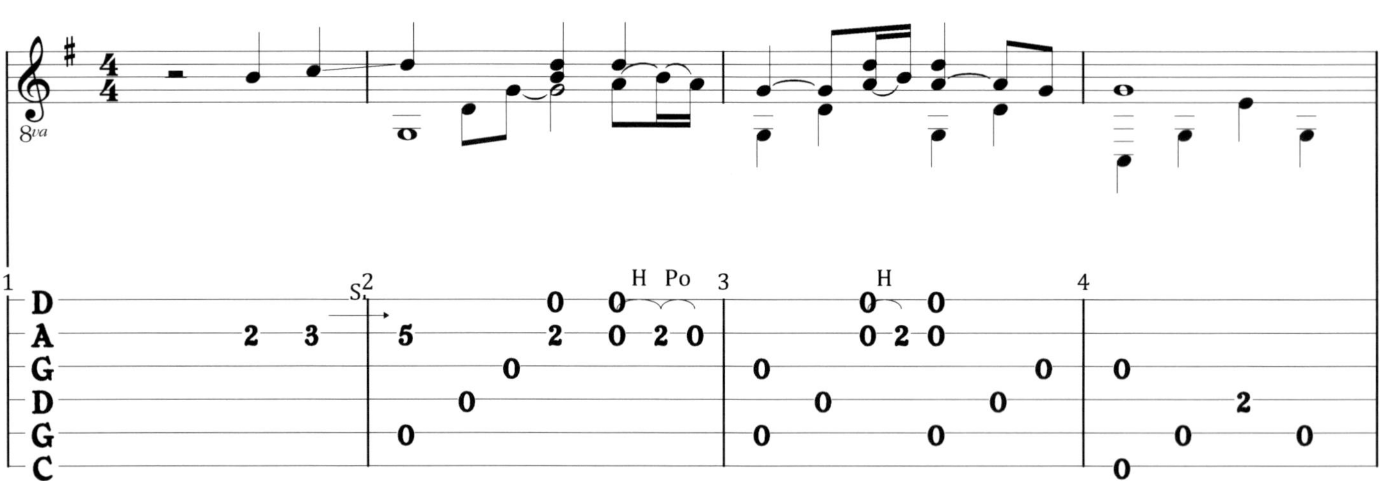

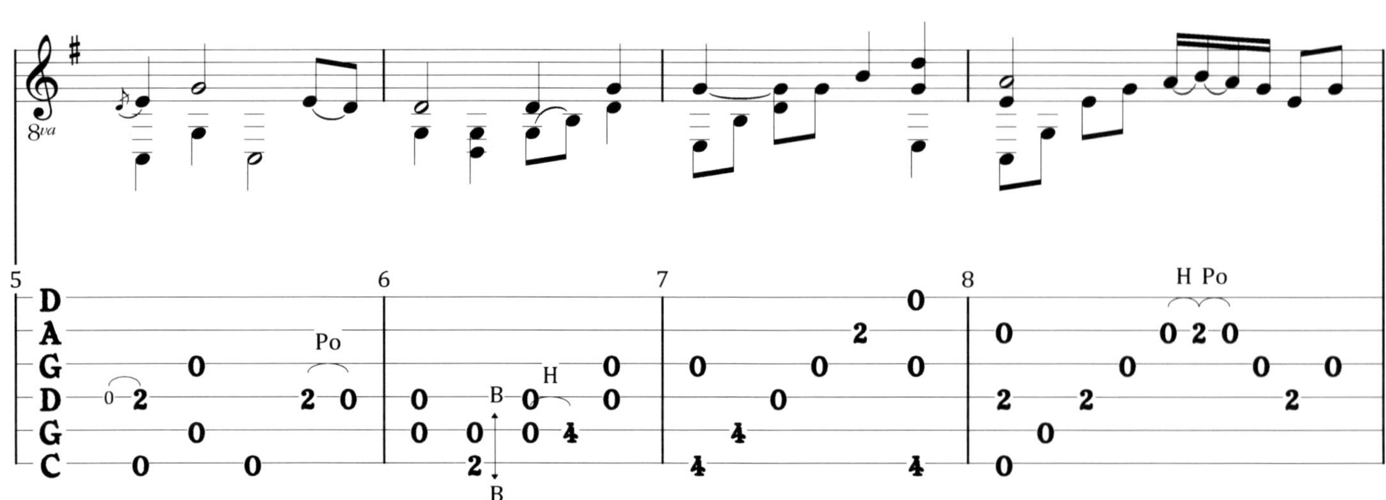

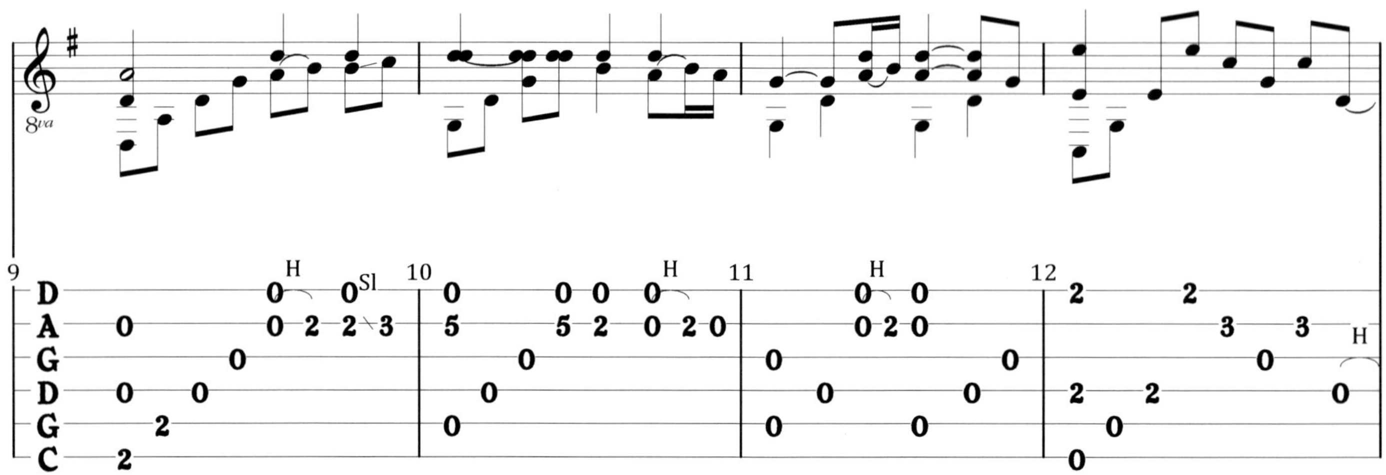

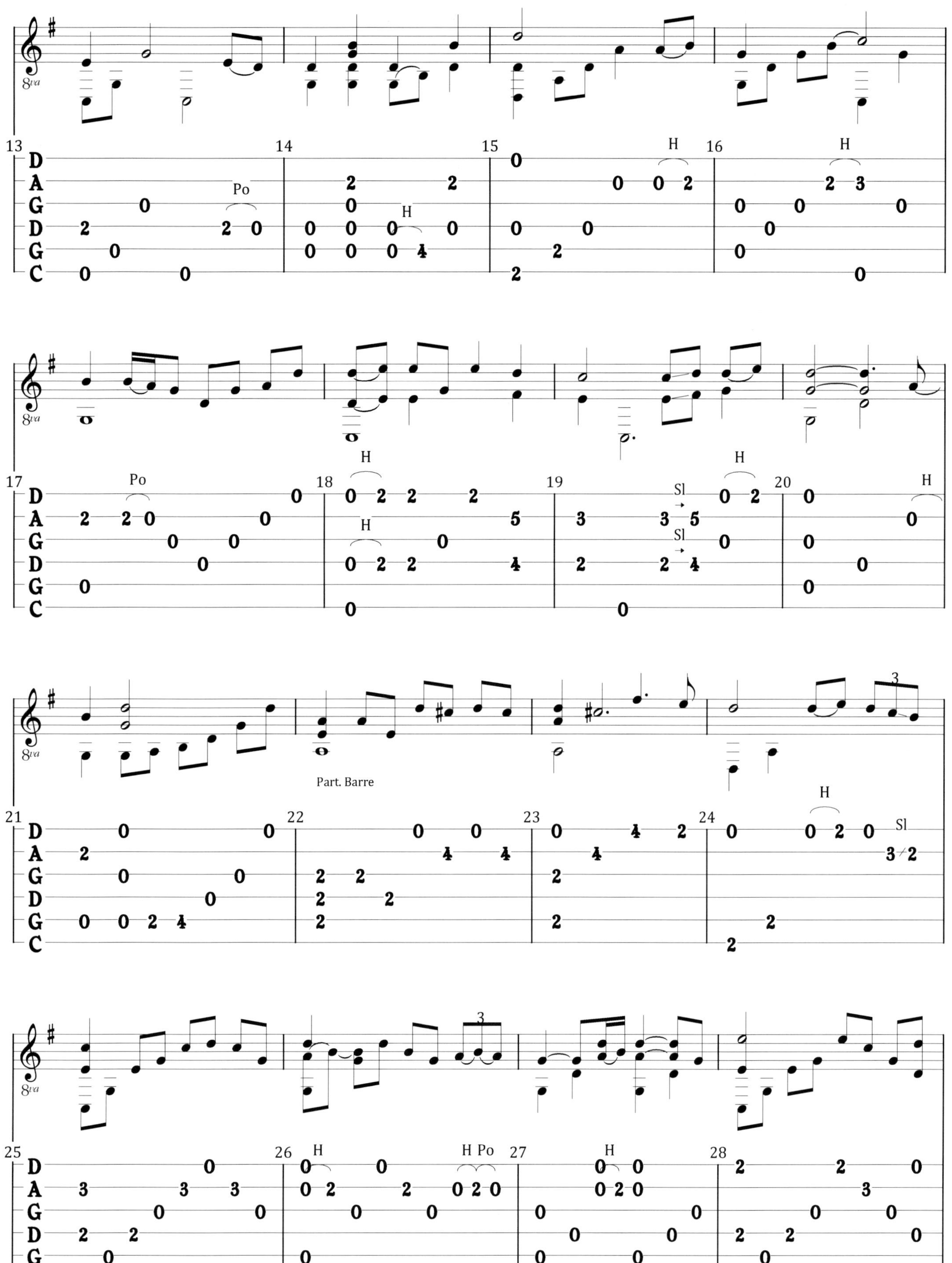
8va
Part. Barre

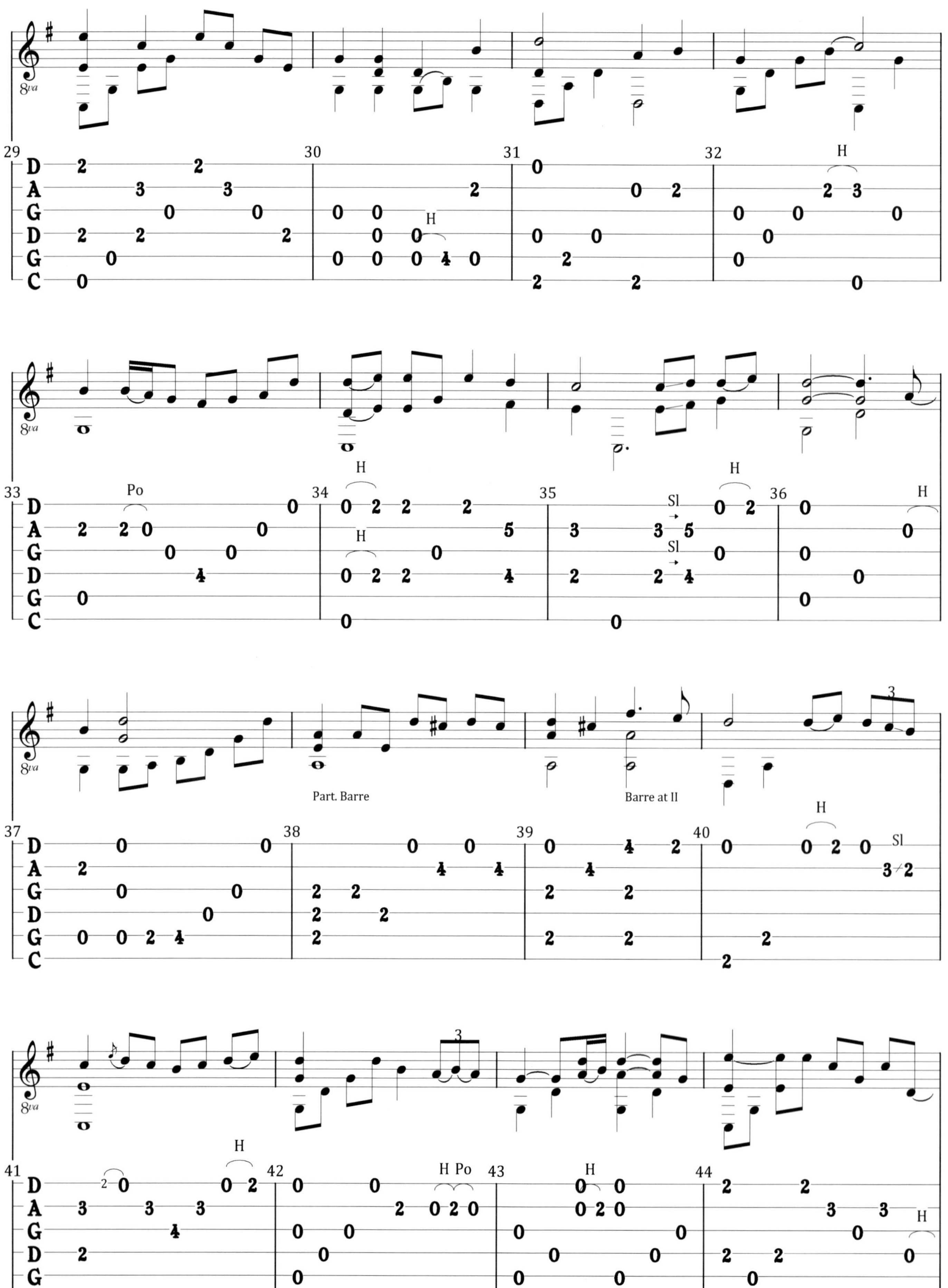
8va
29
30
31
32
33
34
35
36
37
38
39
40
41
42
43
44
D
A
G
D
G
C
H
Po
Sl
Part. Barre
Barre at II

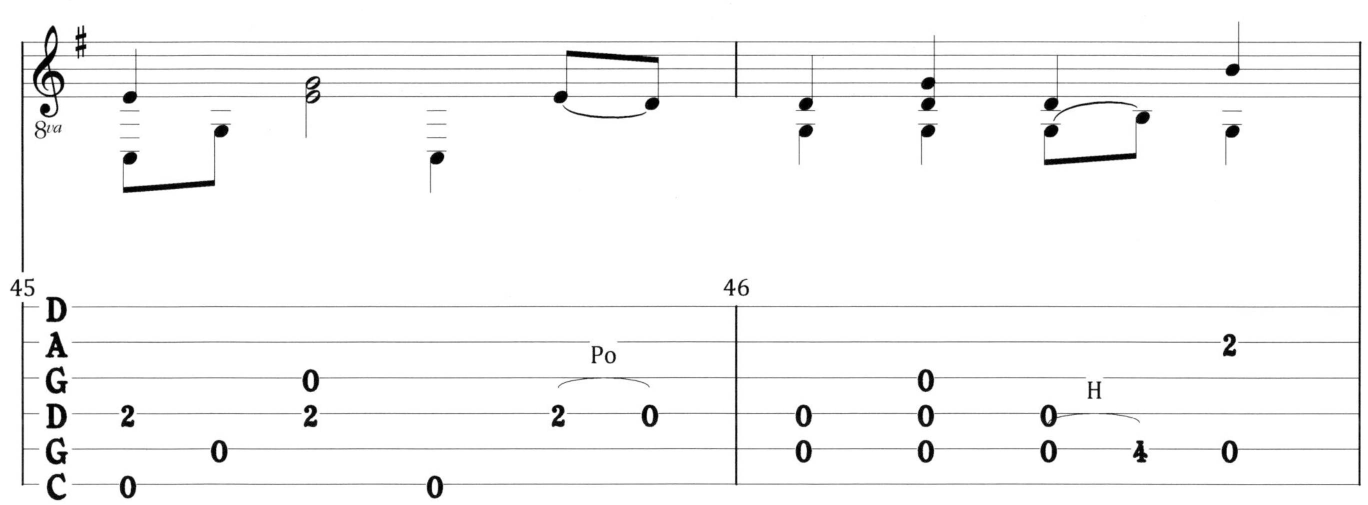

8va
45
46
D
A
G
D
G
C
Po
H

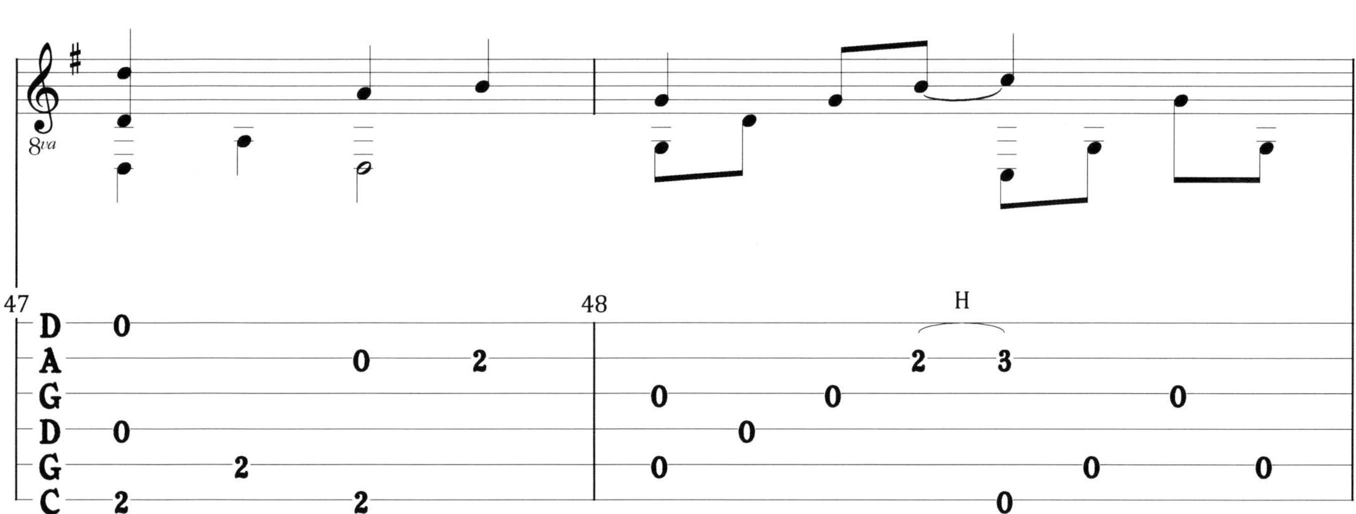

8va
47
48
D
A
G
D
G
C
H

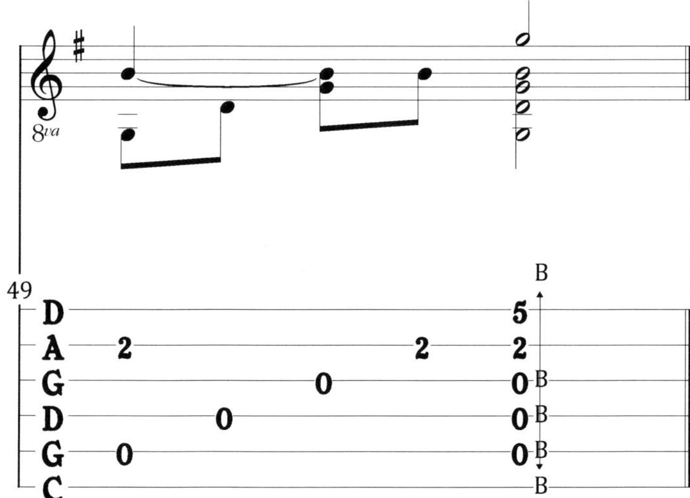

8va
49
D
A
G
D
G
C
B

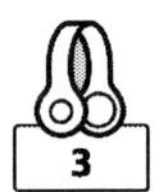

The Humors of Ballyloughlin

(Traditional Jig)

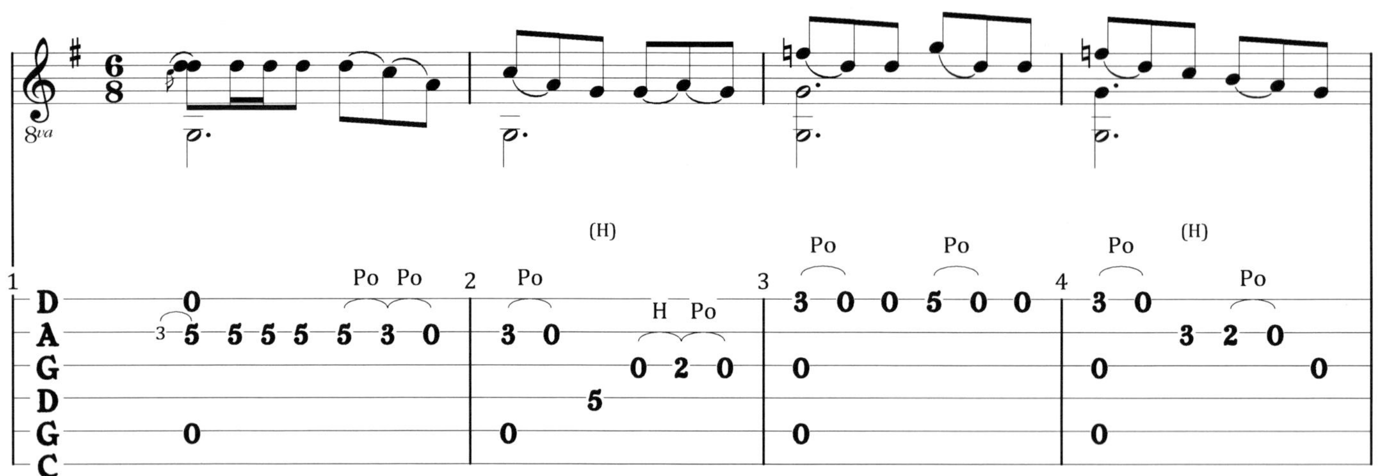

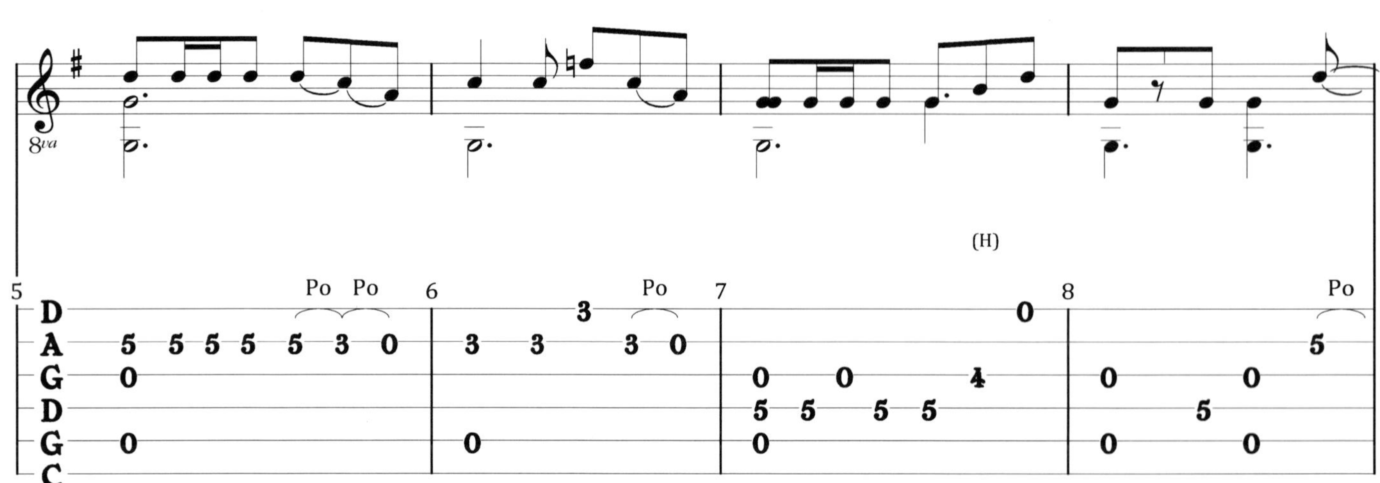

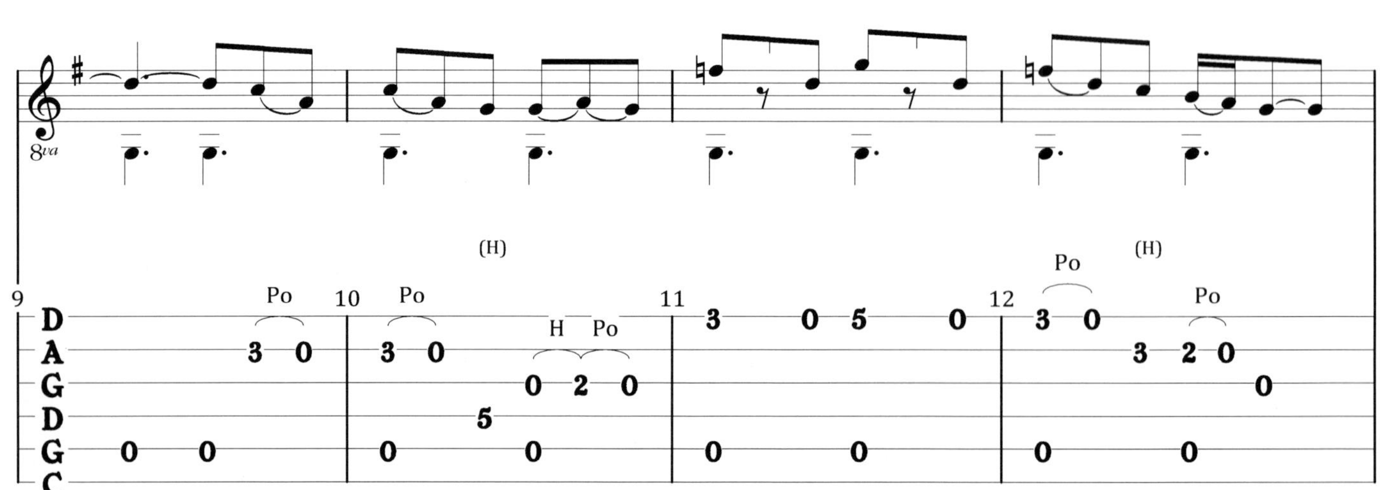

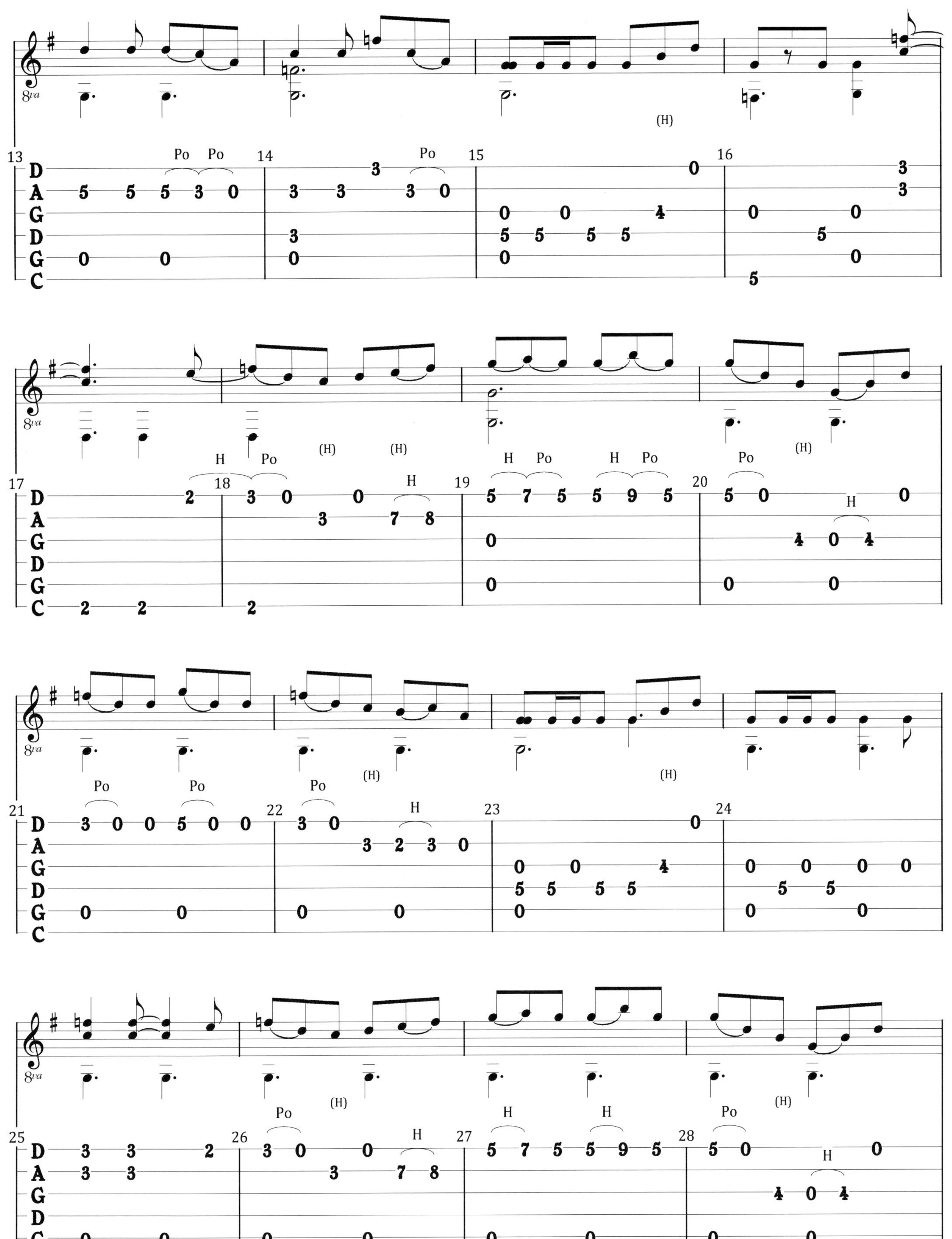
8va
D
A
G
D
G
C
Po
H
(H)

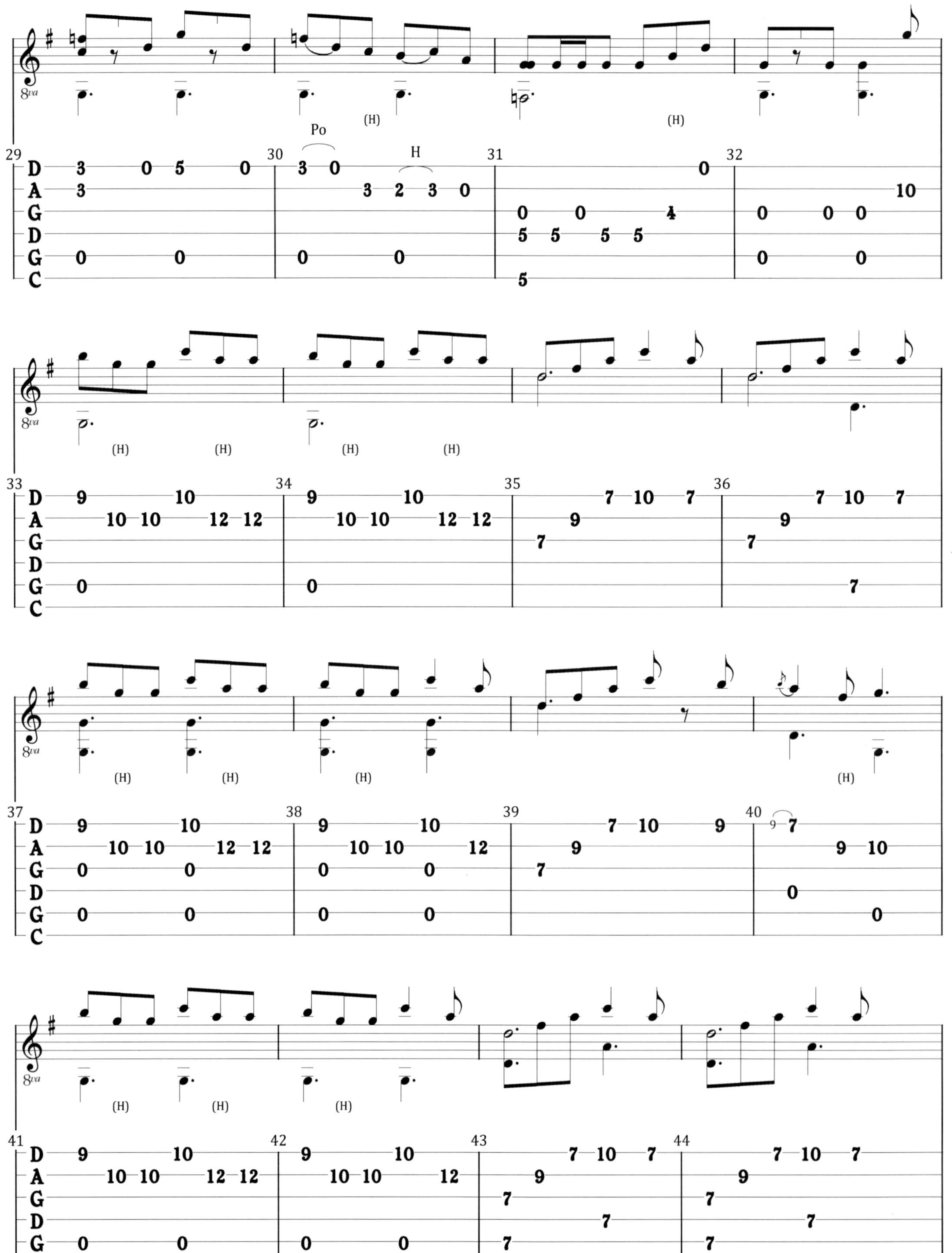
8va
Po
H
(H)
D
A
G
D
G
C

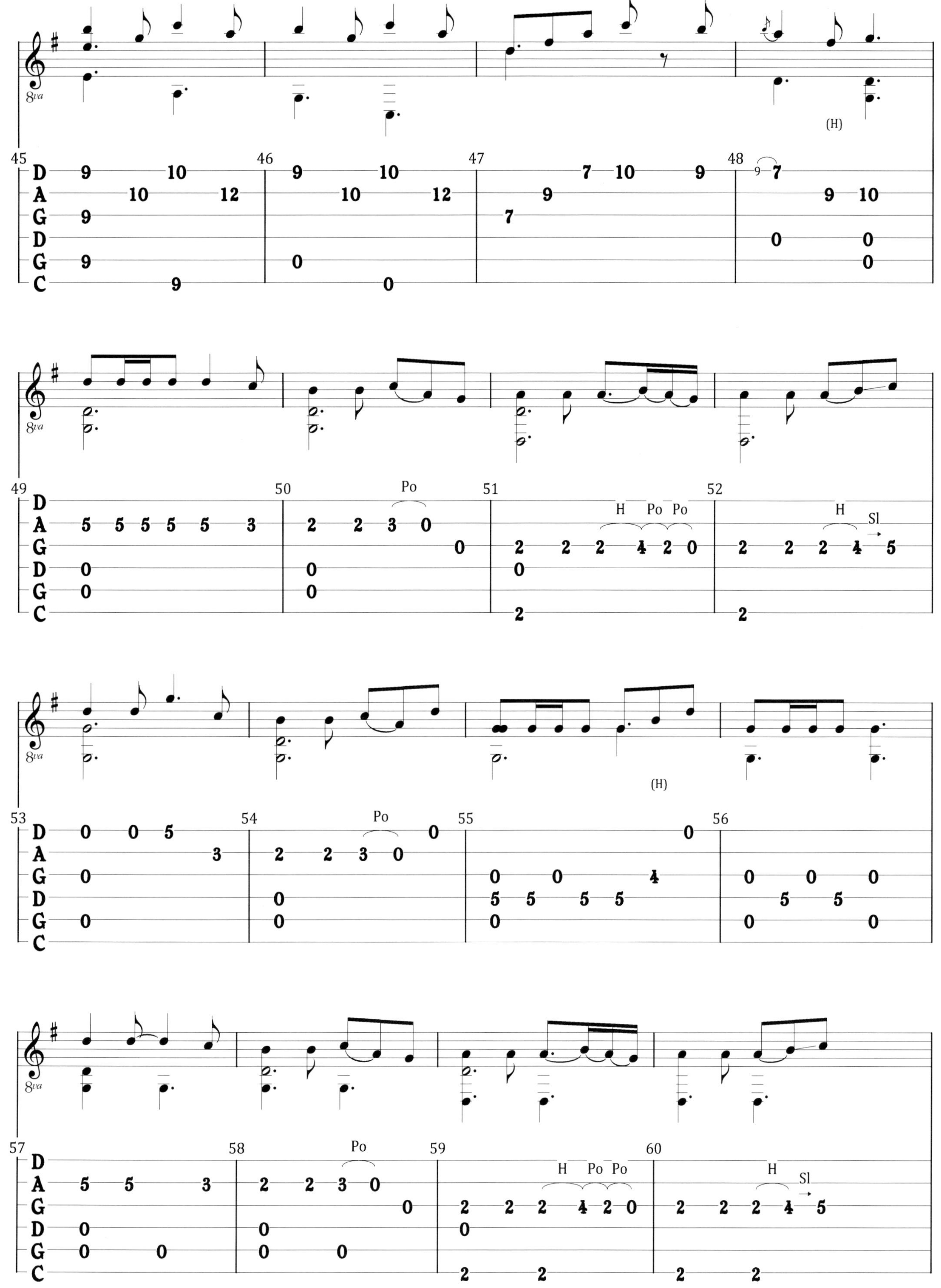
8va
(H)
D
A
G
D
G
C
45
46
47
48
49
50
51
52
Po
H Po Po
H
Sl
53
54
55
56
57
58
59
60

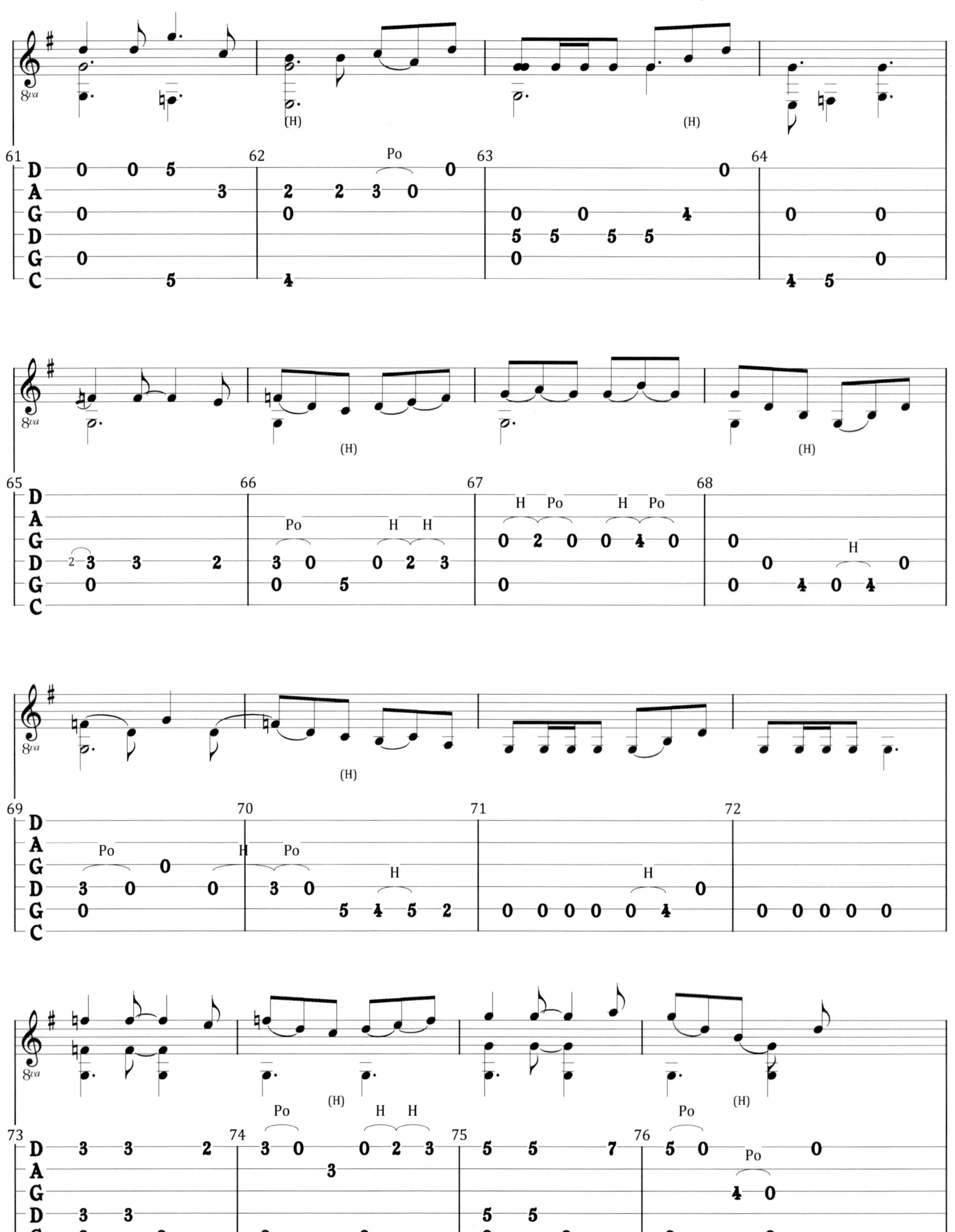
8va
(H)
Po
H
D
A
G
D
G
C
61
62
63
64
65
66
67
68
69
70
71
72
73
74
75
76

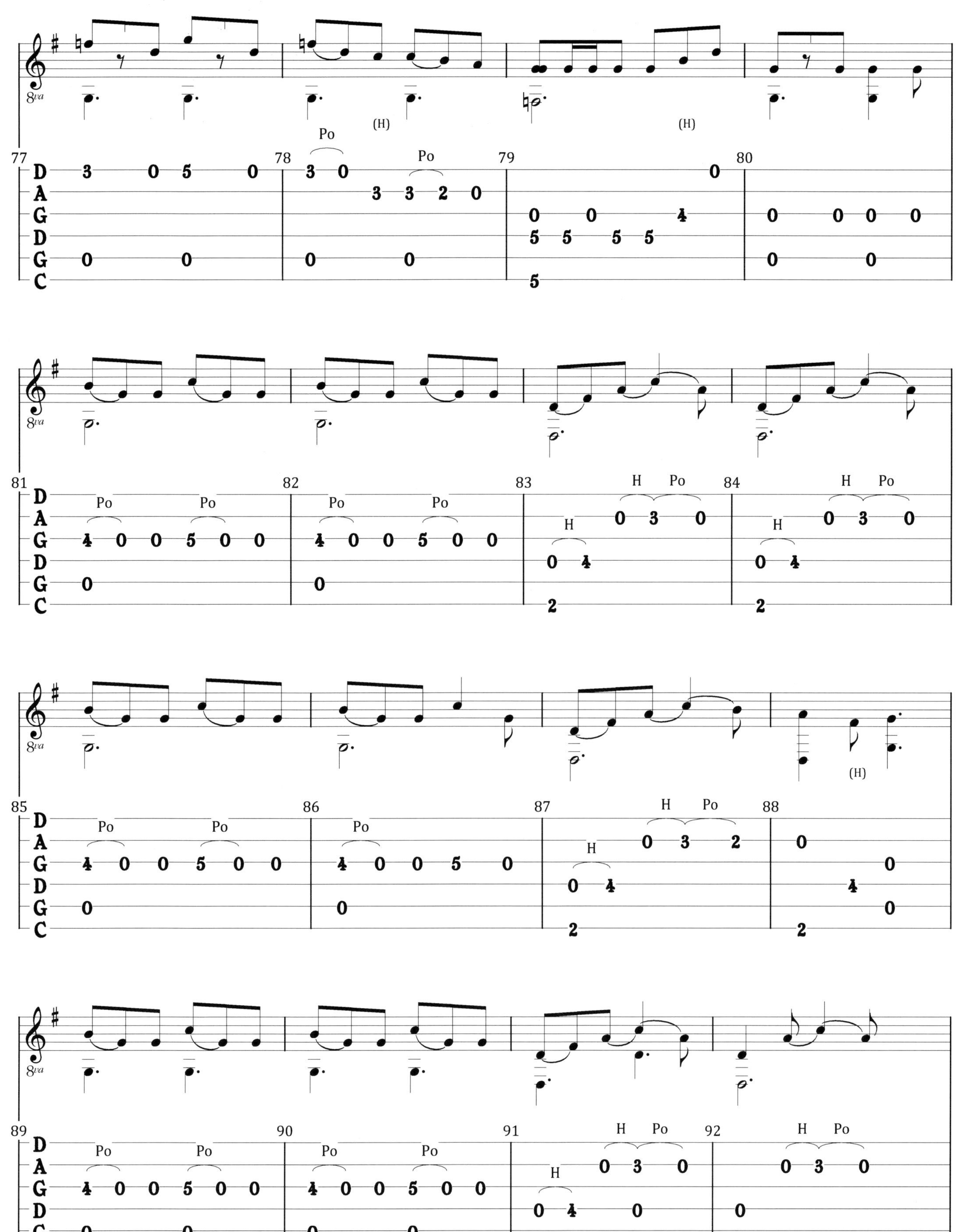
8va
77 78 79 80
81 82 83 84
85 86 87 88
89 90 91 92
D
A
G
D
G
C
Po
H
(H)

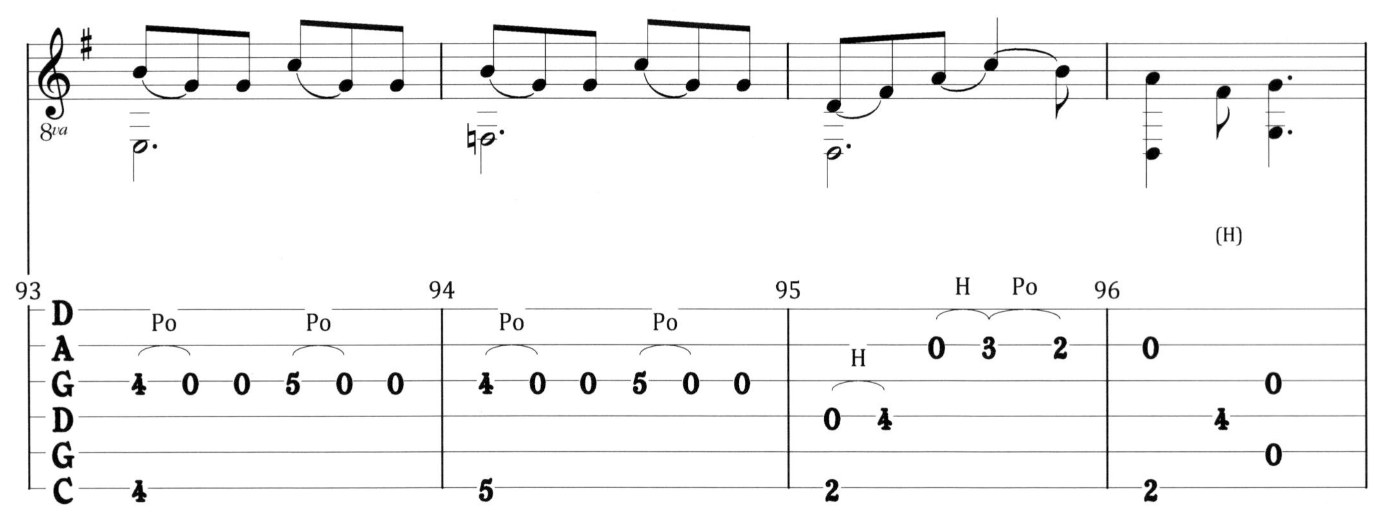
8va
(H)
93
94
95
96
D
A
G
D
G
C
Po
Po
Po
Po
H
H
Po
4 0 0 5 0 0
4 0 0 5 0 0
0 3 2
0 4
0
0
4
0
4
5
2
2

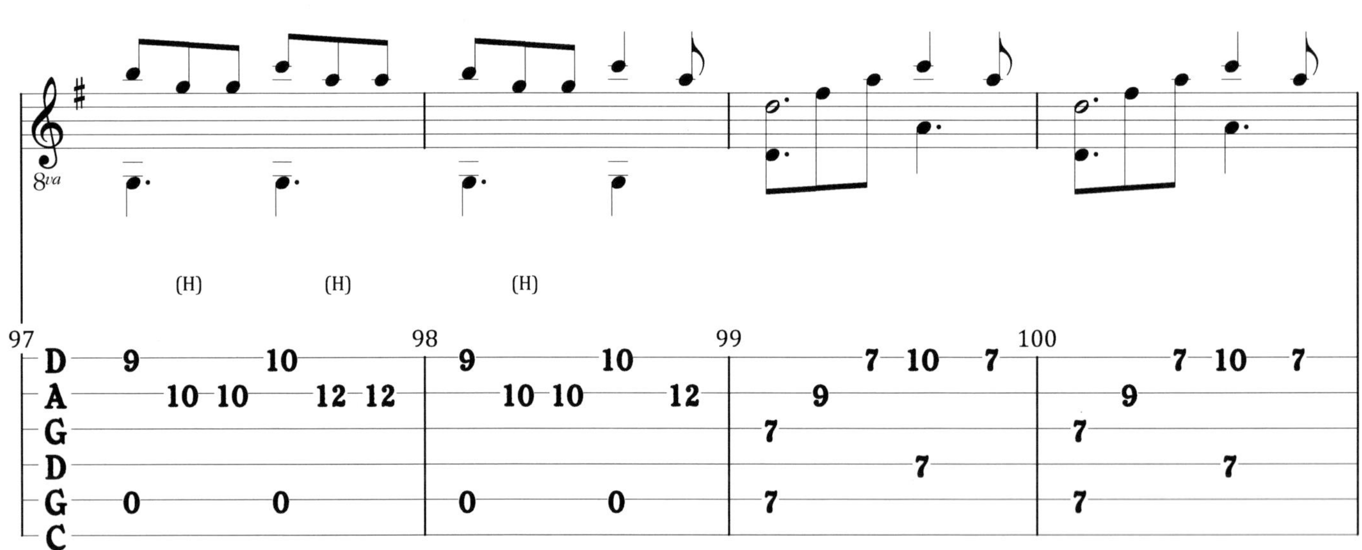
8va
(H)
(H)
(H)
97
98
99
100
D
A
G
D
G
C
9 10
10 10 12 12
0 0
9 10
10 10 12
0 0
7 10 7
9
7
7
7
7 10 7
9
7
7
7

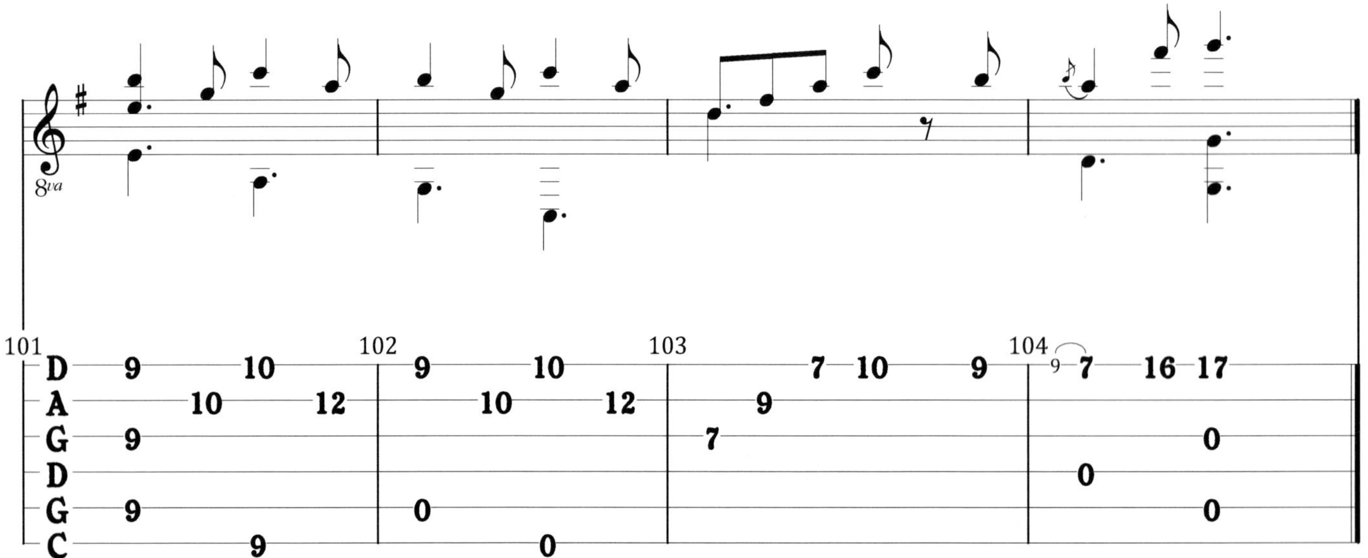
8va
101
102
103
104
D
A
G
D
G
C
9 10
10 12
9
9
9
9 10
10 12
0
0
7 10 9
9
7
9 7 16 17
0
0
0

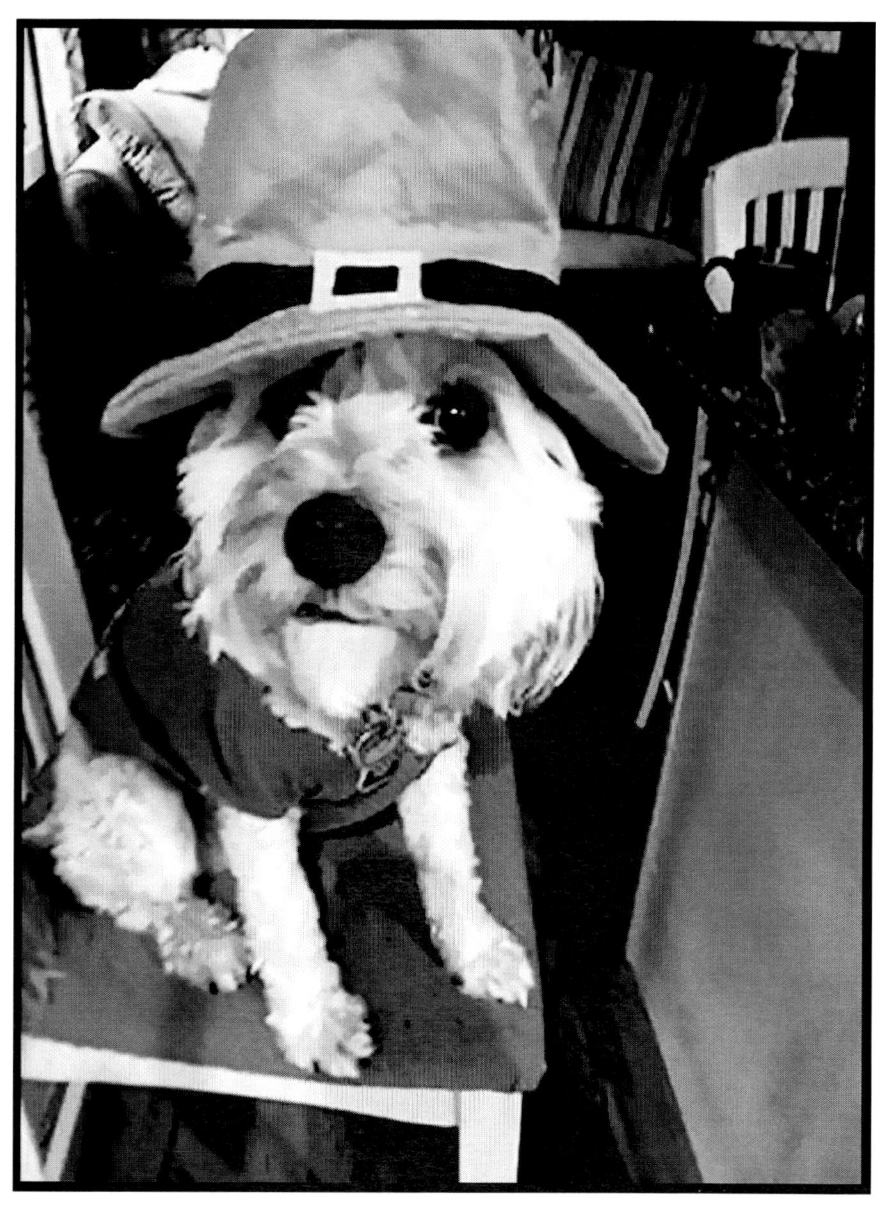

Toby McMeen on St. Patrick's Day 2017

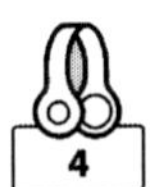

Carolan's Dream

(T.Connellan; tune called "Molly MacAlpin")

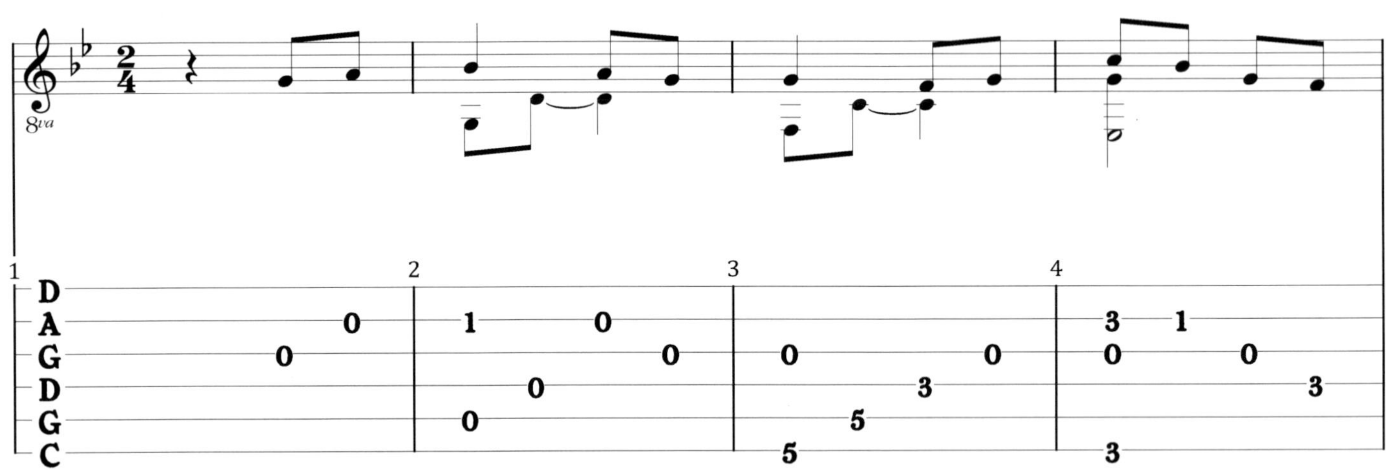

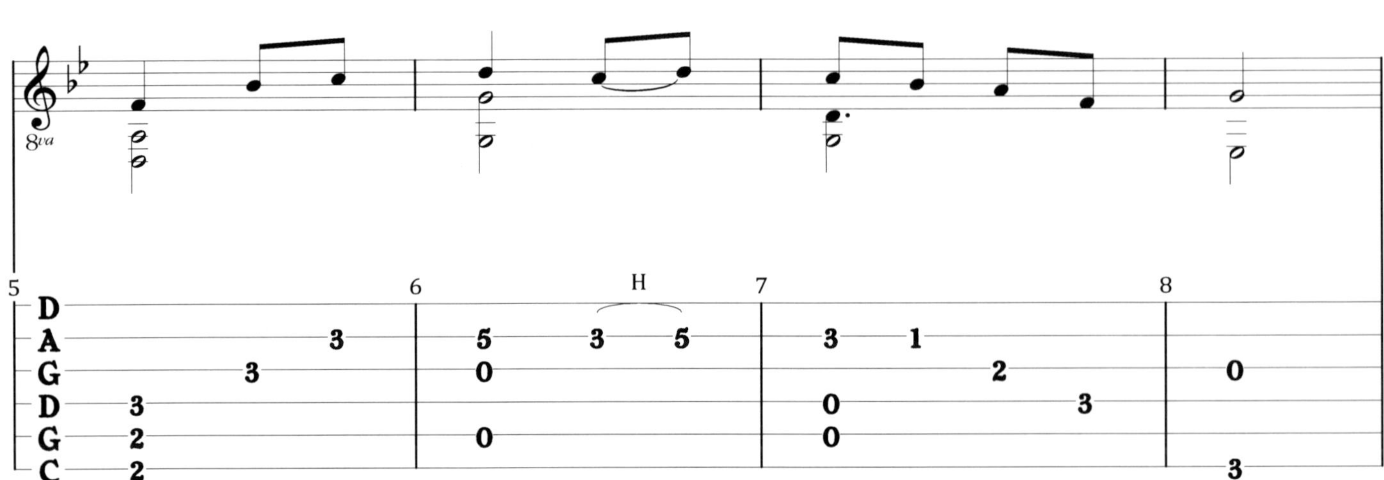

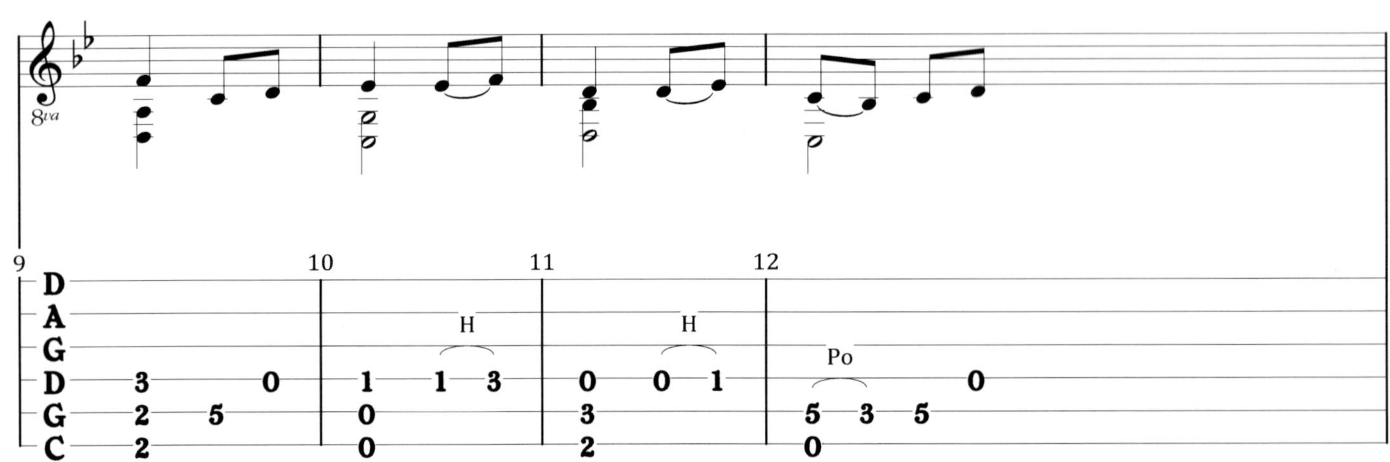

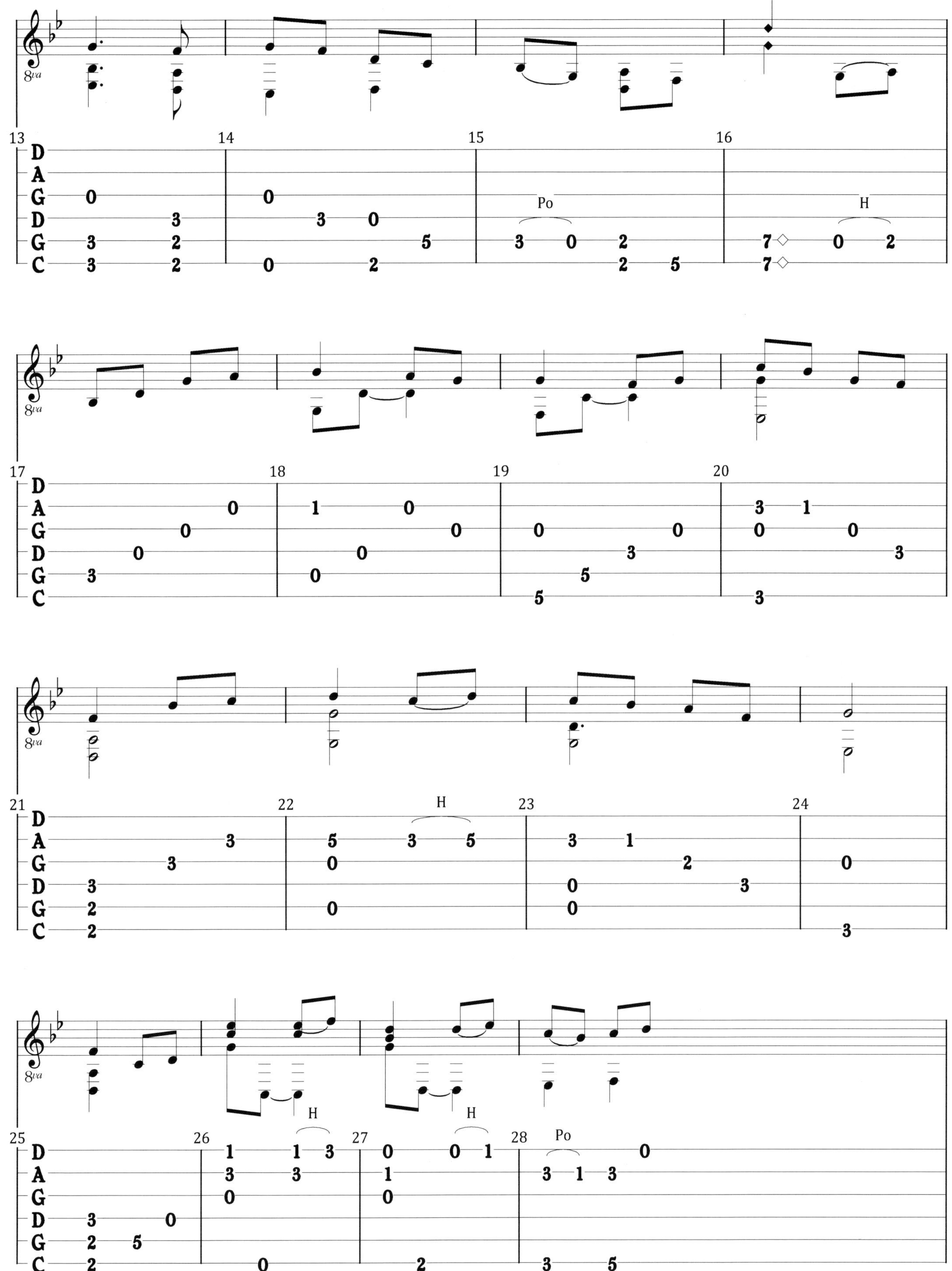
8va
13
14
15
16
D
A
G
D
G
C
Po
H
17
18
19
20
21
22
23
24
25
26
27
28

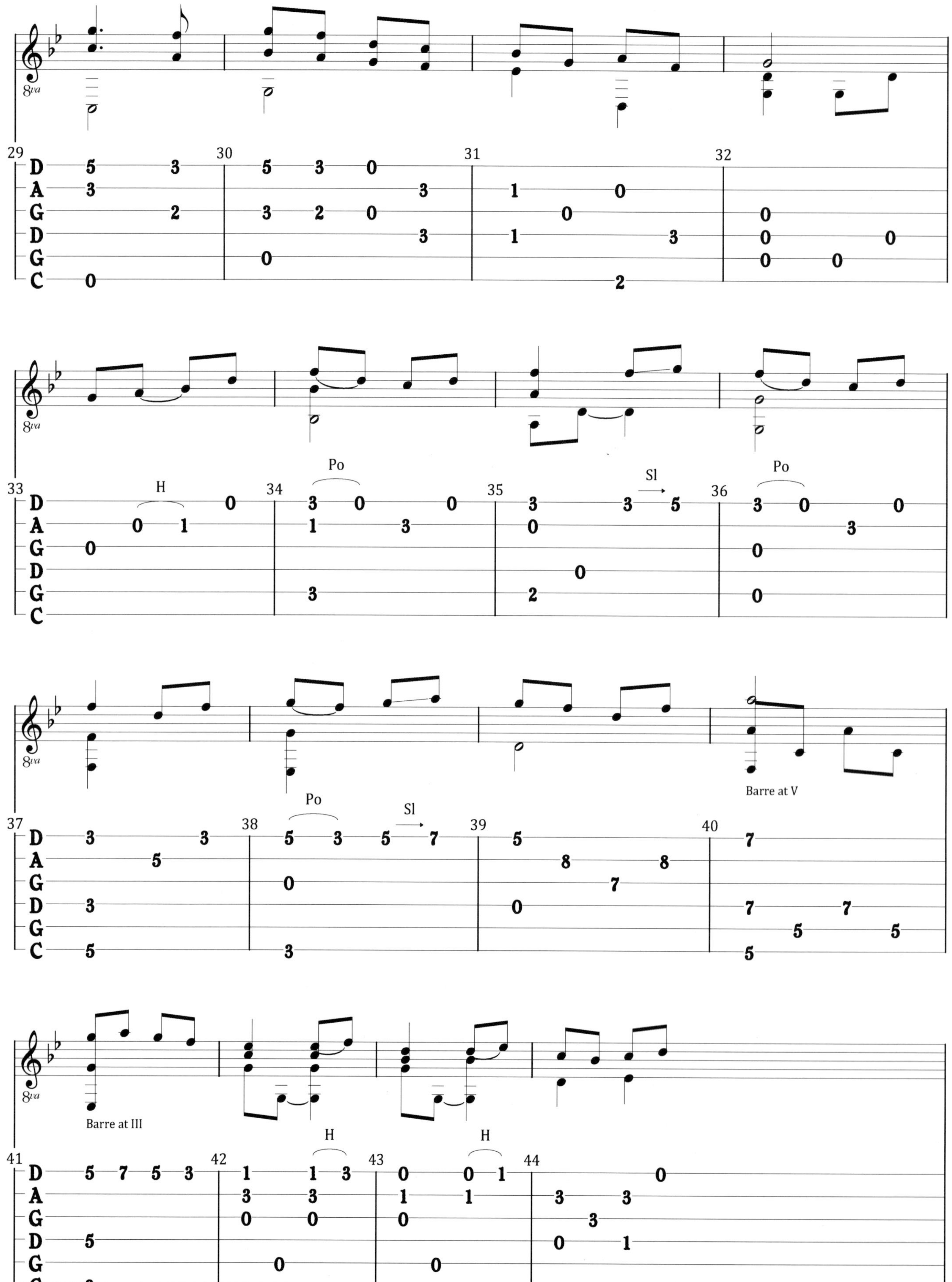
8va
29
30
31
32
D
A
G
D
G
C
33
H
34
Po
35
Sl
36
Po
37
38
Po
Sl
39
40
Barre at V
41
Barre at III
42
H
43
H
44

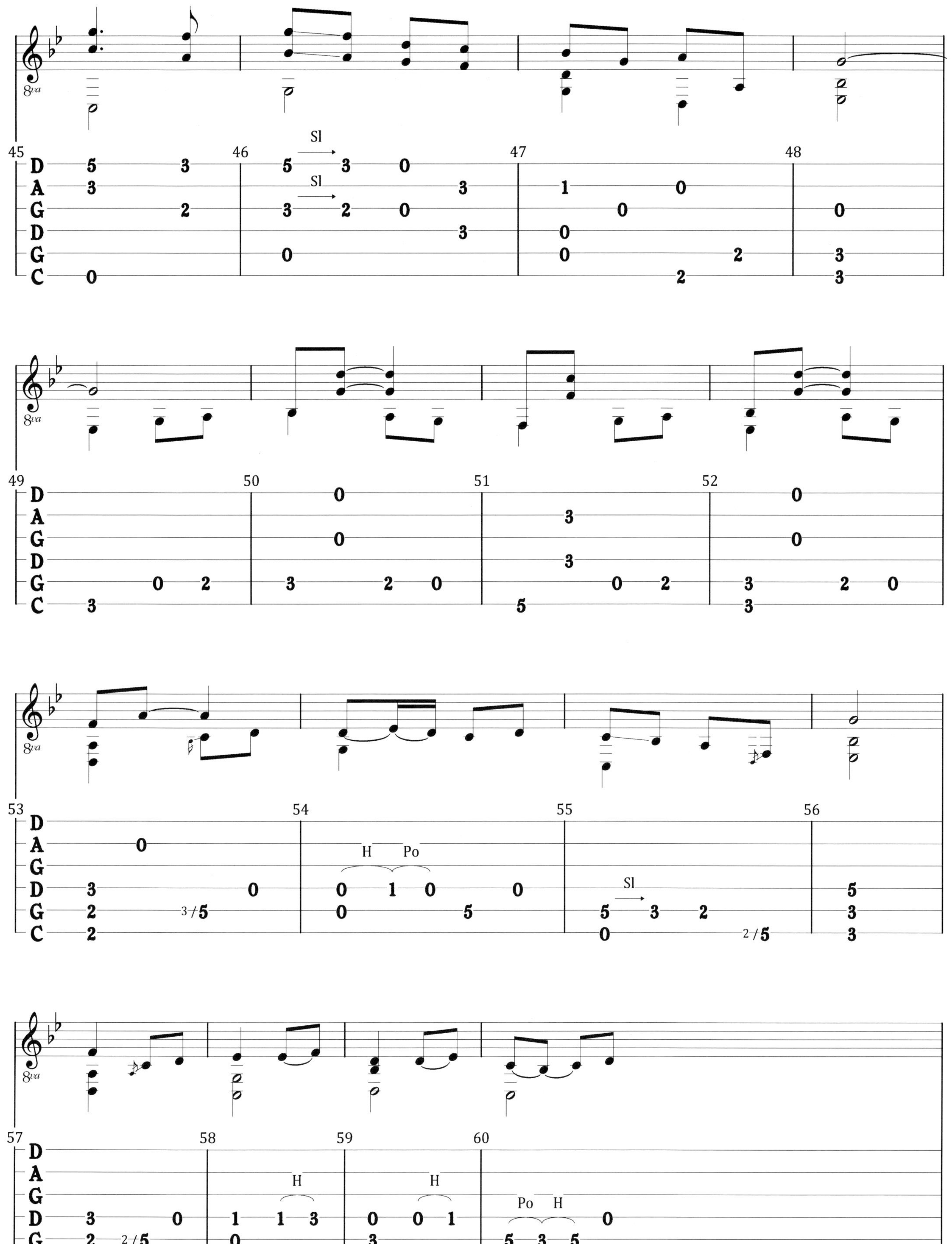
8va
Sl
Sl
H
Po
Sl
H
H
Po
H

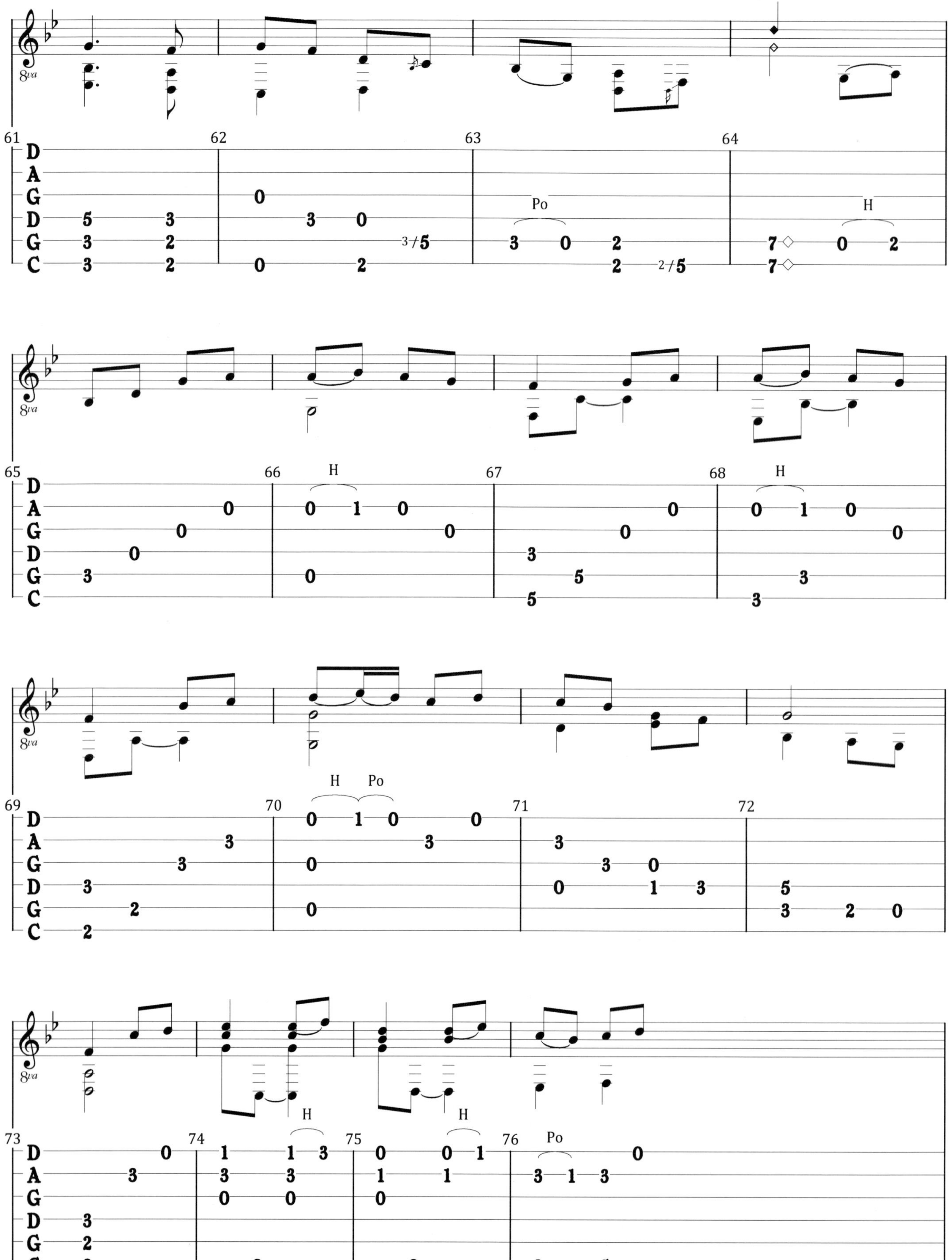
8va
D
A
G
D
G
C
Po
H

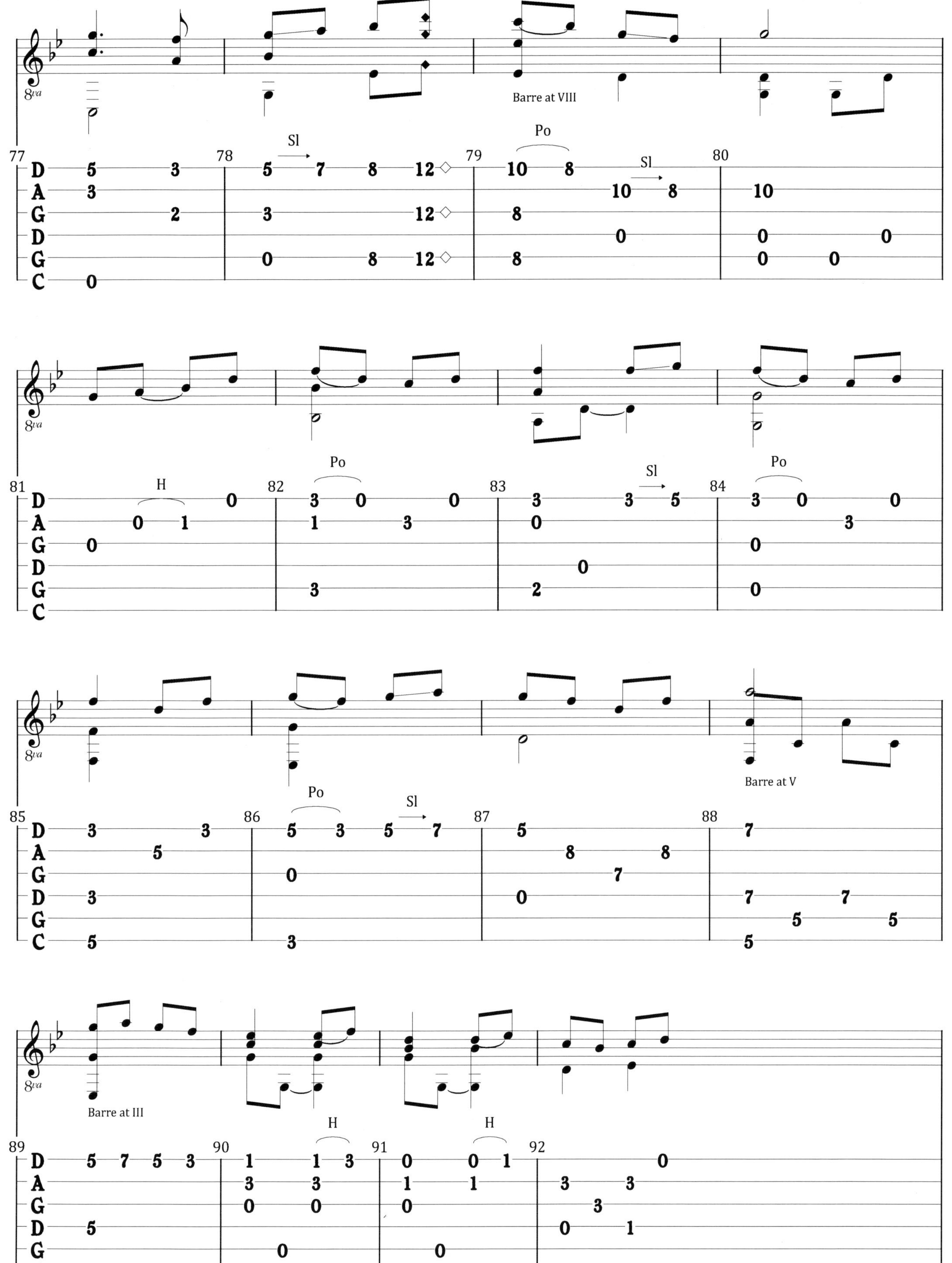
8va
Barre at VIII
Sl
Po
Sl
H
Po
Sl
Po
Po
Sl
Barre at V
Barre at III
H
H

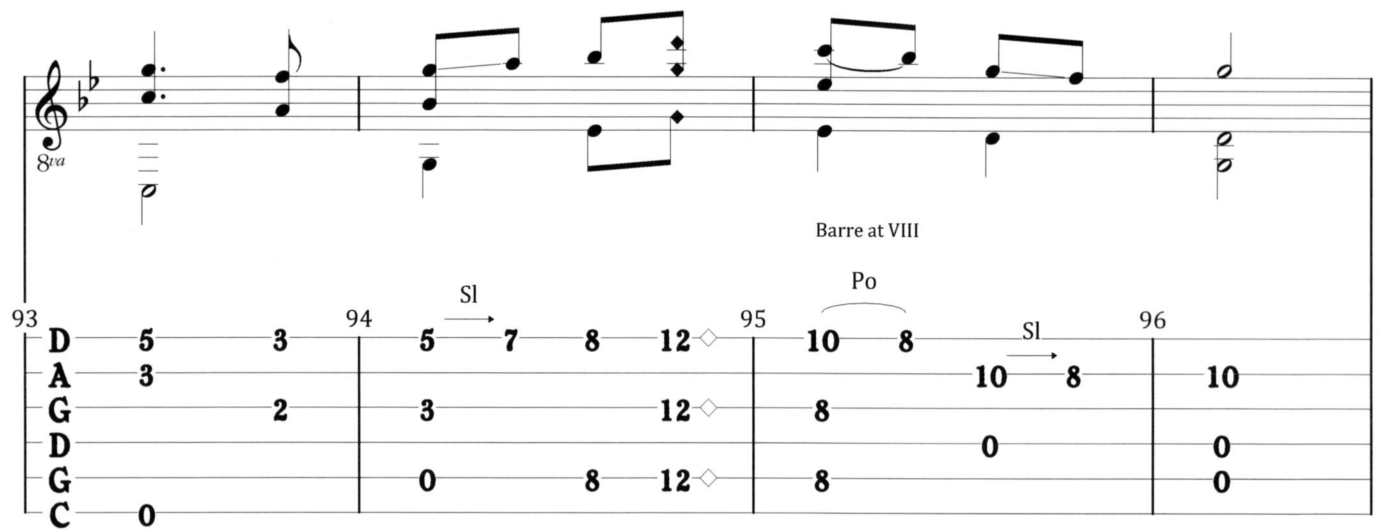
8va
Barre at VIII
Sl
Po
Sl
93
94
95
96
D
A
G
D
G
C

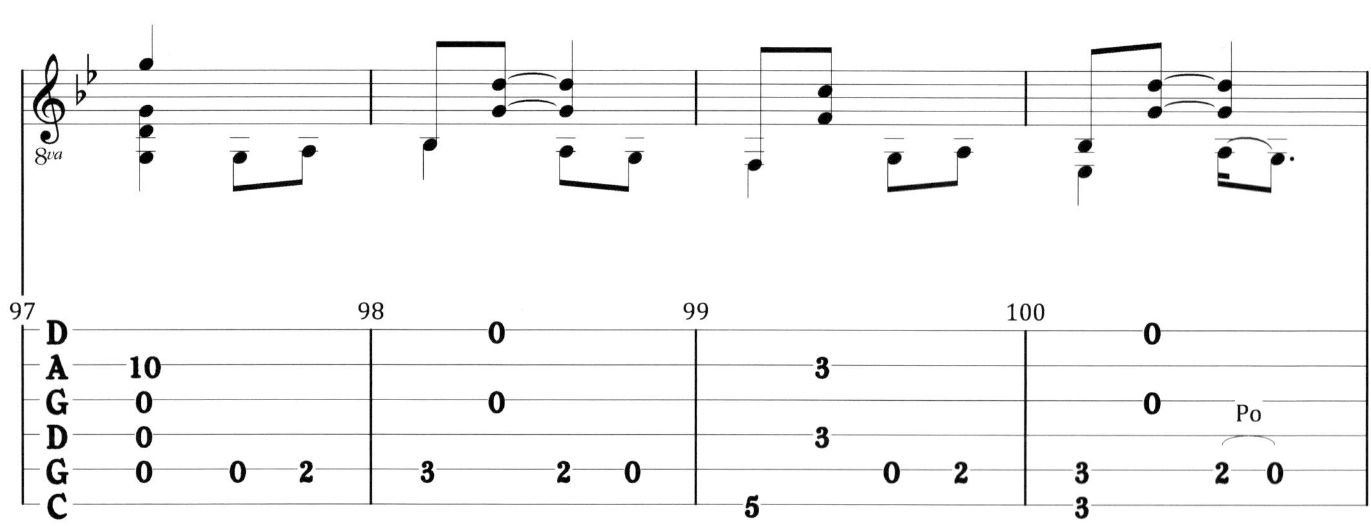
8va
Po
97
98
99
100
D
A
G
D
G
C

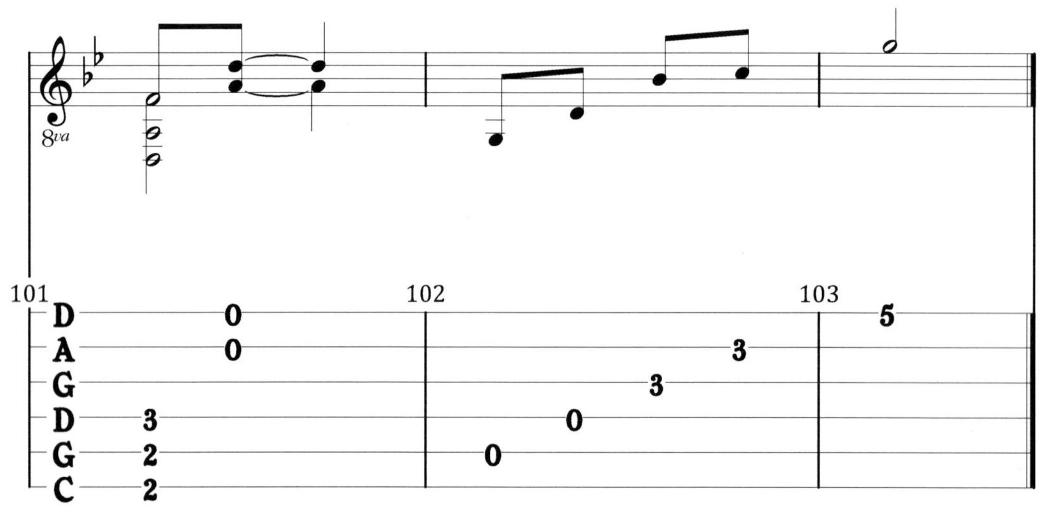
8va
101
102
103
D
A
G
D
G
C

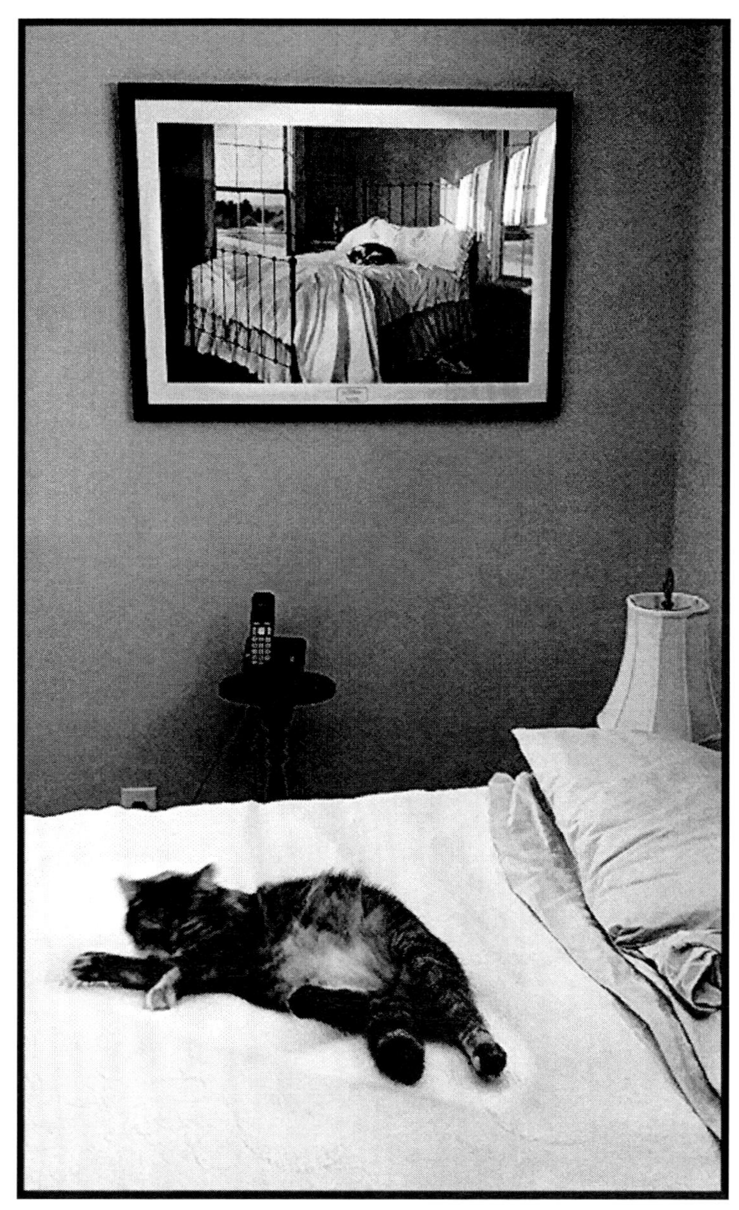

Millie McMeen (Showing that life follows art!)

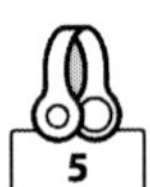

Fanny Power

(T. O'Carolan)

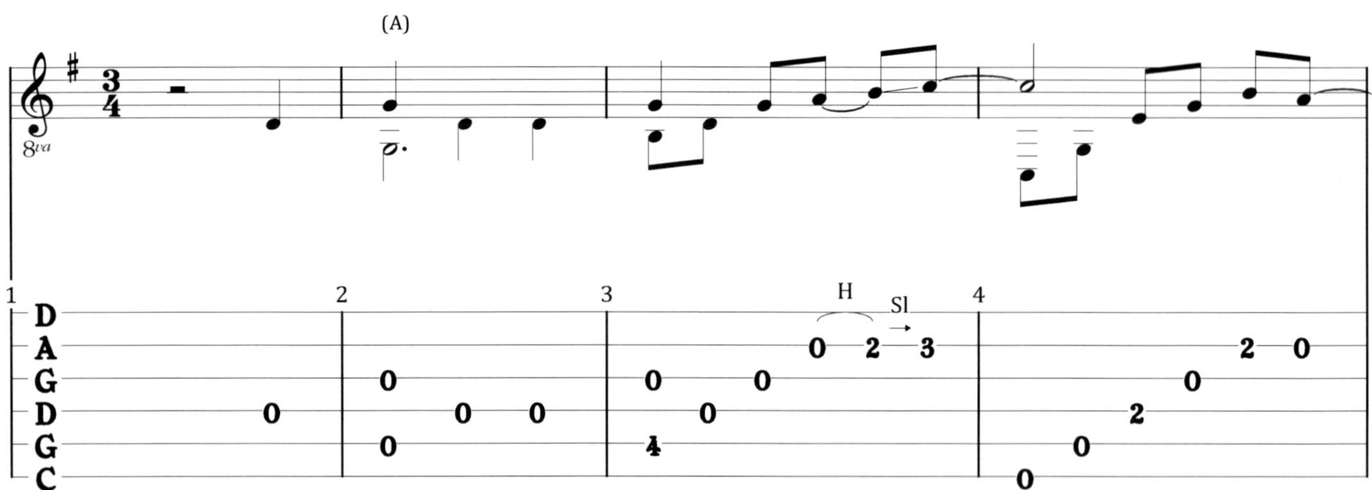

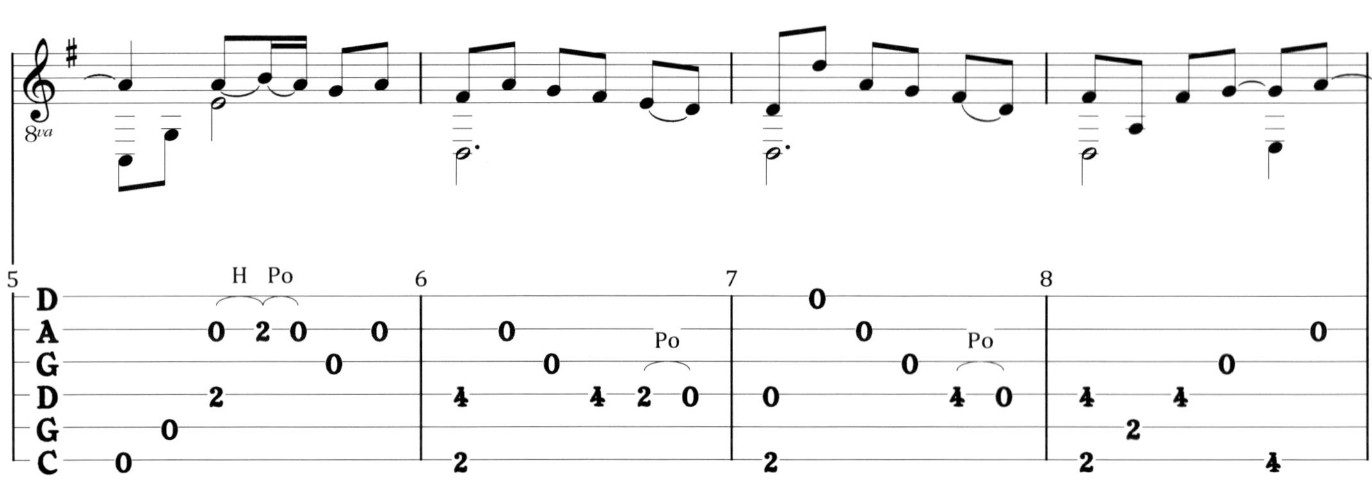

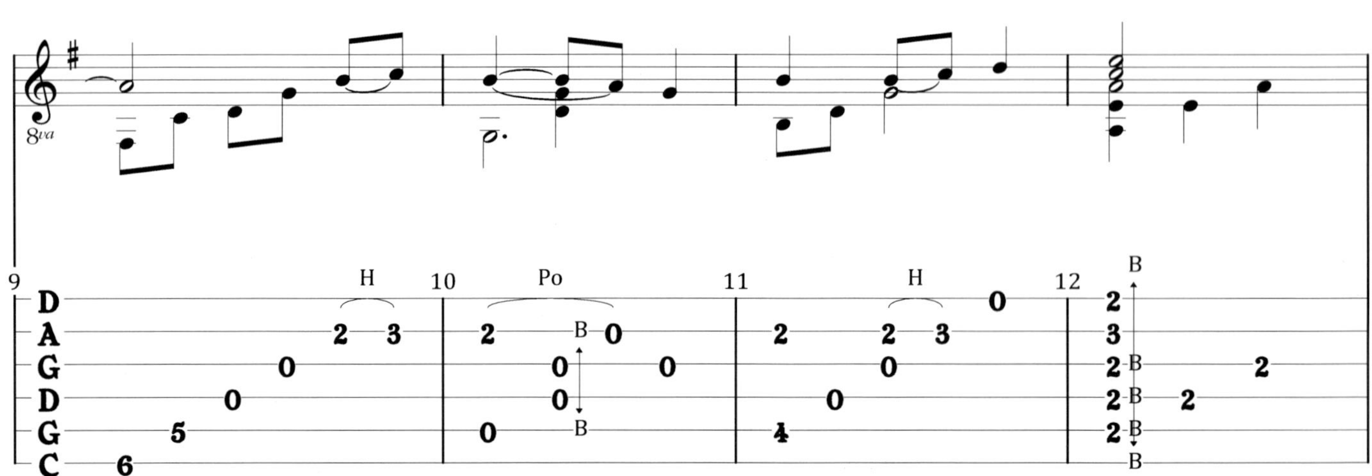

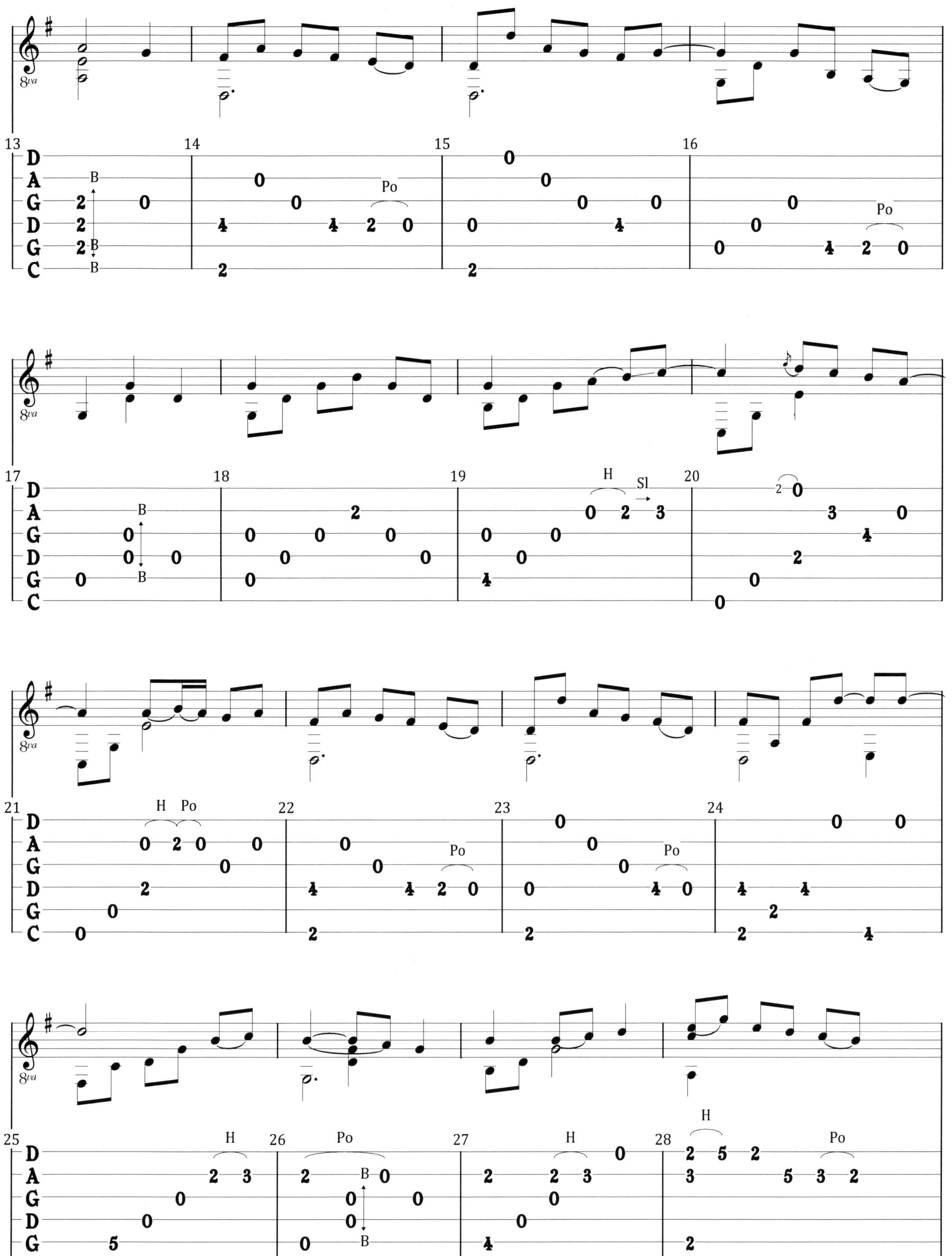
8va
13 14 15 16
D A G D G C
B
Po
17 18 19 20
H
Sl
21 22 23 24
25 26 27 28

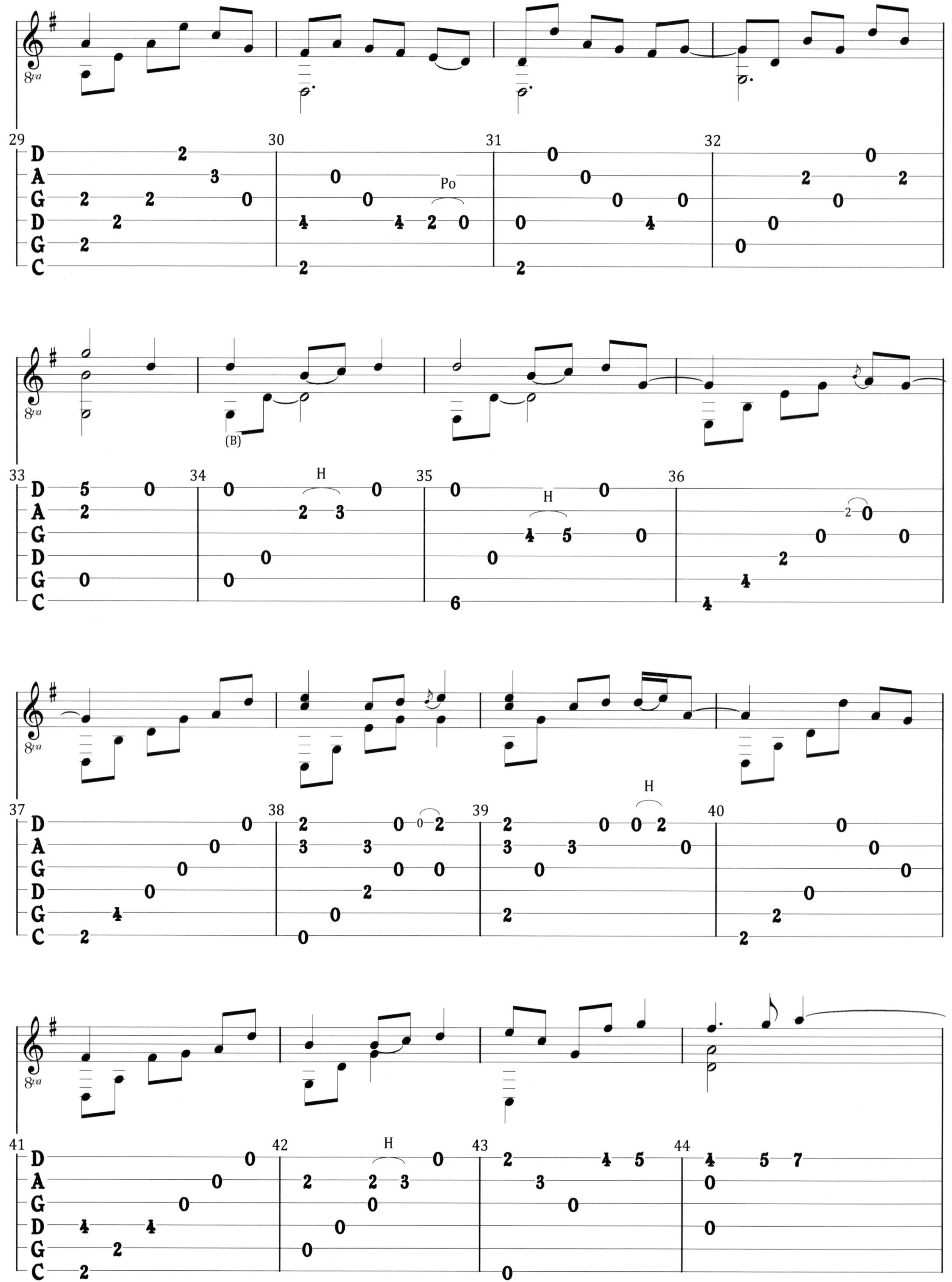
8va
D
A
G
D
G
C
Po
(B)
H

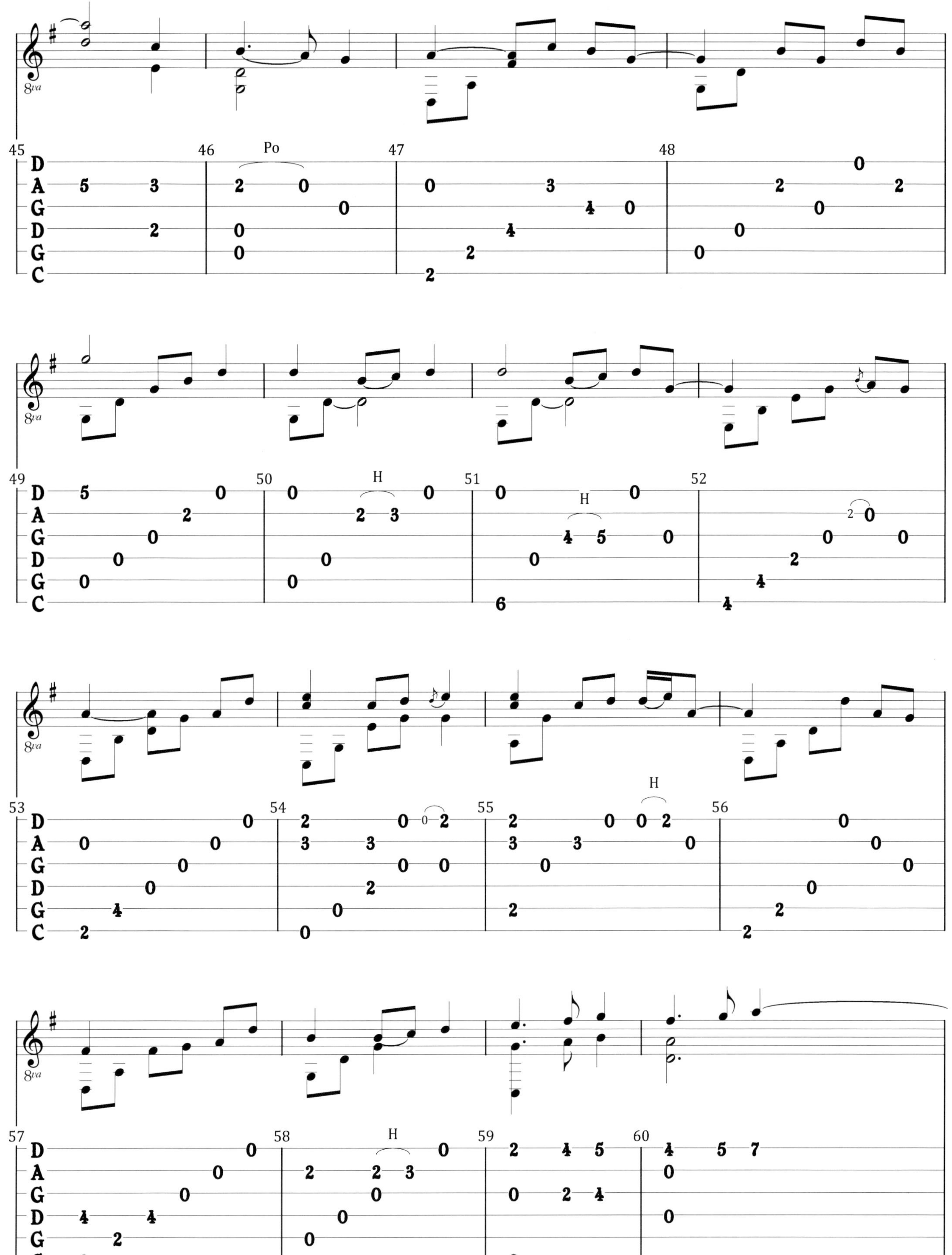
8va
45
46
Po
47
48
D
A
G
D
G
C
49
50
H
51
H
52
53
54
55
H
56
57
58
H
59
60

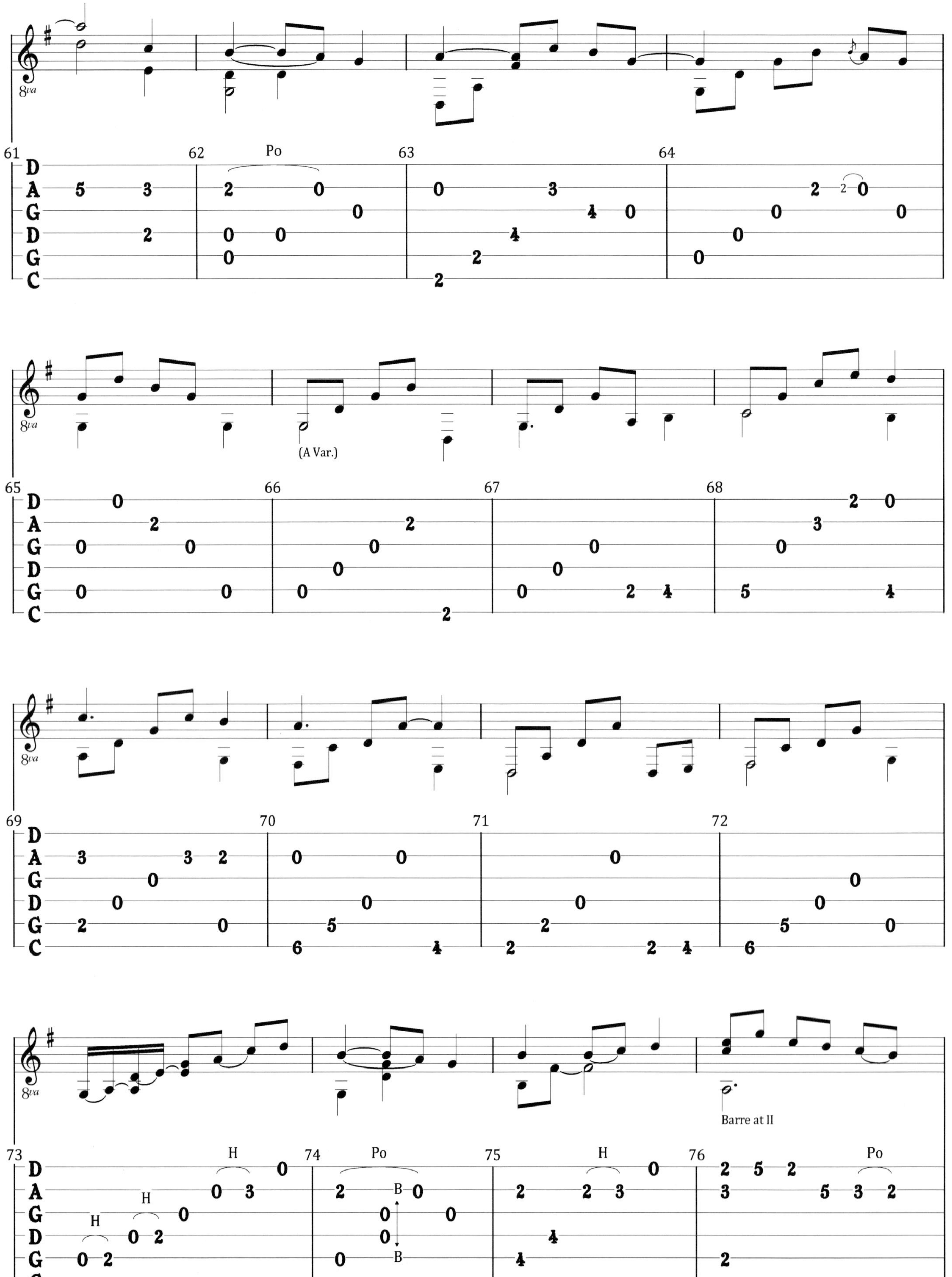
8va
Po
(A Var.)
H
B
Barre at II
D A G D G C

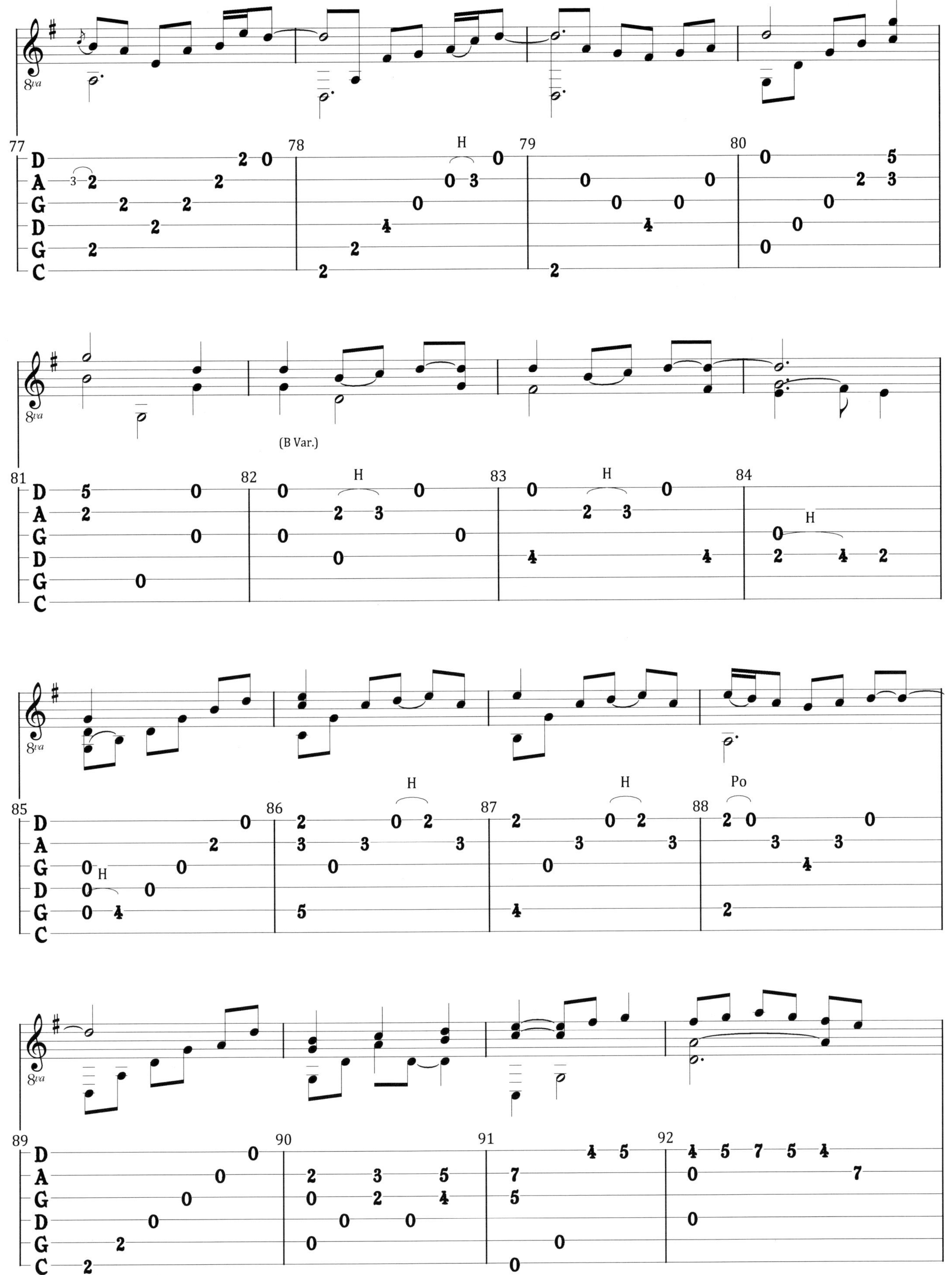
8va
77 78 79 80
D A G D G C
H
(B Var.)
81 82 83 84
85 86 87 88
Po
89 90 91 92

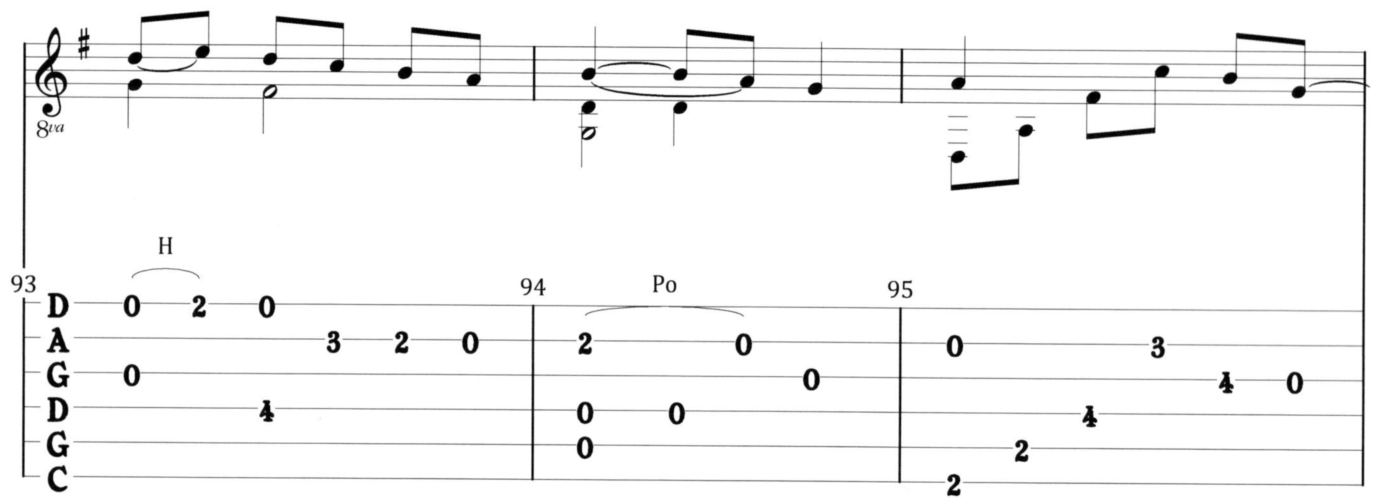
8va
H
Po
93
94
95
D
A
G
D
G
C

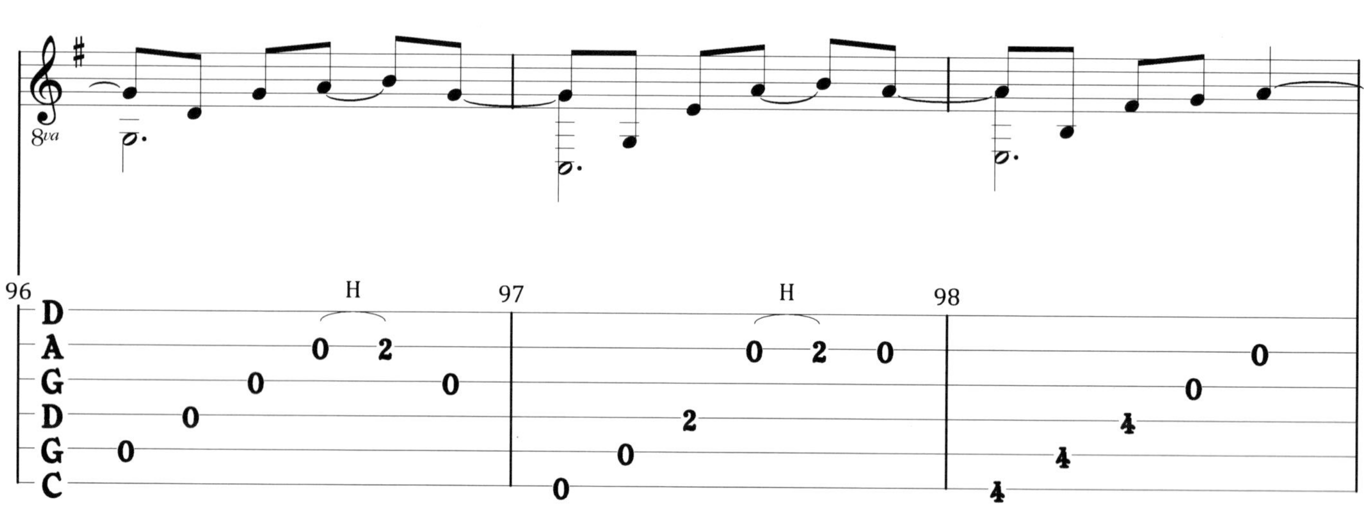
8va
H
H
96
97
98
D
A
G
D
G
C

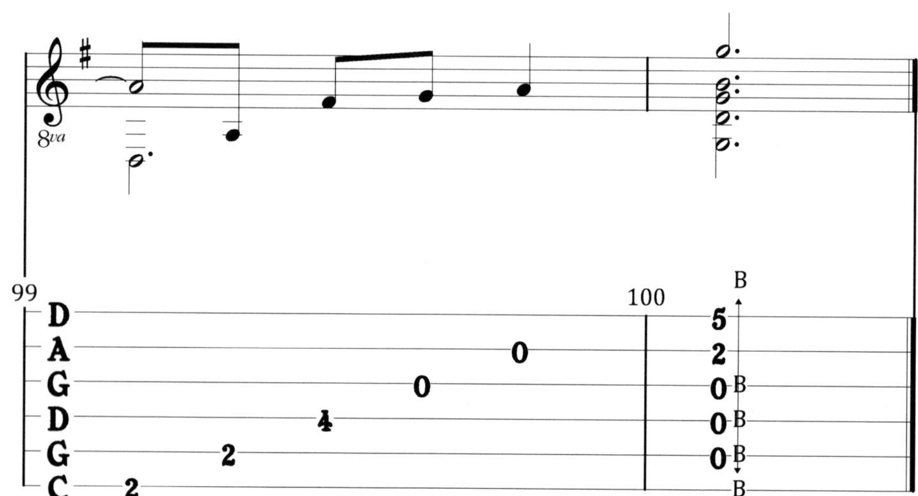
8va
99
100
B
D
A
G
D
G
C

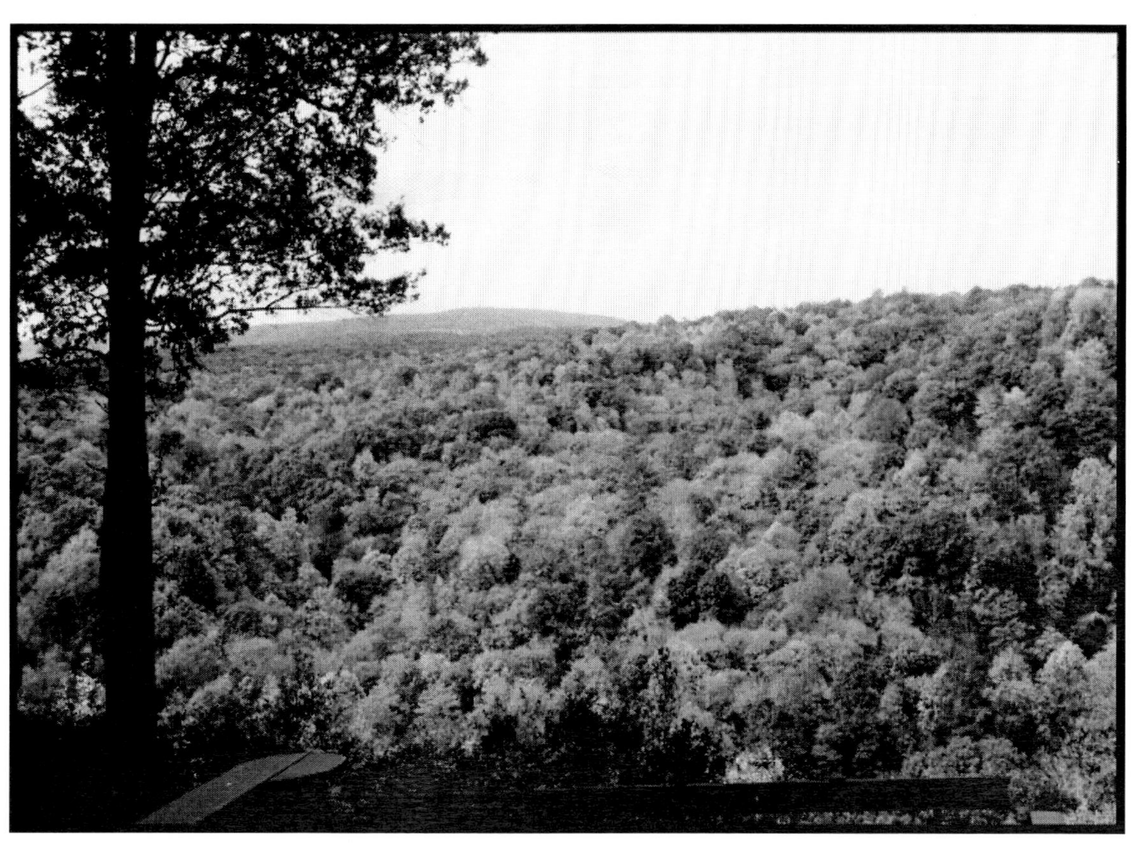

Warrior Ridge, Huntingdon, PA, USA

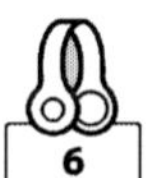

The Kid on the Mountain

(Traditional Slip Jig)

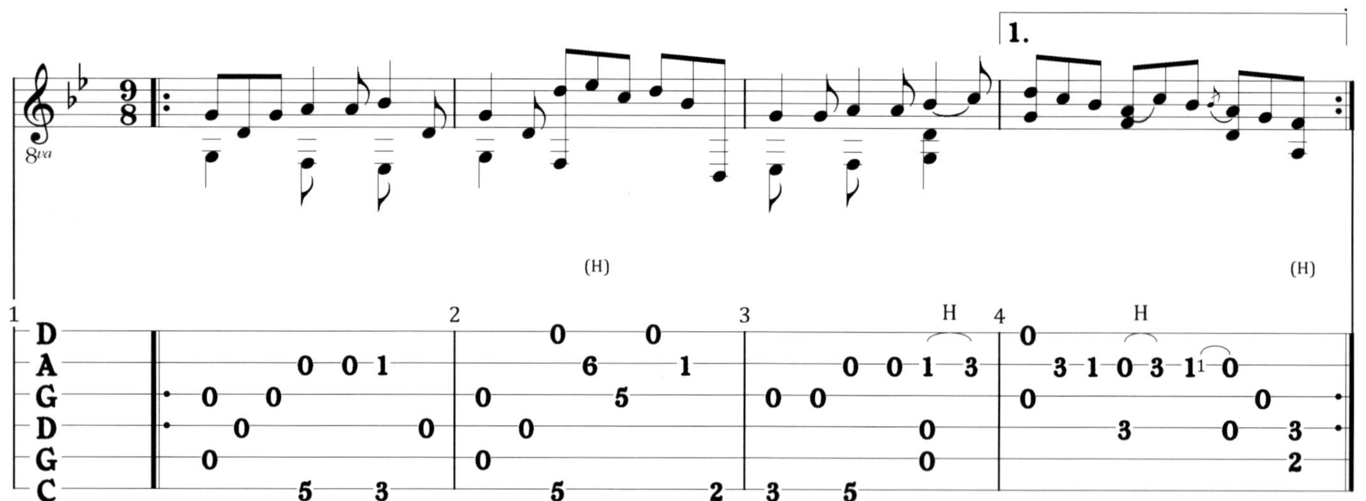

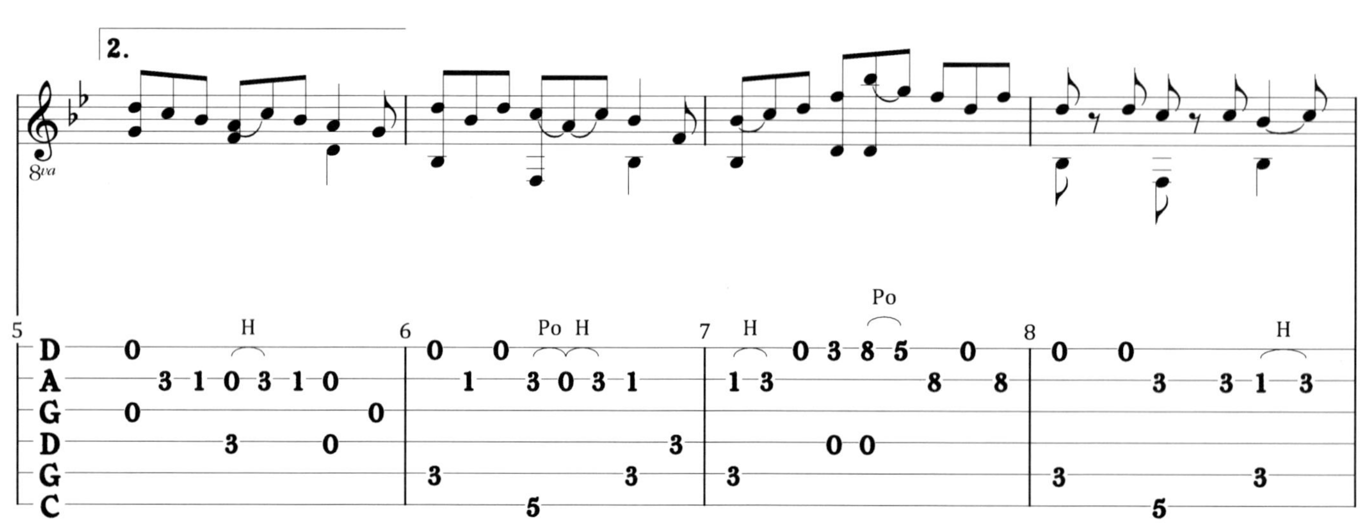

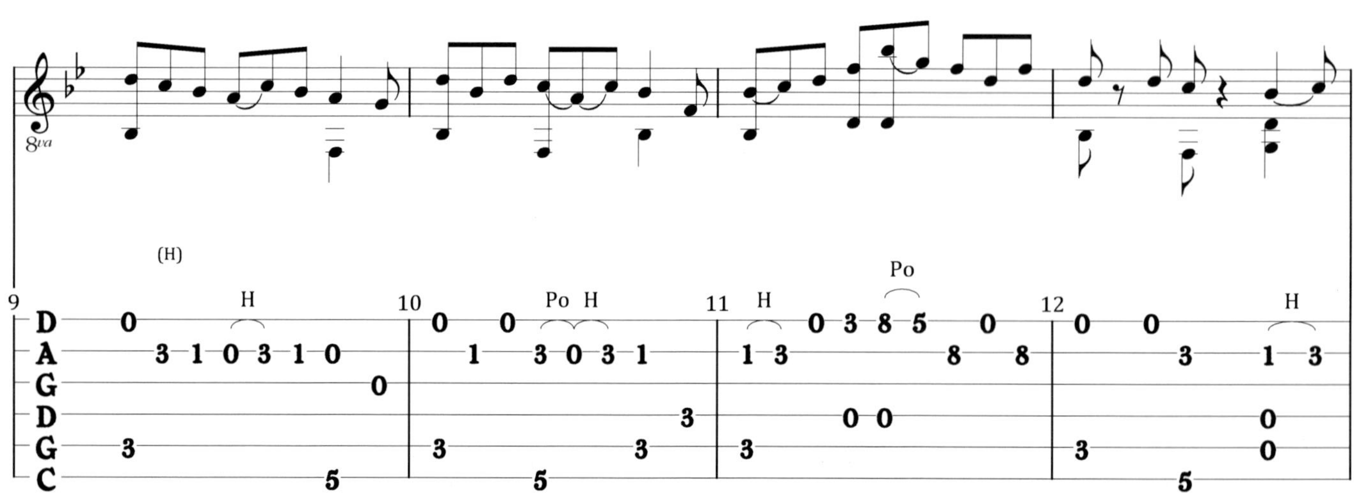

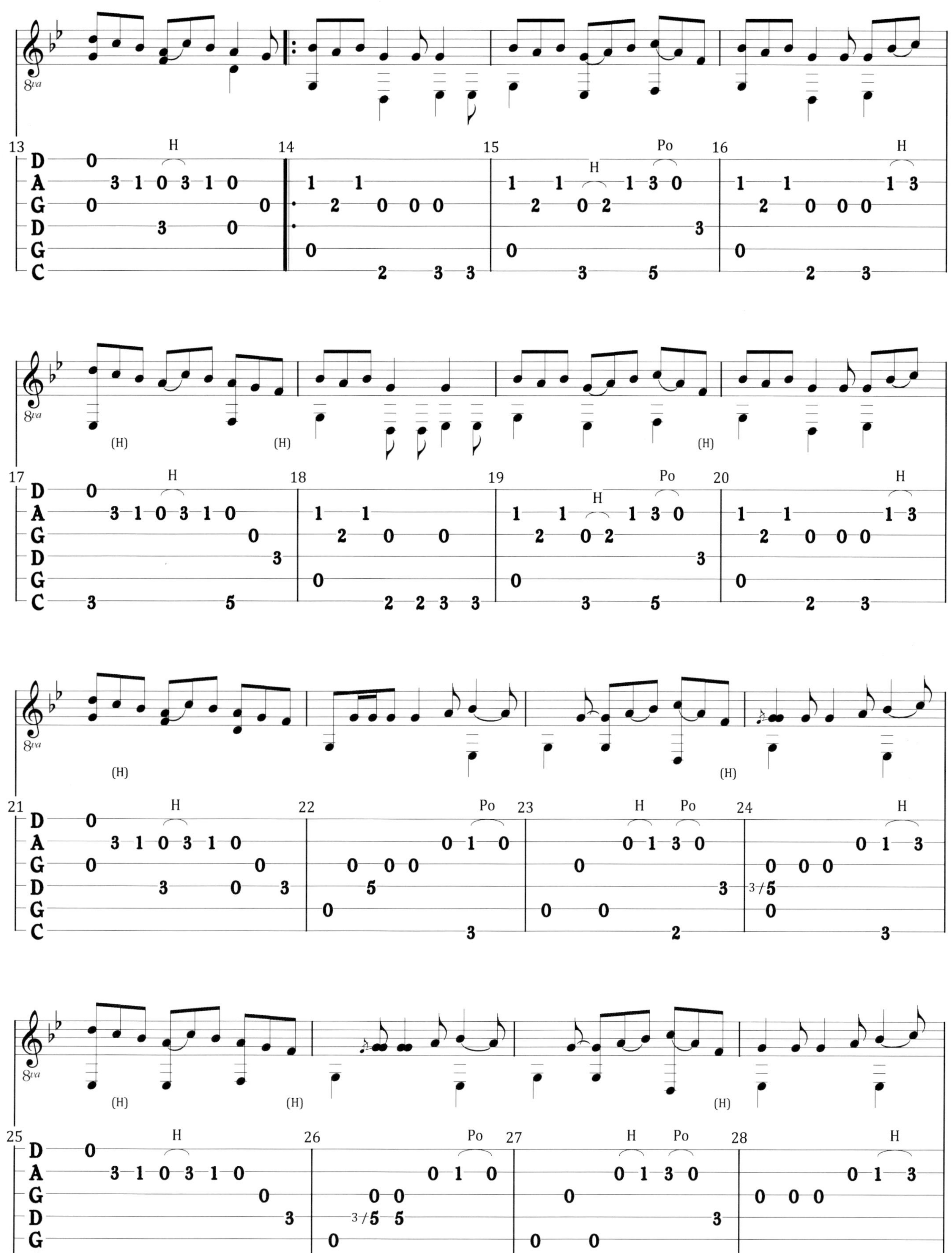
8va
13
14
15
16
17
18
19
20
21
22
23
24
25
26
27
28
D
A
G
D
G
C
H
Po
(H)

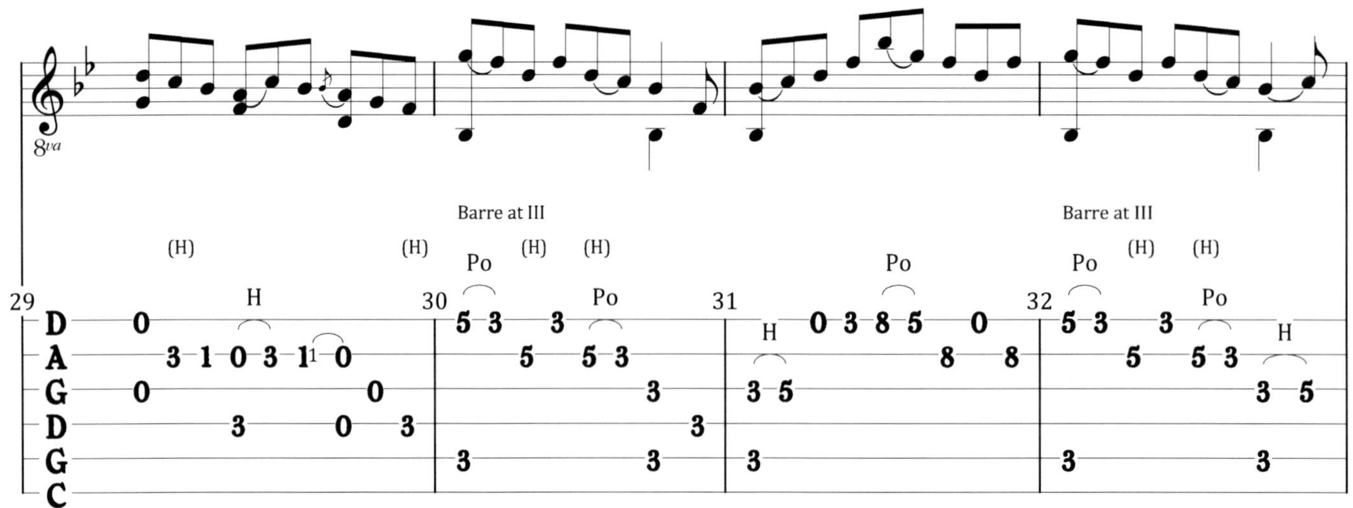
8va
Barre at III
Barre at III
(H)
(H)
Po
(H)
(H)
Po
Po
(H)
(H)
H
Po
H
H
Po
29
30
31
32
D
A
G
D
G
C

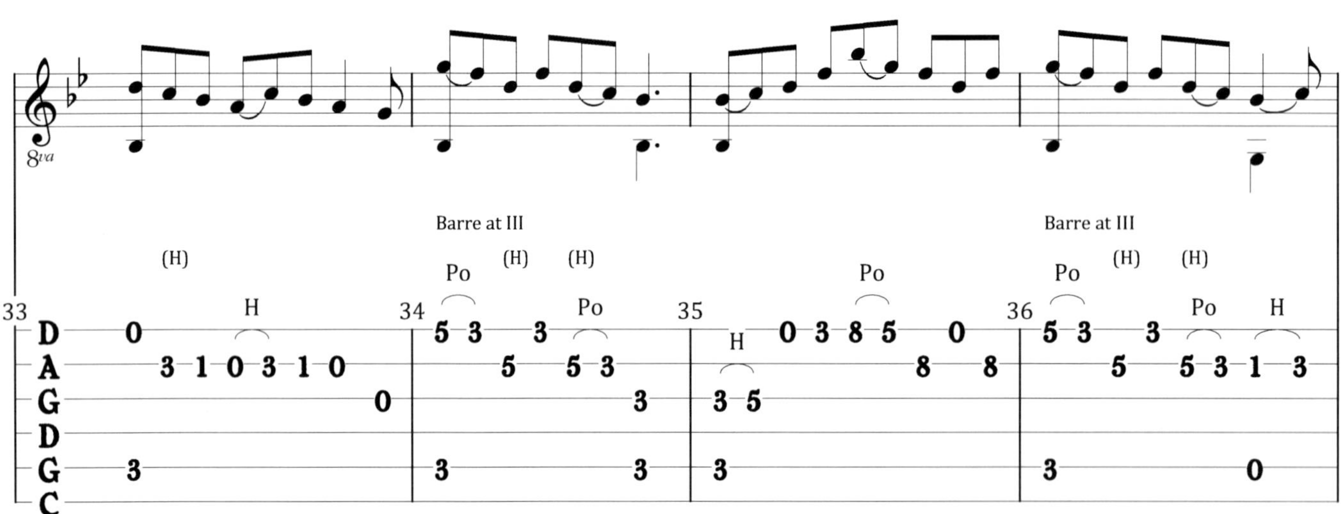
8va
Barre at III
Barre at III
(H)
Po
(H)
(H)
Po
Po
(H)
(H)
H
Po
H
Po
H
33
34
35
36
D
A
G
D
G
C

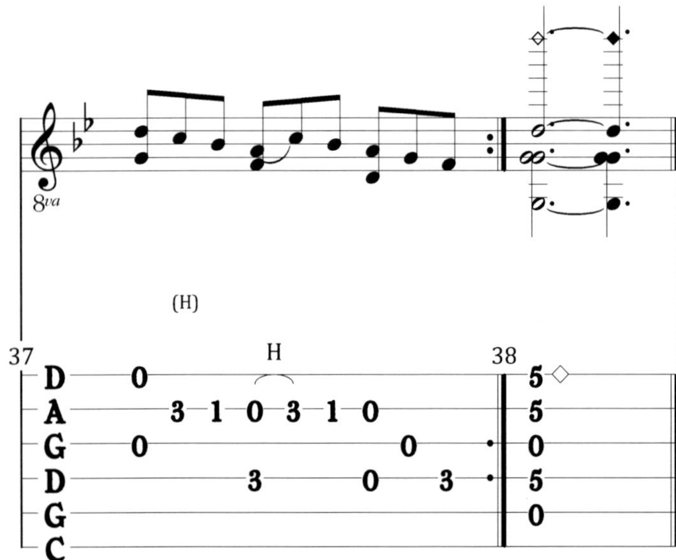
8va
(H)
H
37
38
D
A
G
D
G
C

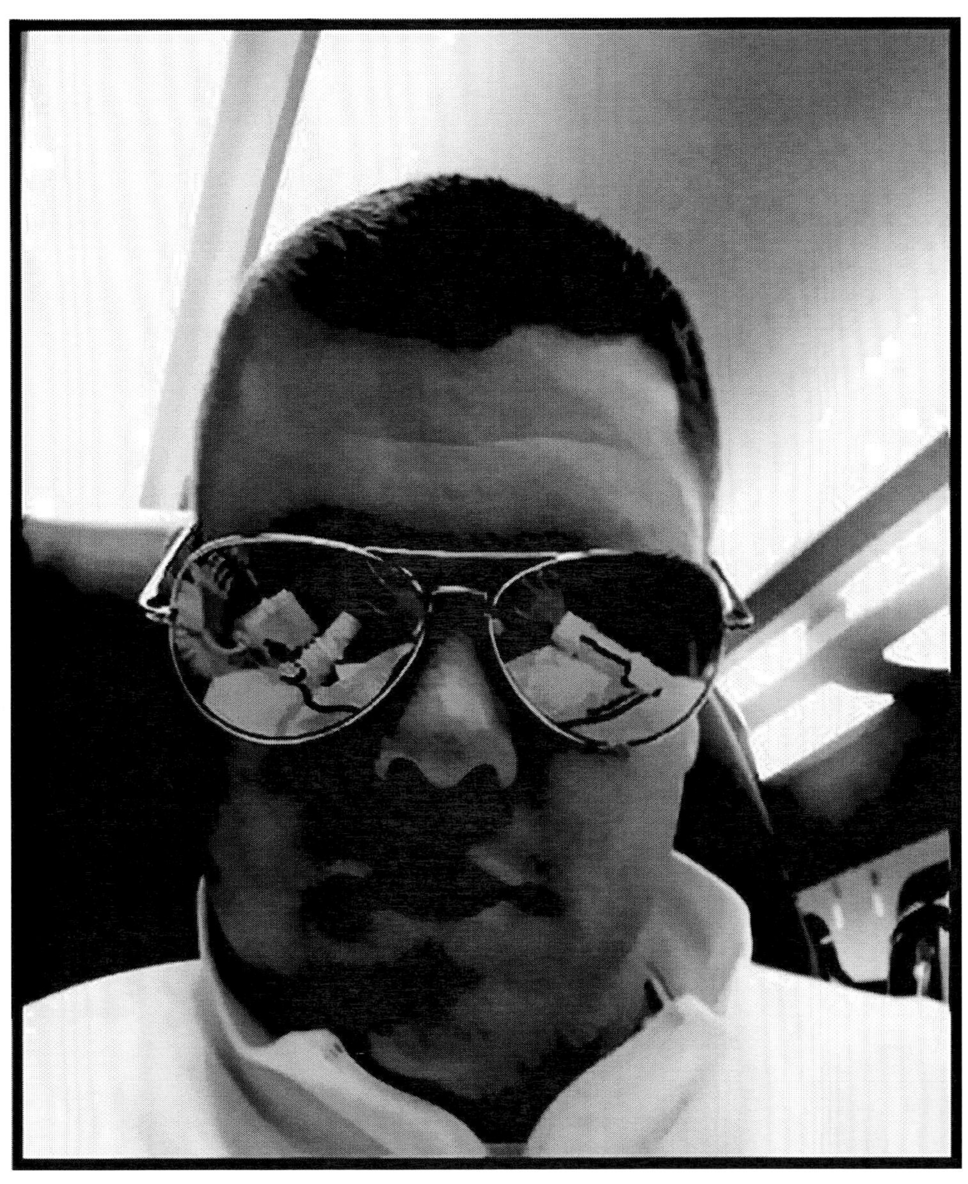

El's son Dan McMeen, with shades

Danny Boy

(Londonderry Air)

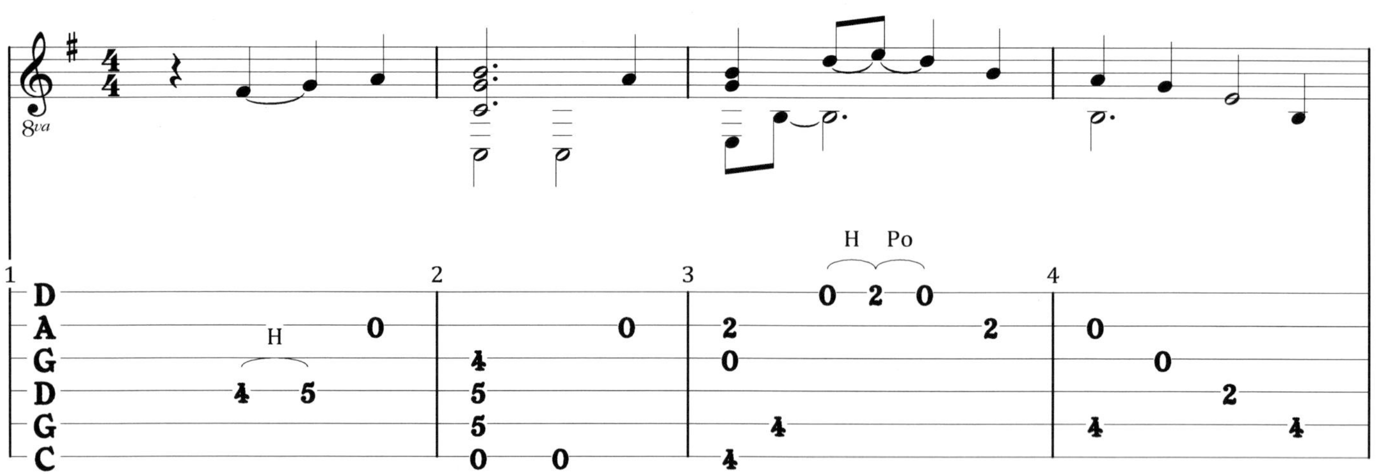

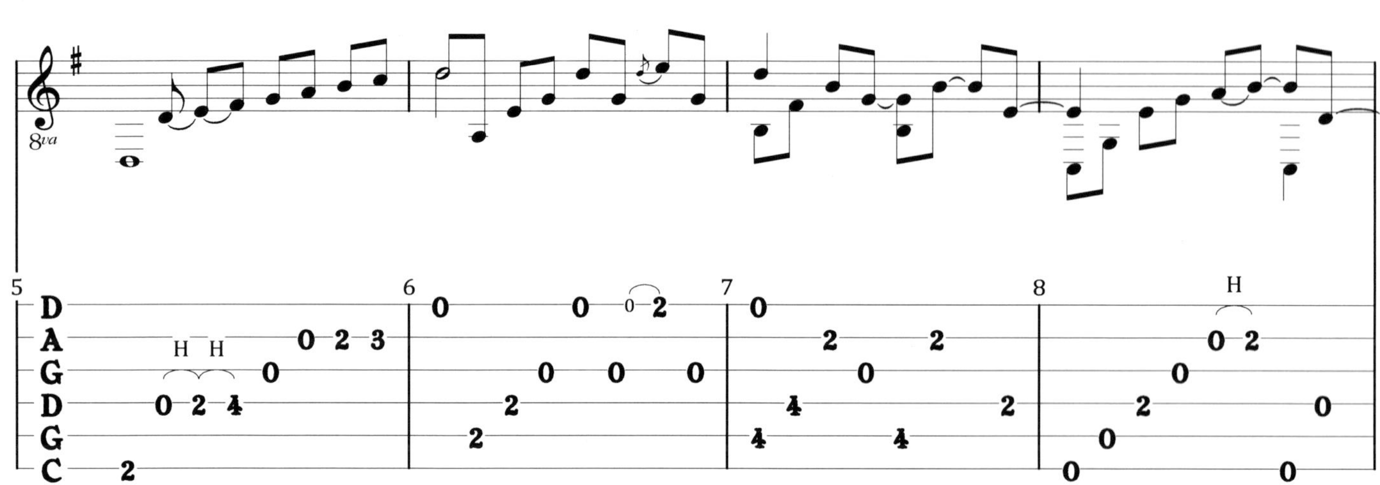

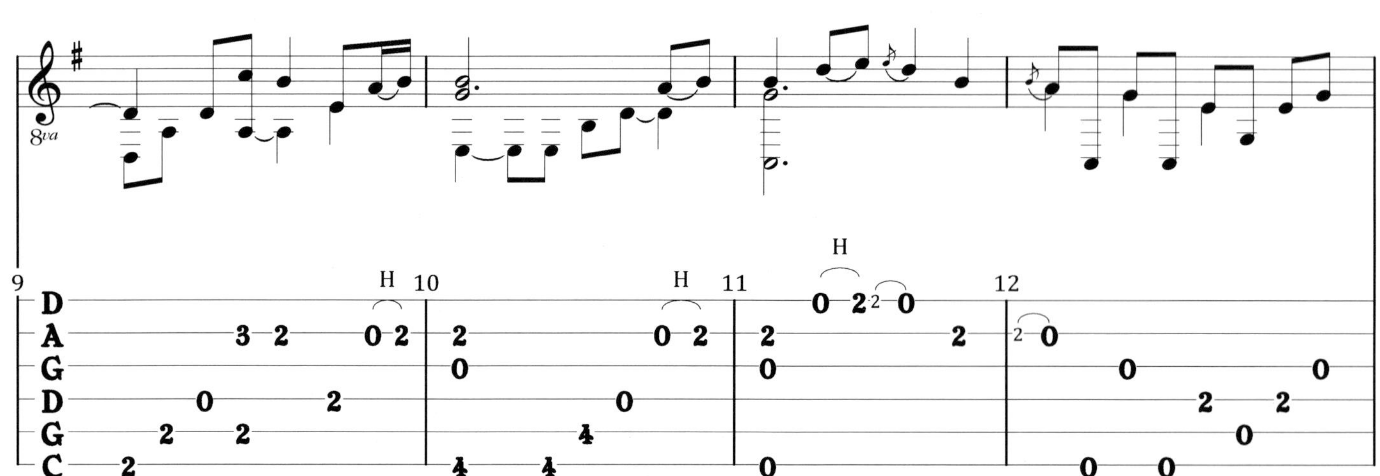

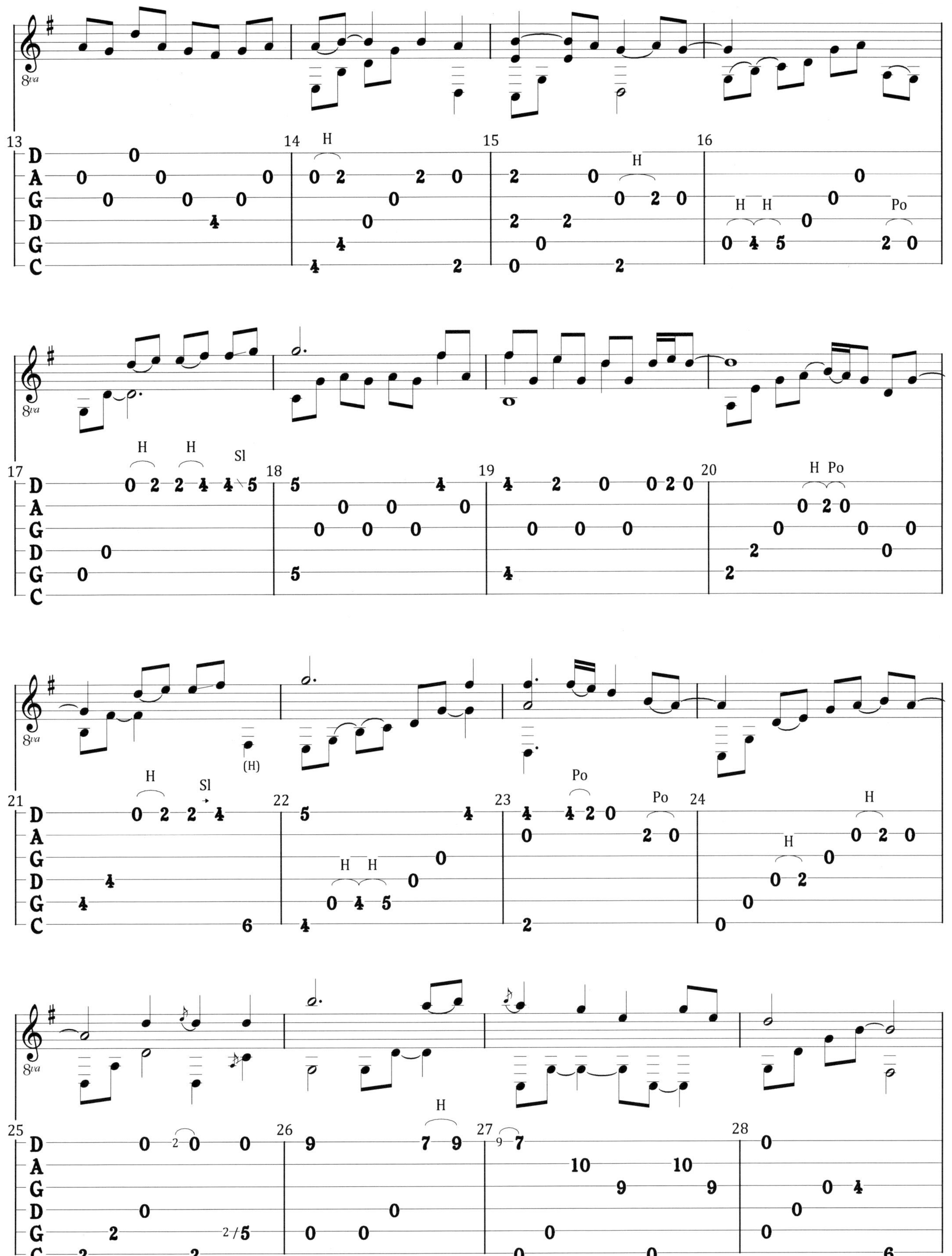
8va
13 14 15 16
D A G D G C
H H H Po
17 18 19 20
H H Sl H Po
21 22 23 24
(H)
H Sl H H Po Po H H
25 26 27 28
H

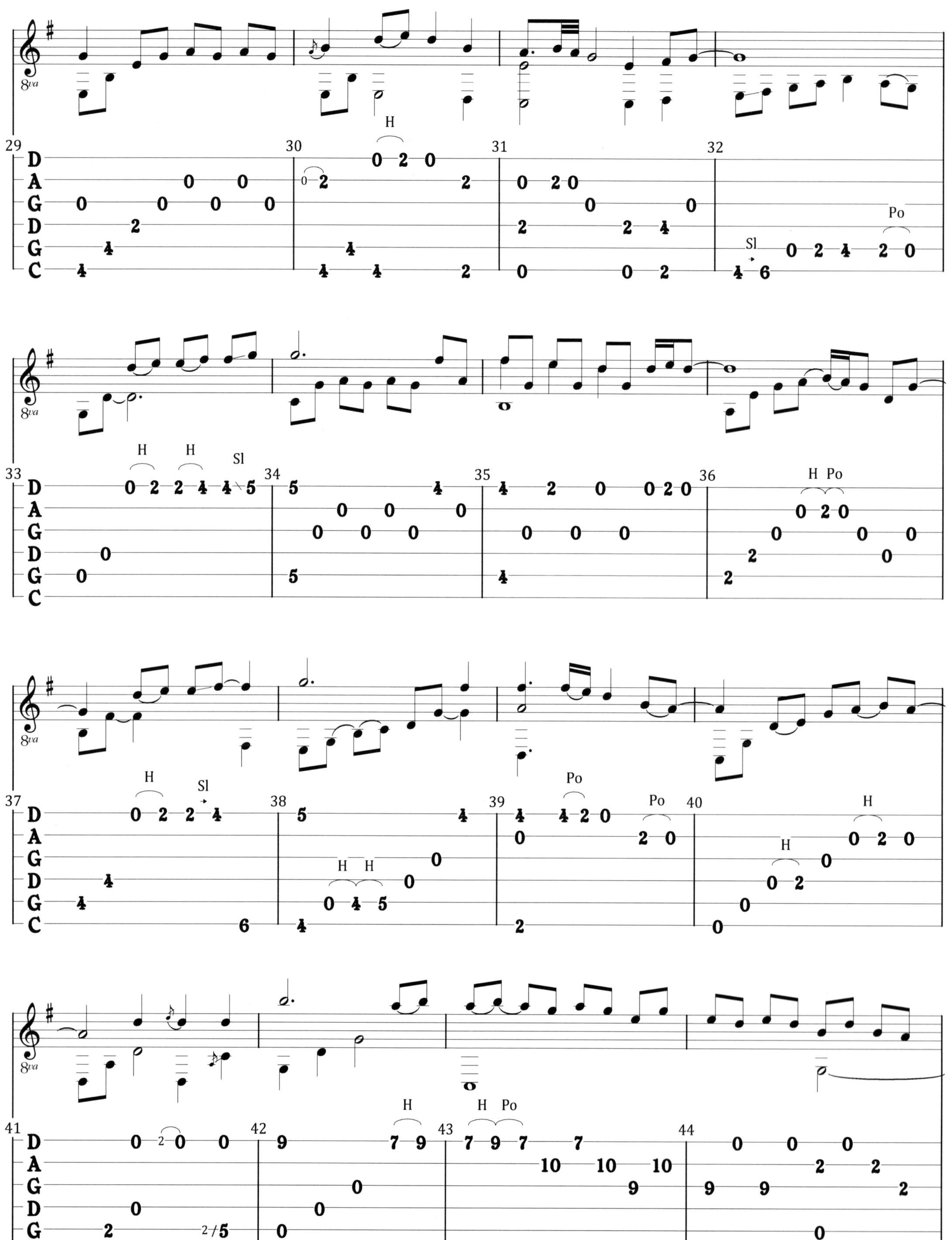
8va
H
Sl
Po
D
A
G
D
G
C

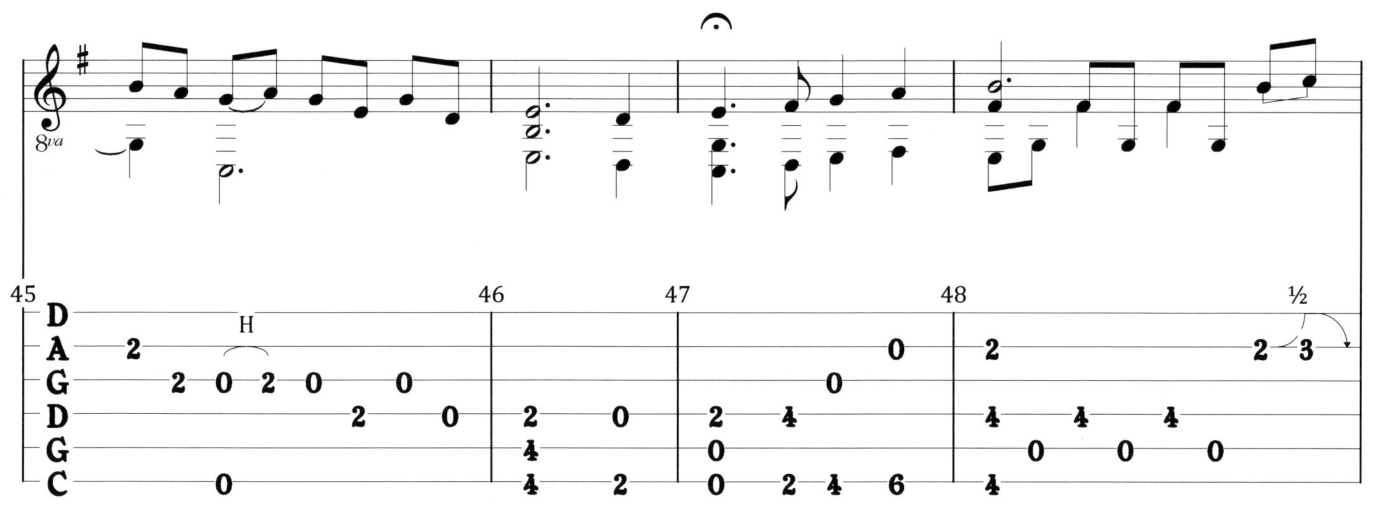
8va
45
46
47
48
½
H
D
A
G
D
G
C

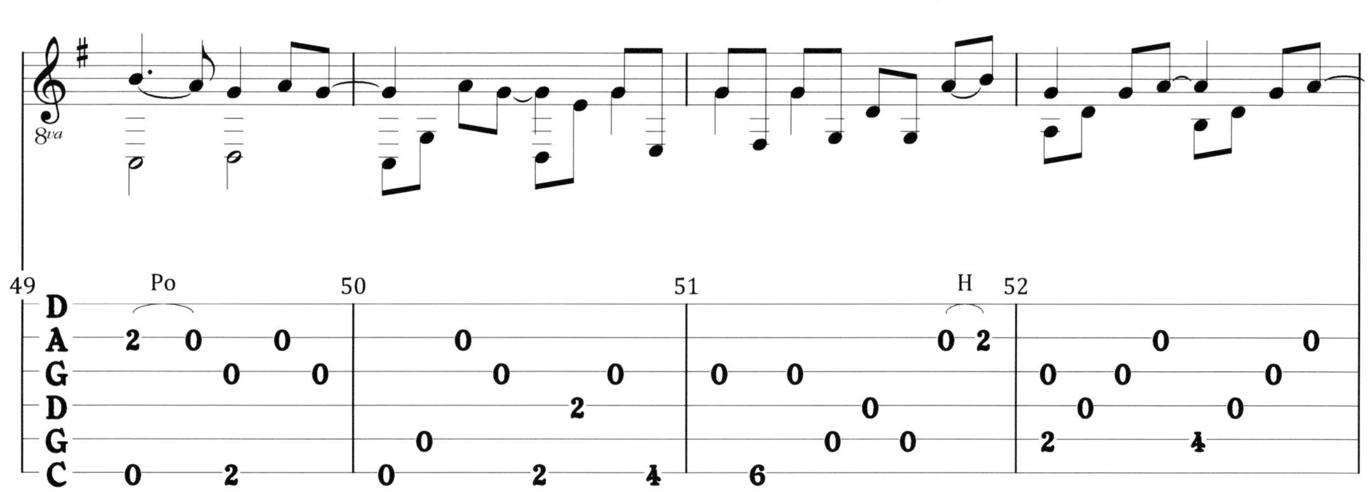
8va
49
50
51
52
Po
H
D
A
G
D
G
C

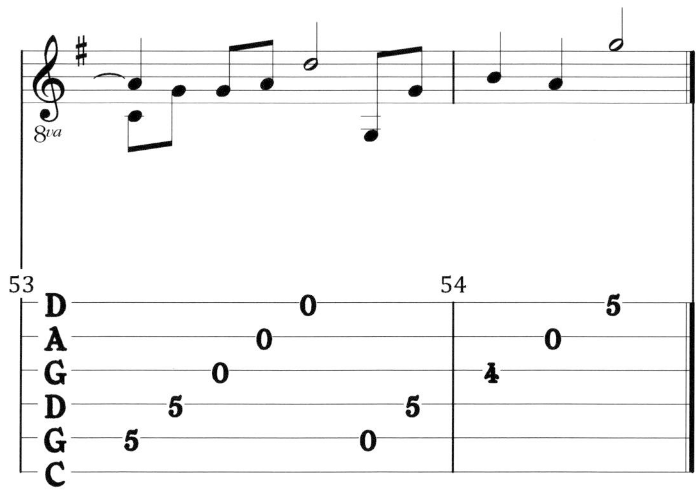
8va
53
54
D
A
G
D
G
C

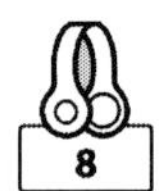

The Fairflower of Northumberland

(Traditional)

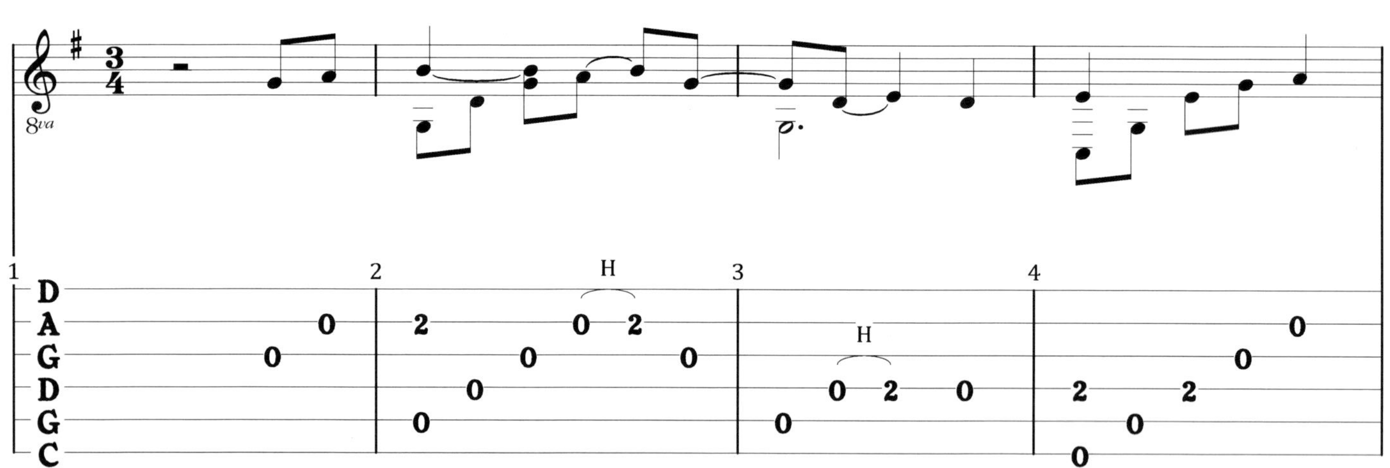

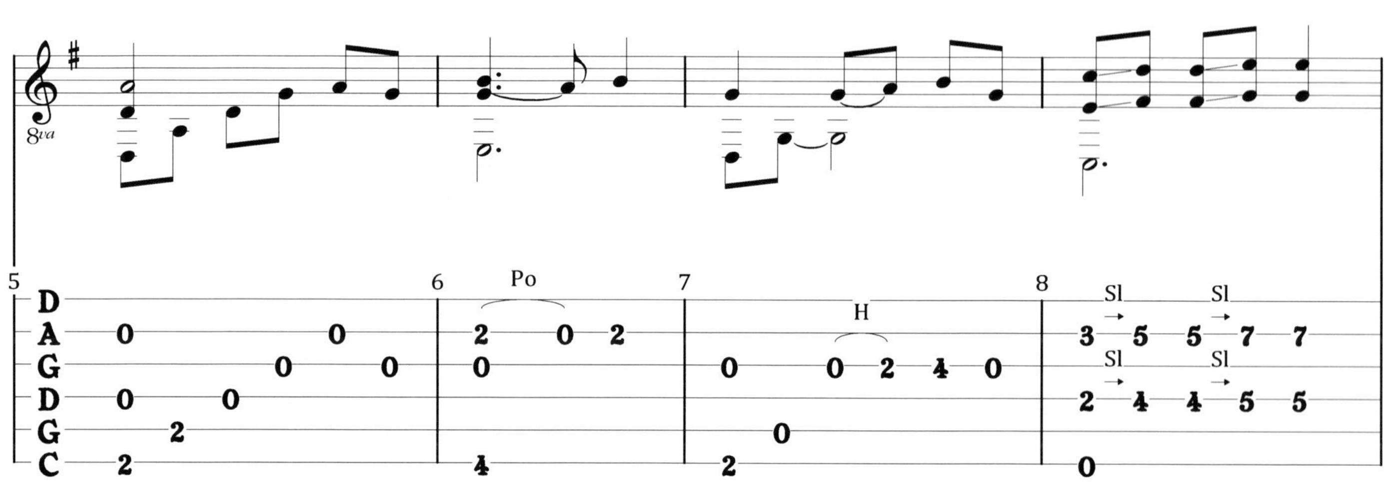

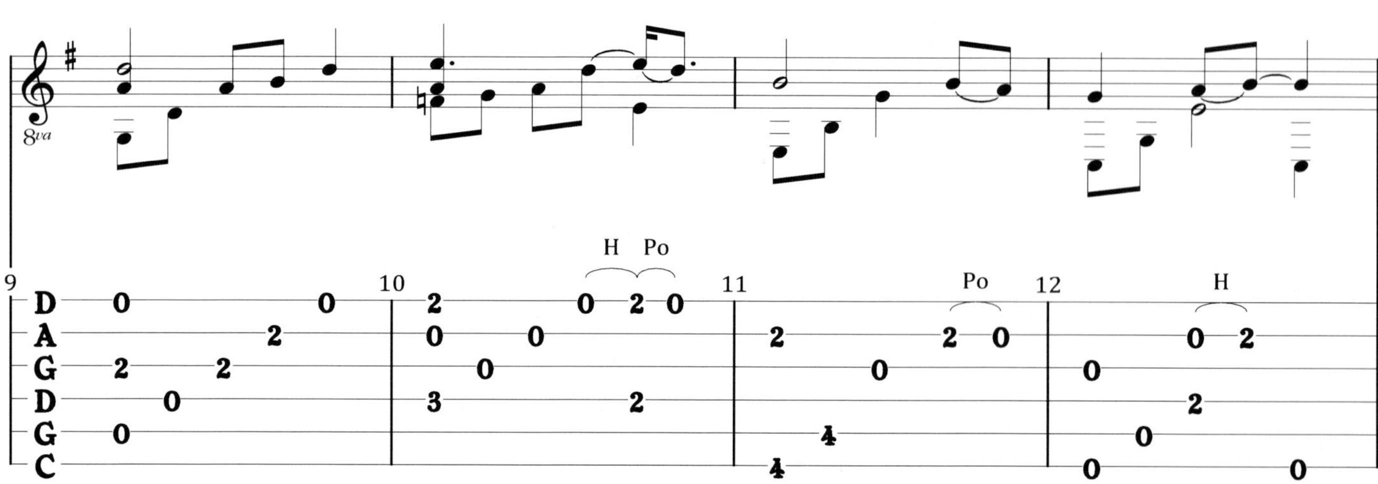

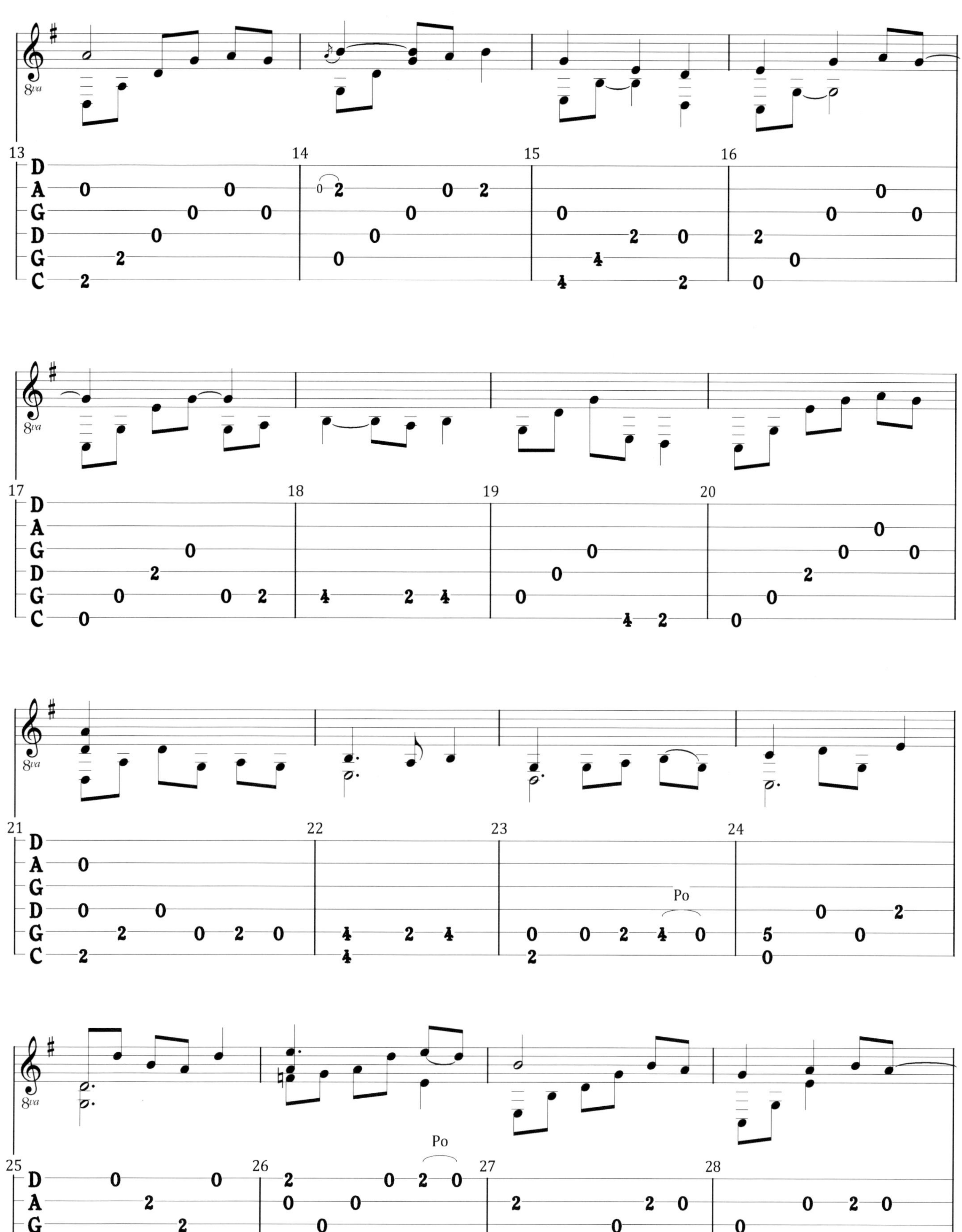
8va
D A G D G C
Po
Po

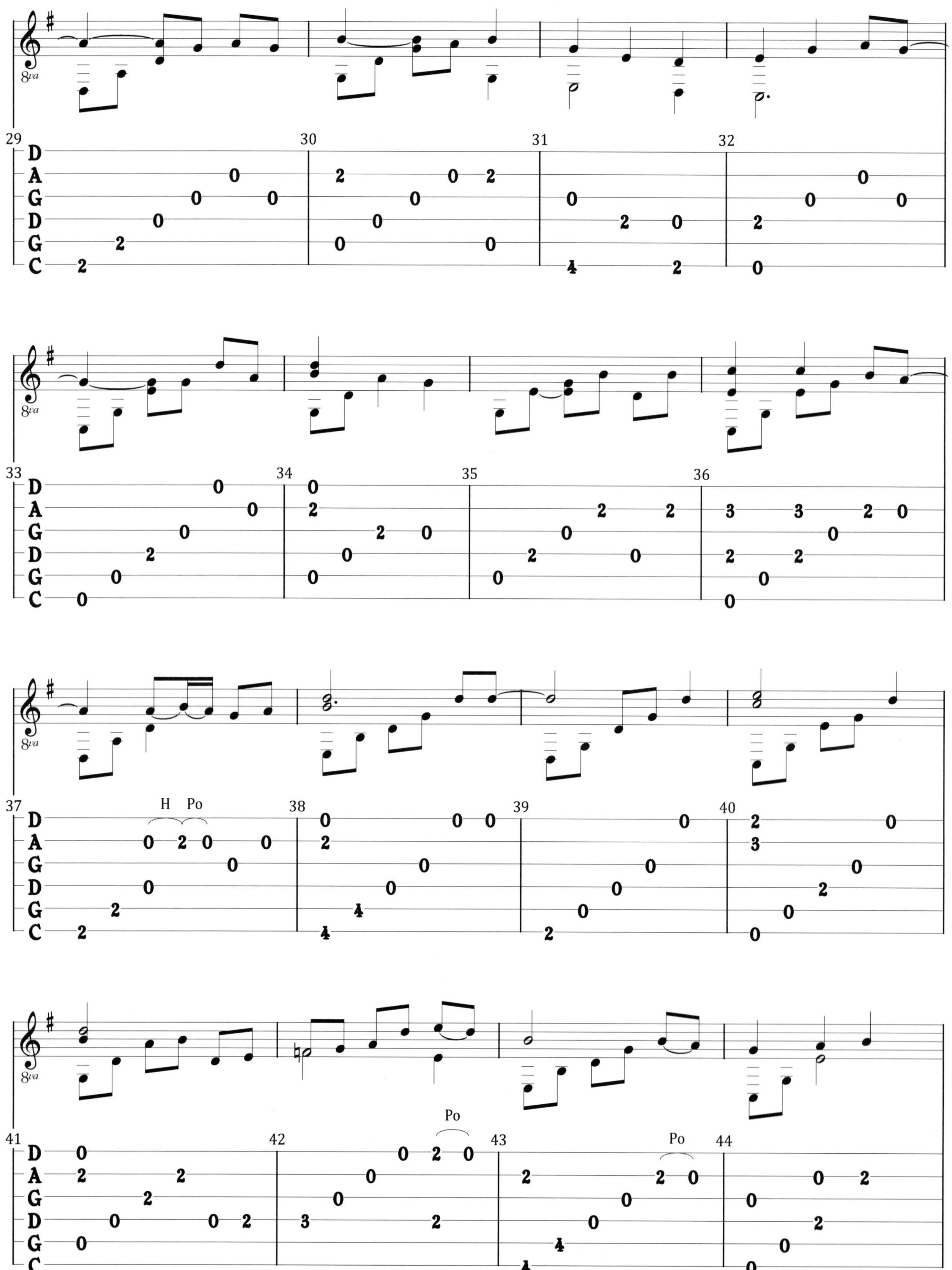
8va
29
30
31
32
D
A
G
D
G
C
33
34
35
36
37
H Po
38
39
40
41
42
Po
43
Po
44

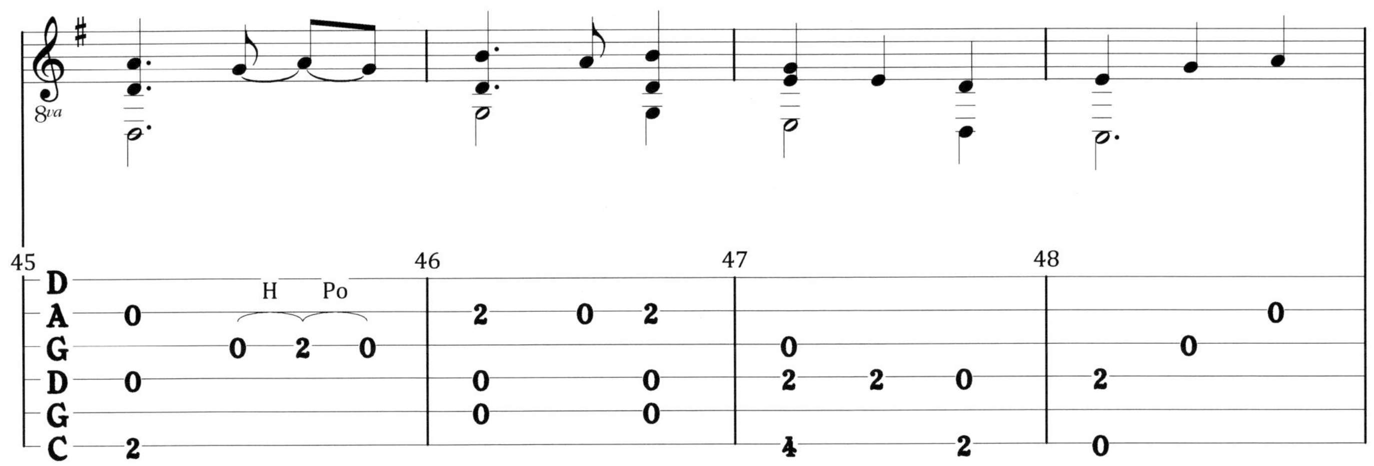
8va
45
46
47
48
D
A
G
D
G
C
H
Po

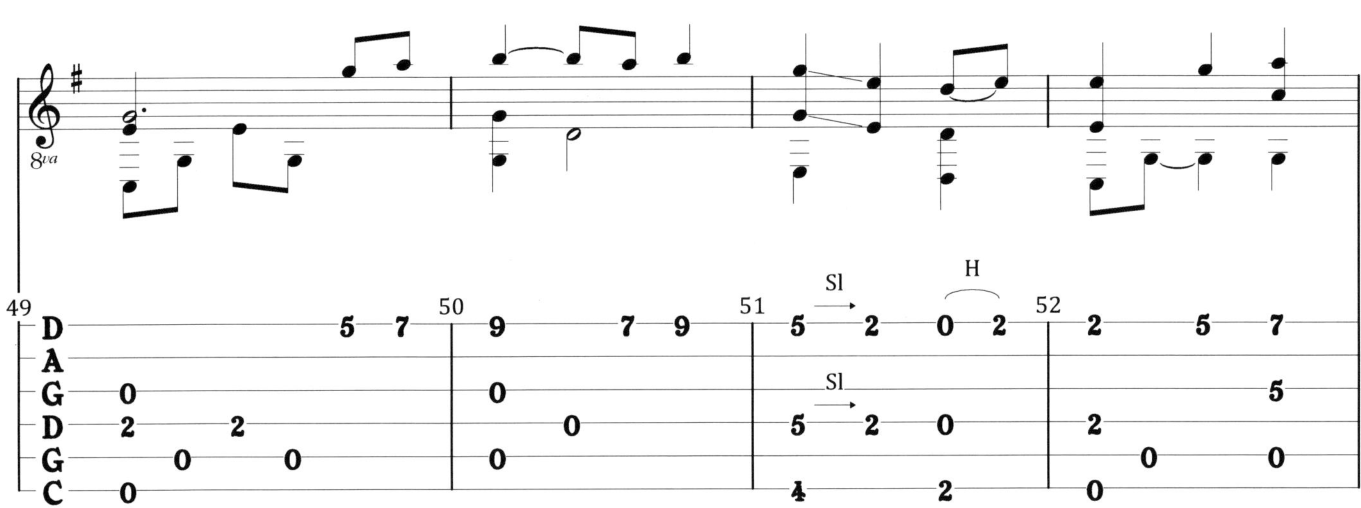
8va
49
50
51
52
D
A
G
D
G
C
Sl
H
Sl

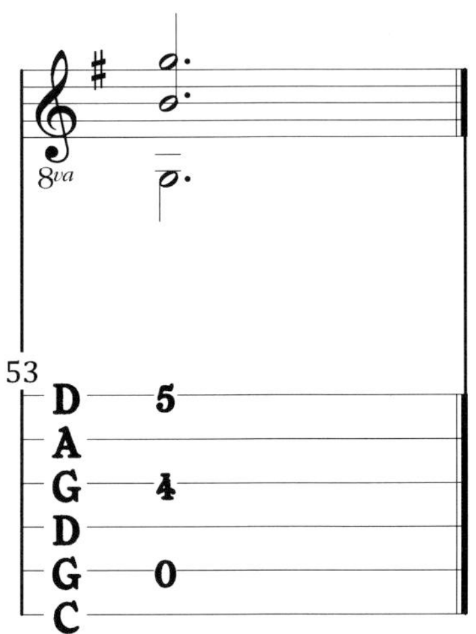
8va
53
D
A
G
D
G
C

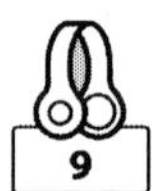

Greensleeves

(Traditional Song)

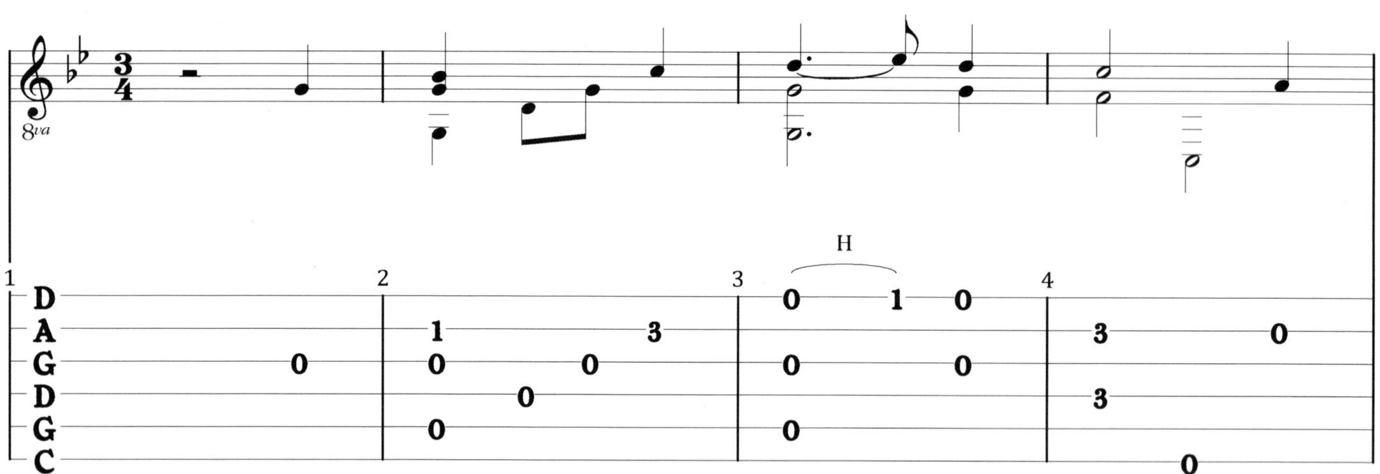

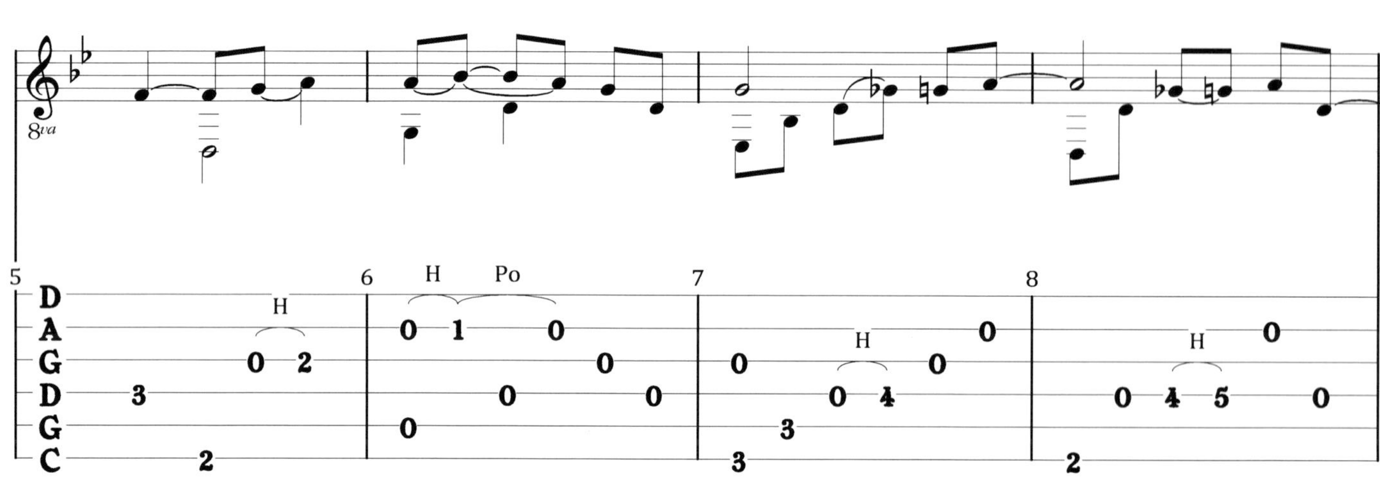

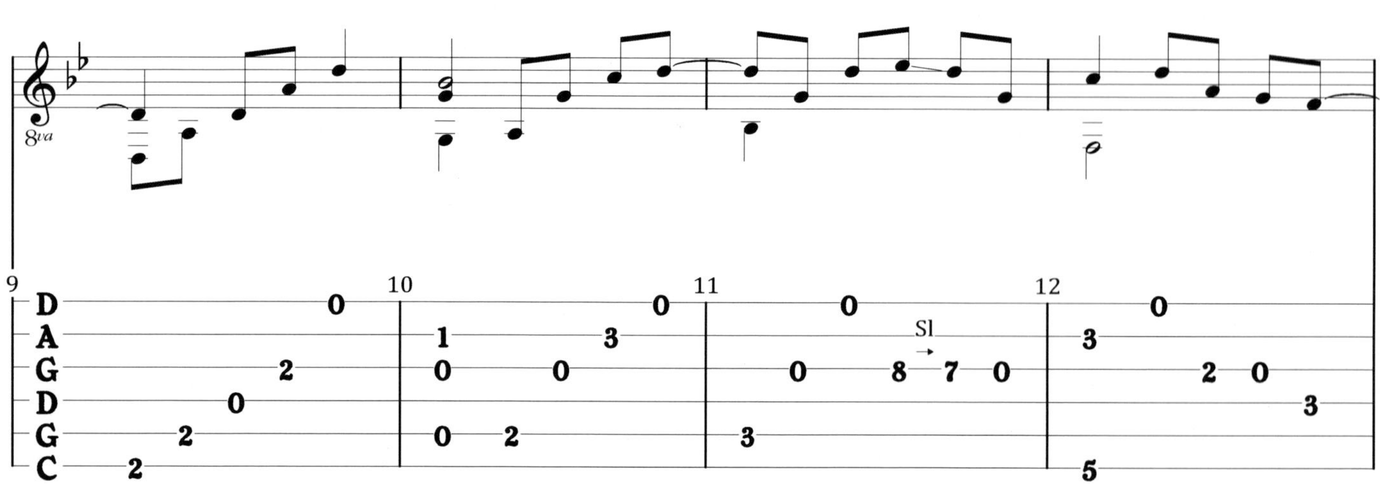

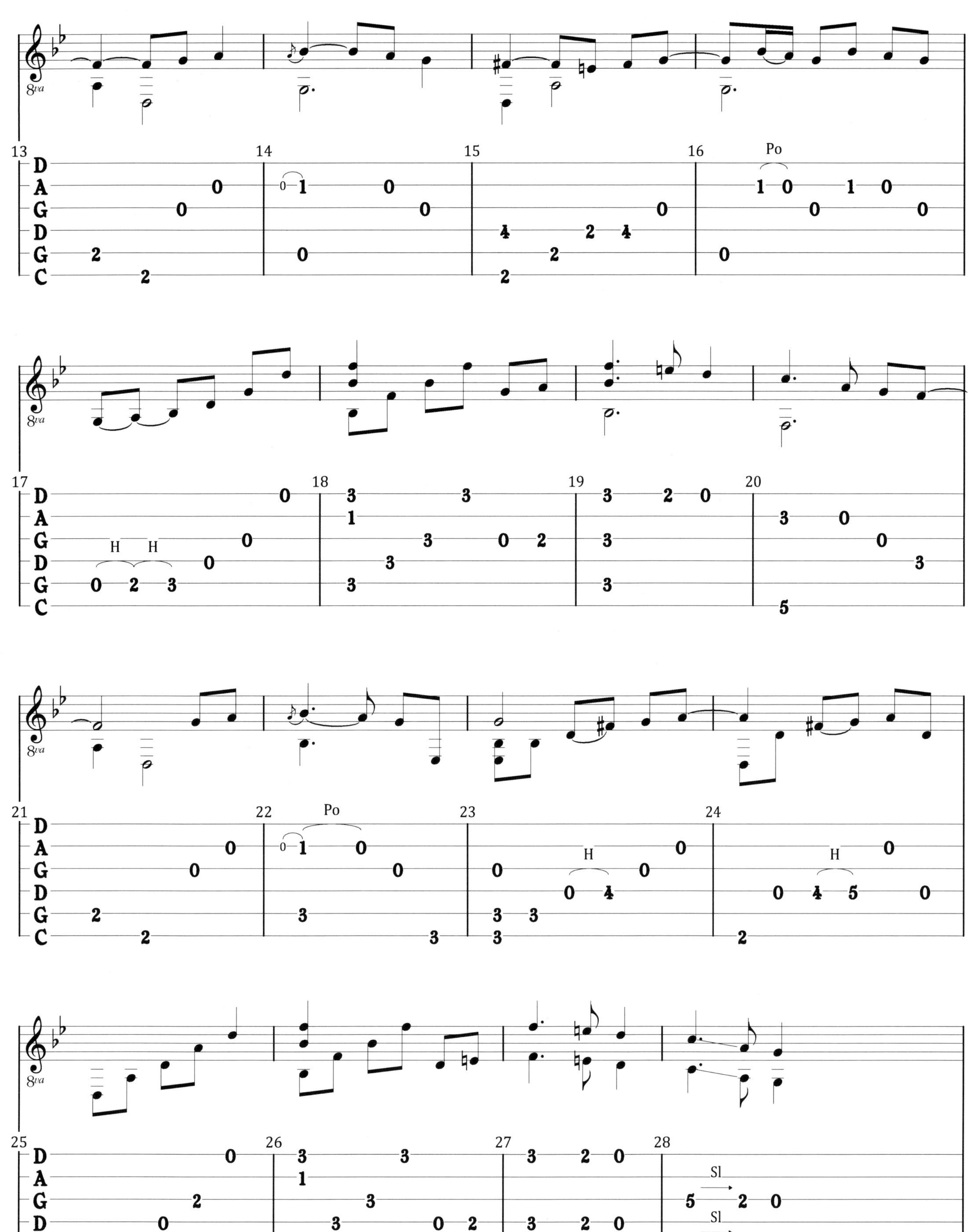
8va
D
A
G
D
G
C
Po
H
Sl

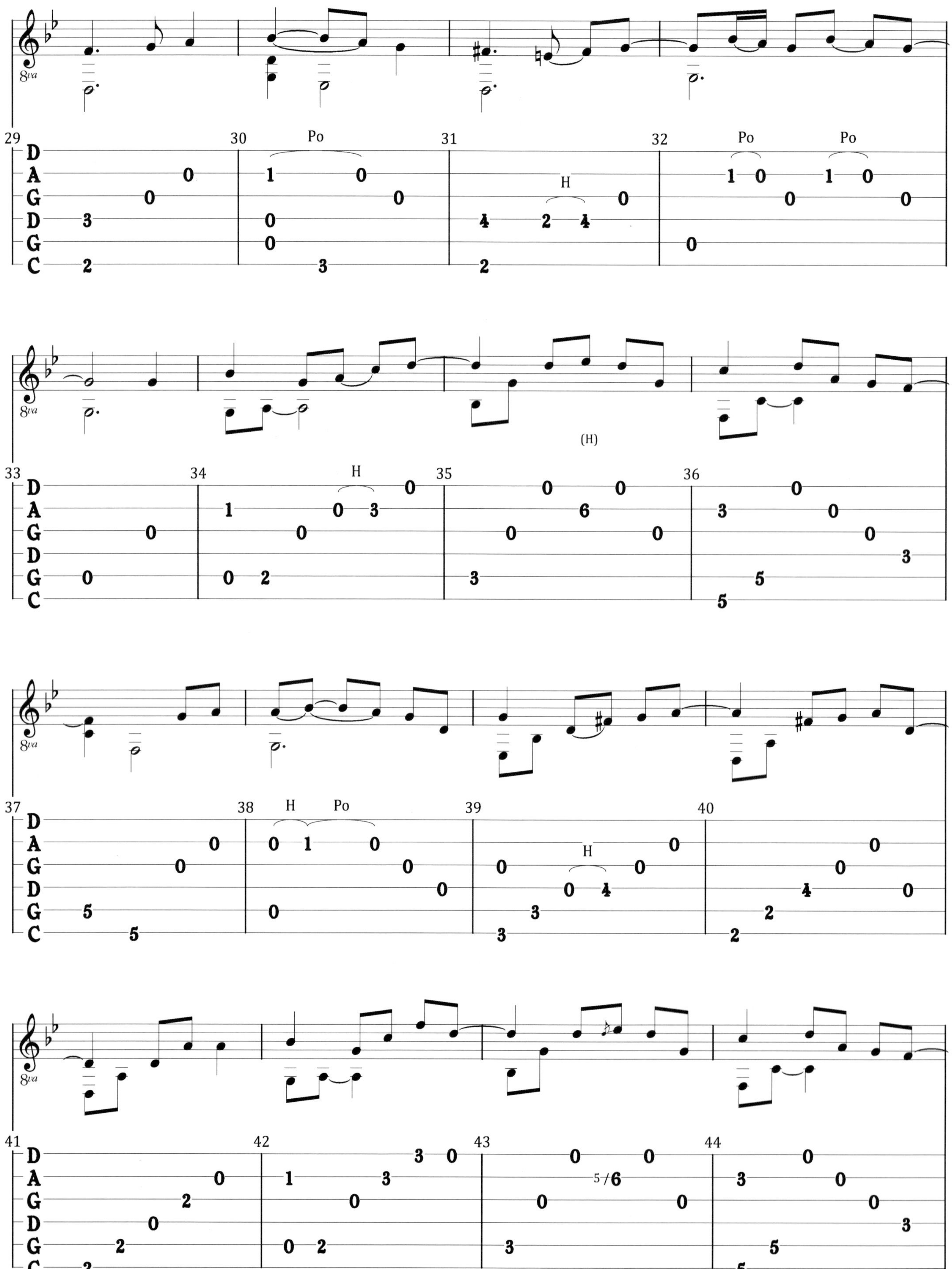
8va
29
30
Po
31
H
32
Po
Po
D
A
G
D
G
C
33
34
H
35
(H)
36
37
38
H
Po
39
H
40
41
42
43
44

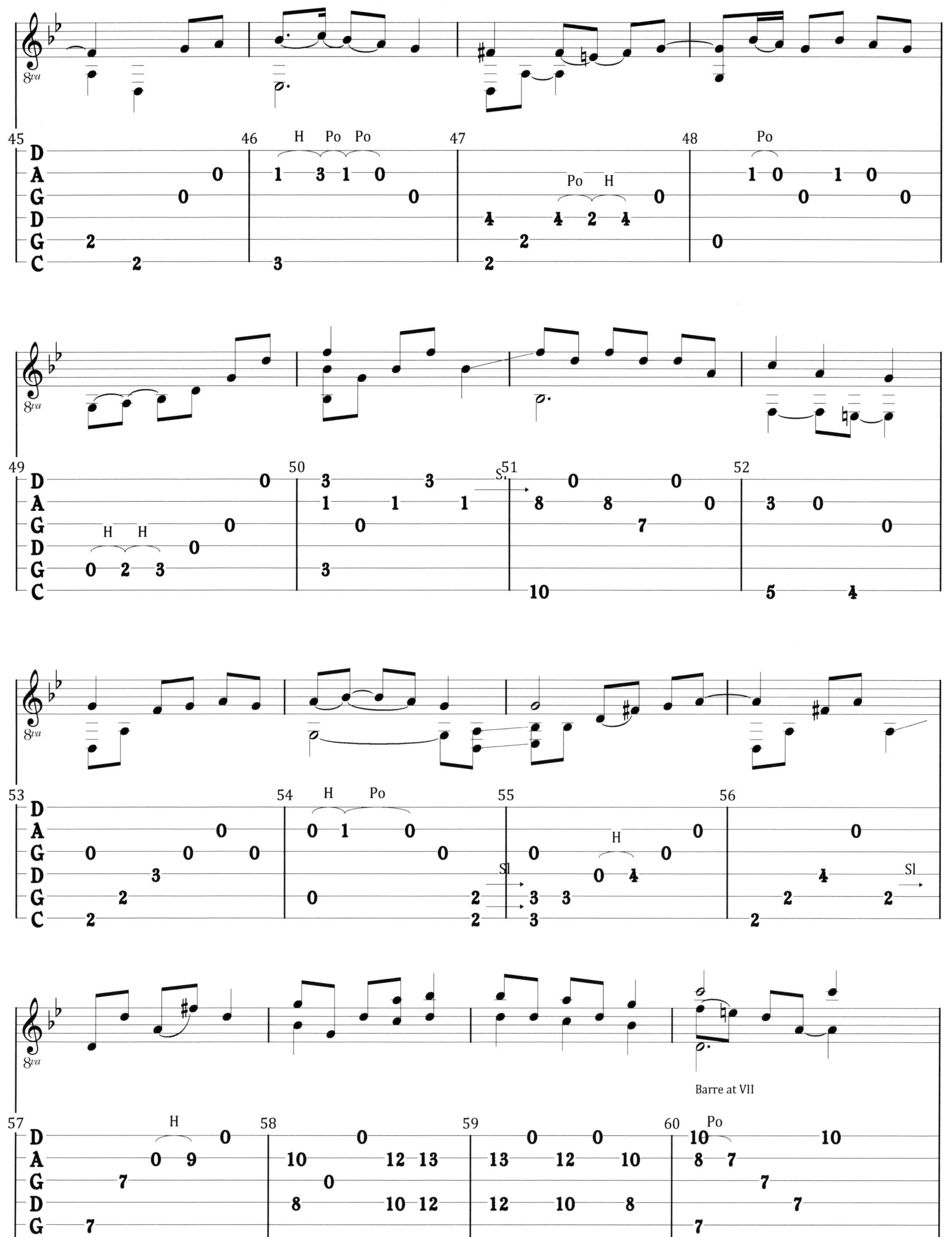
8va
D
A
G
D
G
C
45
46
47
48
H Po Po
Po H
Po
49
50
51
52
H H
S.
53
54
55
56
H Po
H
Sl
Sl
57
58
59
60
H
Po
Barre at VII

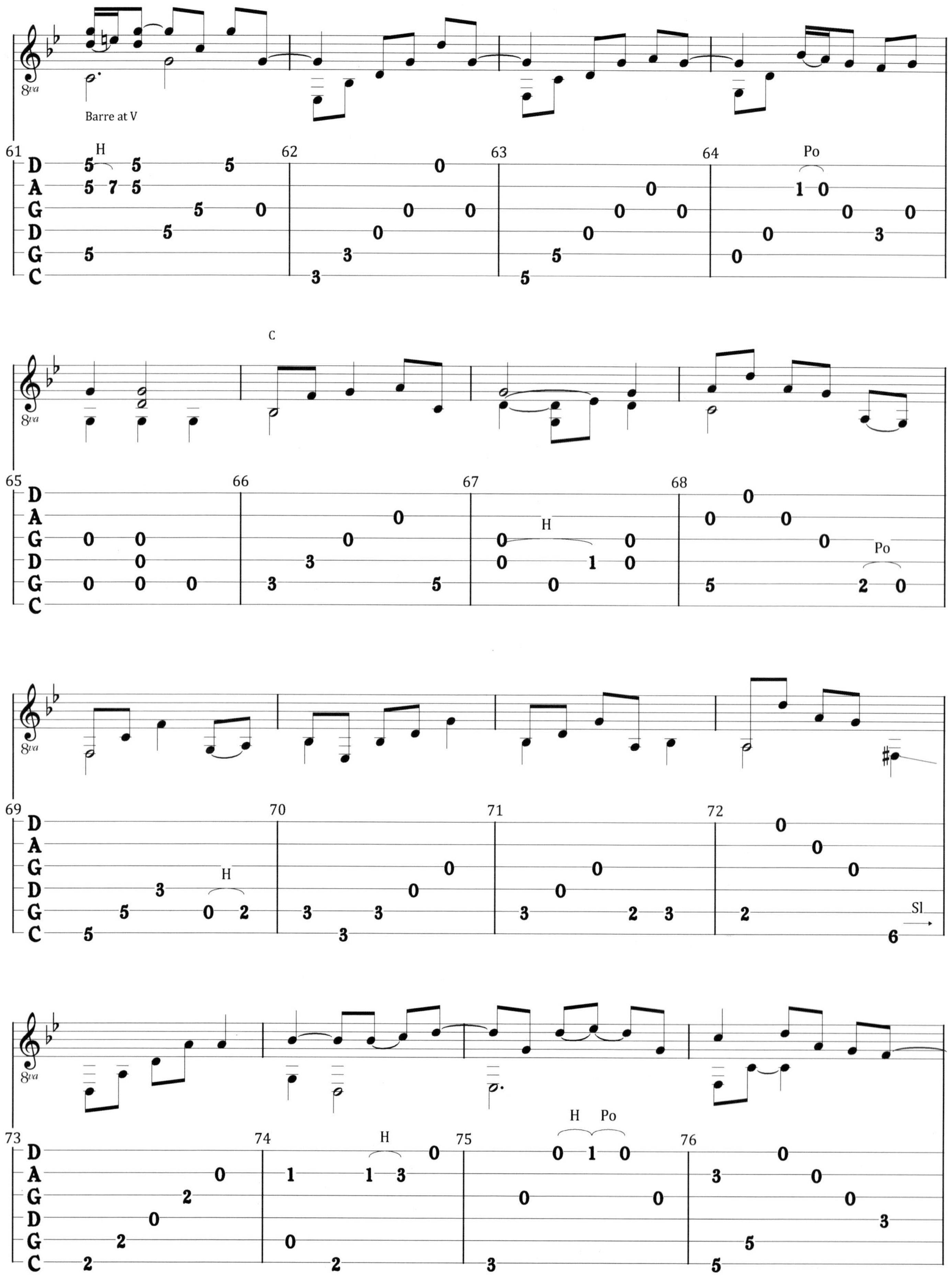
8va
Barre at V
H
Po
C
Sl
61
62
63
64
65
66
67
68
69
70
71
72
73
74
75
76
D
A
G
D
G
C

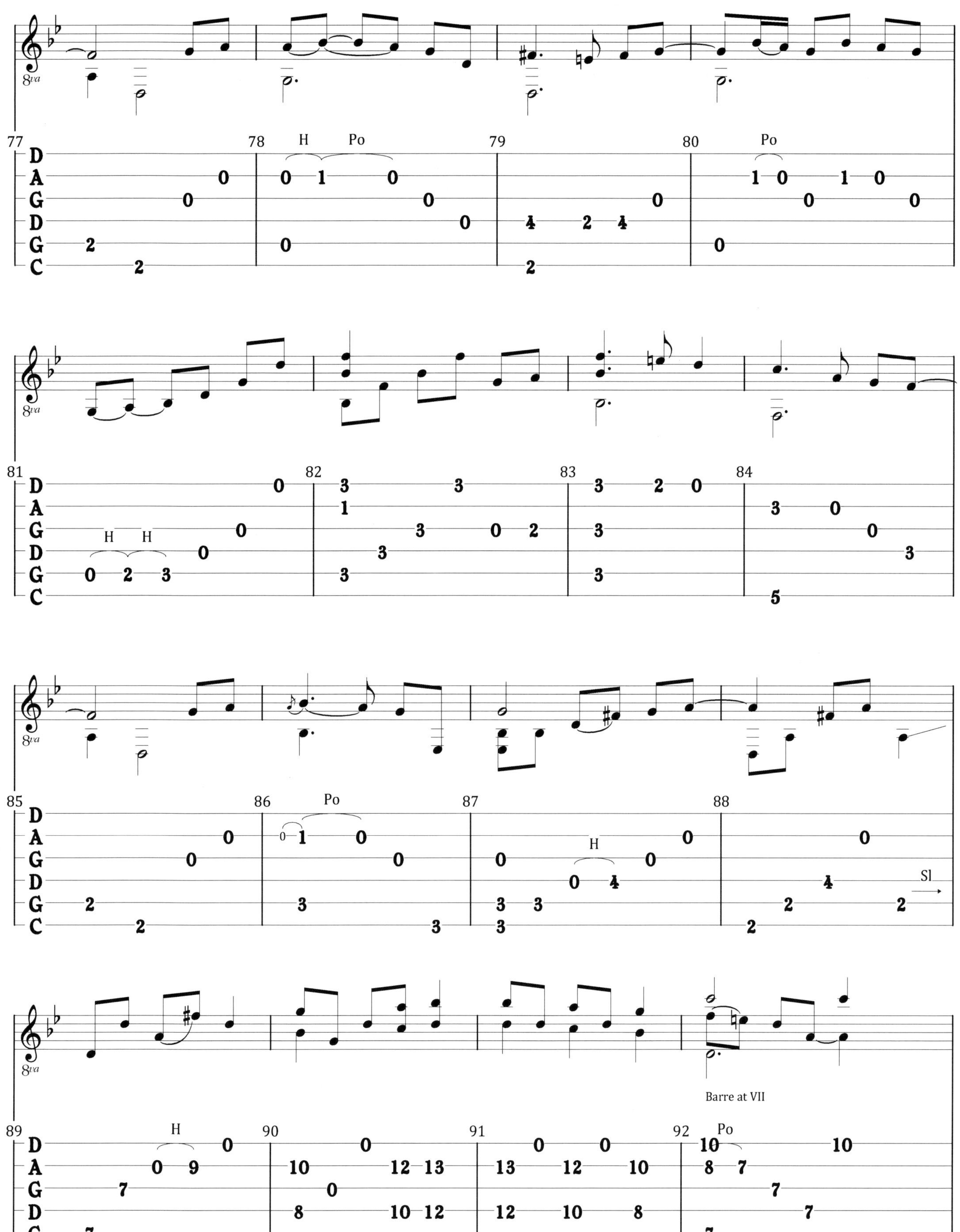
8va
H
Po
Sl
Barre at VII

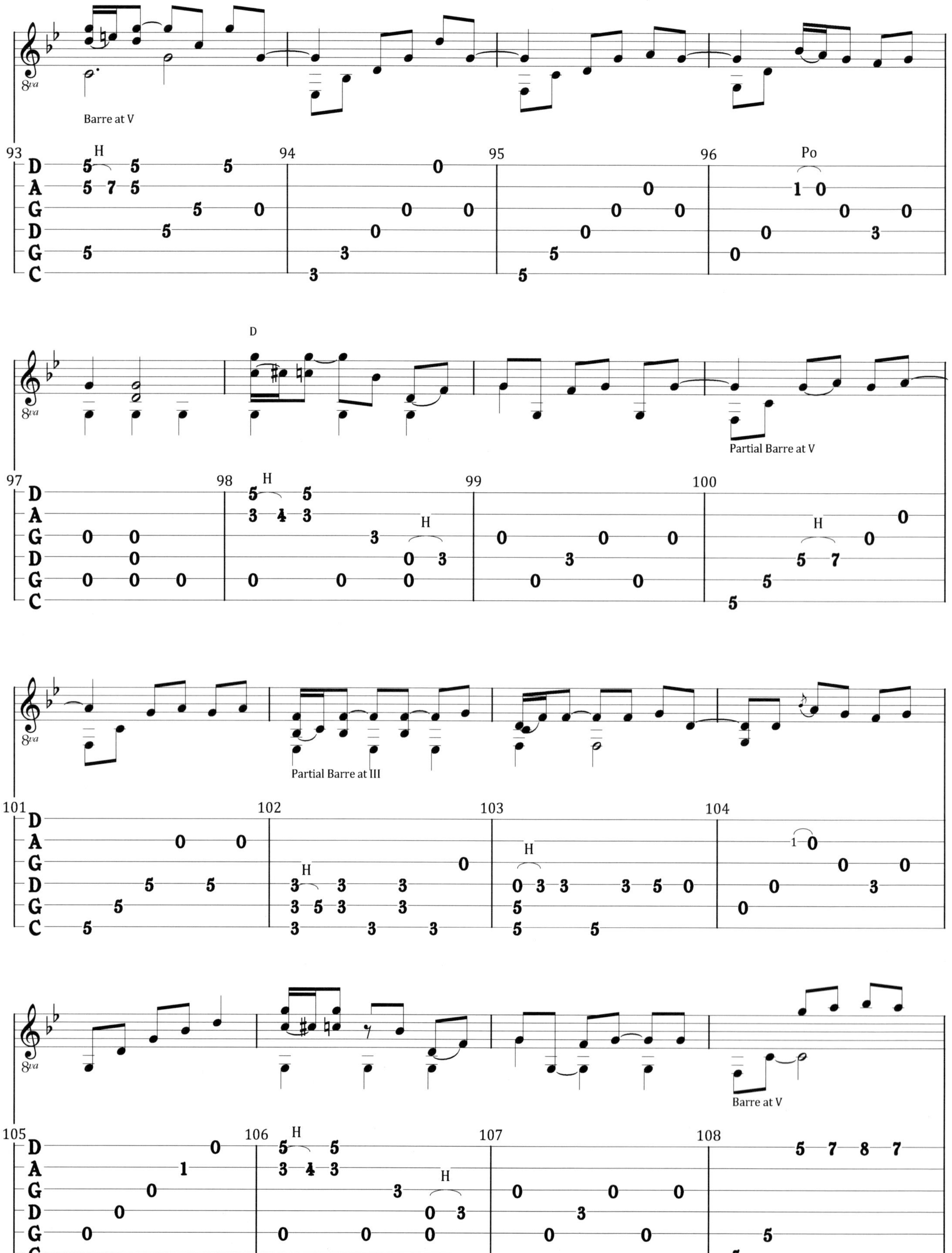
Barre at V
93
94
95
96
D
A
G
D
G
C
H
Po
D
Partial Barre at V
97
98
99
100
H
Partial Barre at III
101
102
103
104
Barre at V
105
106
107
108

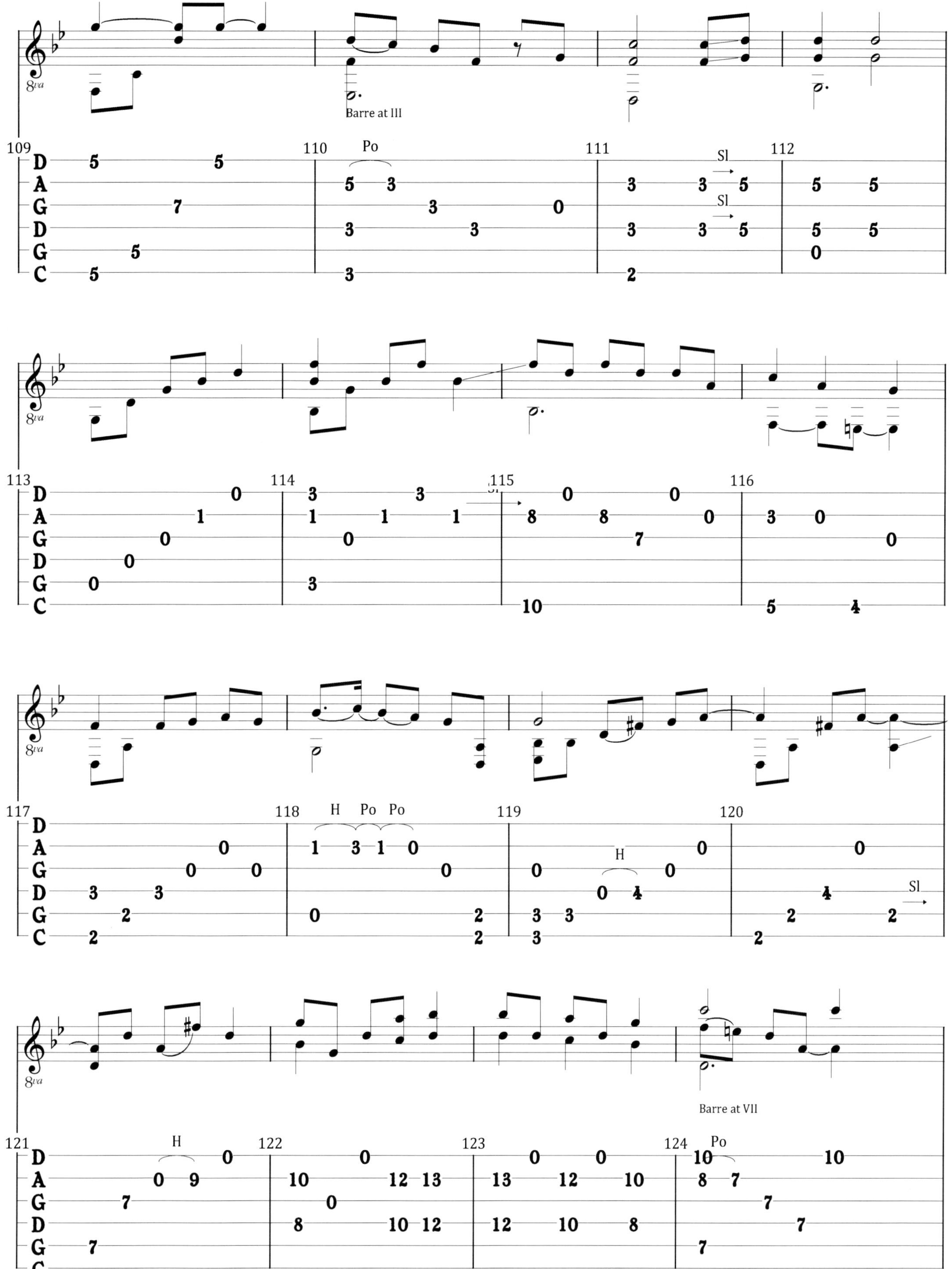
8va
109
110
111
112
Po
Sl
Sl
Barre at III
113
114
115
116
117
118
119
120
H
Po
Po
H
Sl
121
122
123
124
H
Po
Barre at VII

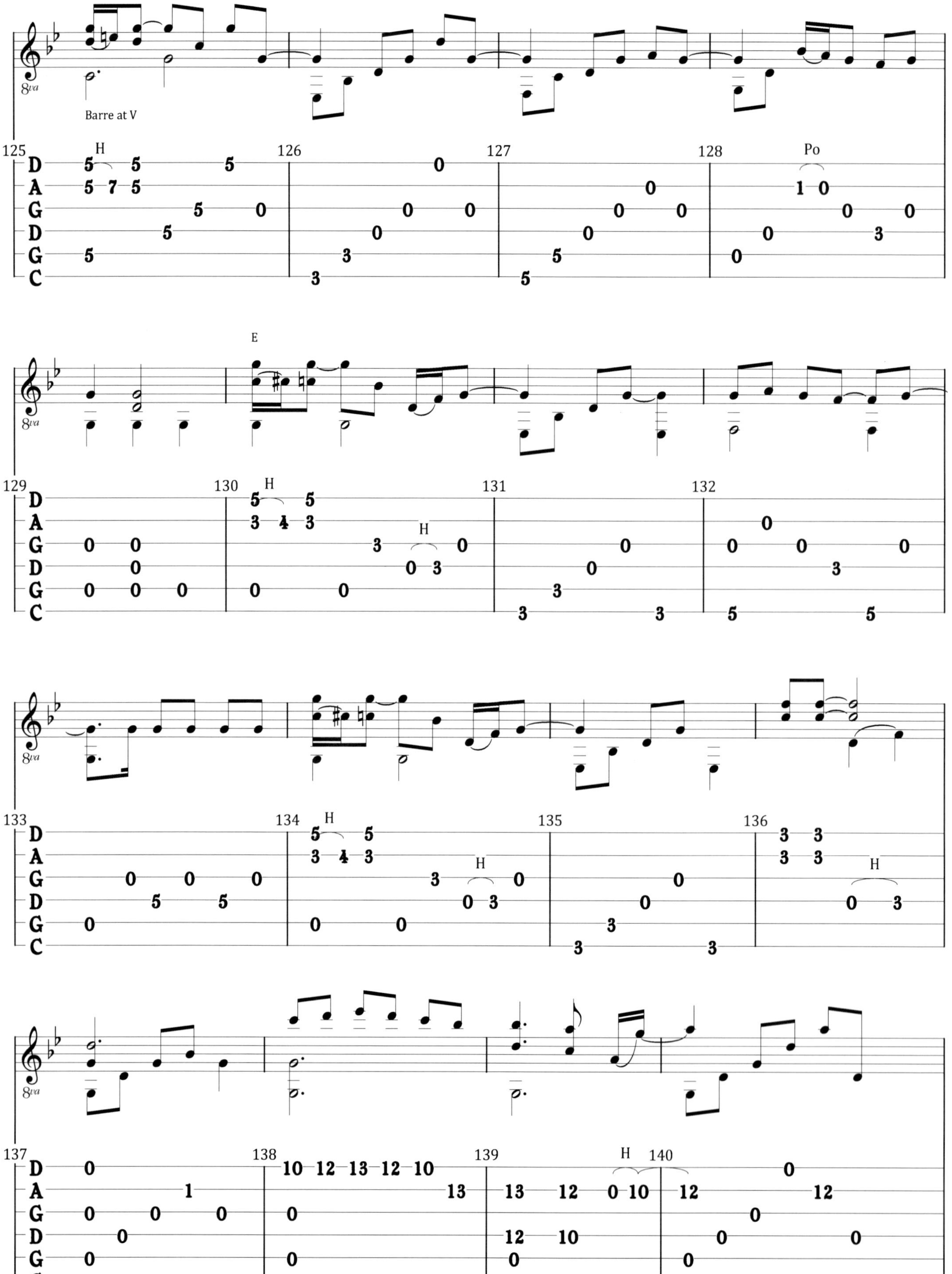
Barre at V
125
126
127
128
H
Po
E
129
130
131
132
133
134
135
136
137
138
139
140
D
A
G
D
G
C

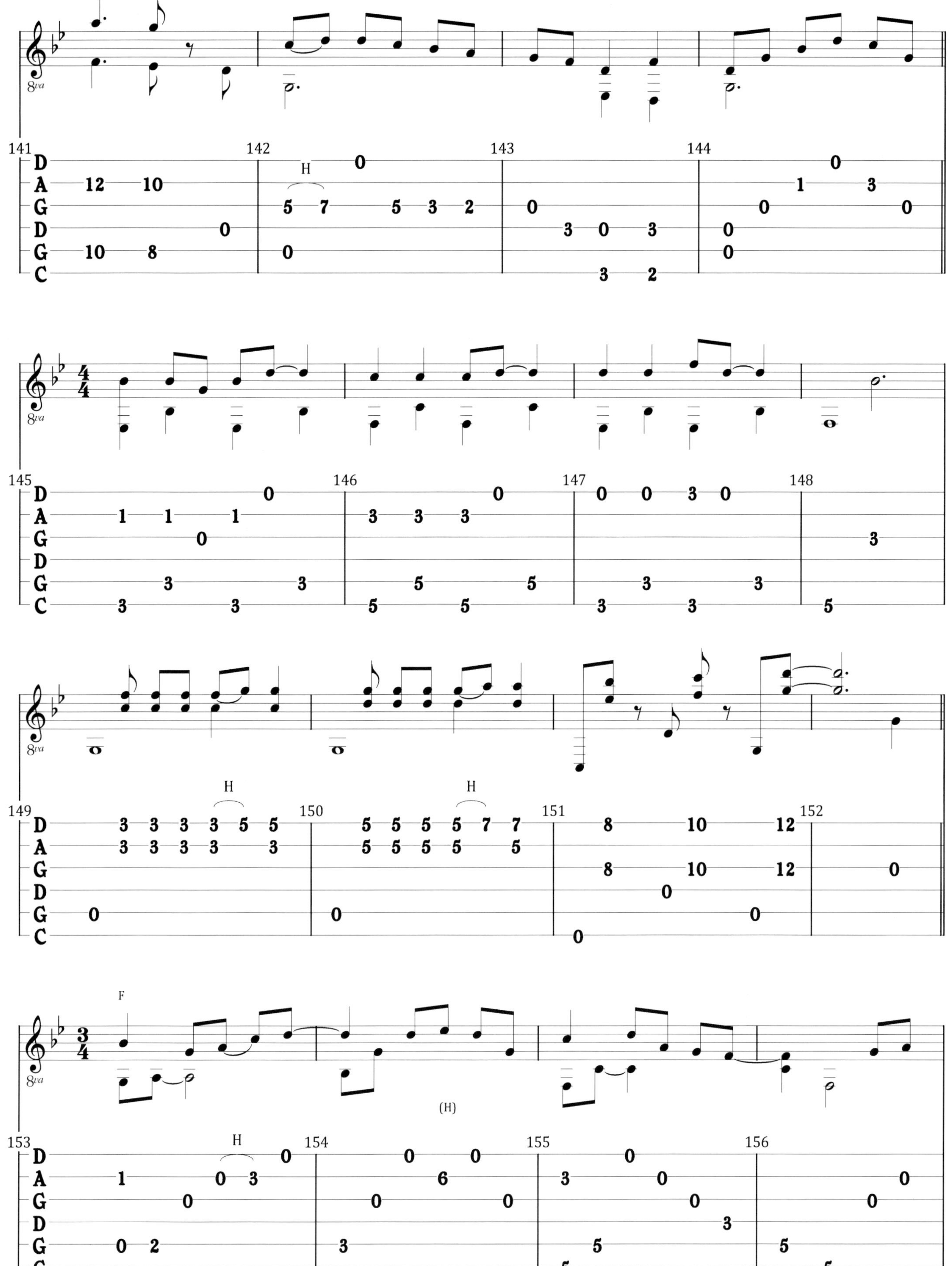
8va
141
142
143
144
H
145
146
147
148
149
150
151
152
F
(H)
153
154
155
156

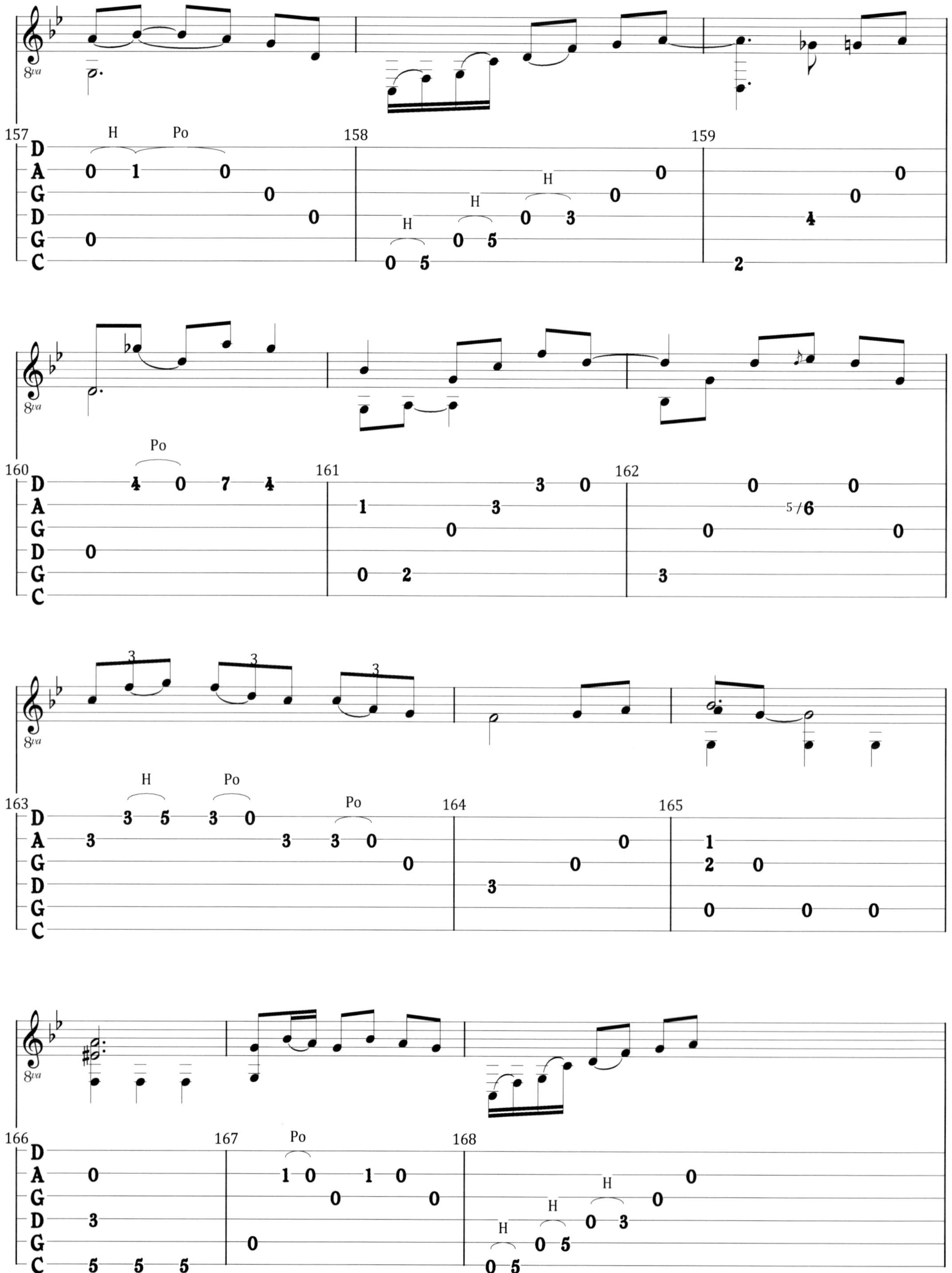
8va
157
158
159
D
A
G
D
G
C
H
Po
160
161
162
163
164
165
166
167
168

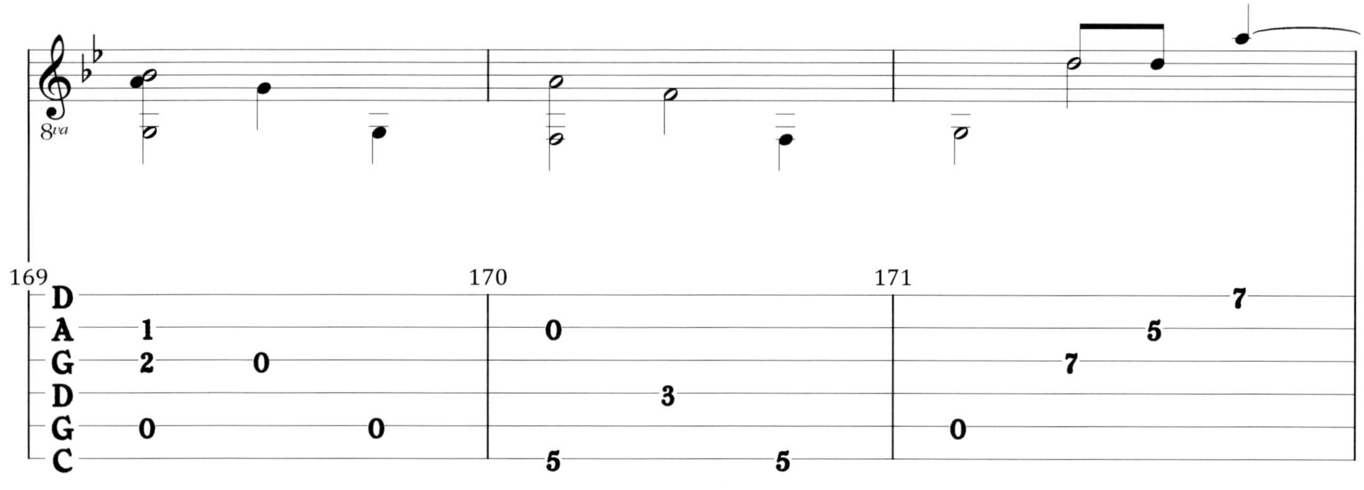
8va
169
170
171
D
A
G
D
G
C
1
2
0
0
0
0
5
3
5
0
7
5
7

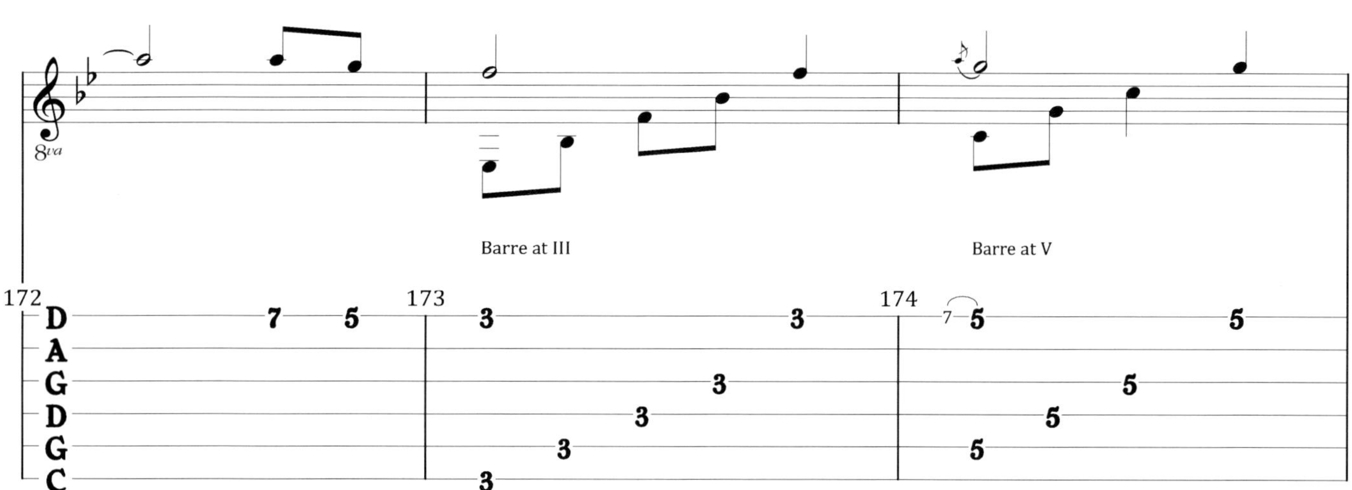
8va
Barre at III
Barre at V
172
173
174
D
A
G
D
G
C
7
5
3
3
3
3
3
7
5
5
5
5
5

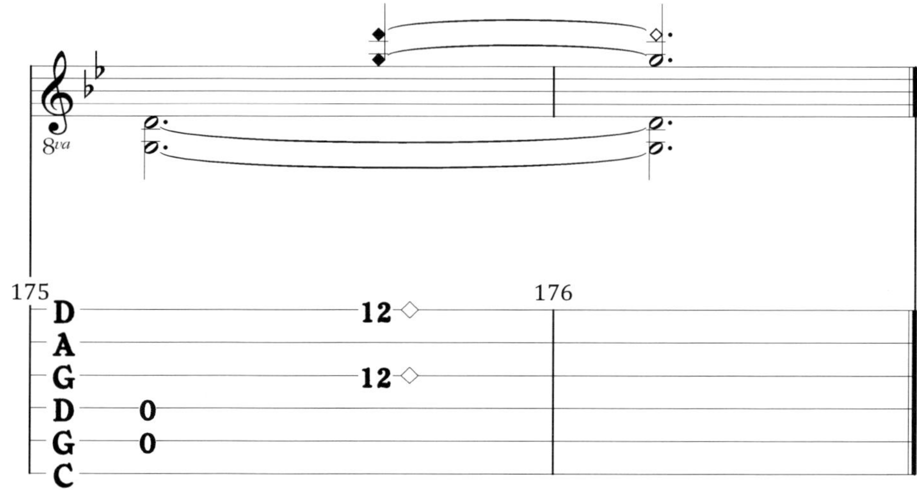
8va
175
176
D
A
G
D
G
C
12
12
0
0

Mo Giolla Mear

(Traditional Song)

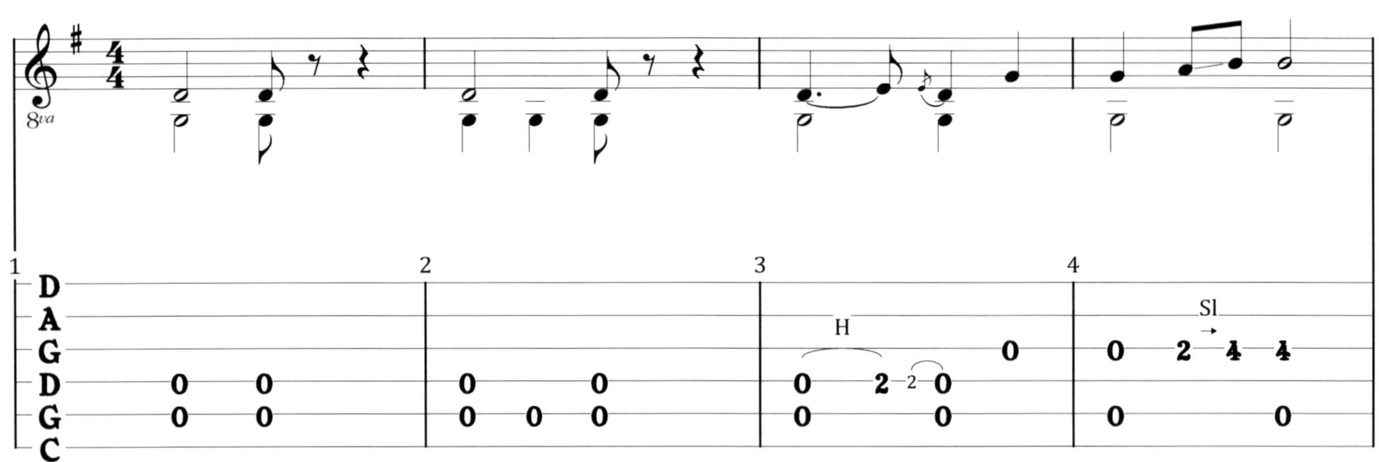

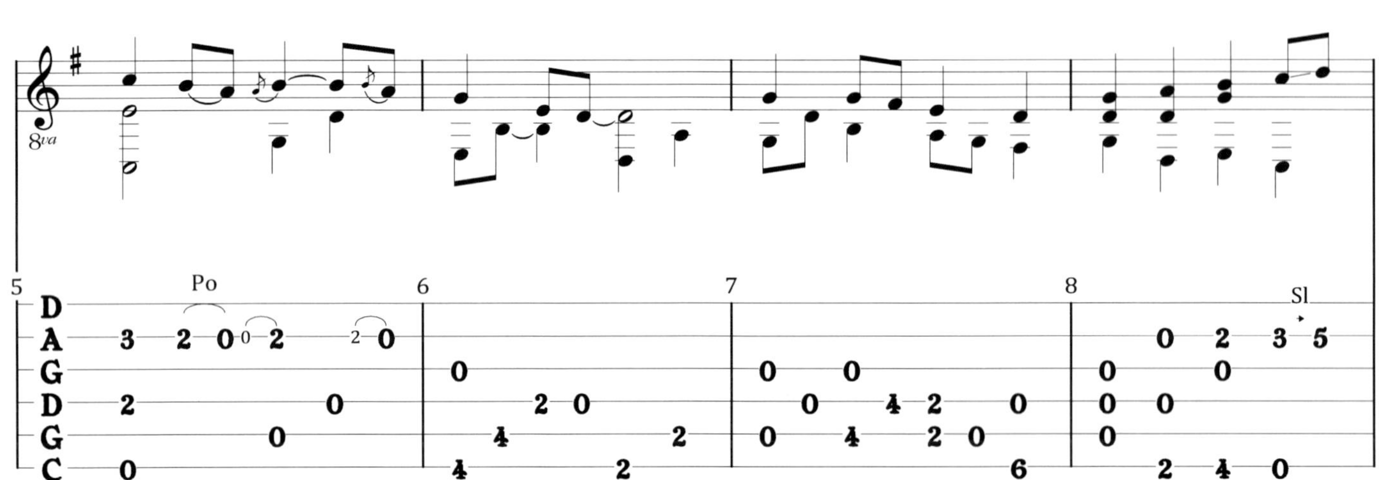

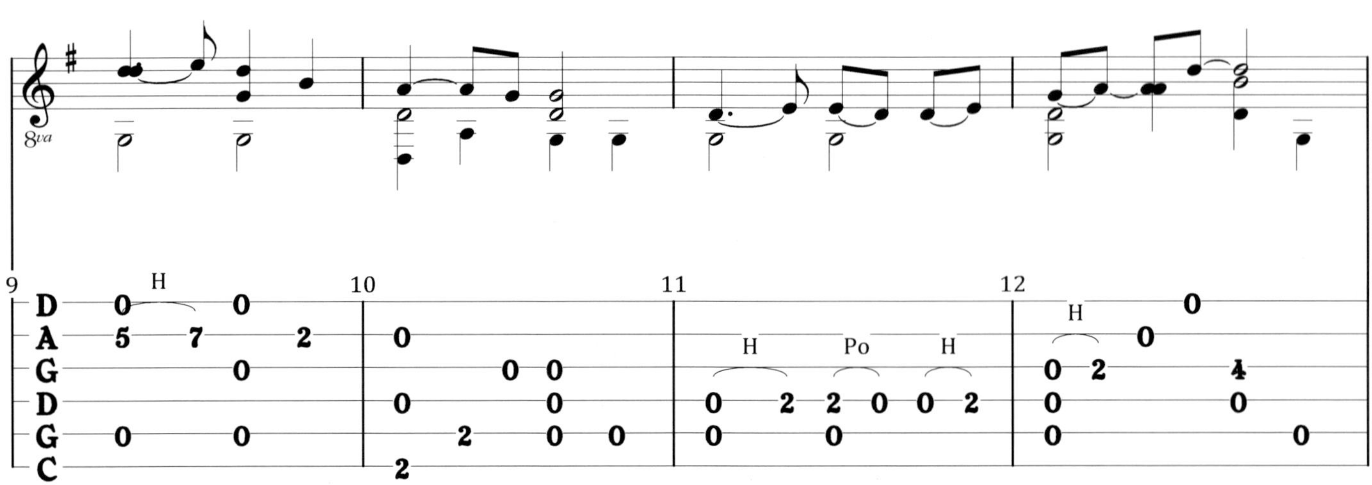

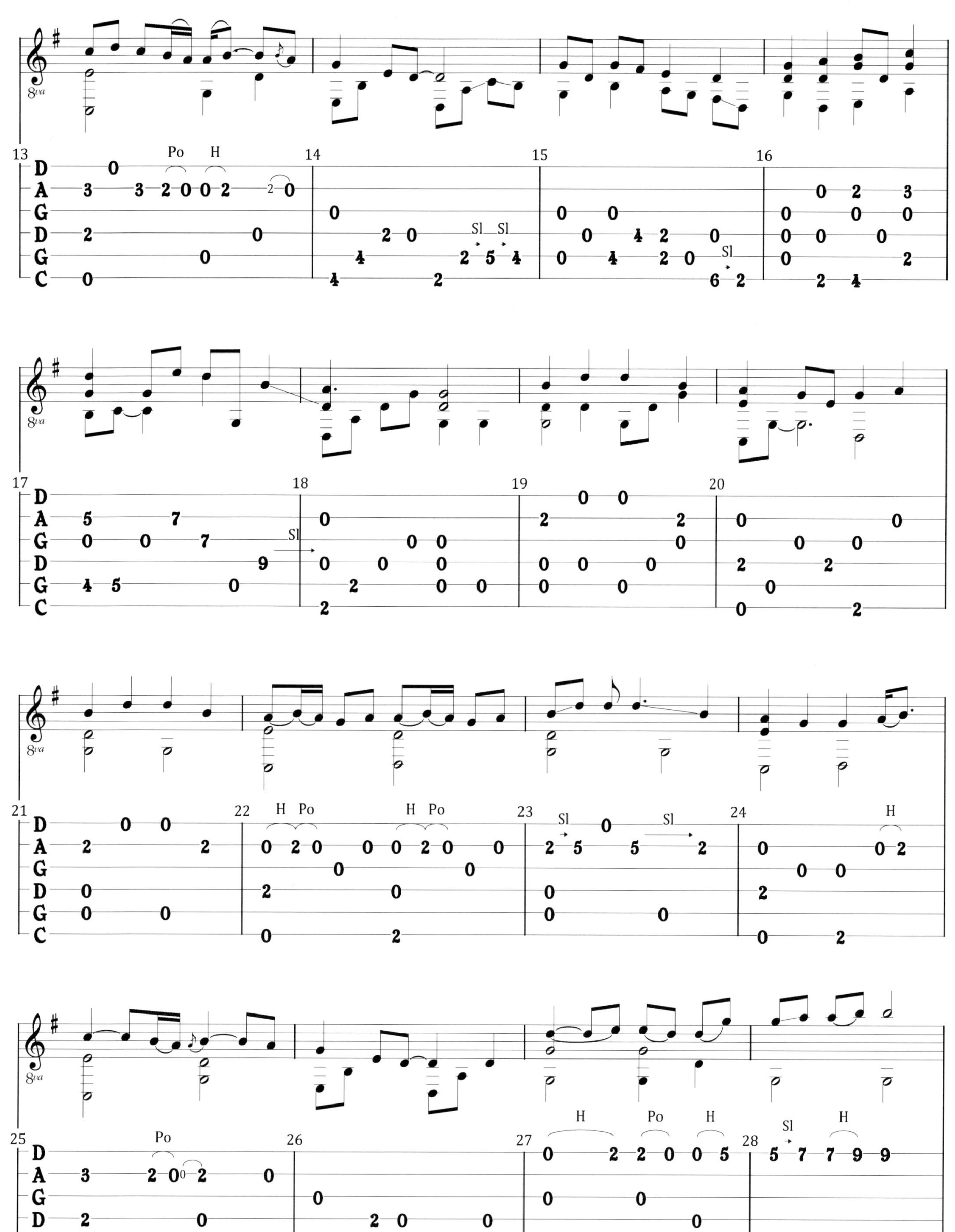
8va
13
14
15
16
17
18
19
20
21
22
23
24
25
26
27
28
D
A
G
D
G
C
Po
H
Sl

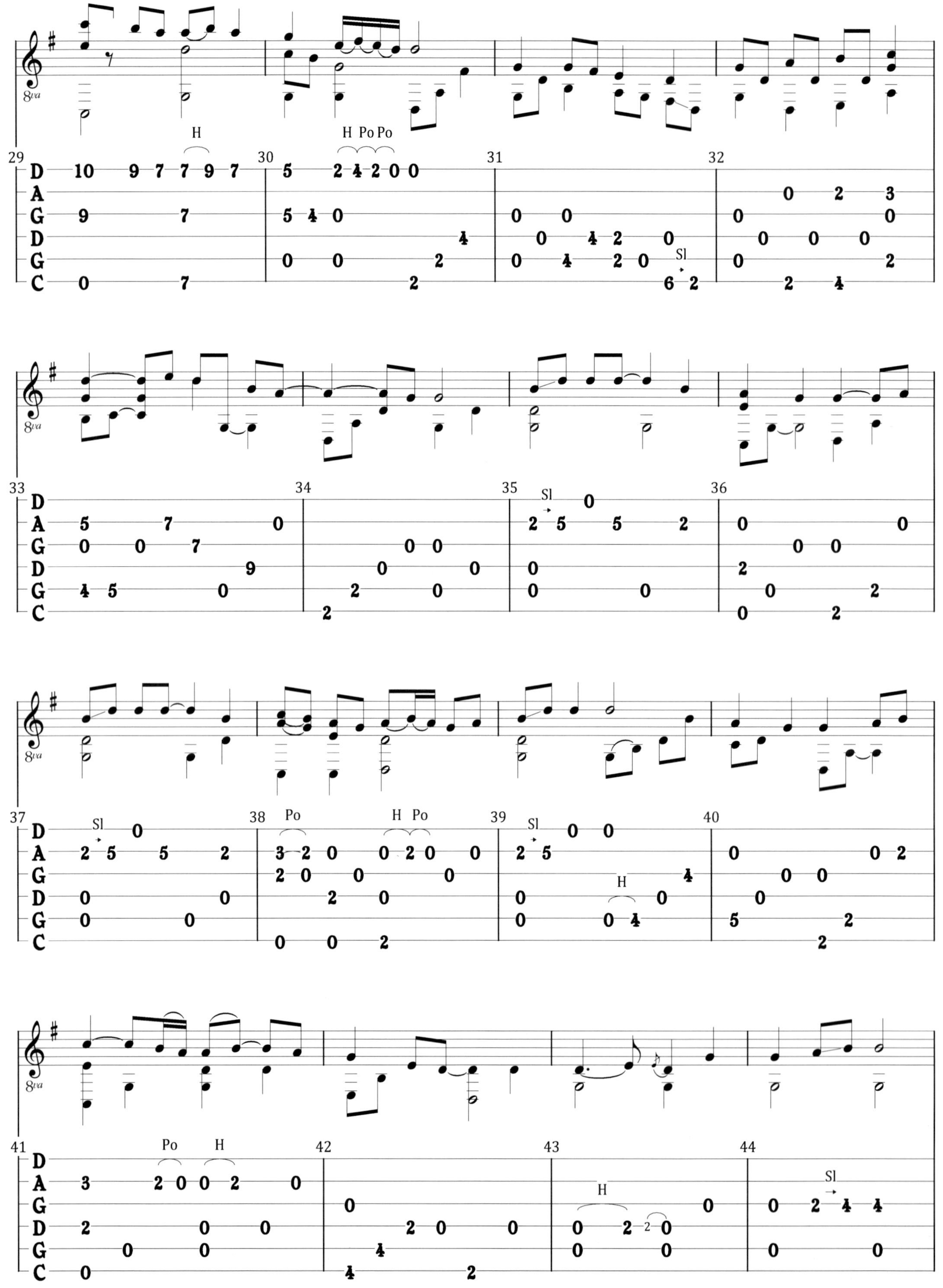
8va
D
A
G
D
G
C
H
Po
Sl

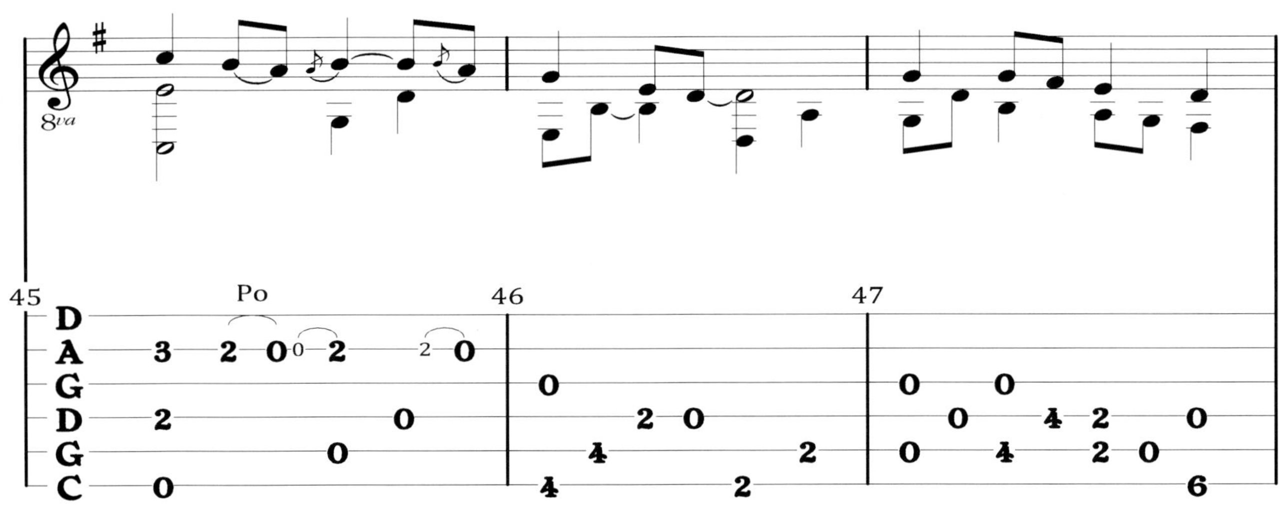
8va
45
46
47
Po
D
A
G
D
G
C

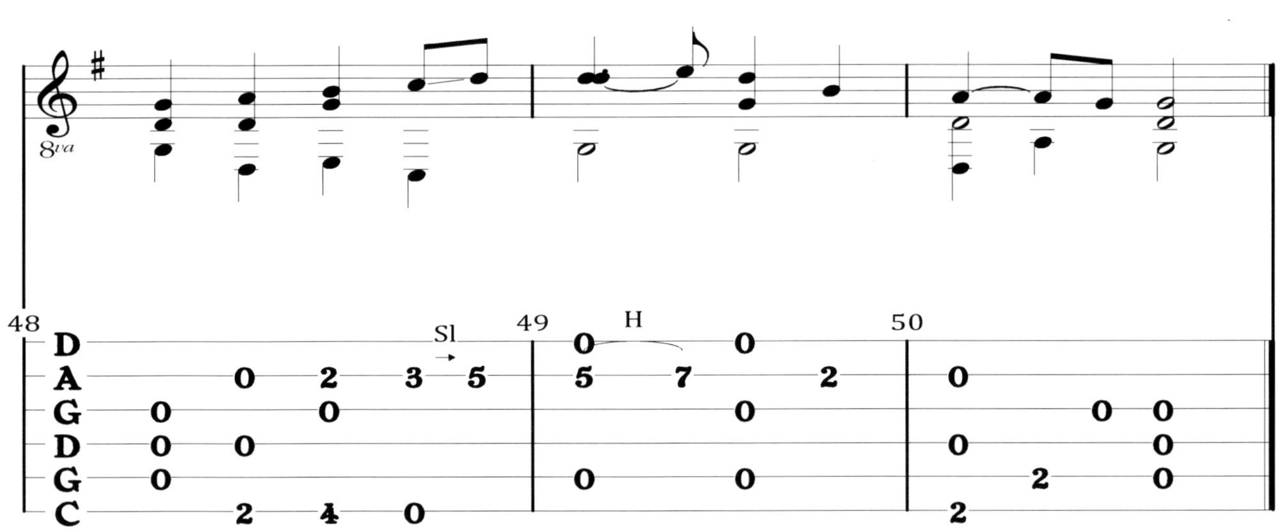
8va
48
49
50
Sl
H
D
A
G
D
G
C

Hugh O'Donnell

(T. O'Carolan)

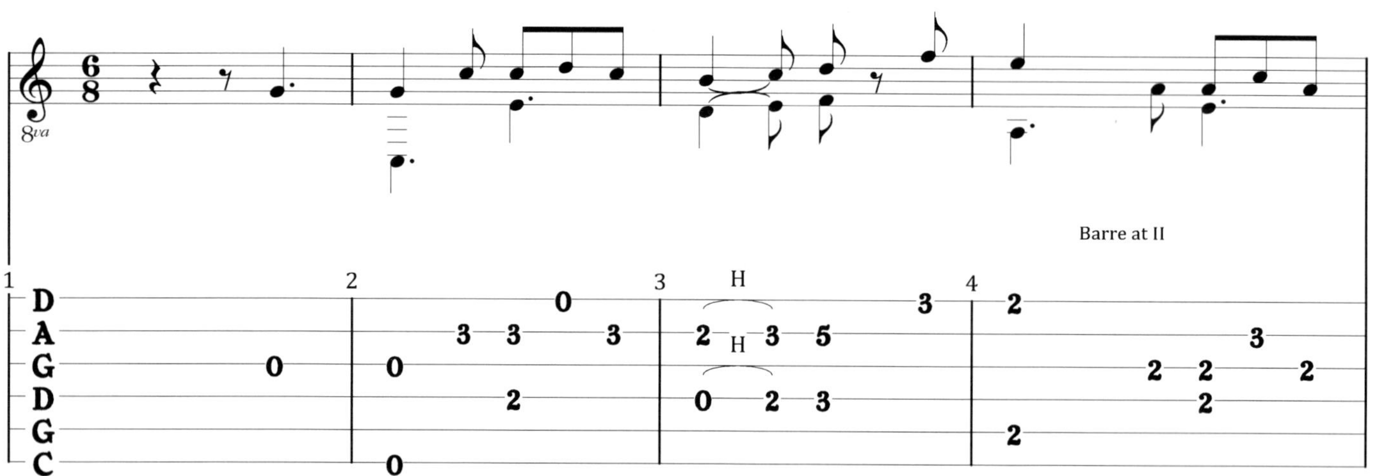

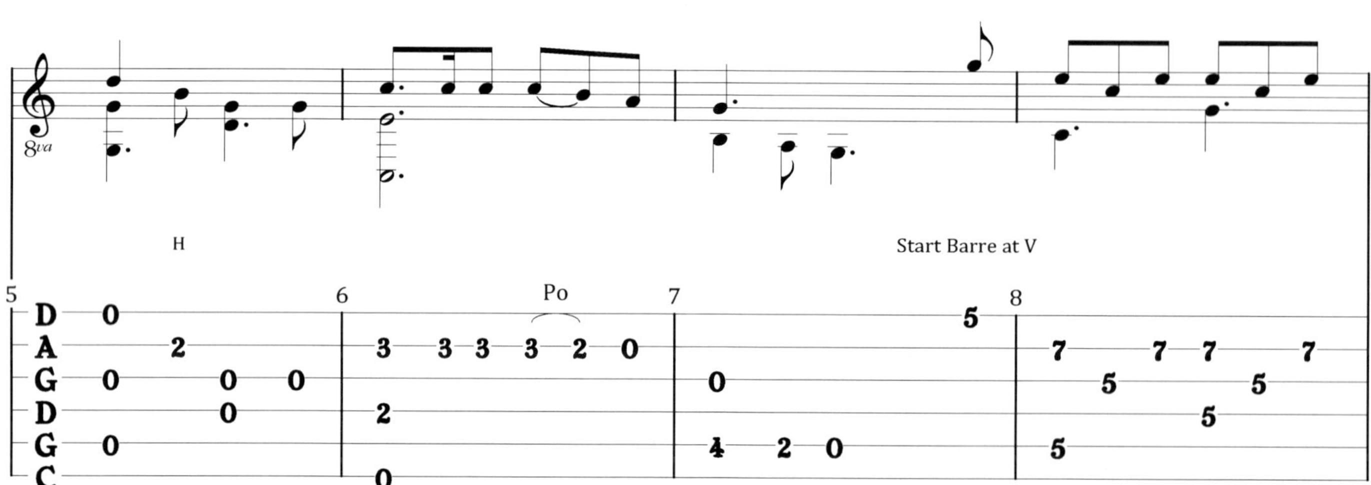

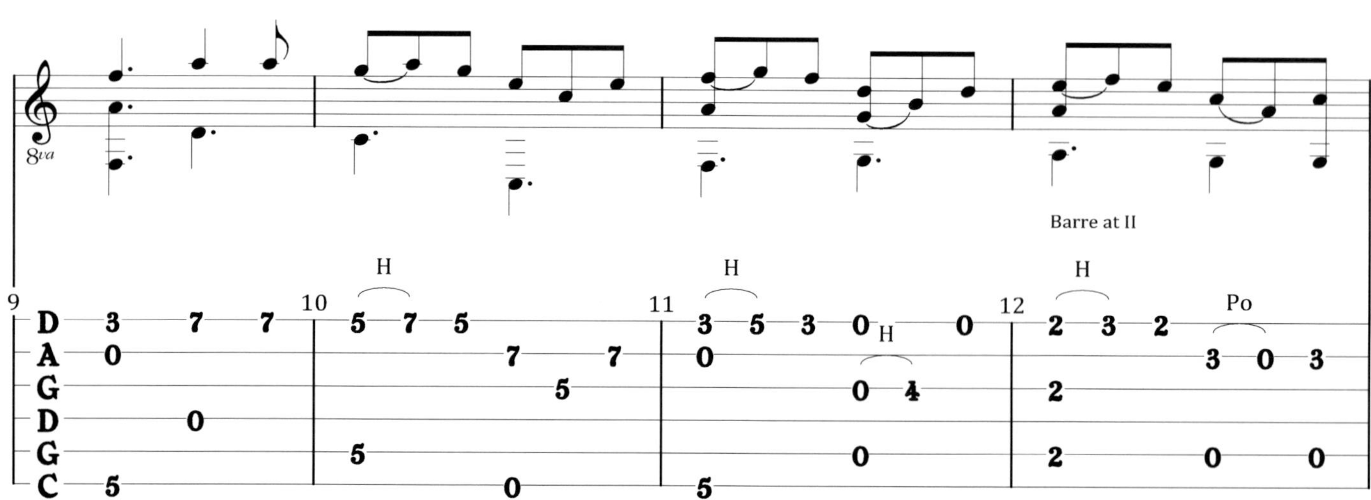

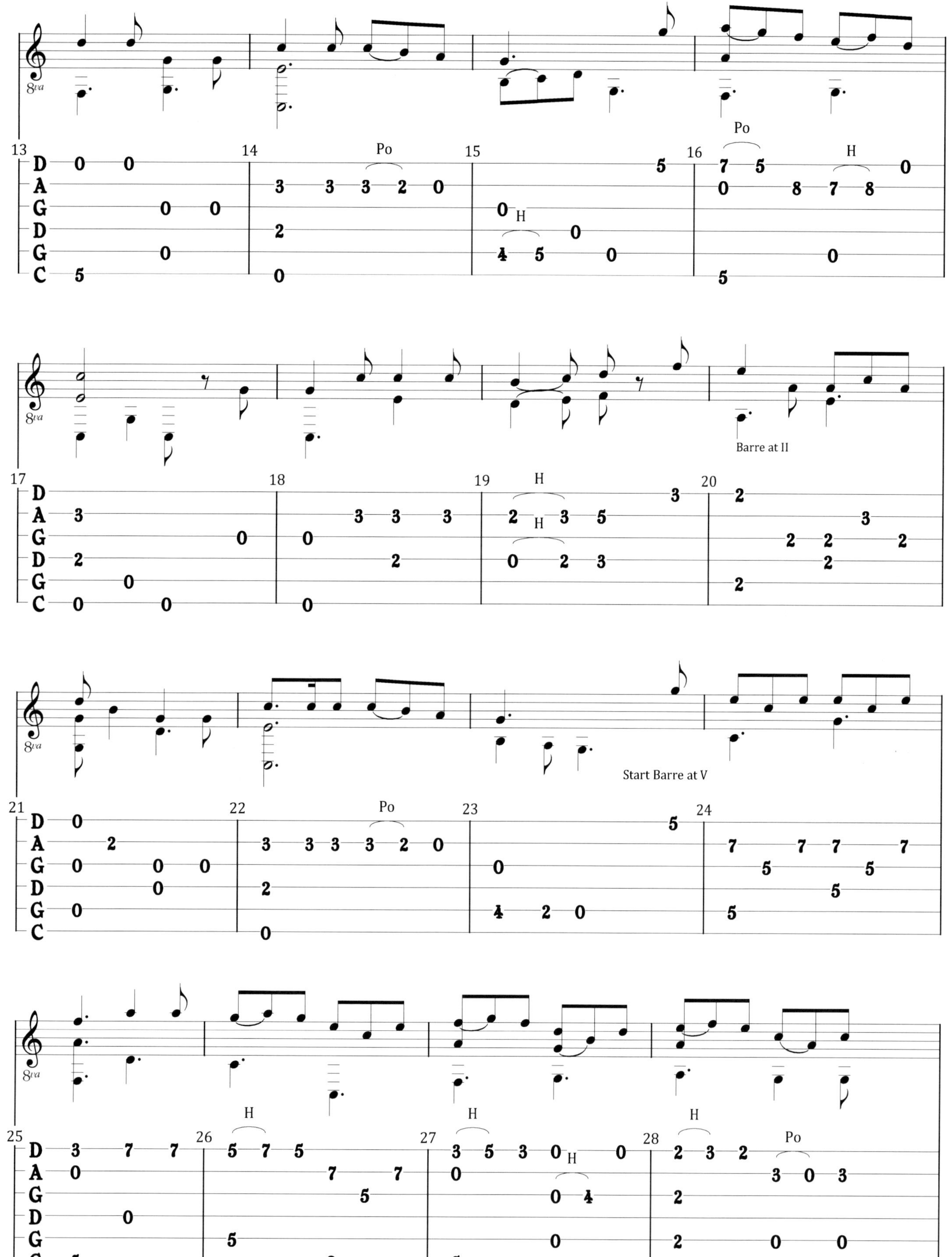
8va
D
A
G
D
G
C
Po
H
Barre at II
Start Barre at V

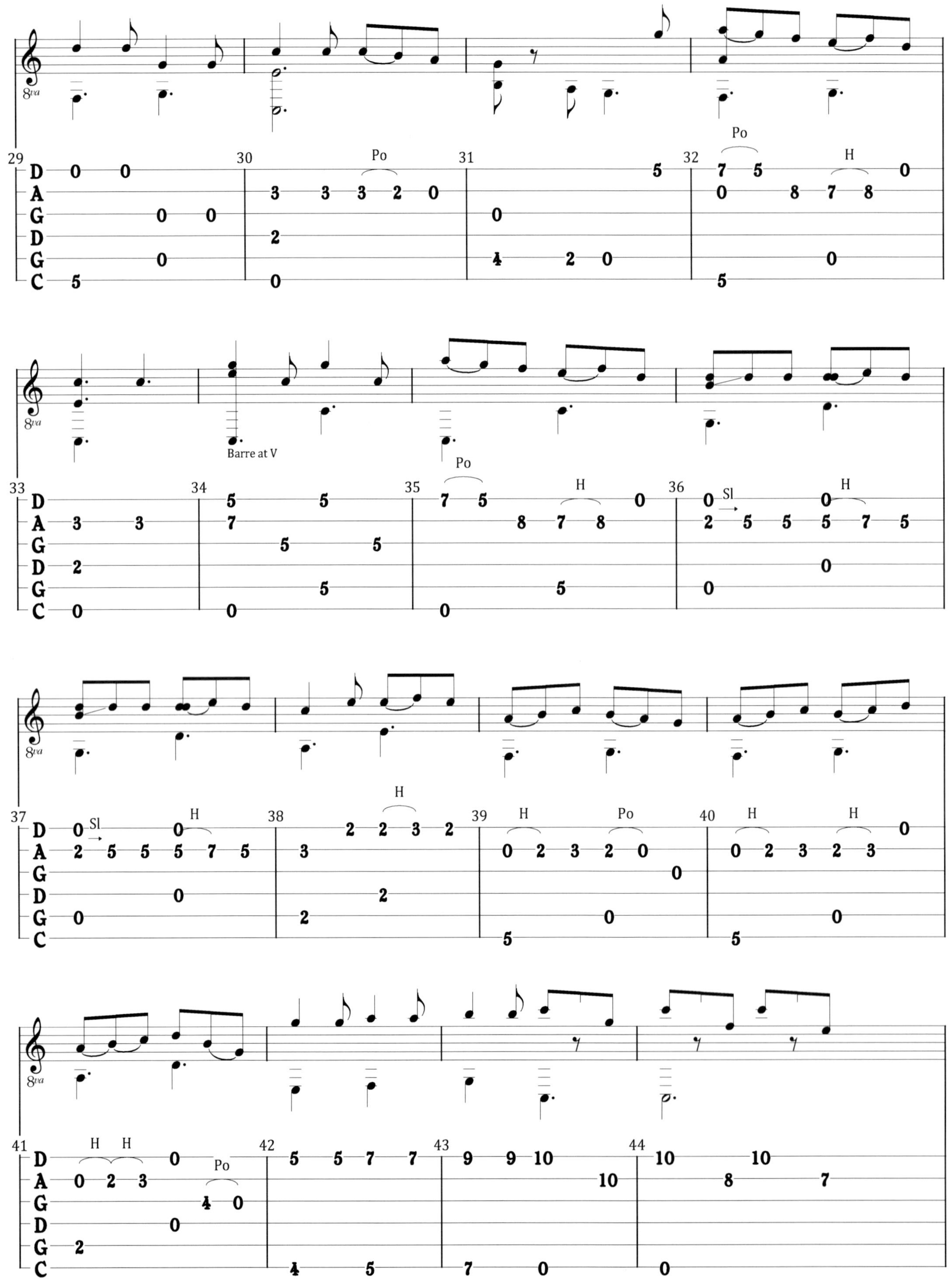
8va
29
30
31
32
Po
H
D
A
G
D
G
C
33
34
35
36
37
38
39
40
41
42
43
44
Barre at V
Sl

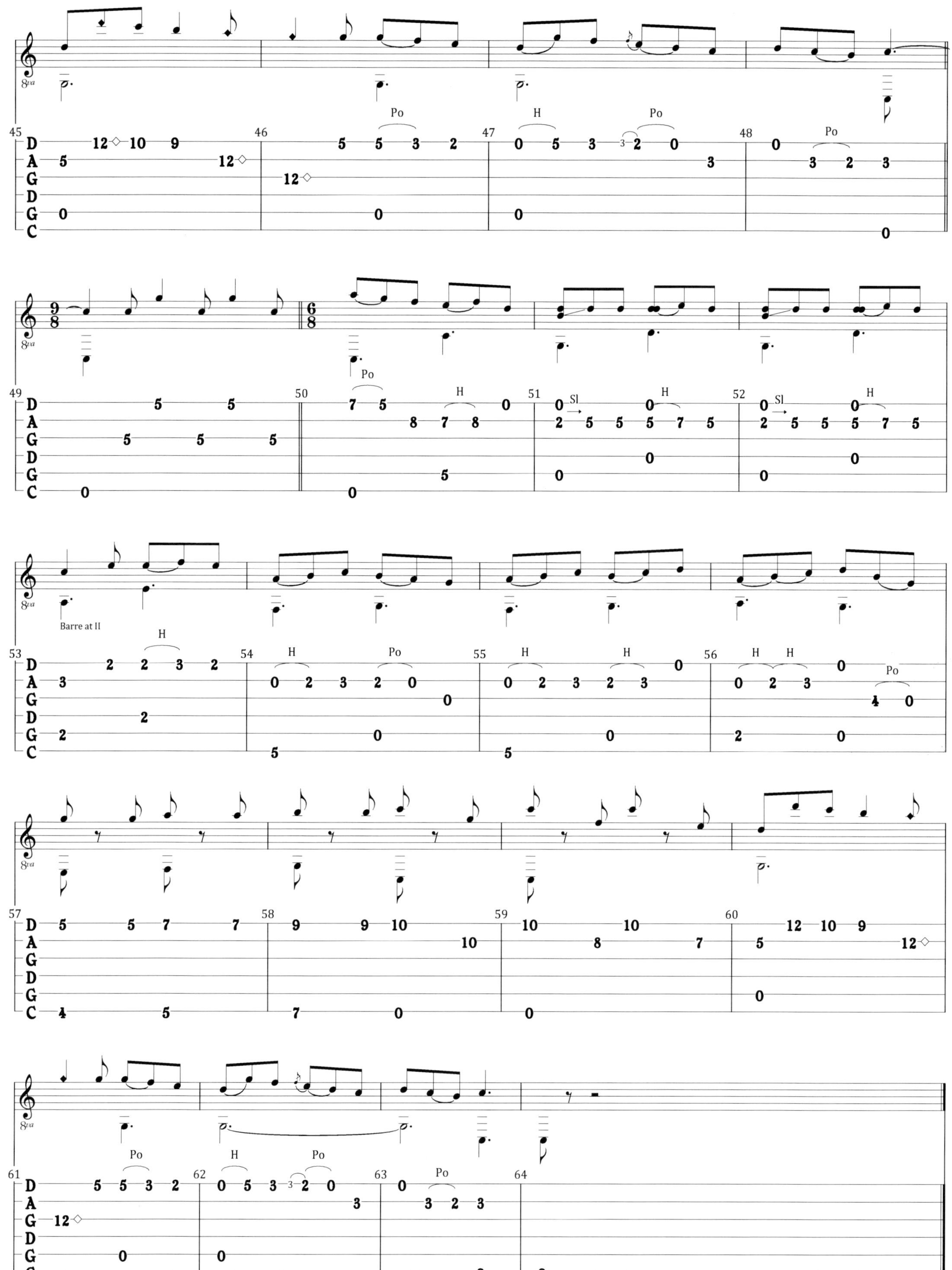
8va
D
A
G
D
G
C
Po
H
Sl
Barre at II

Carolan's Welcome

(T. O'Carolan)

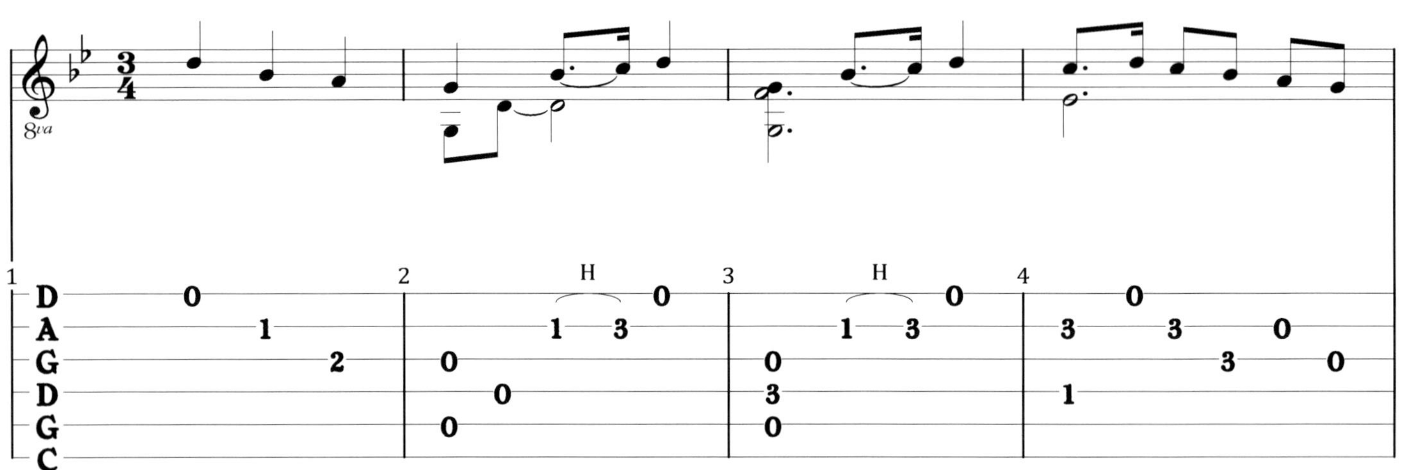

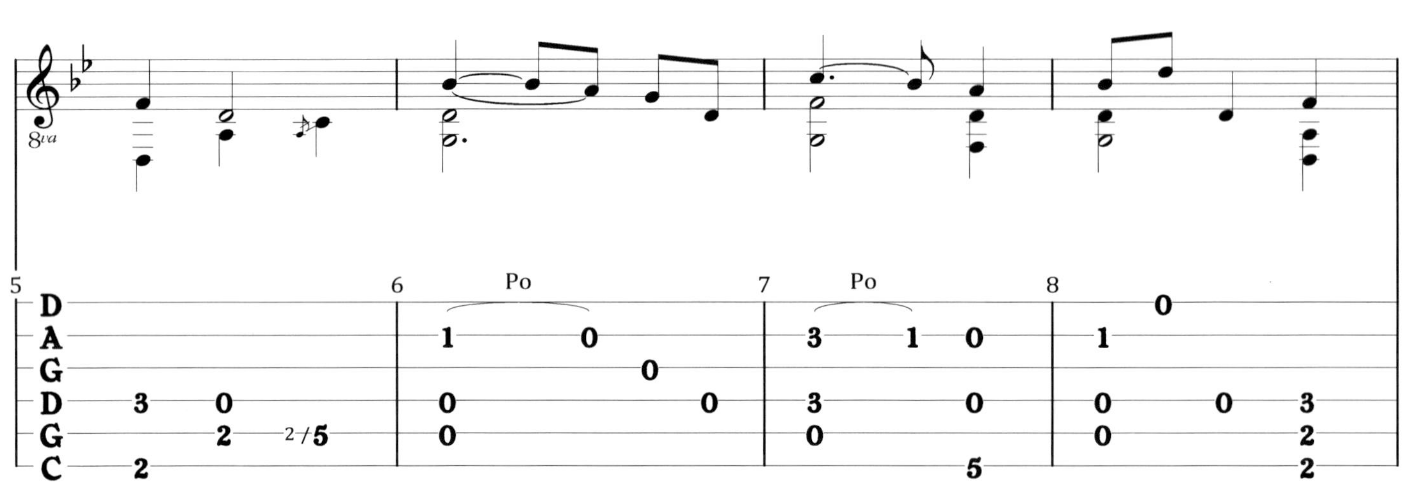

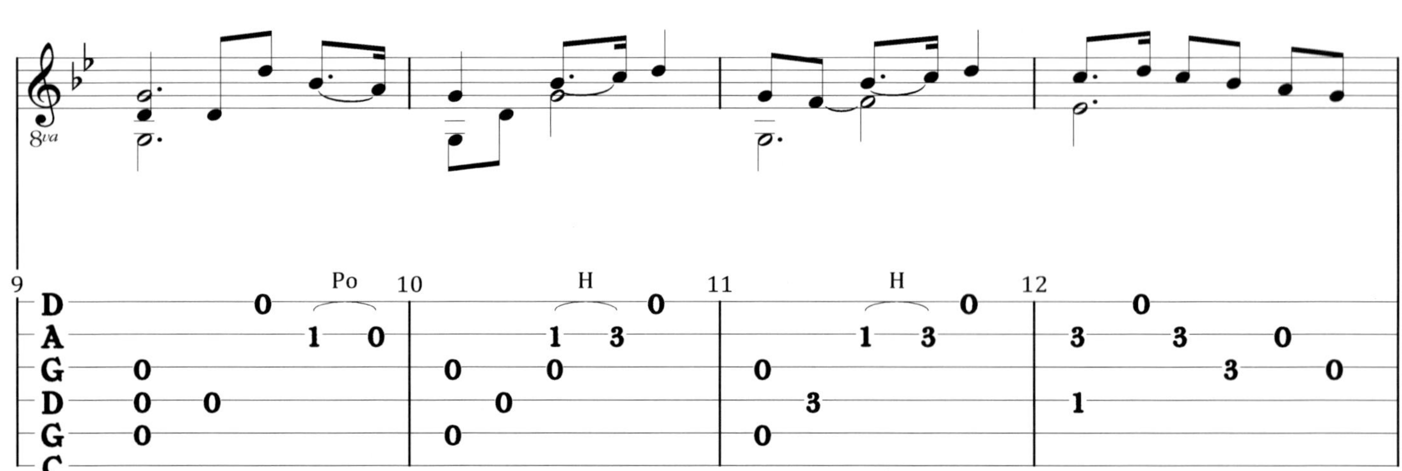

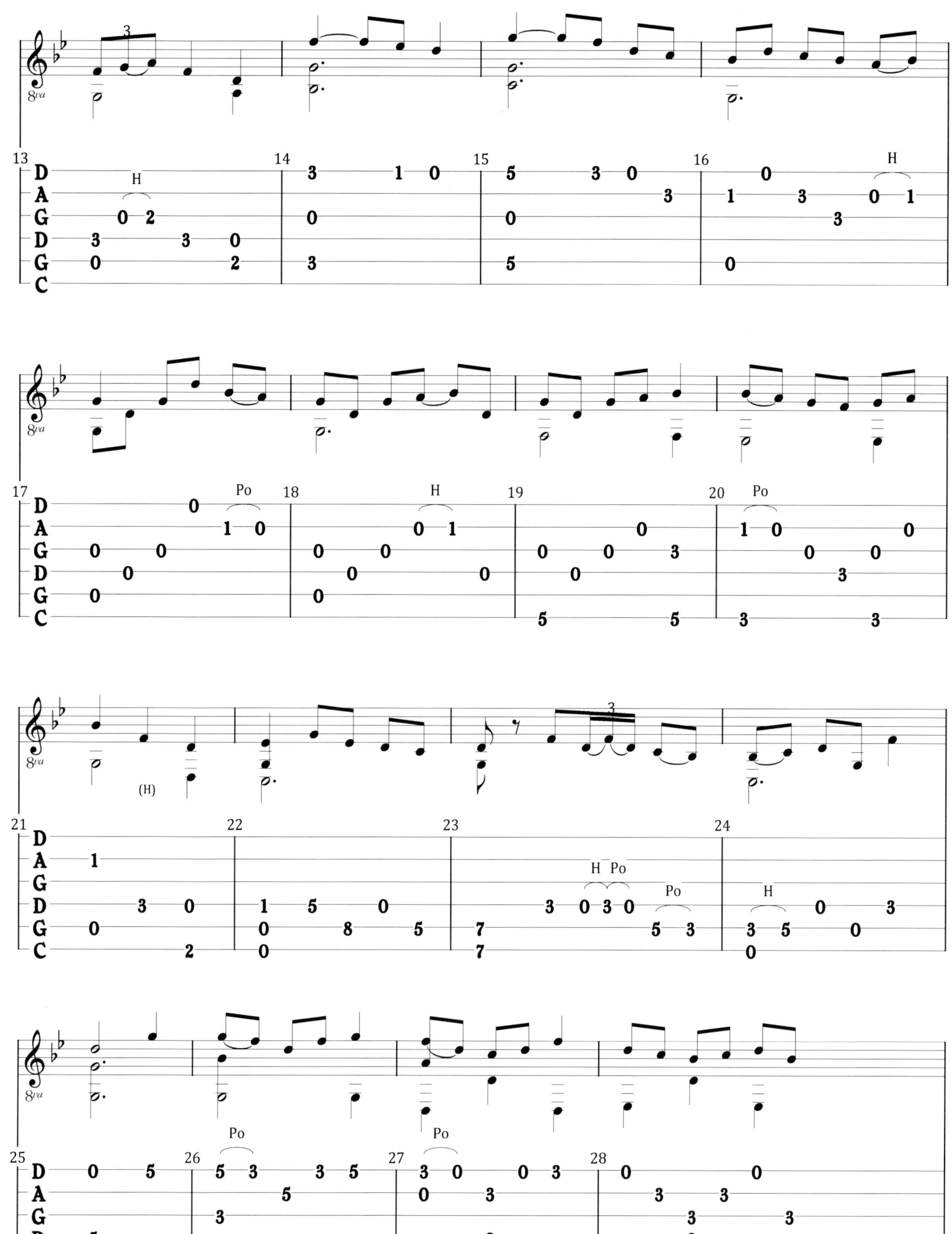
8va
13 14 15 16
D A G D G C
H
17 18 19 20
Po H Po
21 22 23 24
(H)
H Po Po H
25 26 27 28
Po Po

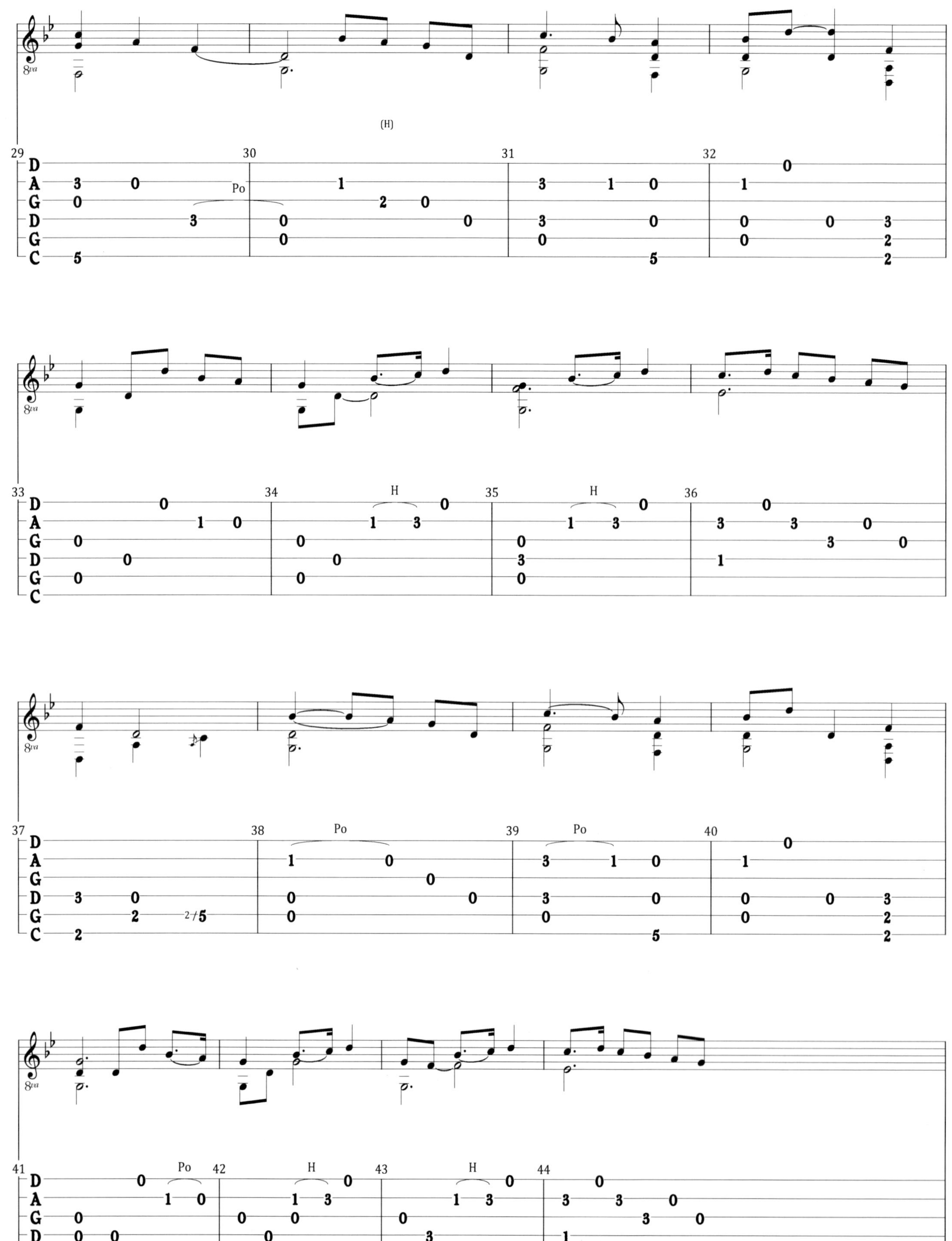
8va
(H)
Po
H
D A G D G C
29 30 31 32 33 34 35 36 37 38 39 40 41 42 43 44

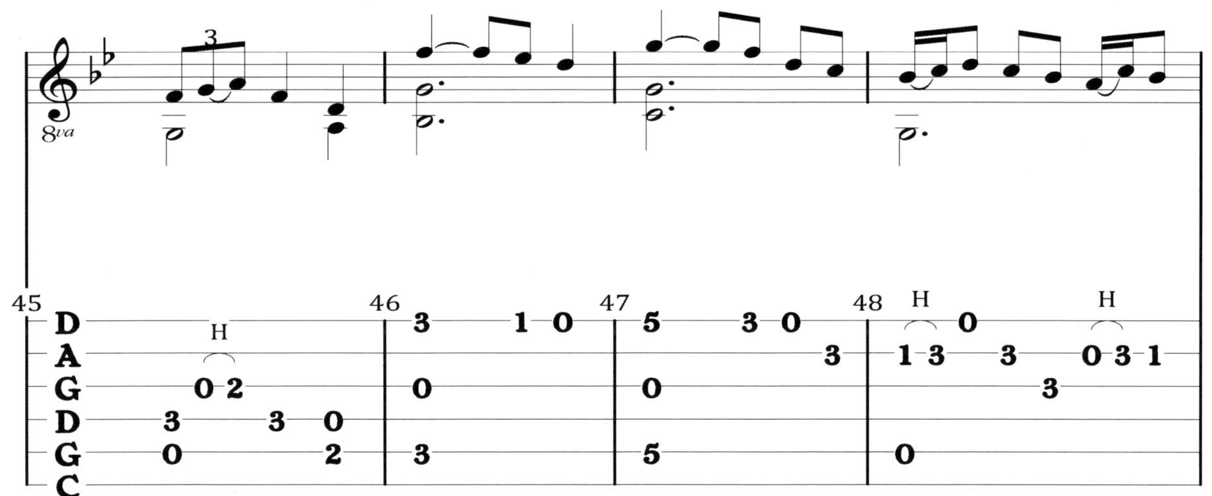
8va
45
46
47
48
D
A
G
D
G
C
H

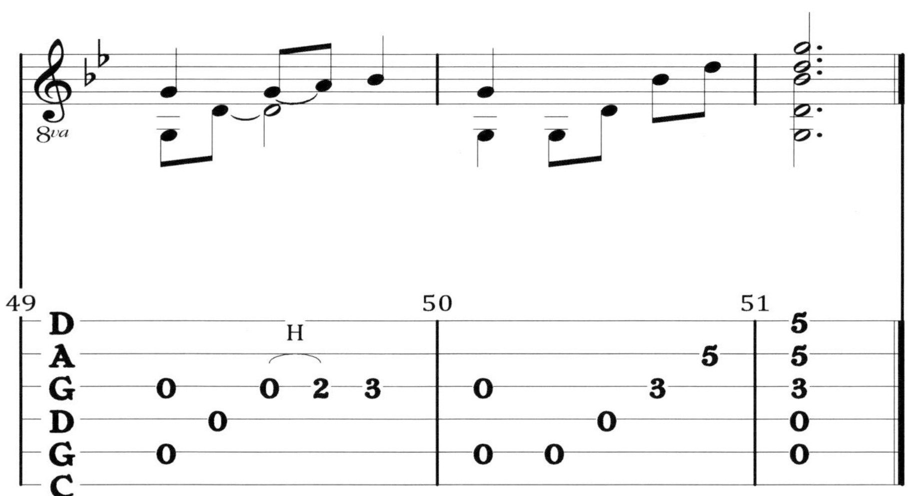
8va
49
50
51
D
A
G
D
G
C
H

Carolan's Receipt

(T. O'Carolan)

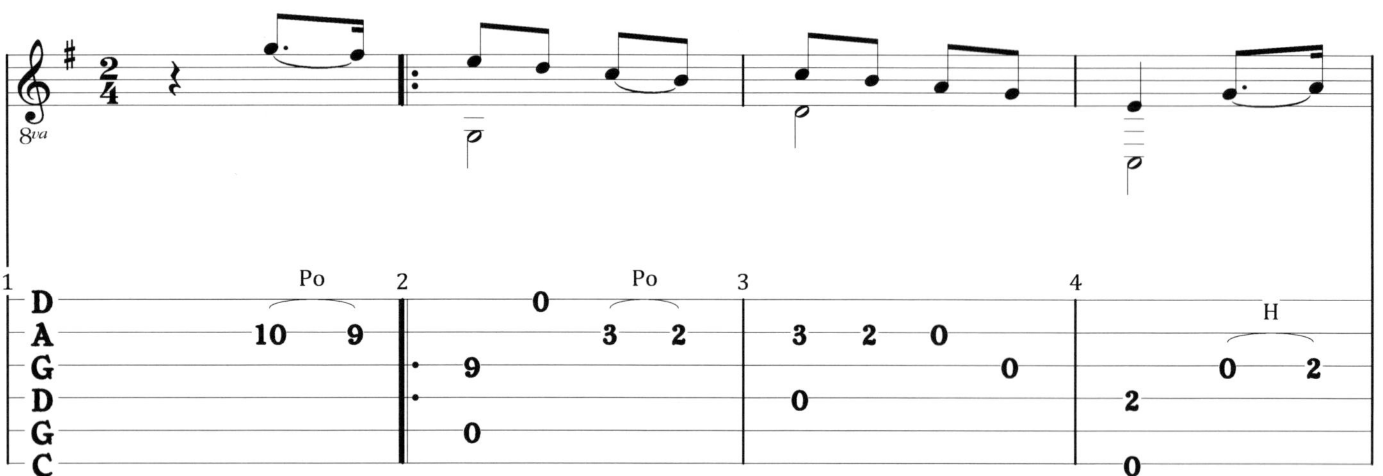

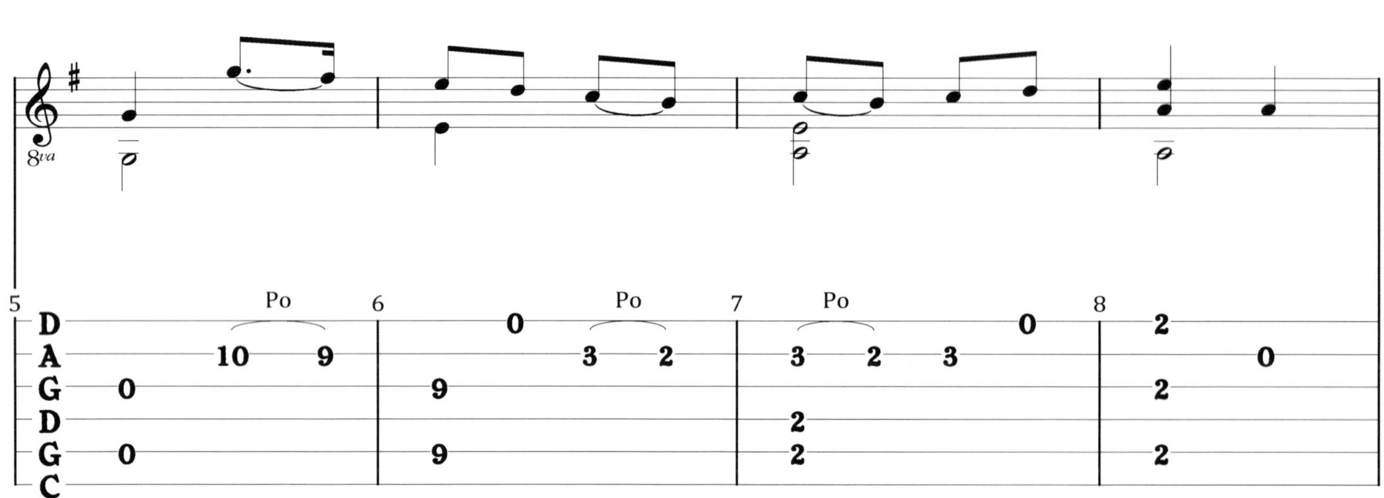

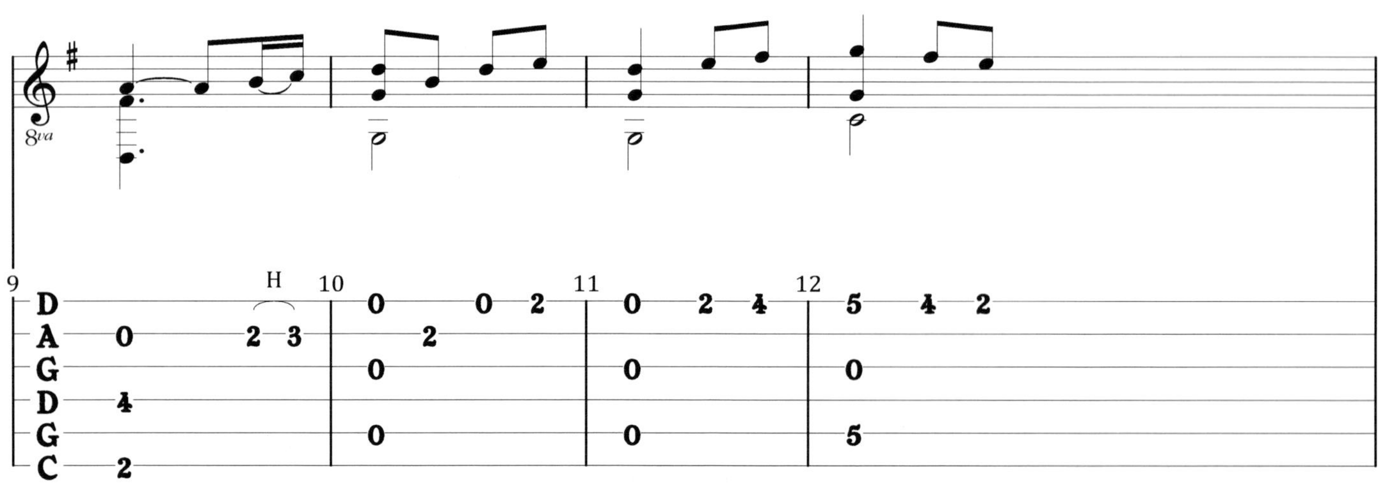

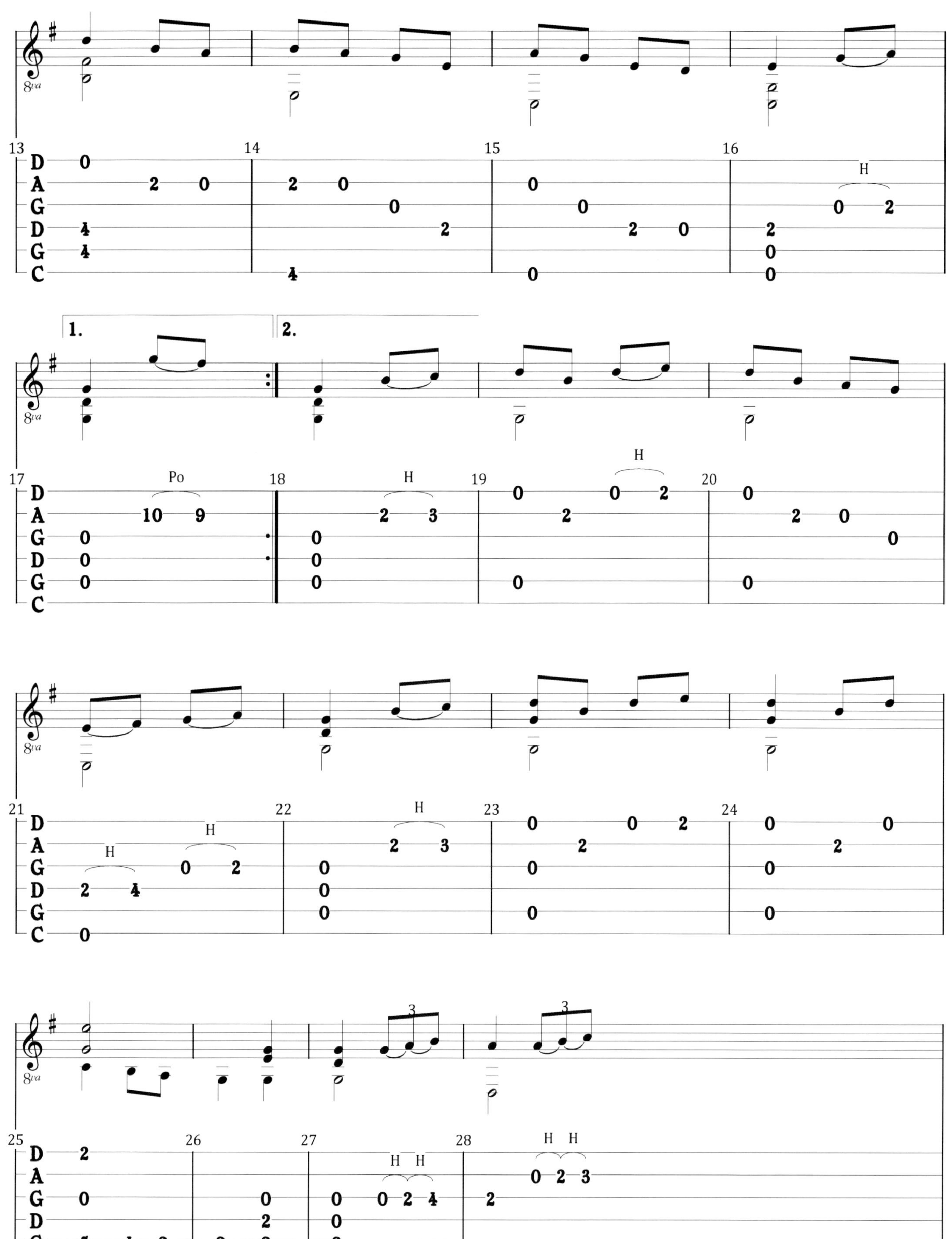

13
14
15
16
17
18
19
20
21
22
23
24
25
26
27
28
1.
2.
8va
D
A
G
D
G
C
H
Po

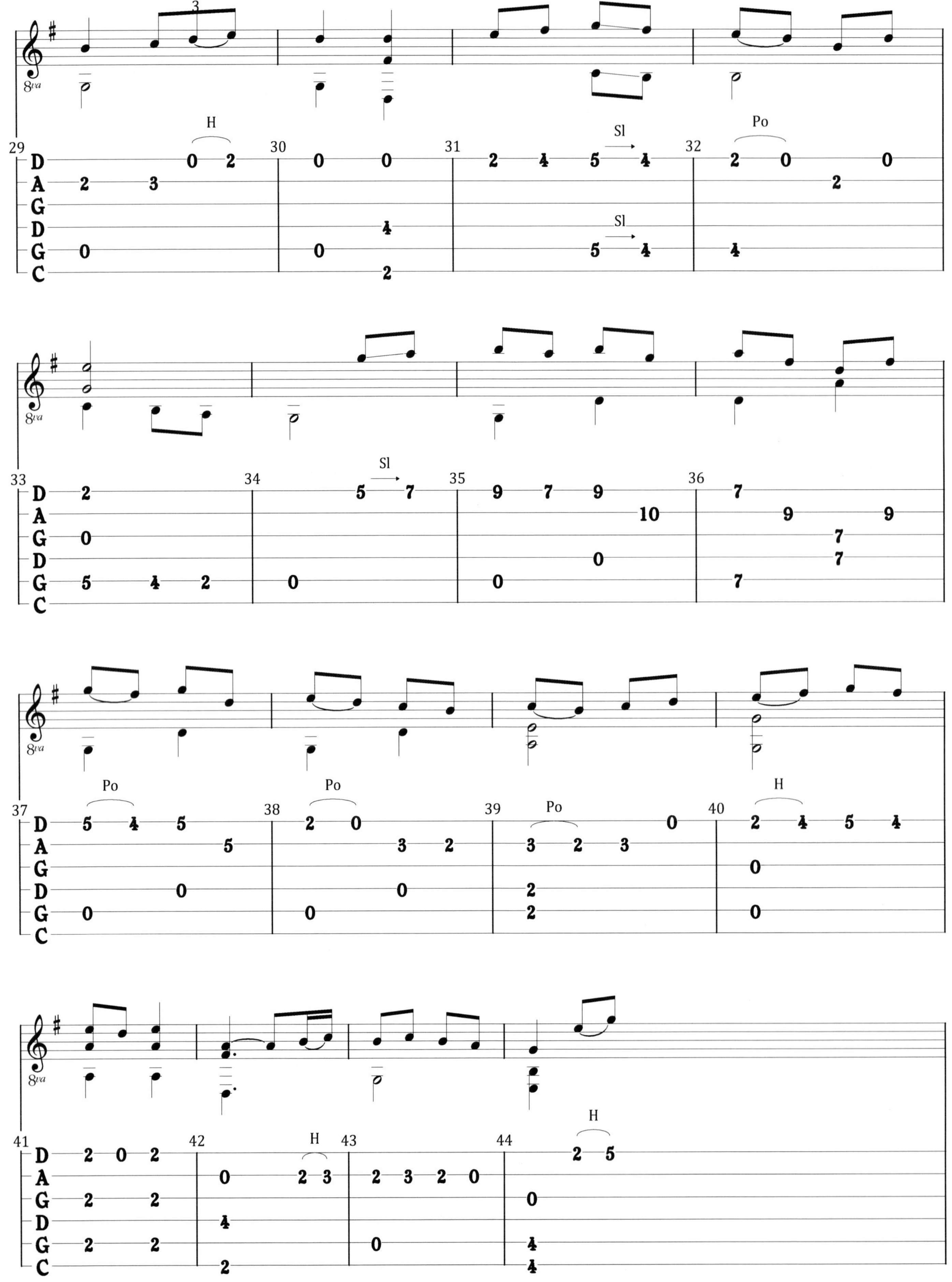
8va
3
H
Po
Sl
D
A
G
D
G
C

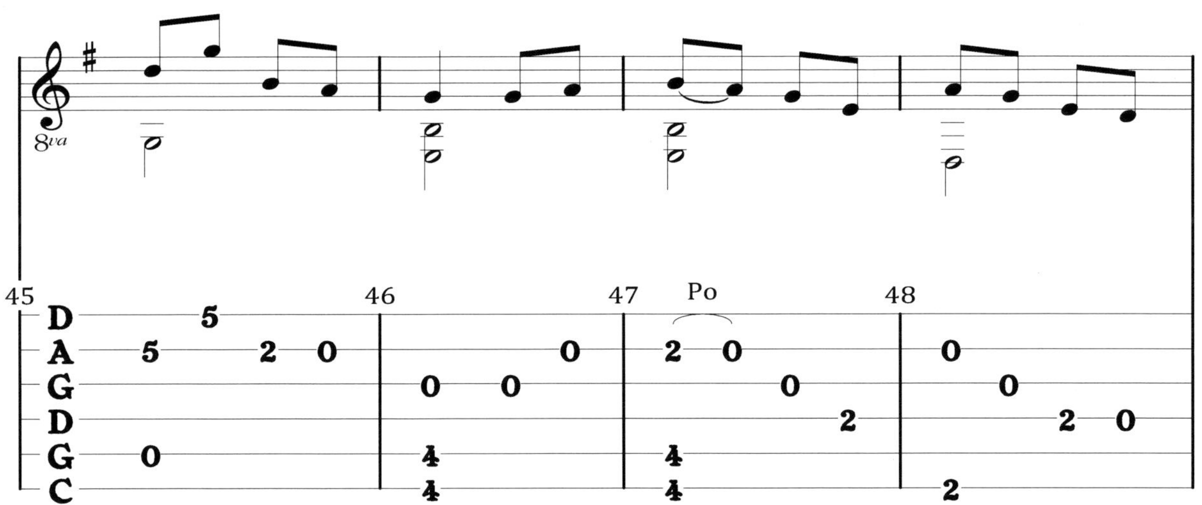

8va
45
46
47
48
Po
D
A
G
D
G
C
5
5 2 0
0
0 0 0
4
4
2 0
0
2
4
4
0
0
2 0
2

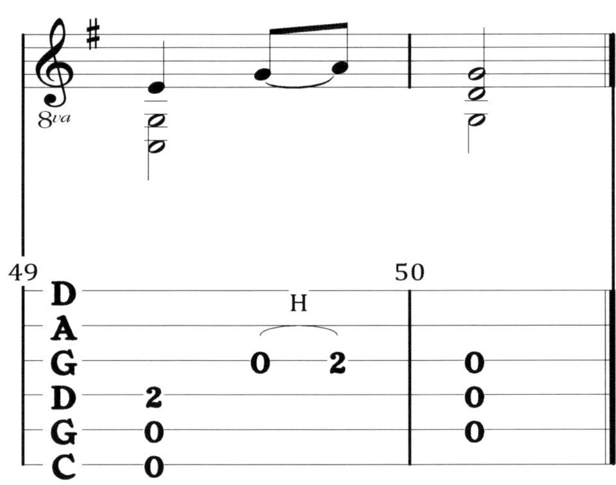

8va
49
50
H
D
A
G
D
G
C
0 2
0
2
0
0
0
0

Morgan Magan

(T. O'Carolan)

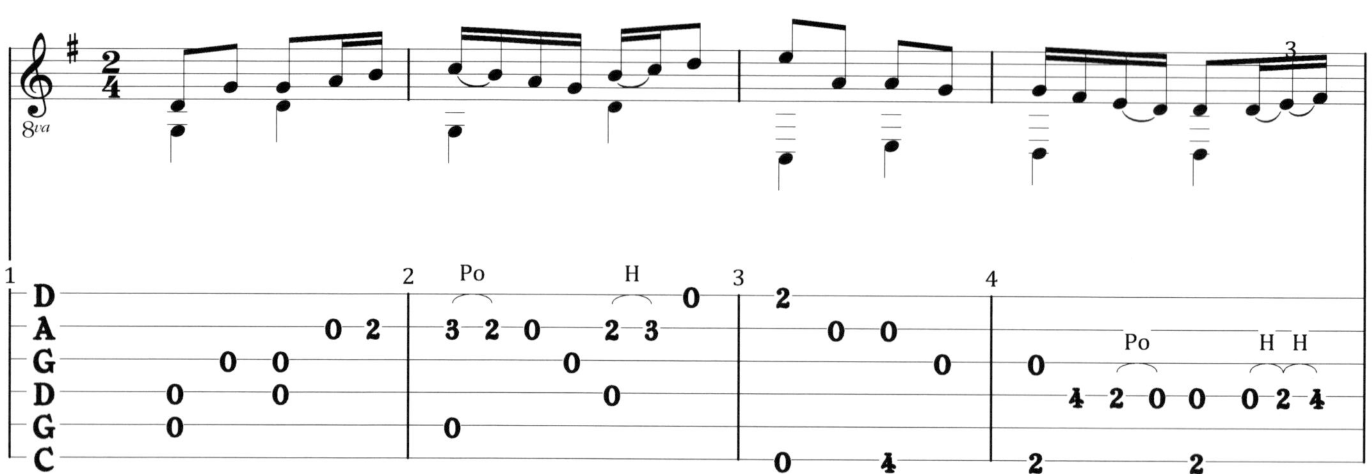

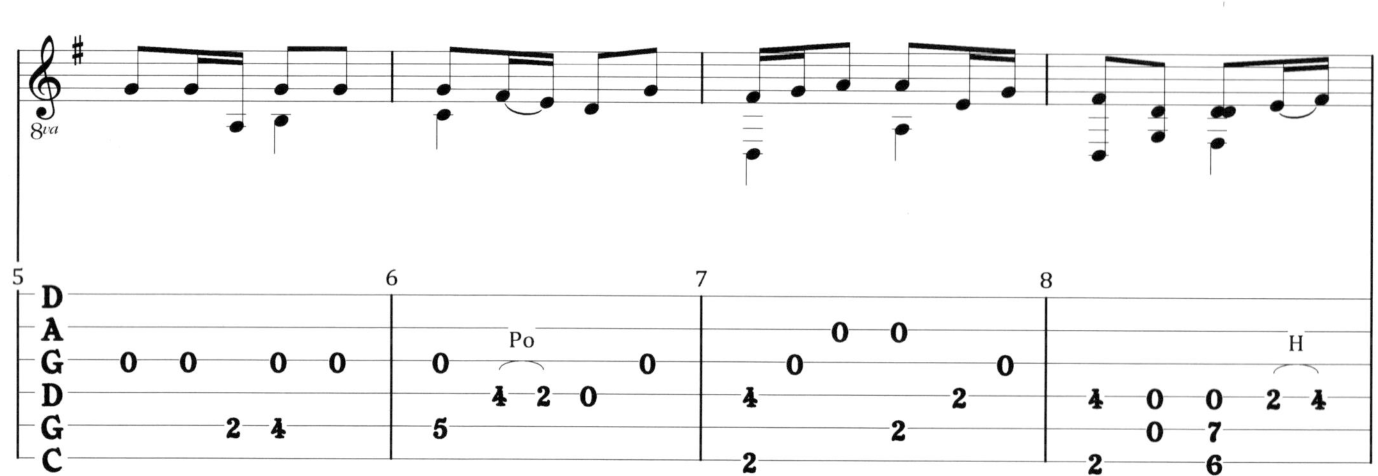

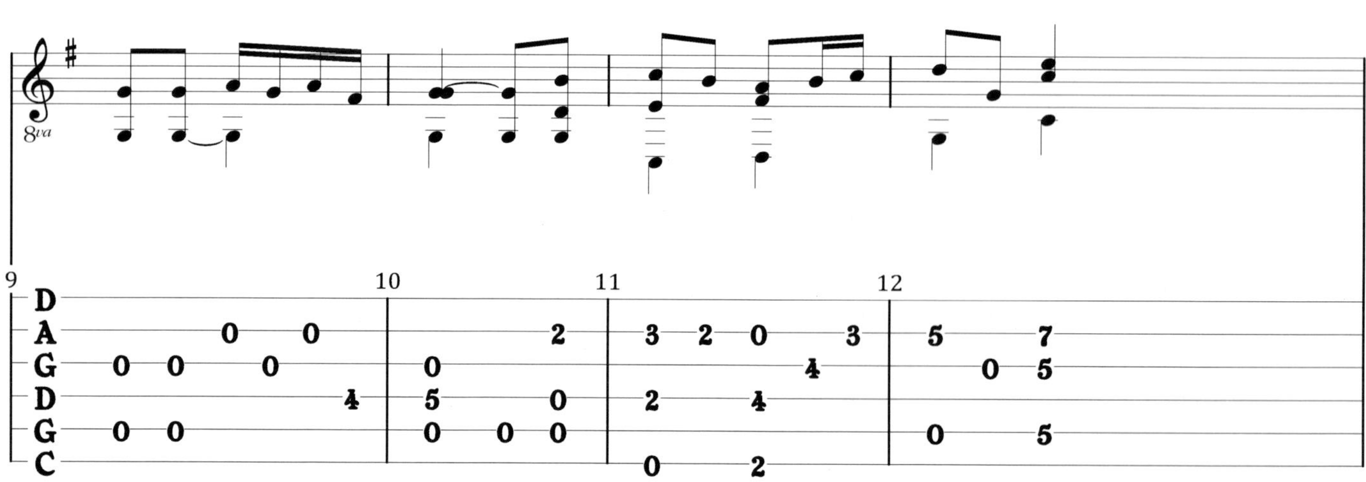

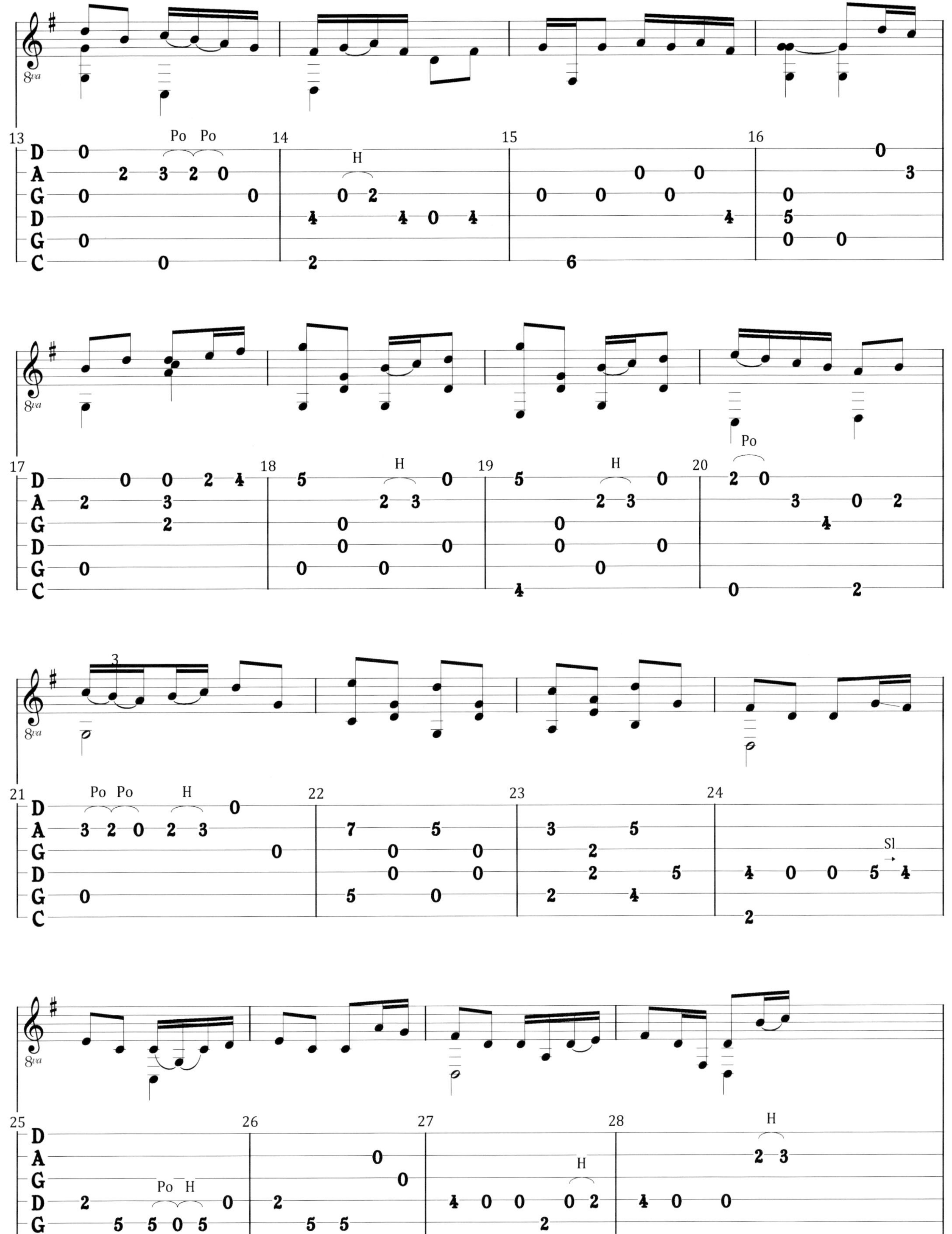
8va
13
14
15
16
D
A
G
D
G
C
Po Po
H
17
18
19
20
Po
H
H
21
22
23
24
Po Po
H
Sl
25
26
27
28
Po H
H
H

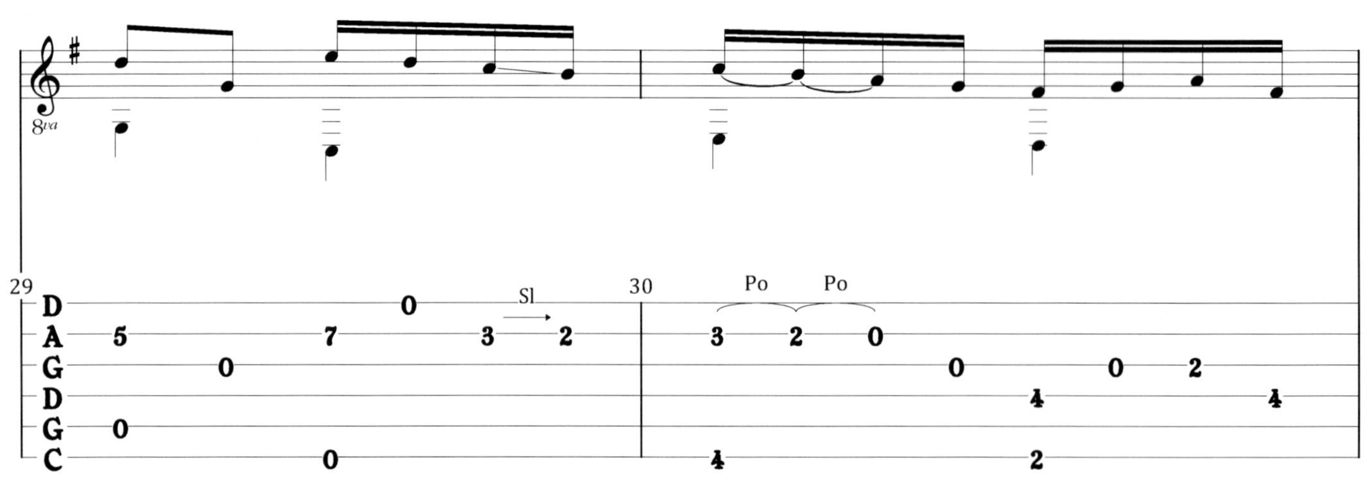
8va
29
D
A
G
D
G
C
5 0 0 7 0 0 3 Sl 2
30
Po Po
3 4 2 0 0 4 2 0 2 4

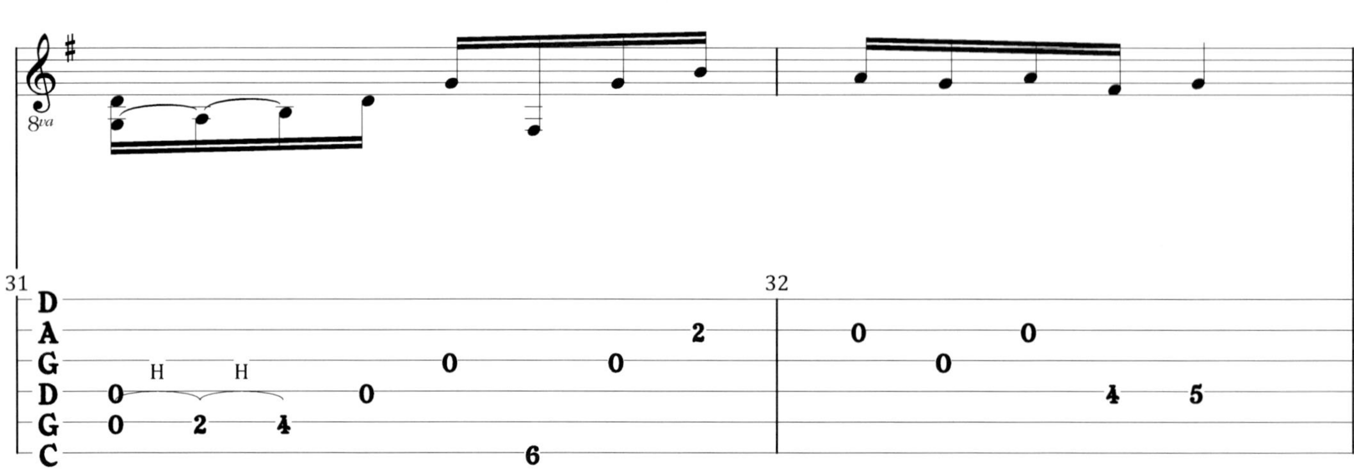
8va
31
D
A
G
D
G
C
H H
0 0 2 4 0 0 6 0 2
32
0 0 0 4 5

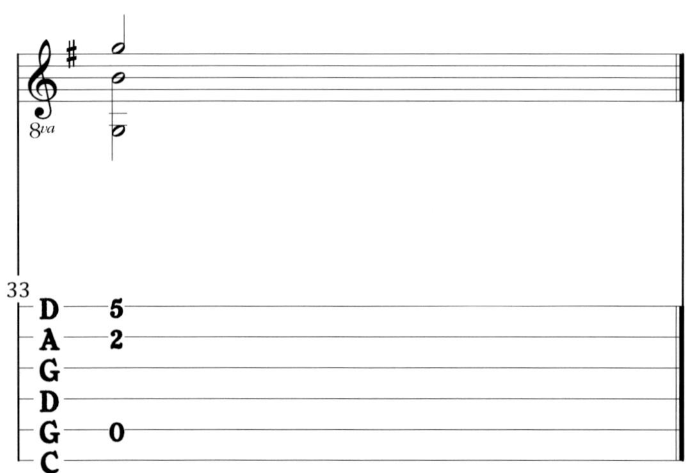
8va
33
D
A
G
D
G
C
5 2 0

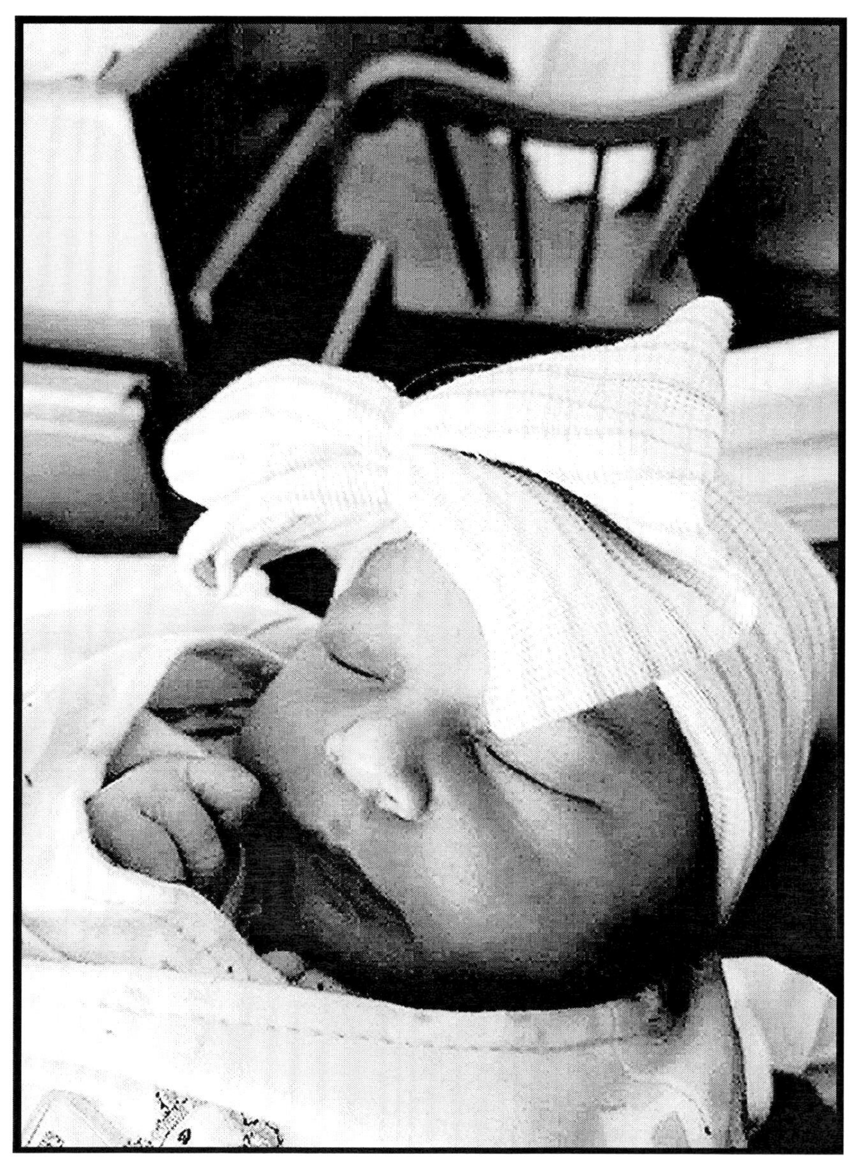

El's Granddaughter Kelsey McMeen enters the scene in Aug. 2018!

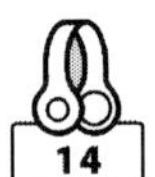

Jock O'Hazeldean

(Traditional Song)

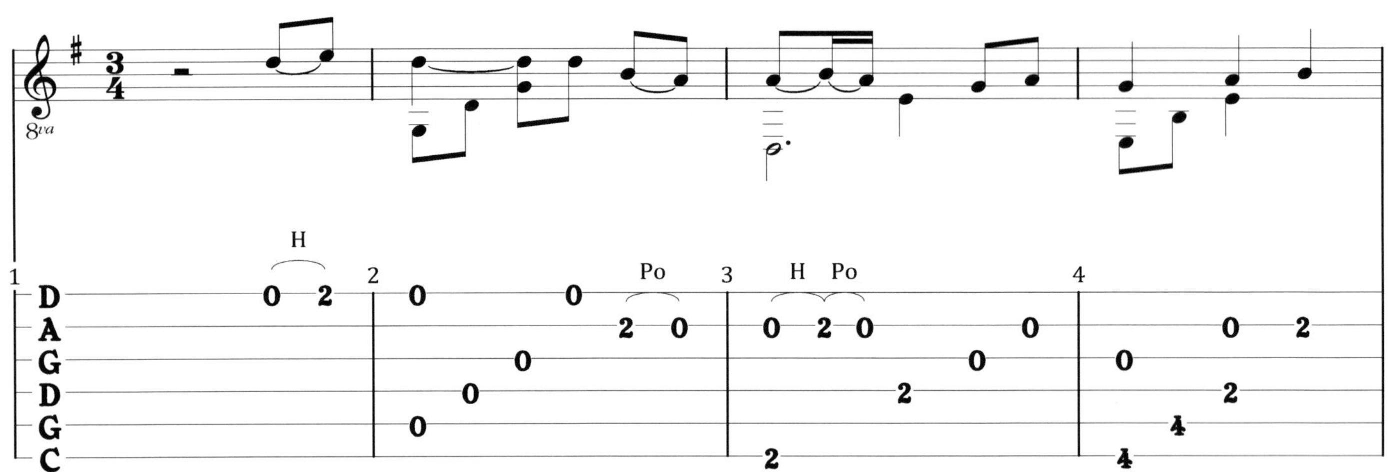

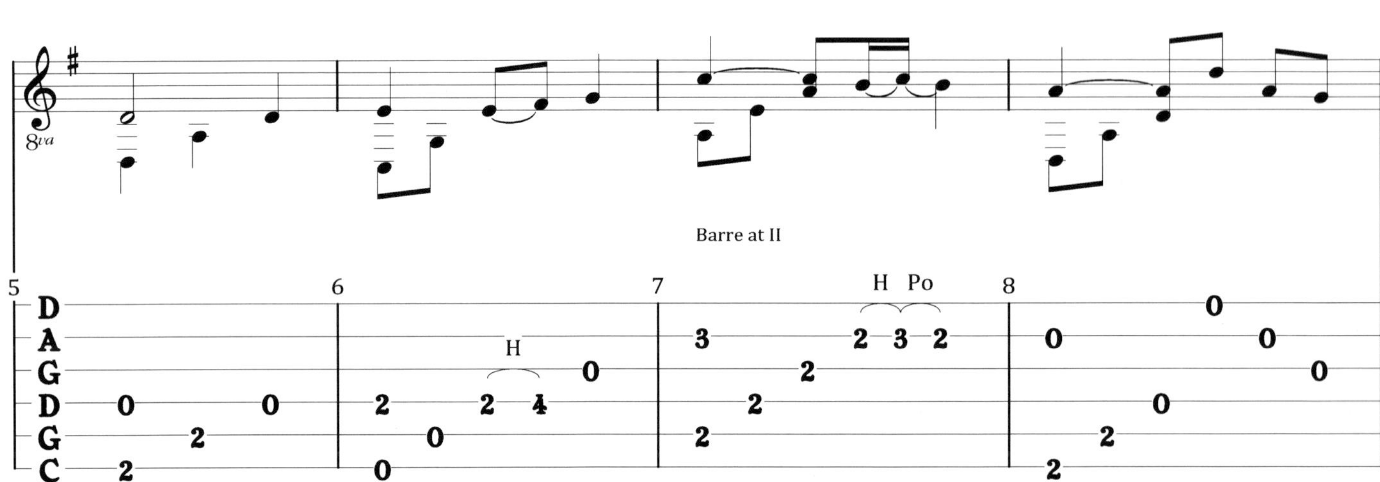

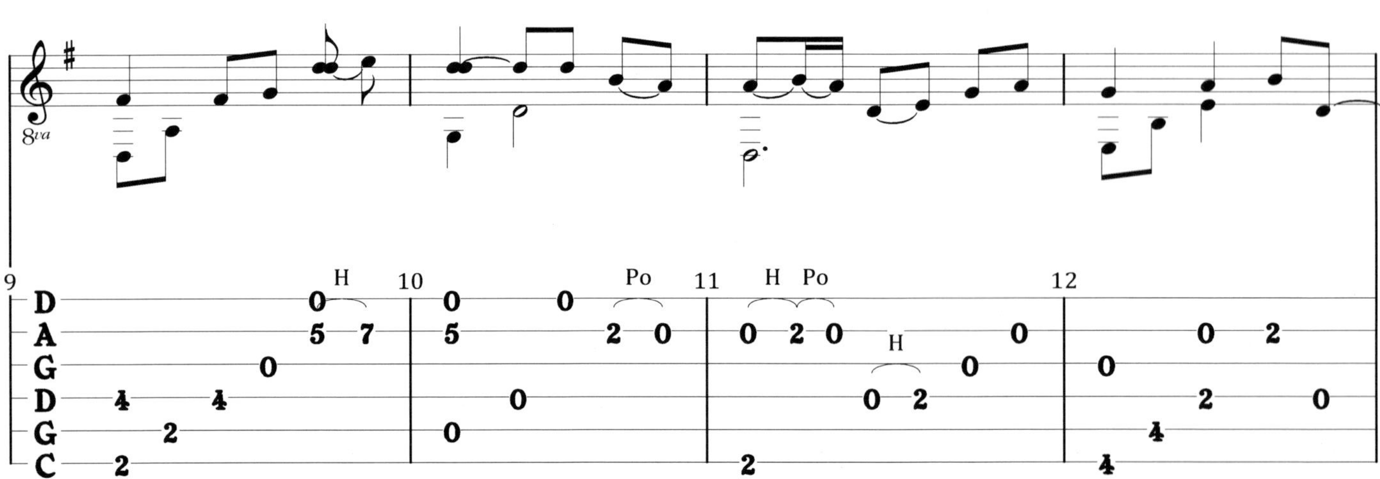

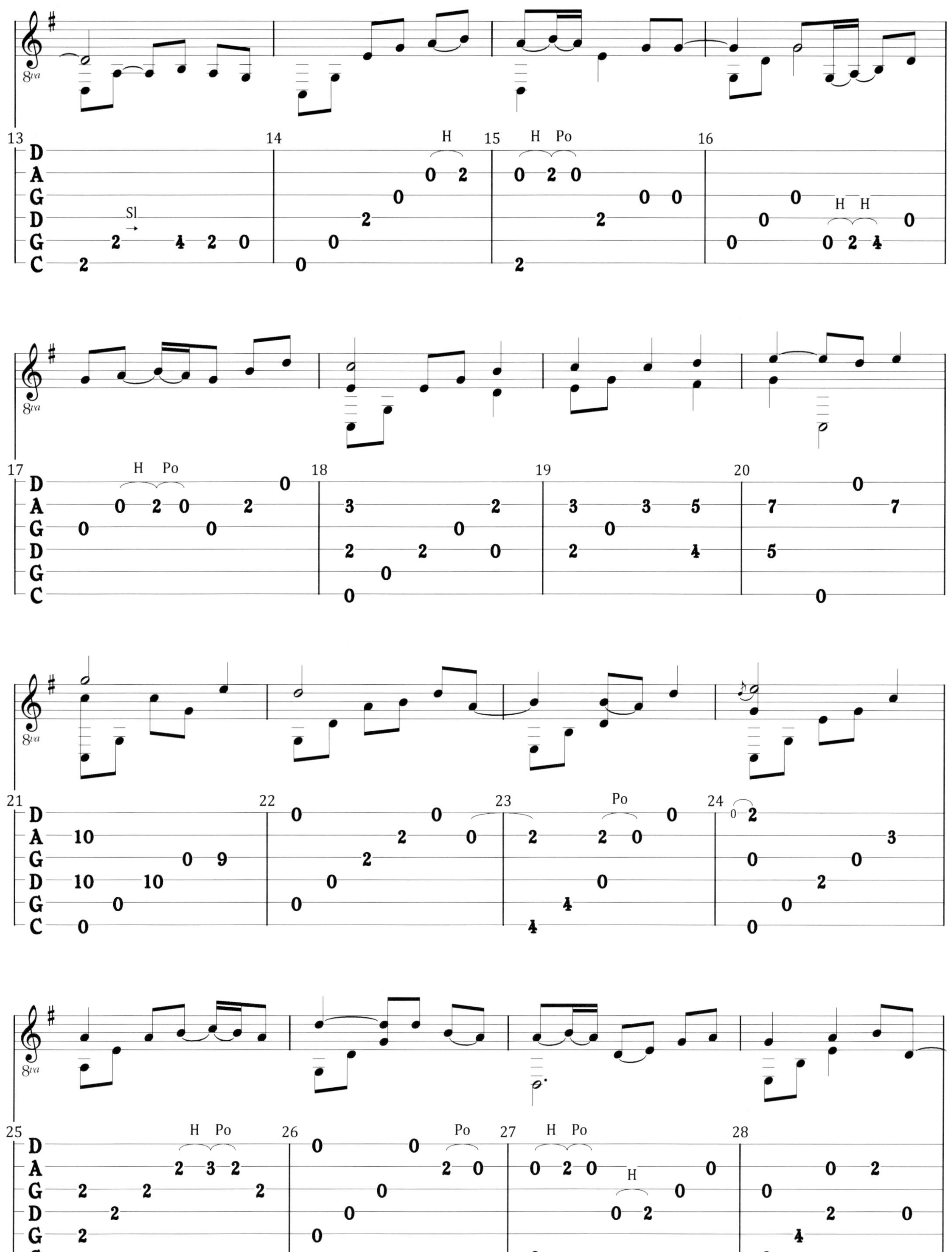
8va
13
14
15
16
D
A
G
D
G
C
Sl
H
H Po
H H
17
18
19
20
H Po
21
22
23
24
Po
25
26
27
28
H Po
Po
H Po
H

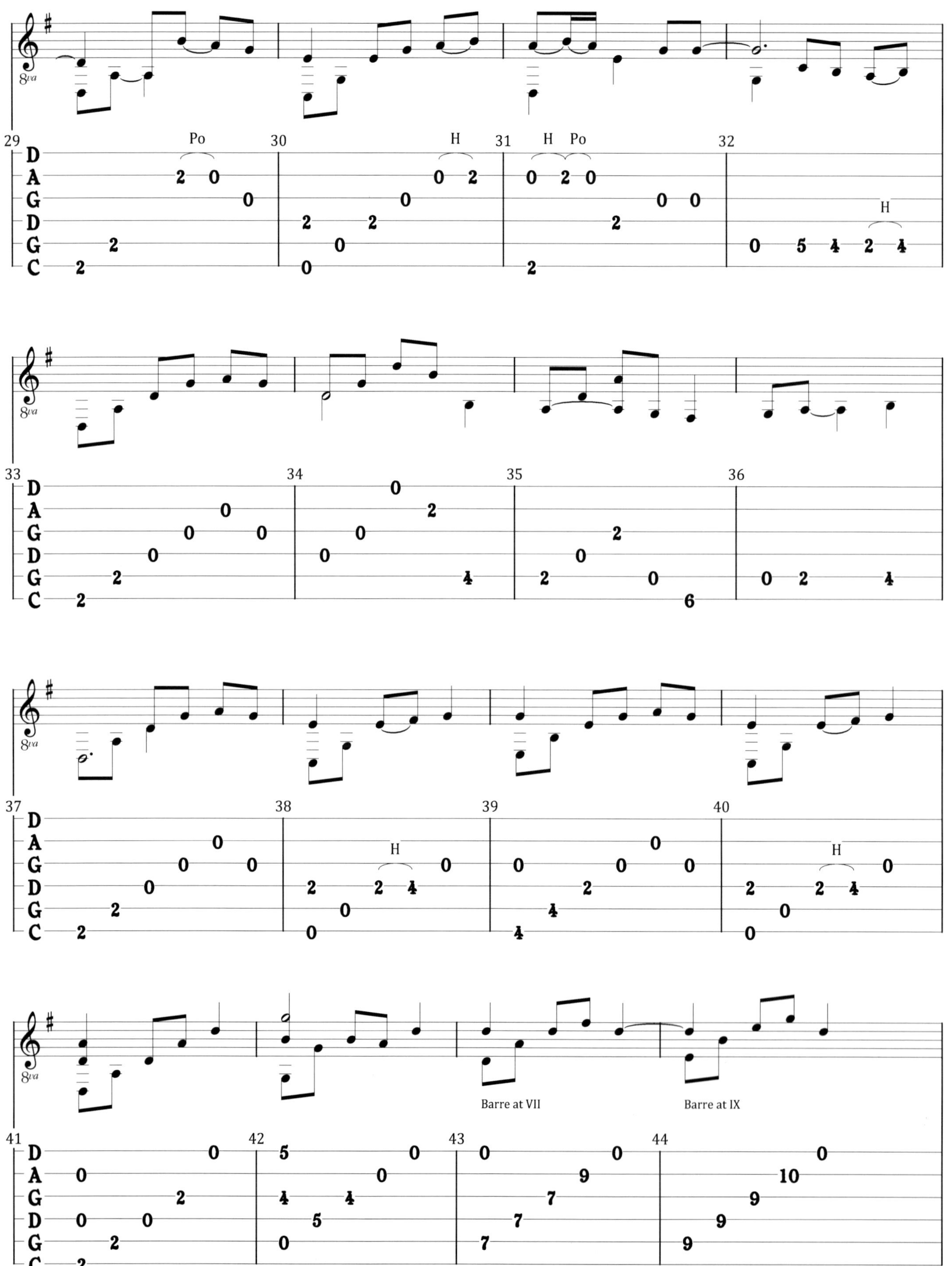
8va
Po
H
H Po
H
Barre at VII
Barre at IX

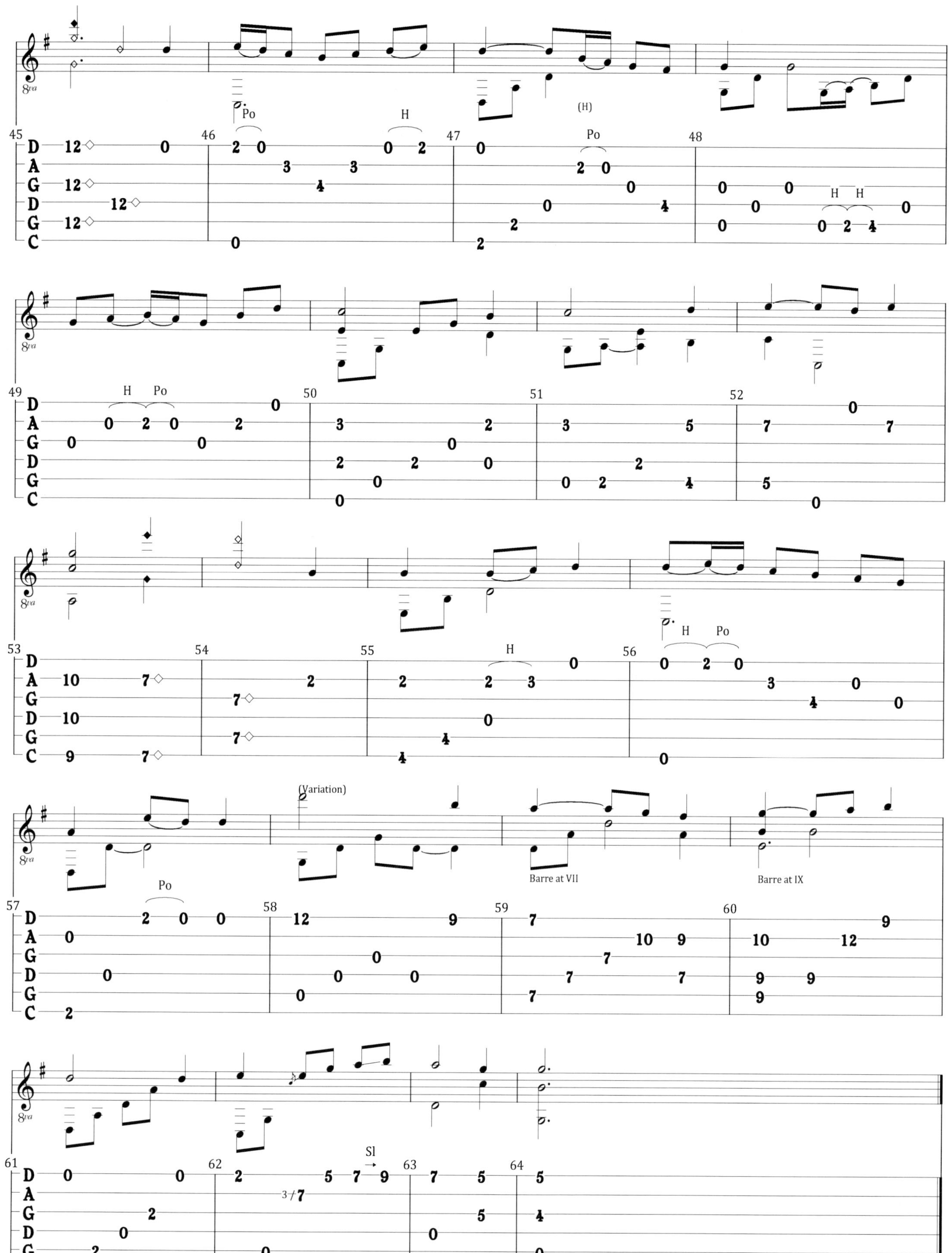
8va
Po
H
(H)
D
A
G
D
G
C
(Variation)
Barre at VII
Barre at IX
Sl

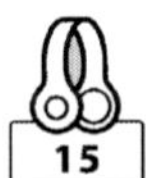

The Star of the County Down

(Traditional Song)

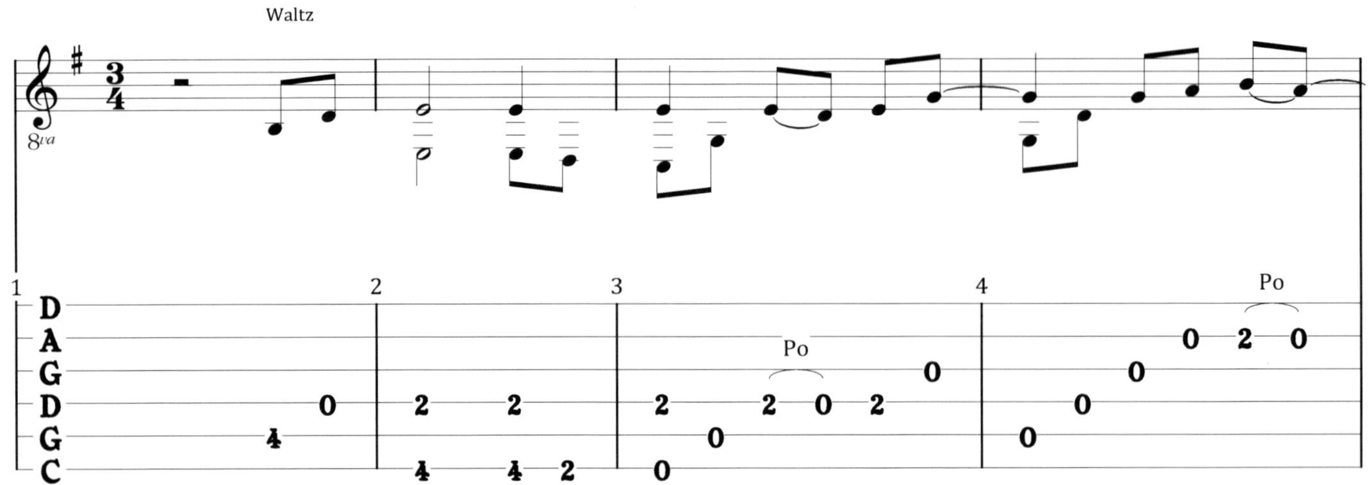

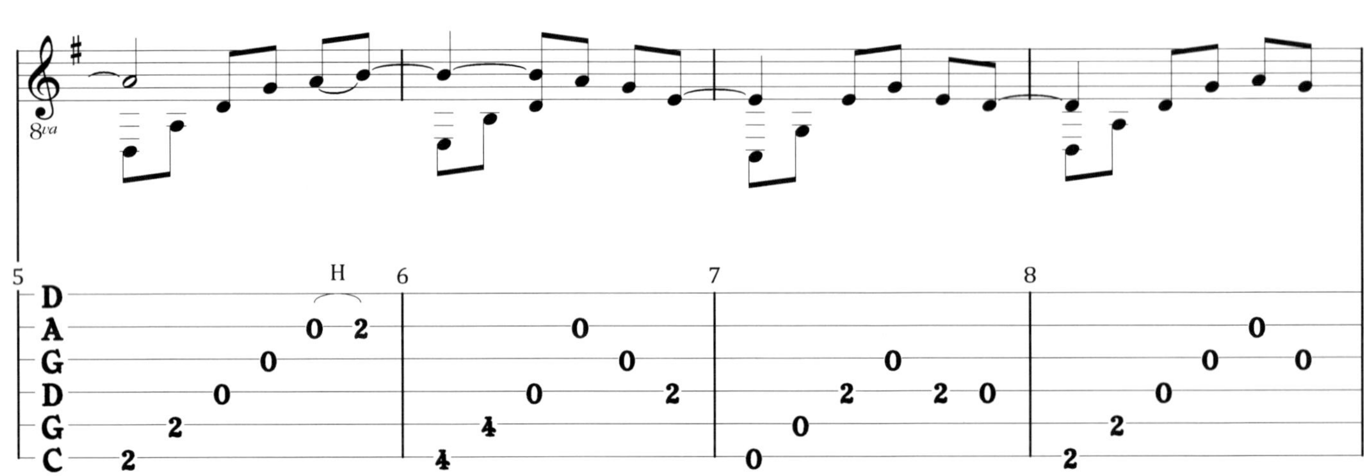

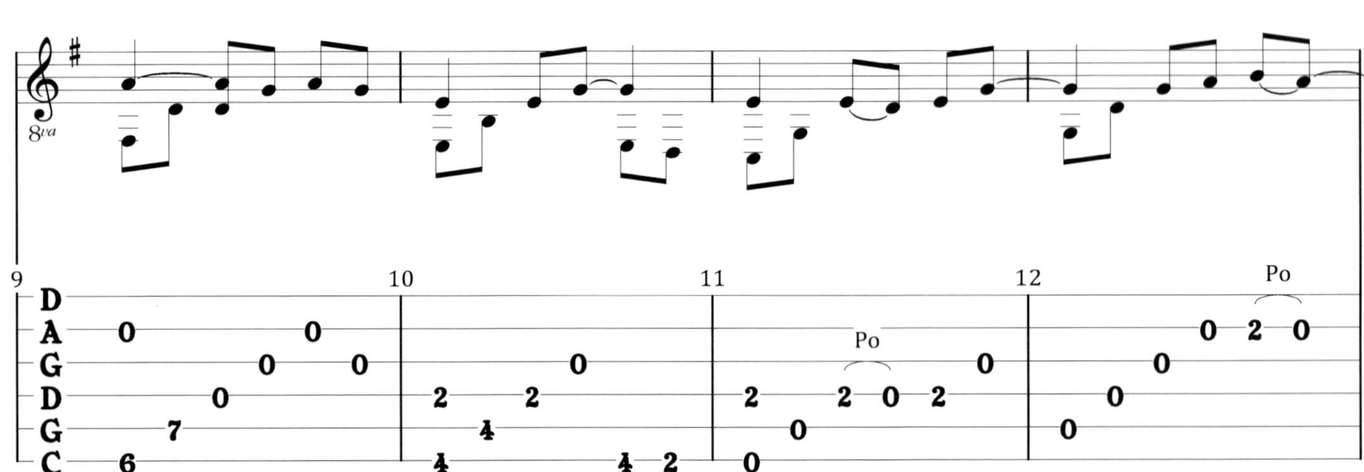

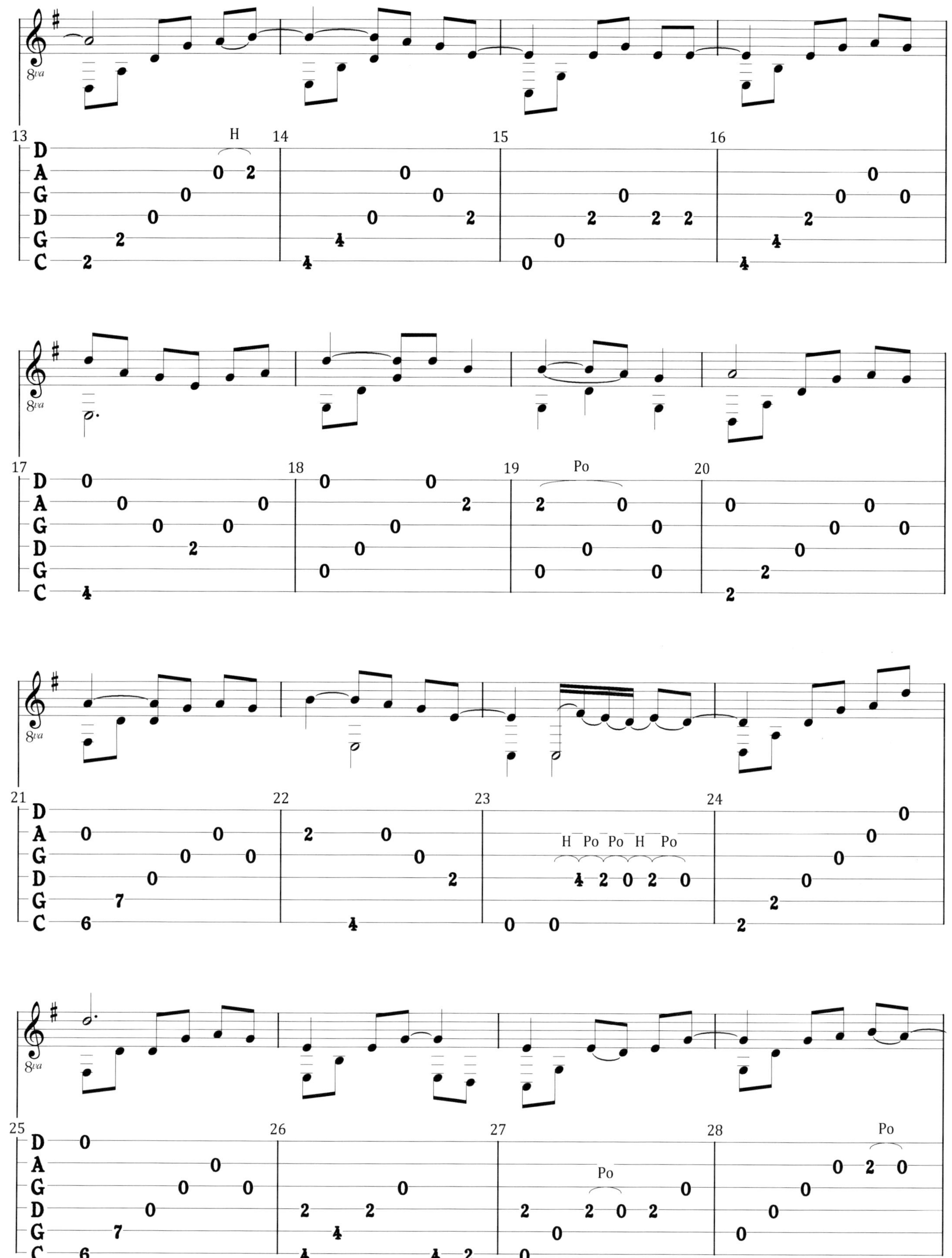
8va
13
14
15
16
17
18
19
20
21
22
23
24
25
26
27
28
D
A
G
D
G
C
H
Po
H Po Po H Po

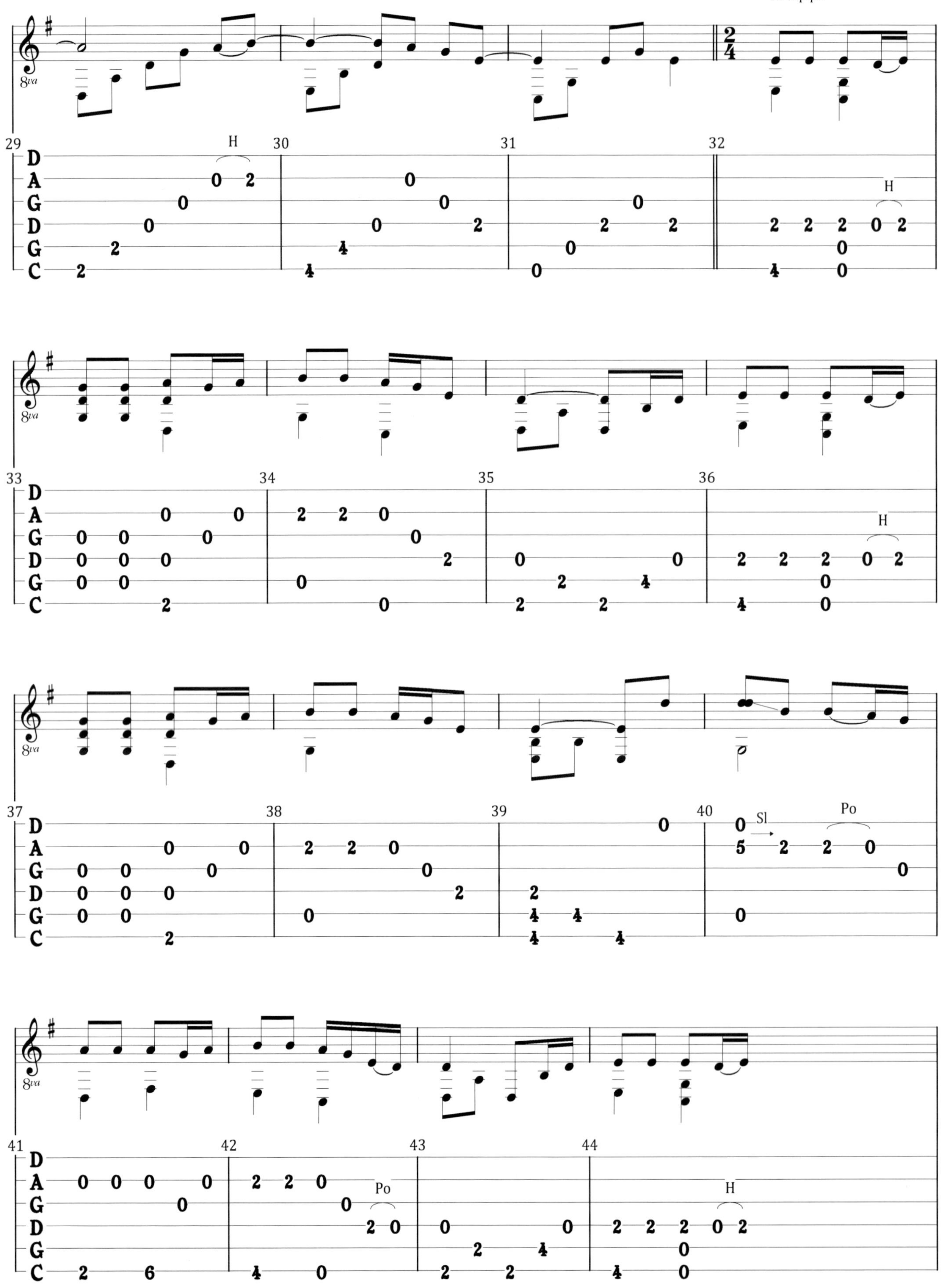
Hornpipe
8va
29
30
31
32
33
34
35
36
37
38
39
40
41
42
43
44
D
A
G
D
G
C
H
Sl
Po

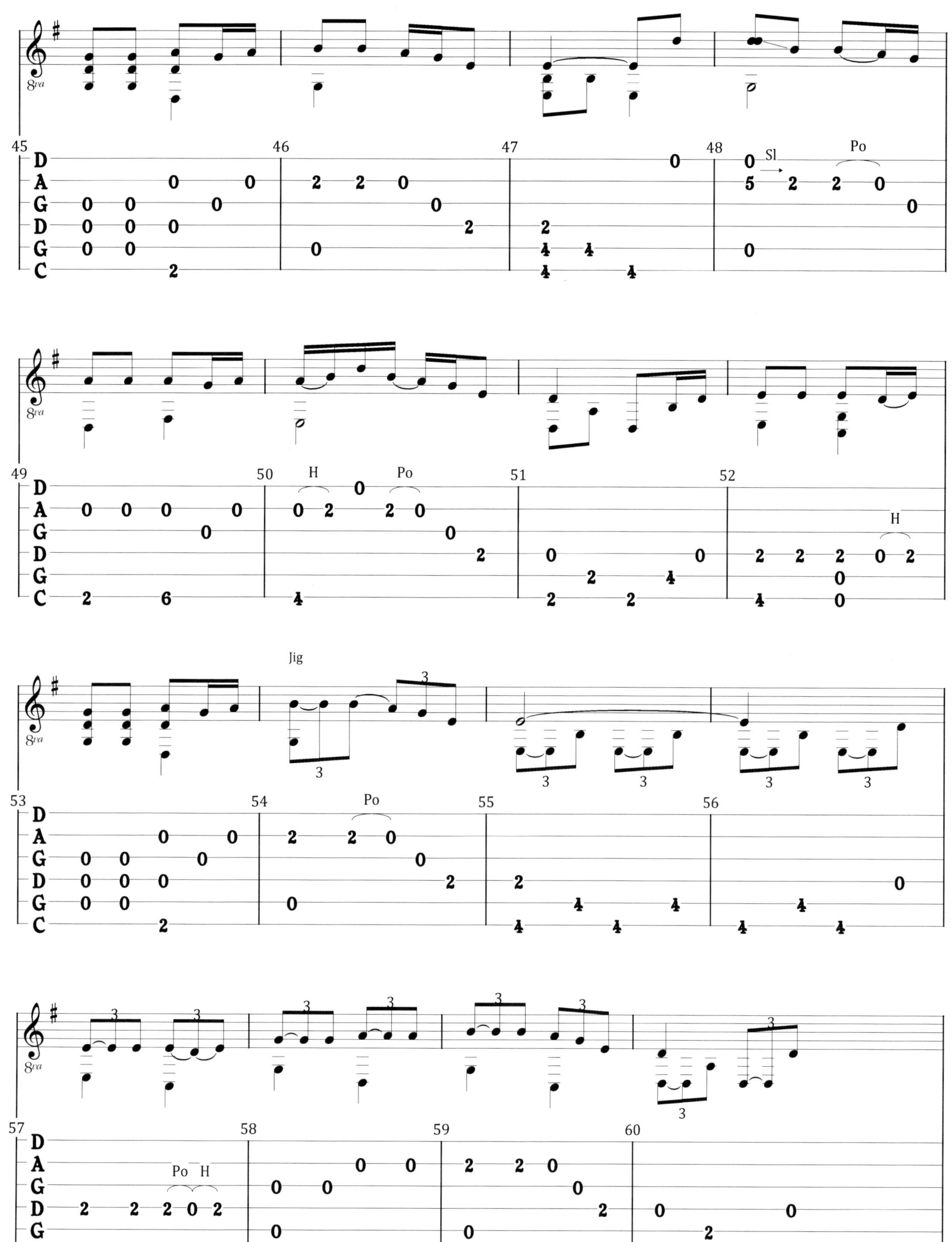
8va
D
A
G
D
G
C
Sl
Po
H
Jig

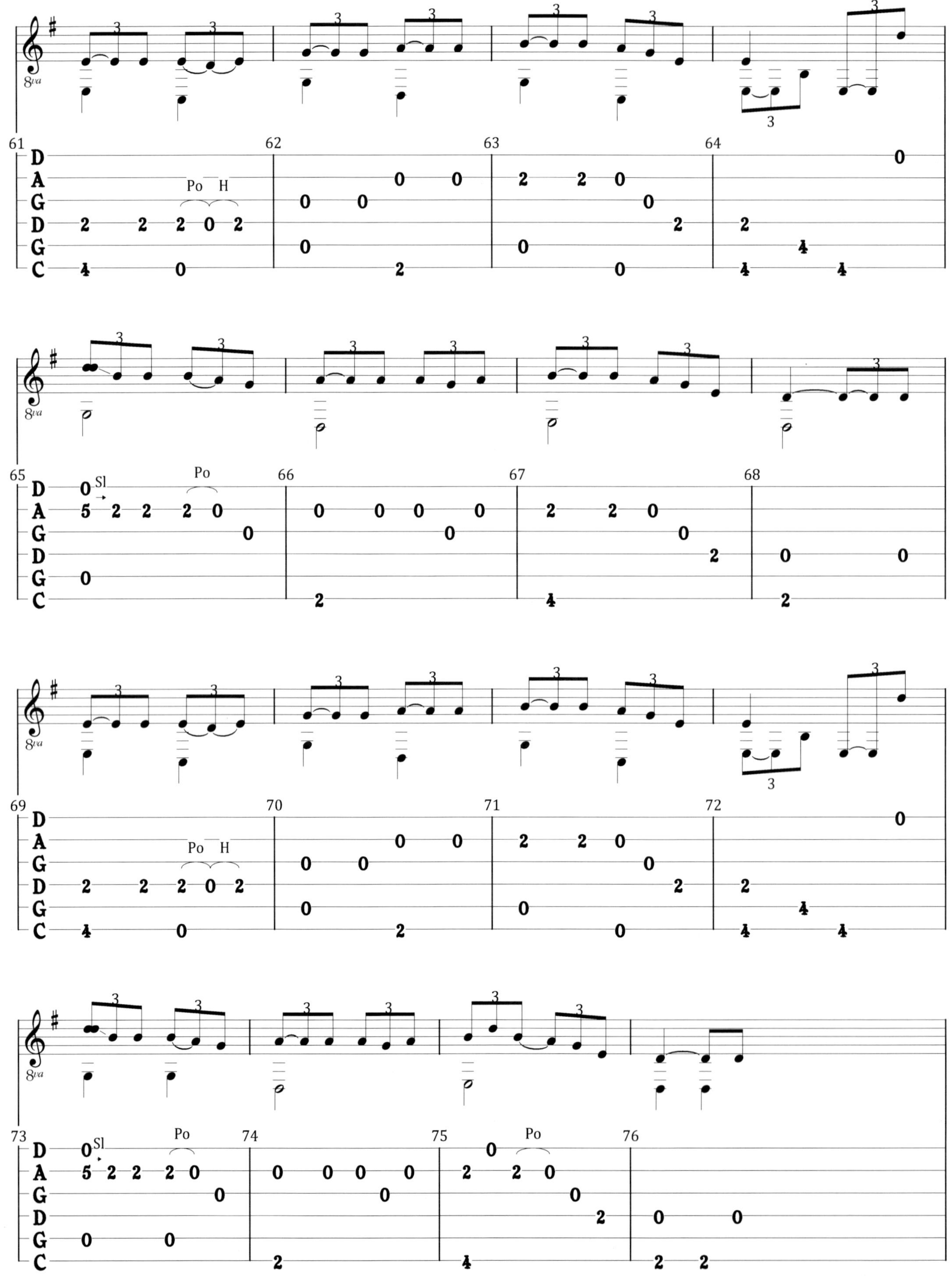
8va
61
62
63
64
Po
H
Sl
65
66
67
68
69
70
71
72
73
74
75
76

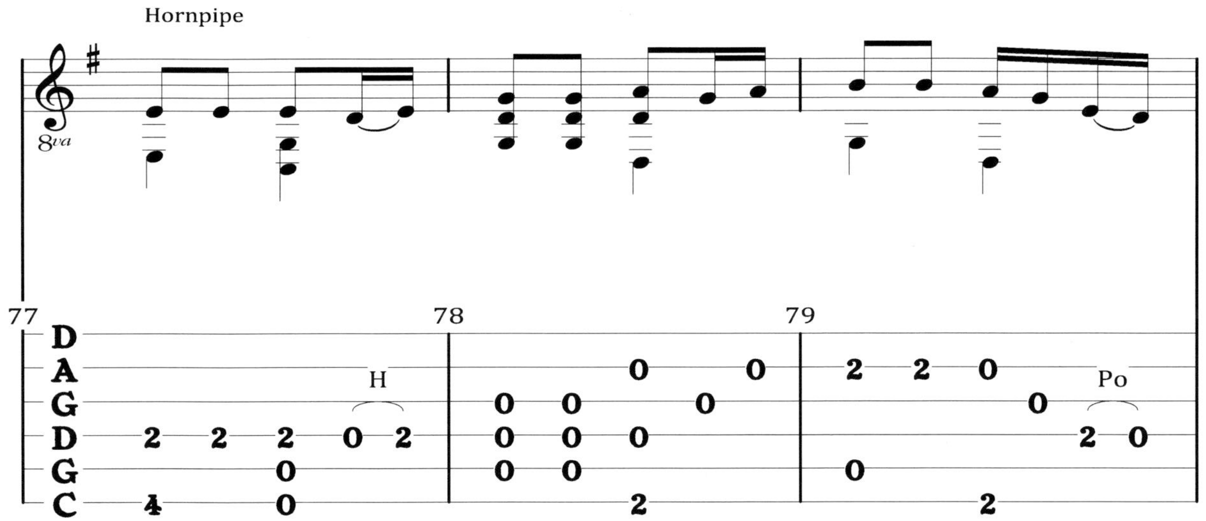
Hornpipe
8va
77
D
A
G
D
G
C
2 2 2 0 2
H
4 0
0
78
0 0 0
0 0 0 0
0 0
2
0
79
2 2 0
0
Po
2 0
0
2

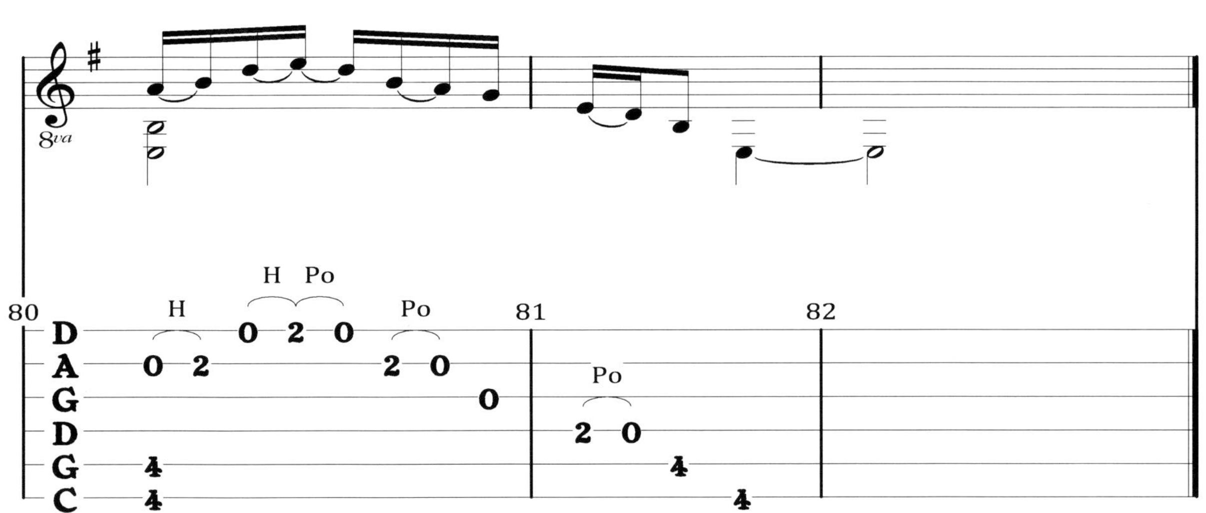
8va
80
D
A
G
D
G
C
H
H Po
Po
0 2 0
0 2 2 0
0
4
4
81
Po
2 0
4
4
82

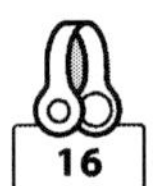

George Brabazon, 2d Air

(T. O'Carolan)

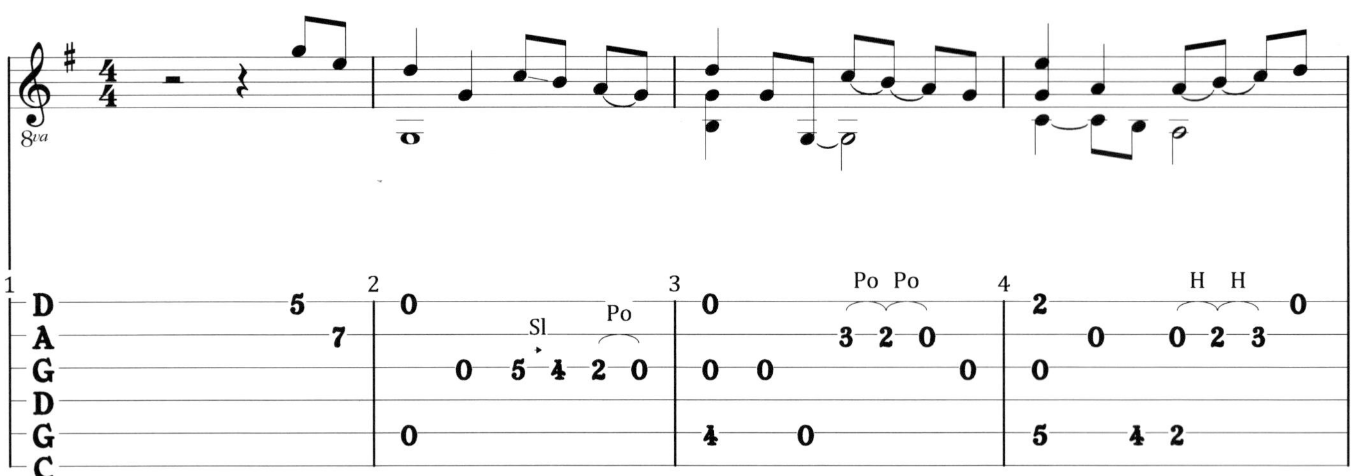

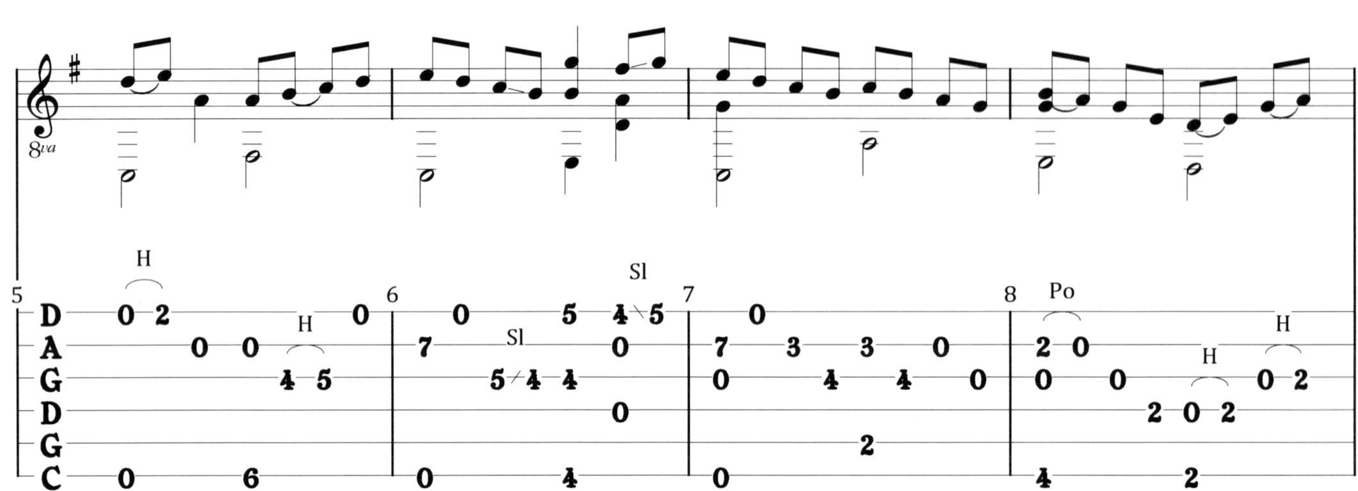

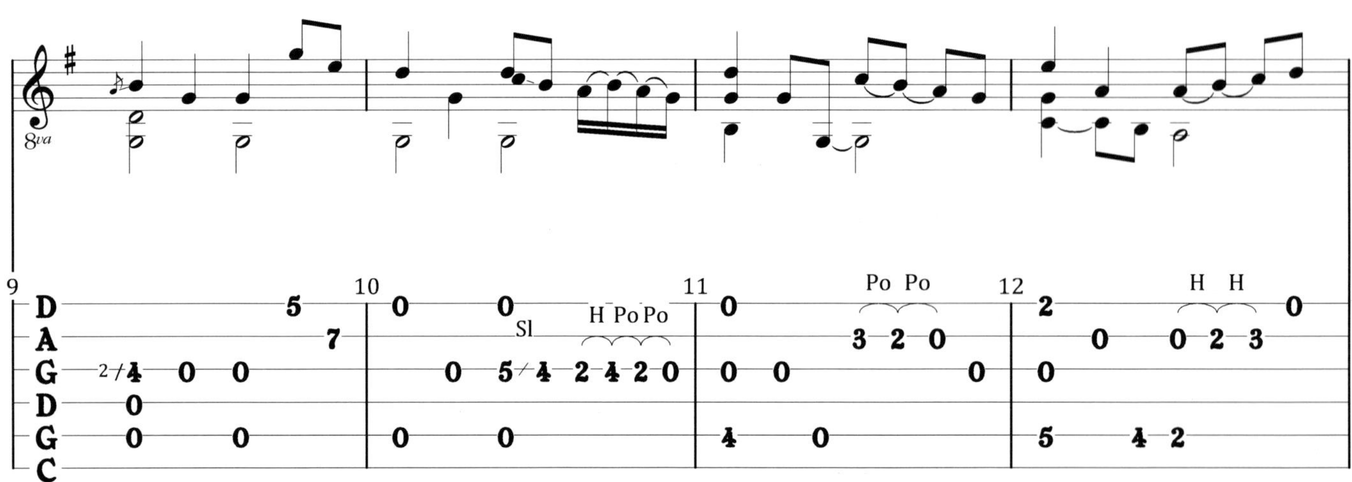

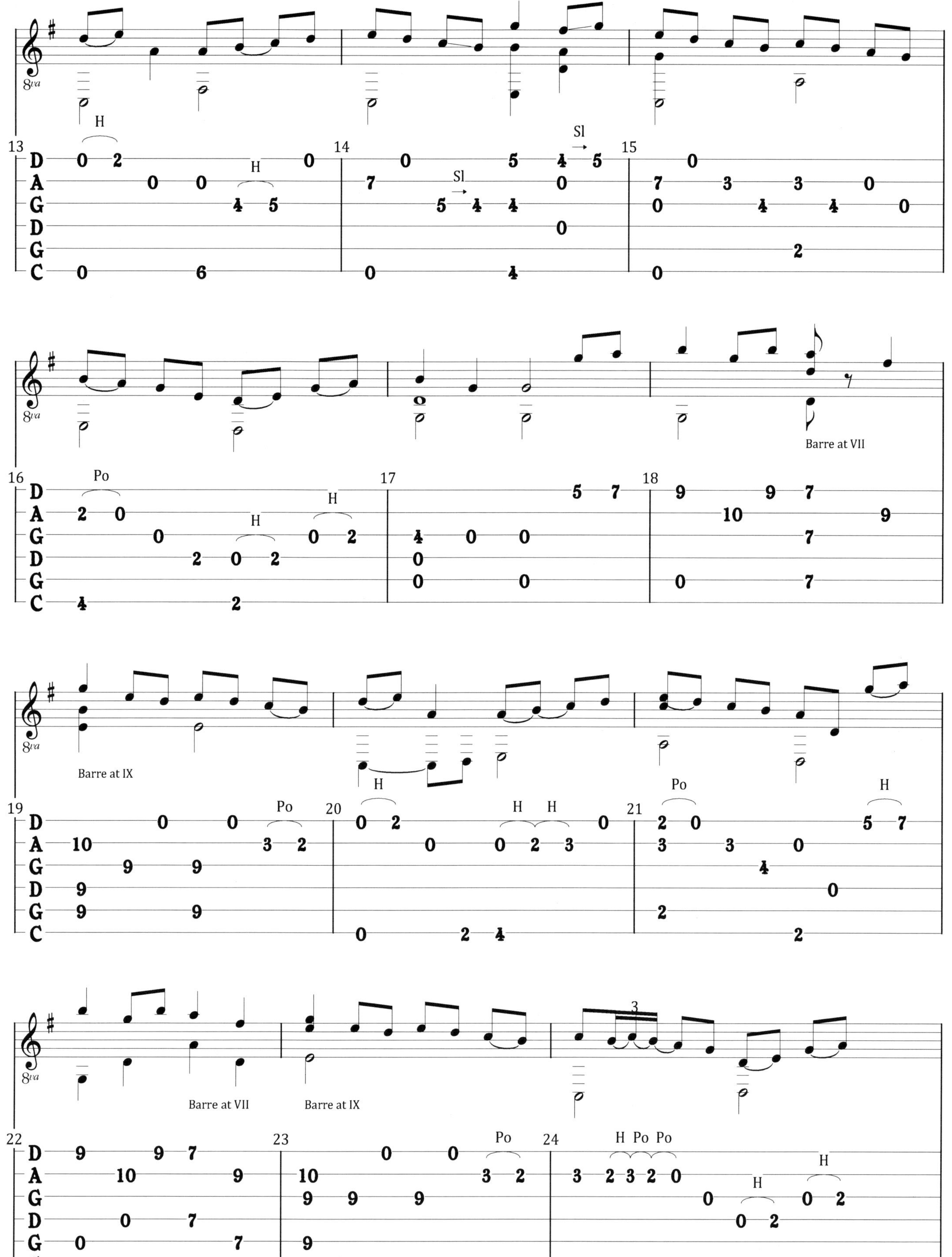
8va
13
14
15
16
17
18
19
20
21
22
23
24
D
A
G
D
G
C
H
Po
Sl
Barre at VII
Barre at IX
3

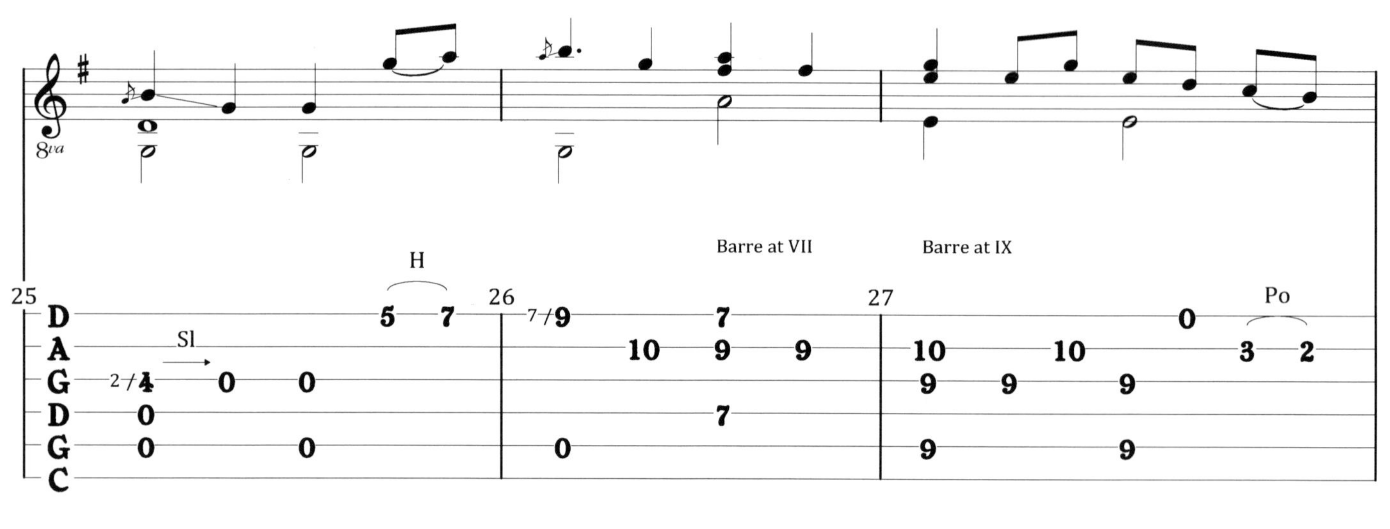
8va
Barre at VII
Barre at IX
H
Sl
Po
25
26
27
D
A
G
D
G
C

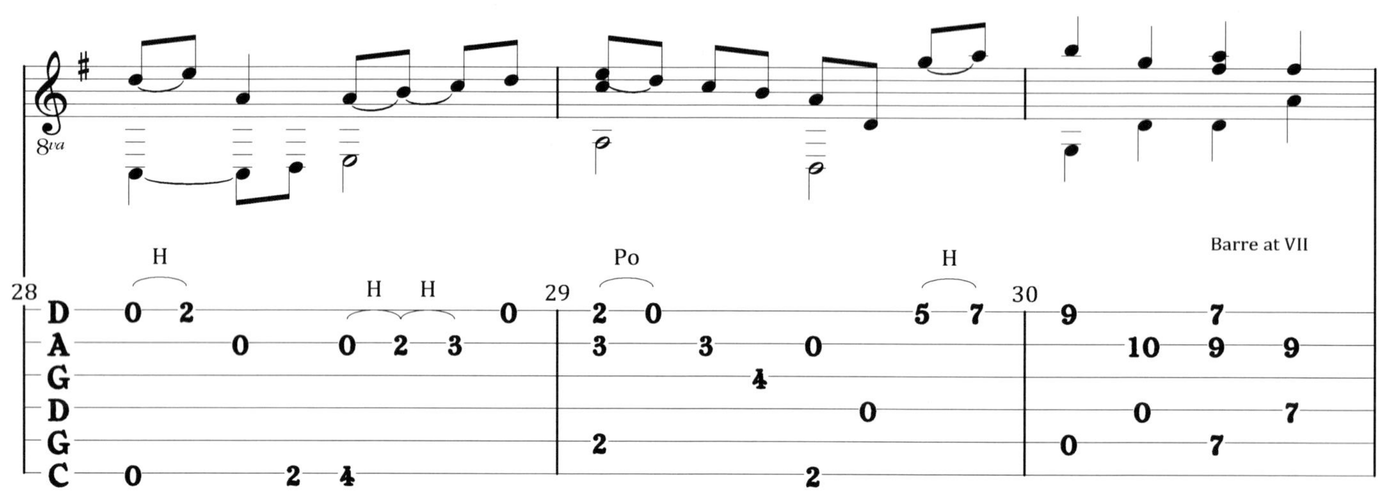
8va
Barre at VII
H
Po
28
29
30
D
A
G
D
G
C

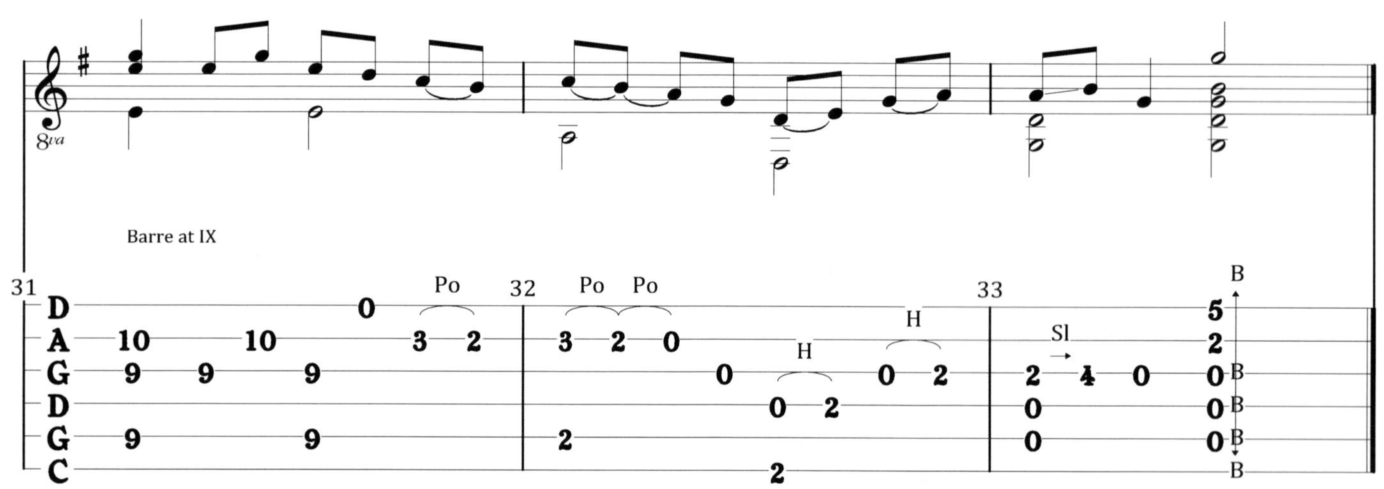
8va
Barre at IX
Po
H
Sl
B
31
32
33
D
A
G
D
G
C

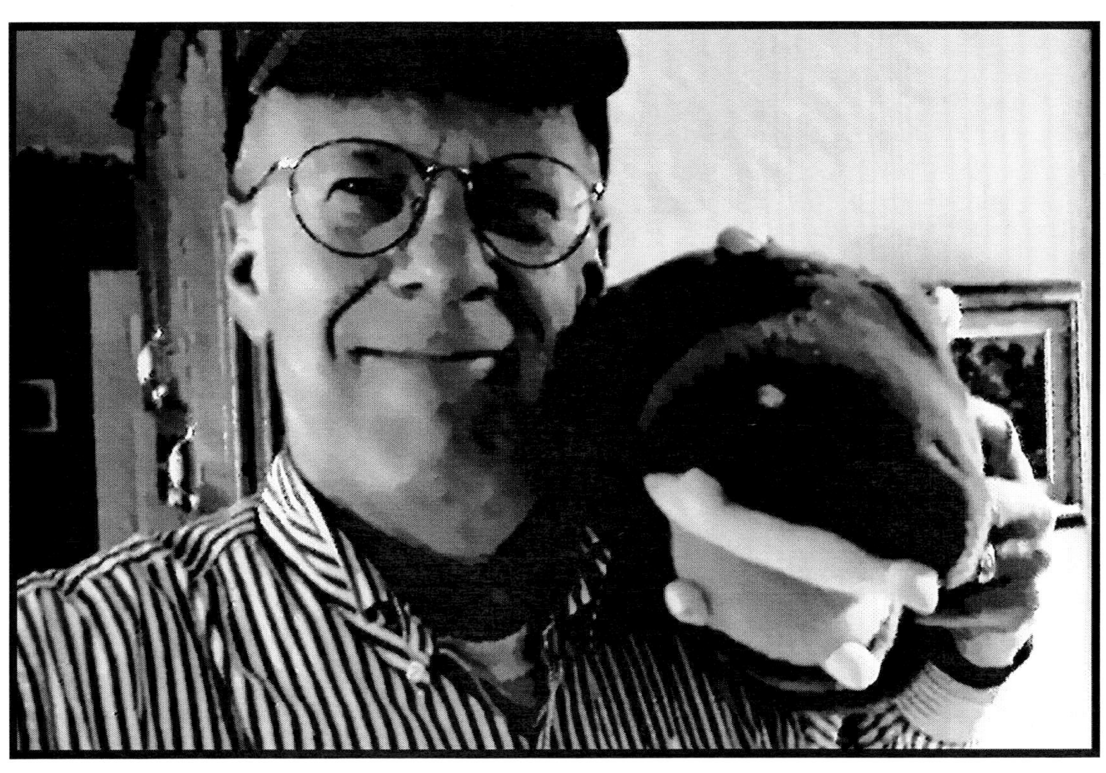

El with stuffed hippo given to him as gift

The South Wind

(Traditional)

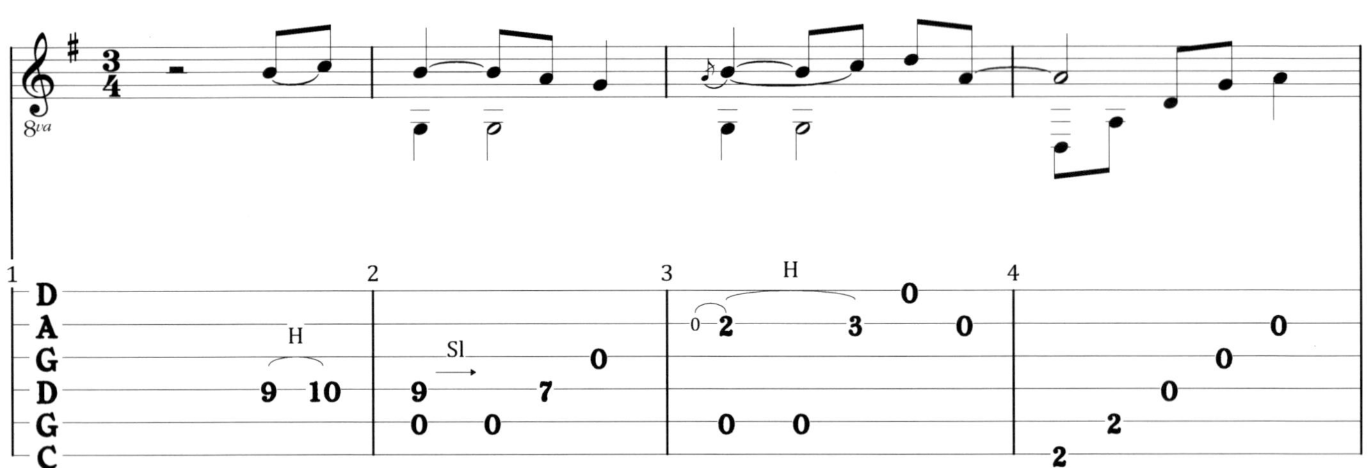

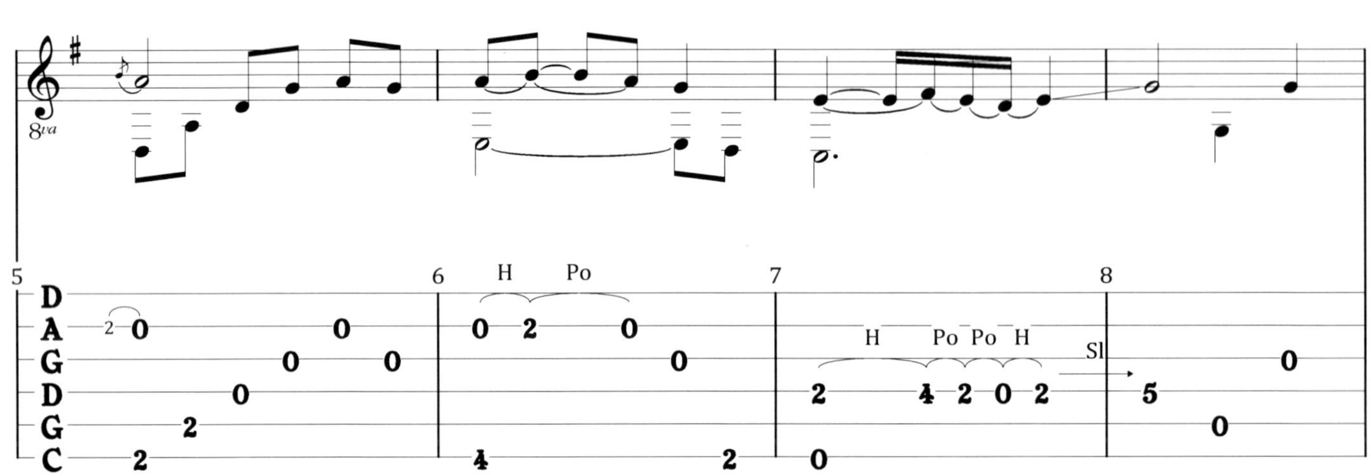

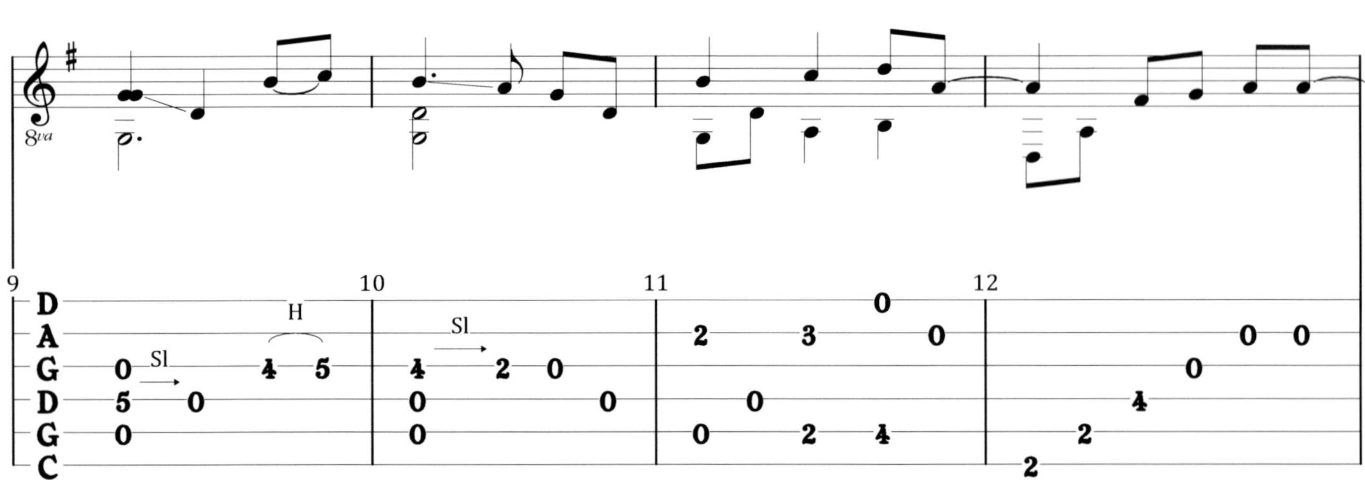

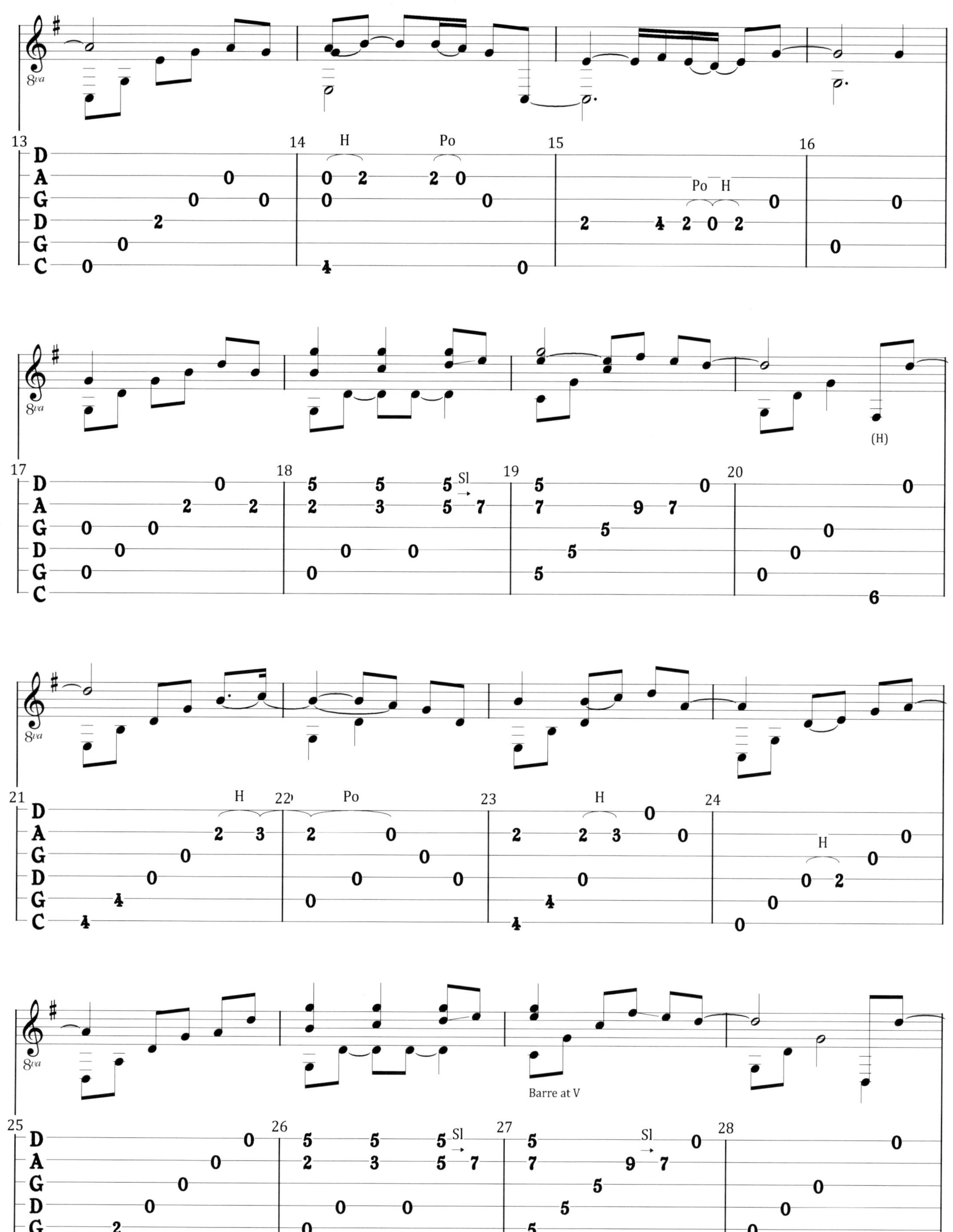

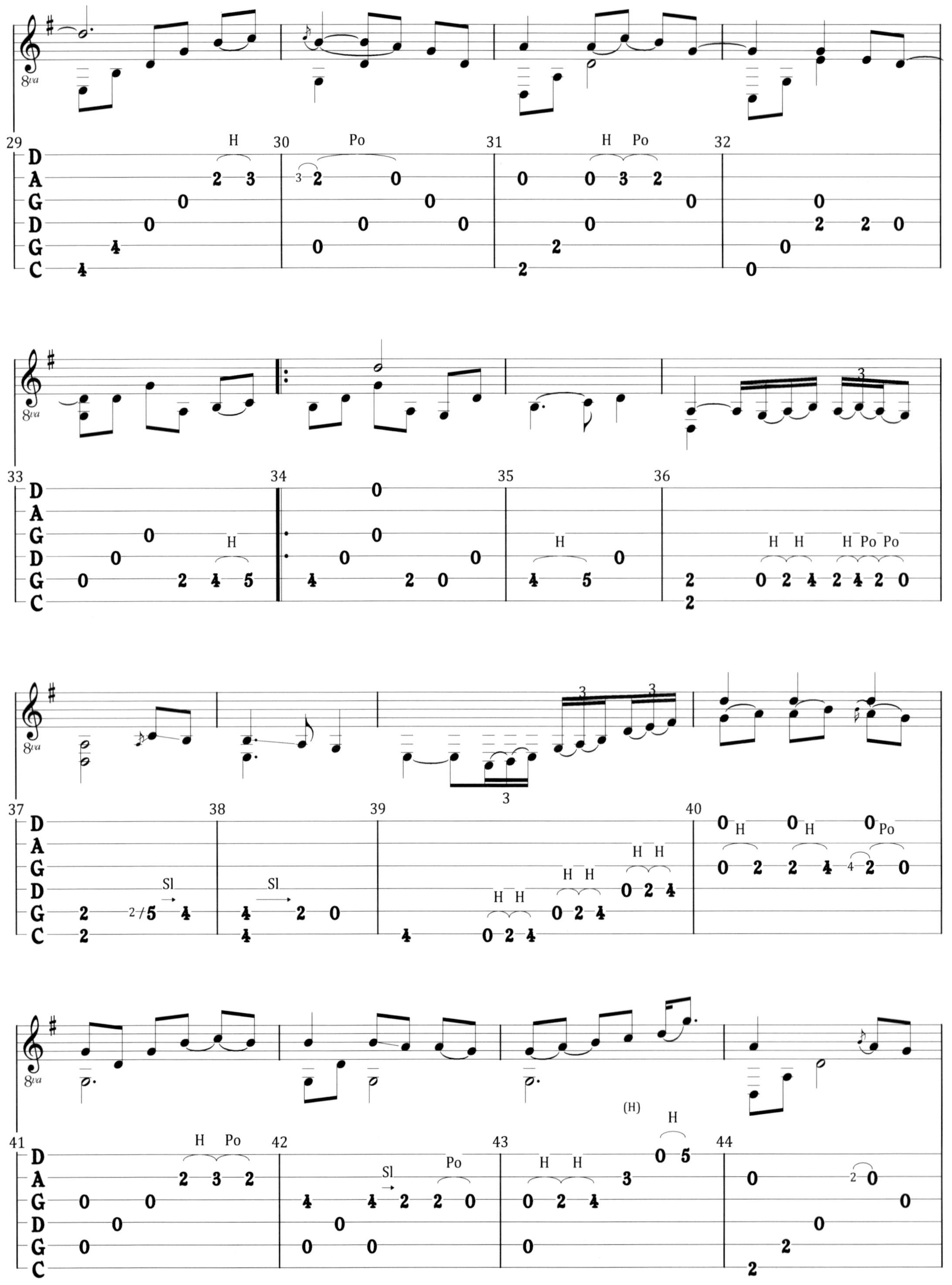
8va
29 30 31 32
D A G D G C
H Po H Po
33 34 35 36
H H H H H Po Po
37 38 39 40
Sl Sl H H H H H H H H Po
41 42 43 44
H Po Sl Po H H (H) H

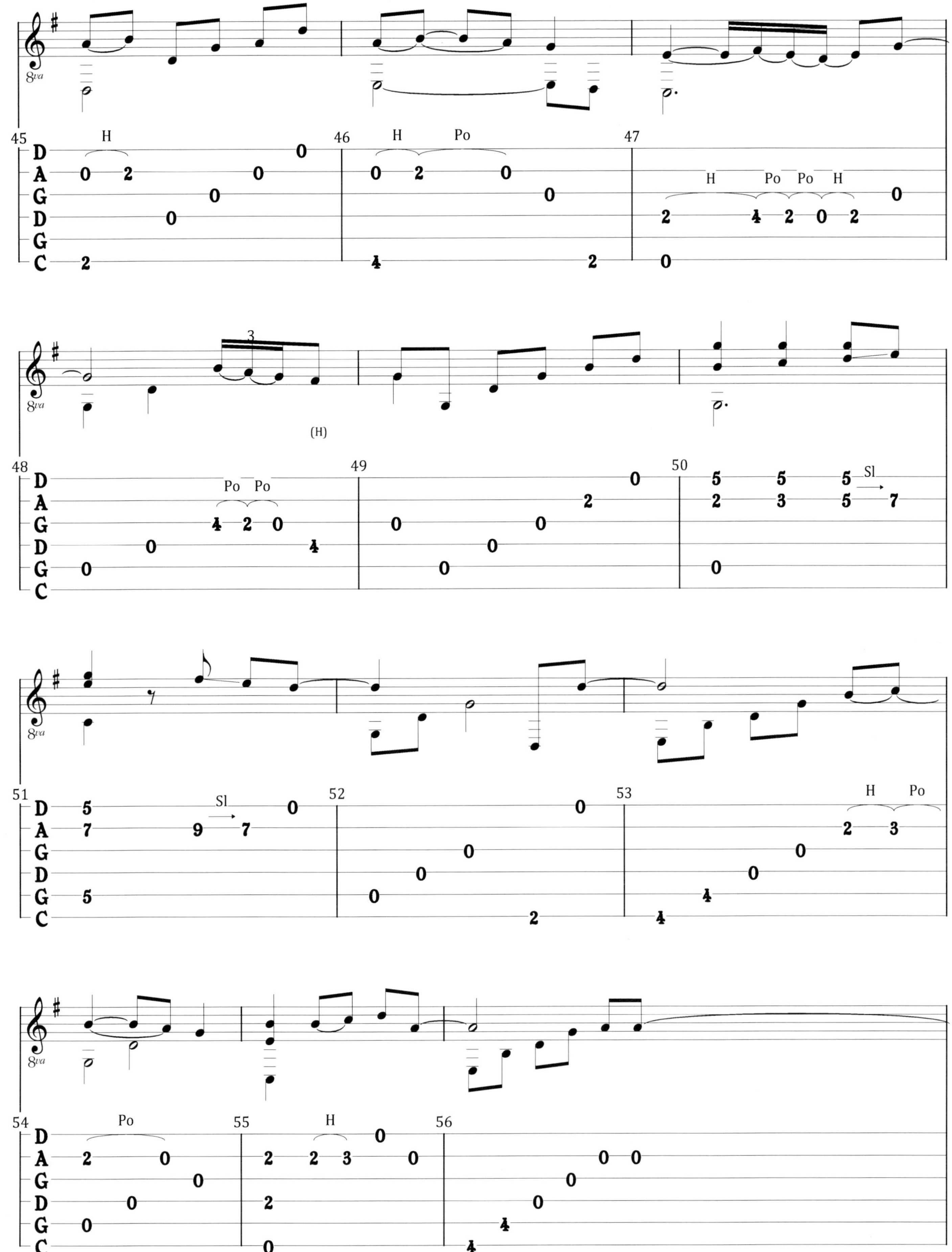

8va
45
H
D A G D G C
46
H Po
47
H Po Po H
3
(H)
48
Po Po
49
50
Sl
51
Sl
52
53
H Po
54
Po
55
H
56

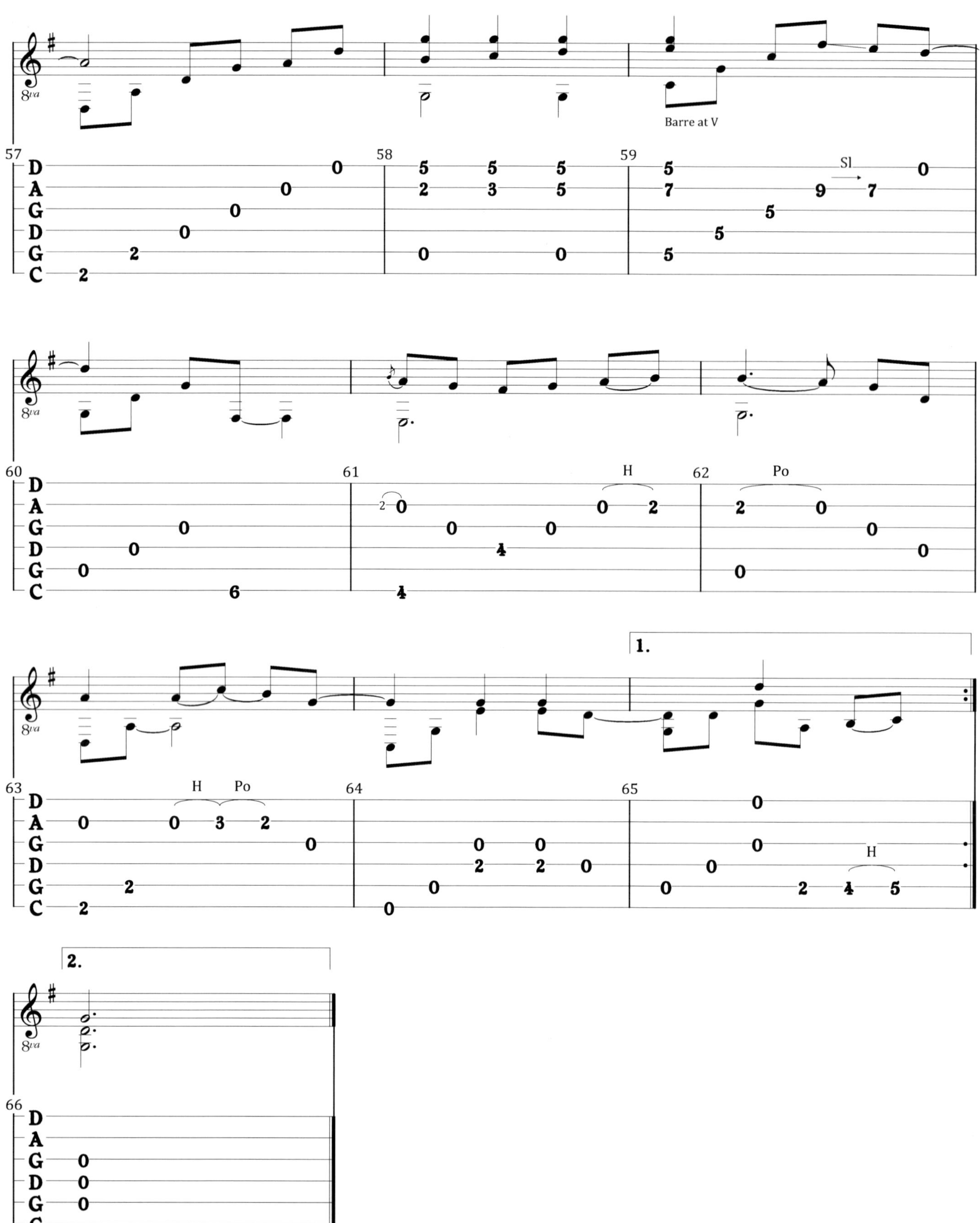
8va
Barre at V
Sl
H
Po
1.
2.

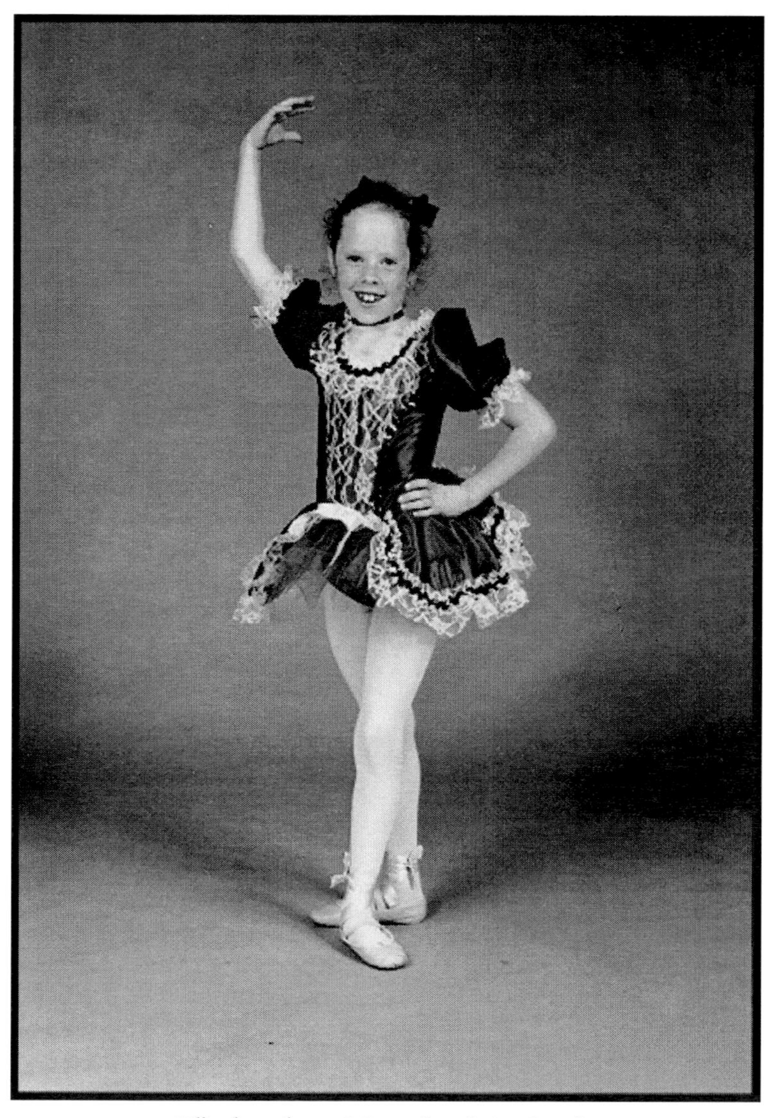

El's daughter Mary, back in the day

Pretty Maid Milking A Cow

(Traditional)

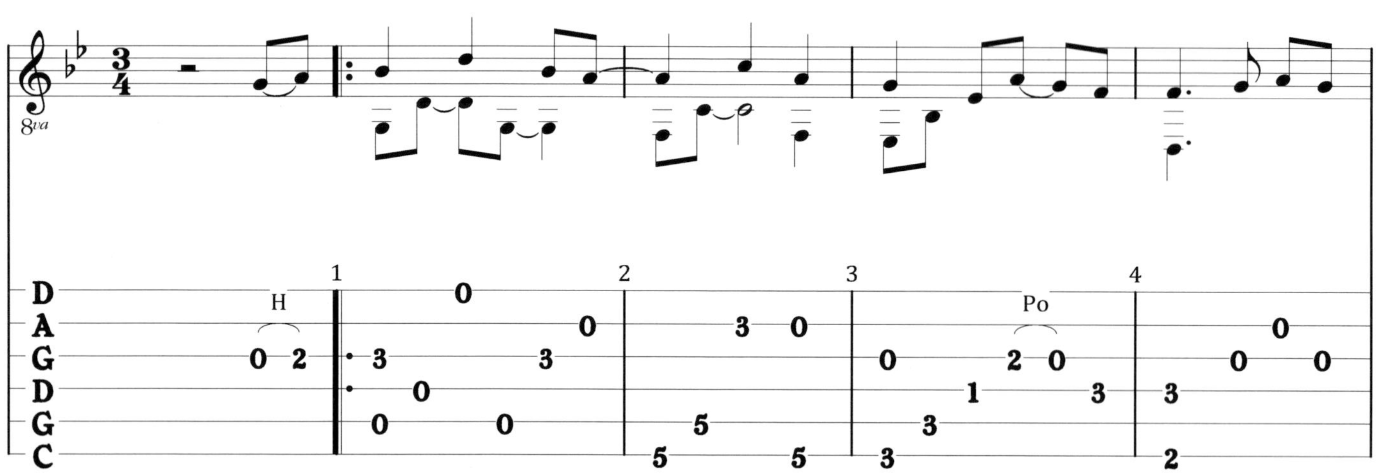

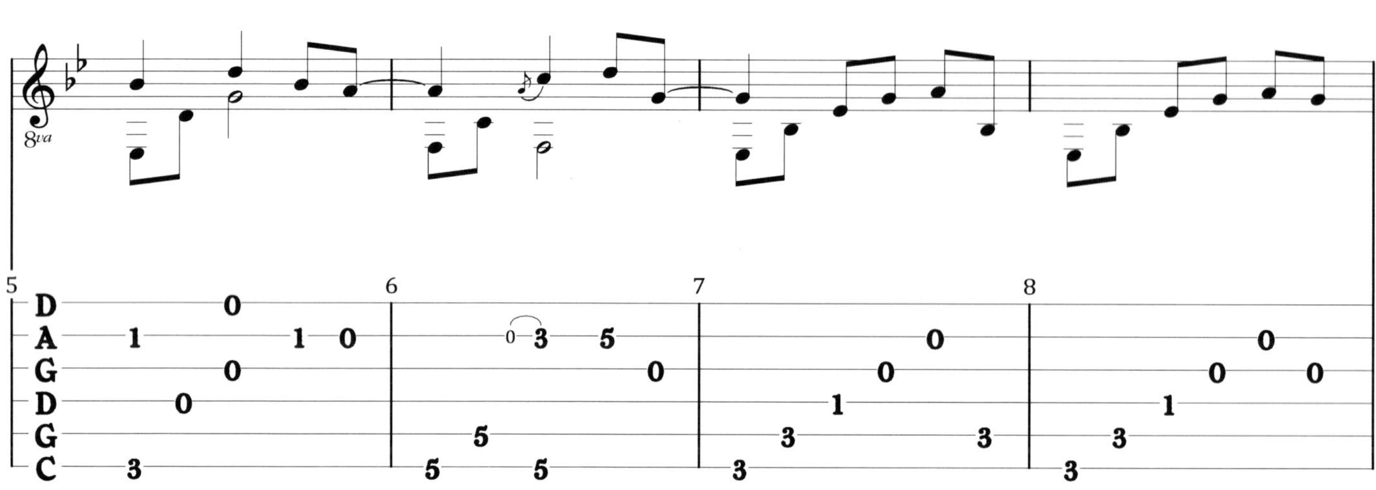

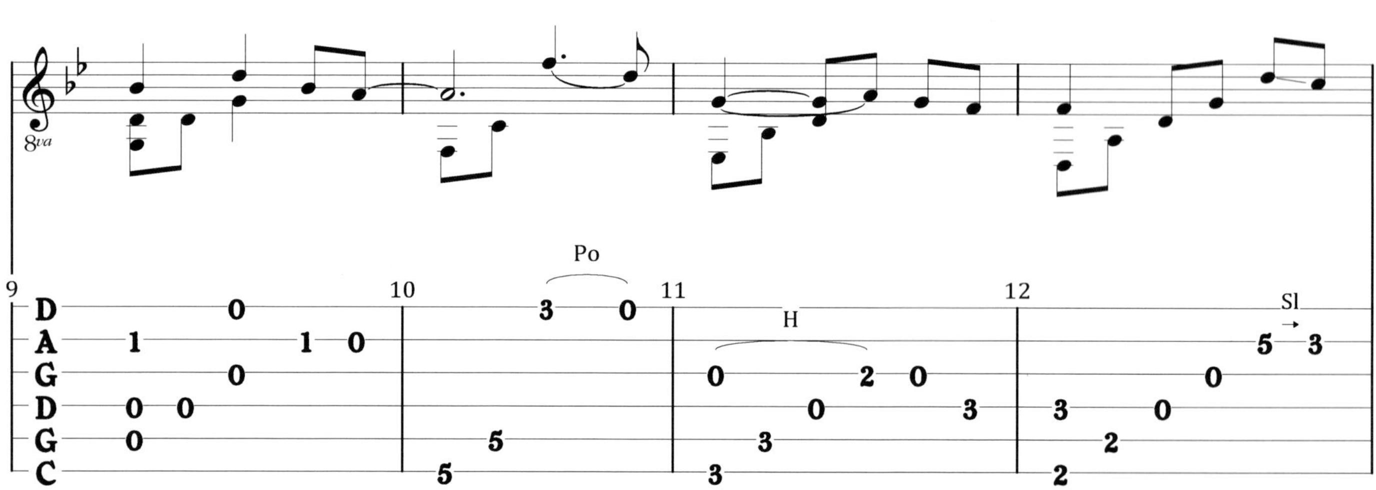

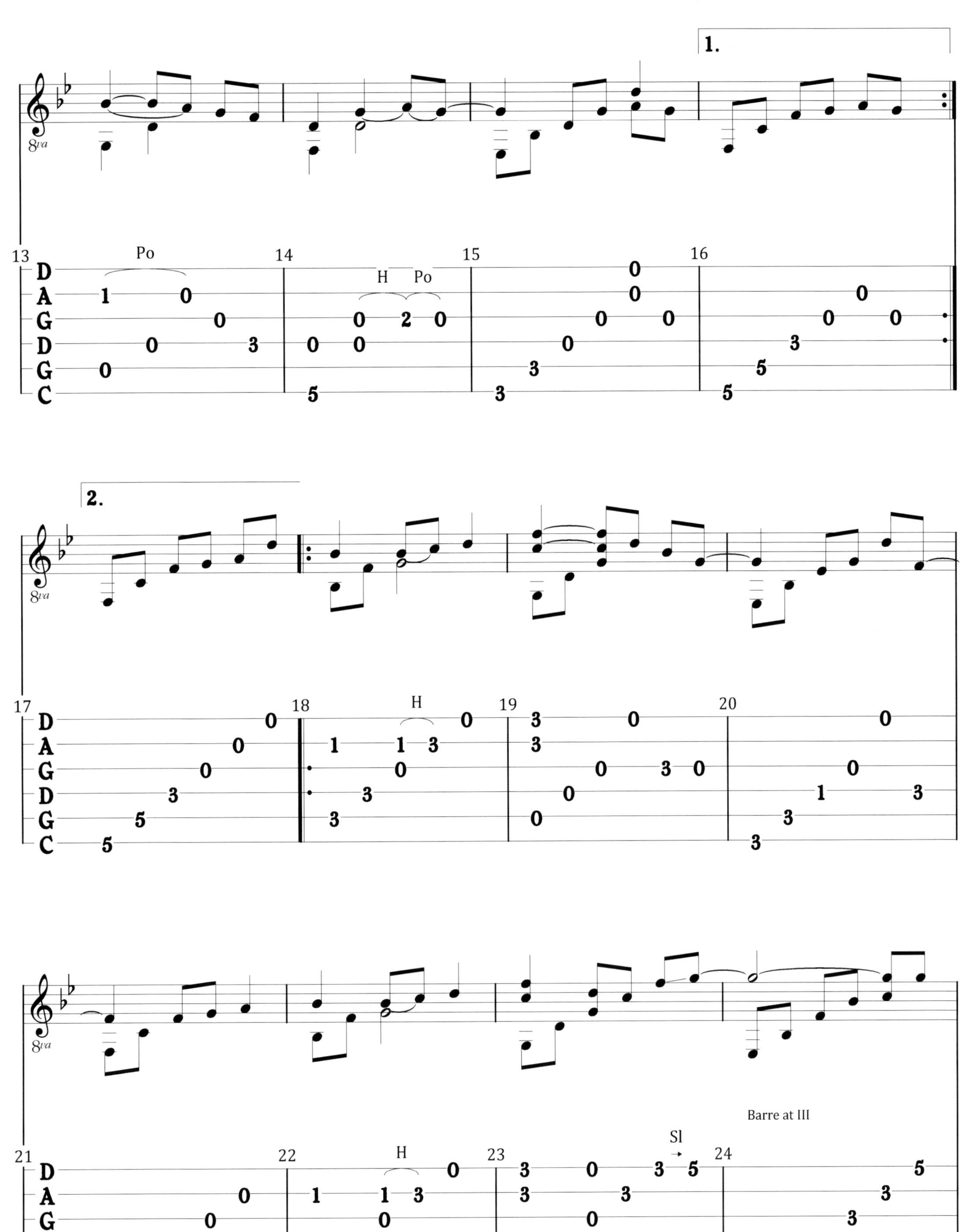
1.
8va
13
Po
D
A
G
D
G
C
14
H Po
15
16
2.
17
18
H
19
20
21
22
H
23
Sl
24
Barre at III

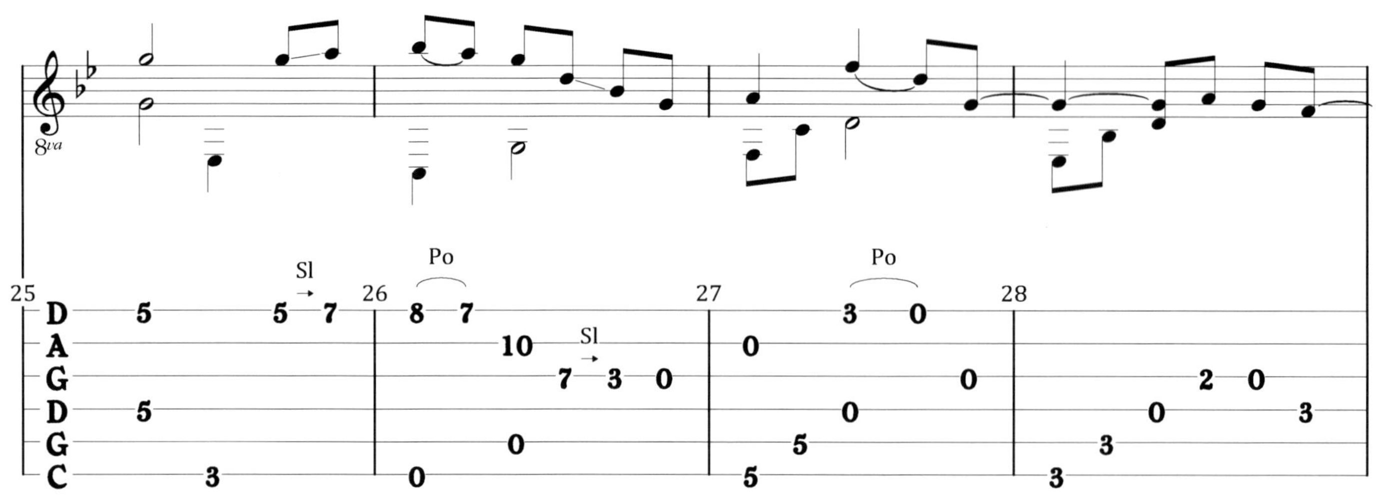
8va
Sl
Po
Sl
Po
25
26
27
28
D
A
G
D
G
C

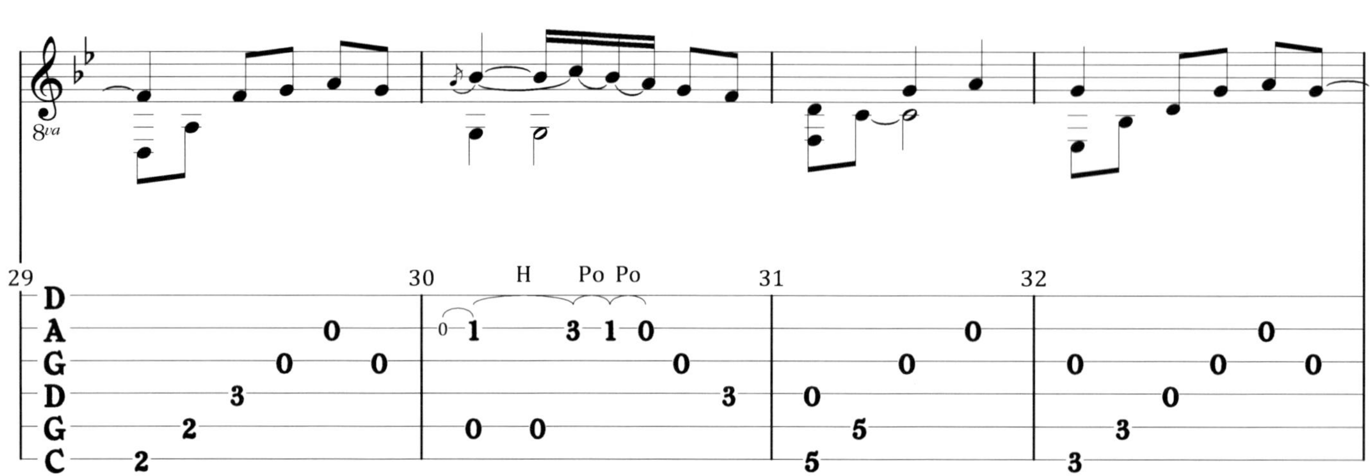
8va
H
Po Po
29
30
31
32
D
A
G
D
G
C

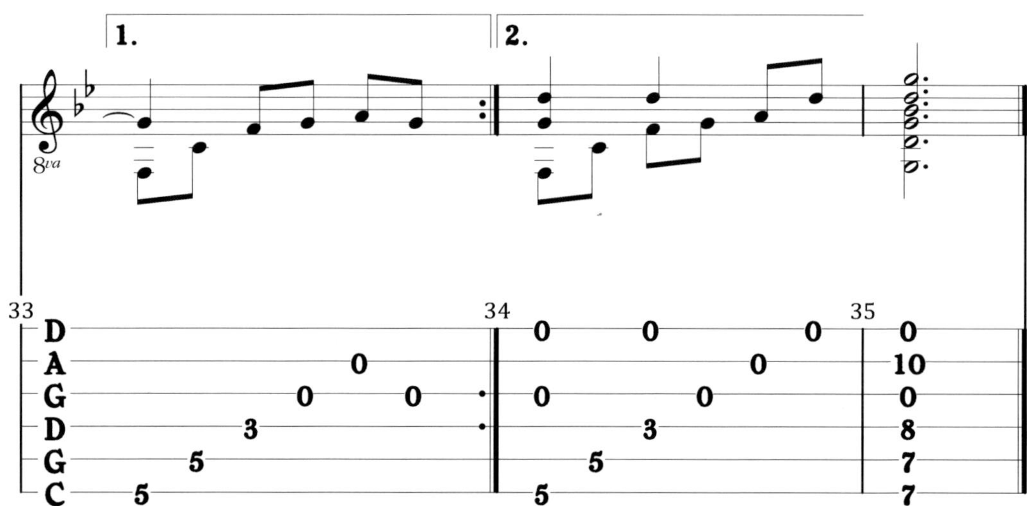
1.
2.
8va
33
34
35
D
A
G
D
G
C

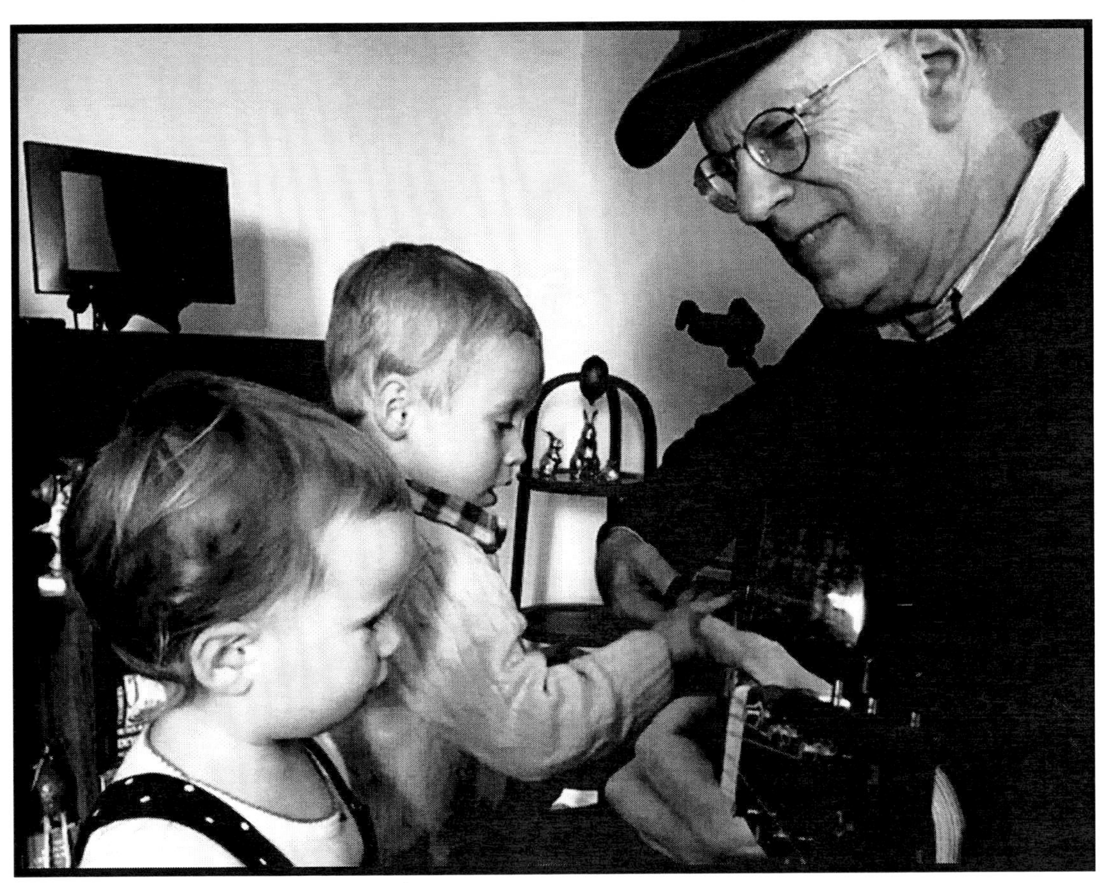

El showing grandchildren Conner McMeen and Evelyn Kohan the magic of guitar

Carolan's No. 179

(T. O'Carolan)

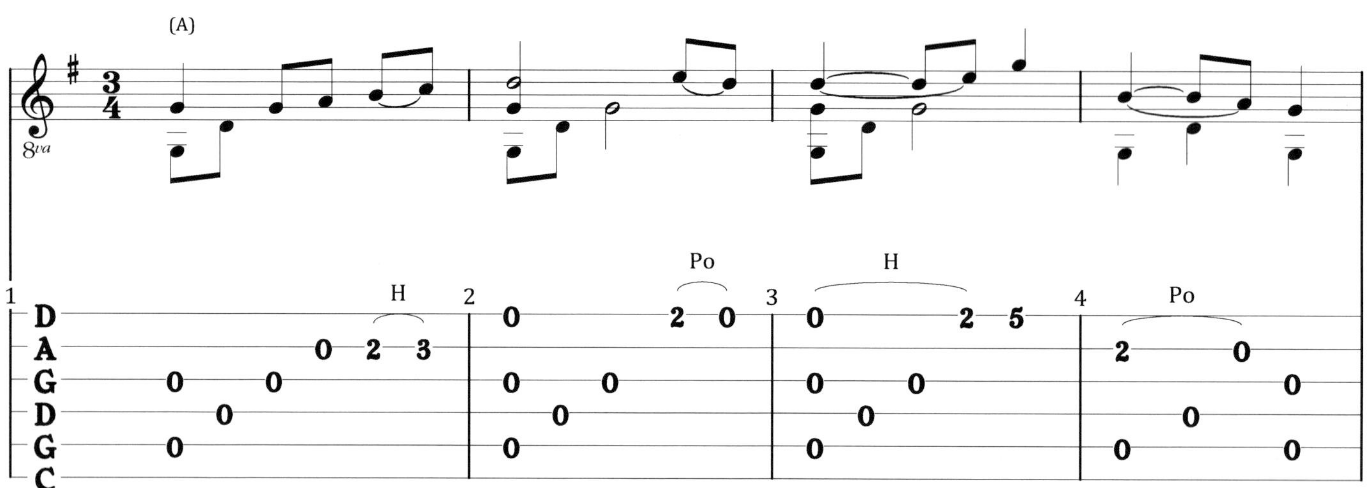

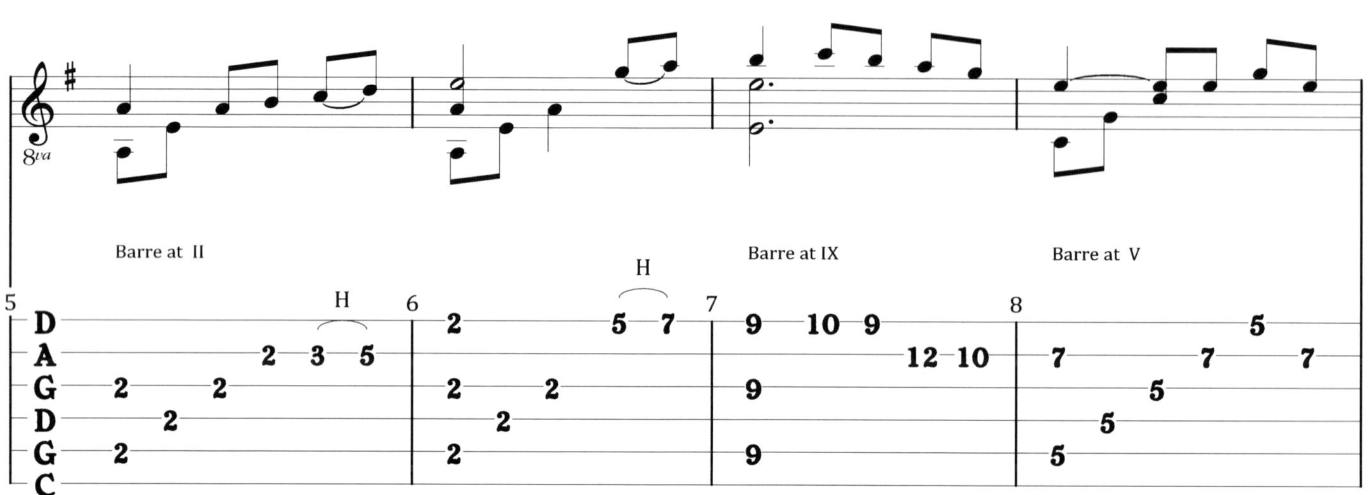

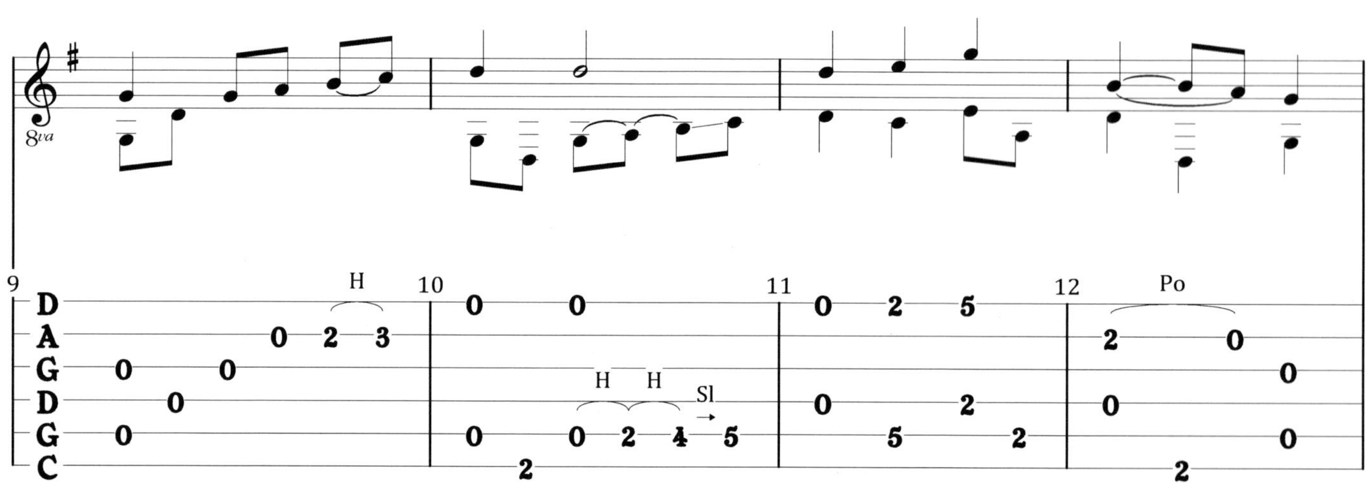

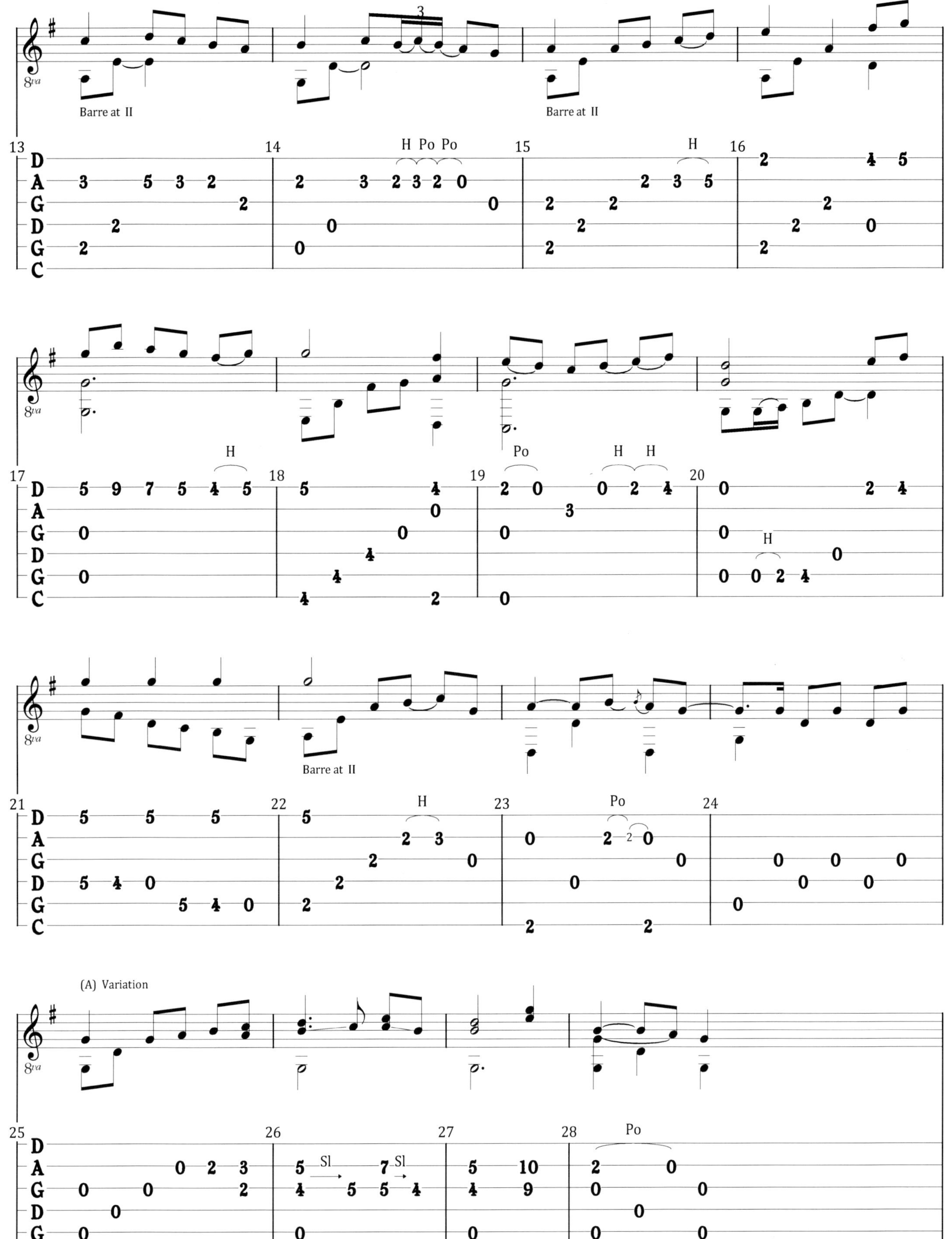
8va
Barre at II
Barre at II
Barre at II
(A) Variation
13
14
15
16
17
18
19
20
21
22
23
24
25
26
27
28
H Po Po
H
Po
H H
H
Sl
Sl
D
A
G
D
G
C

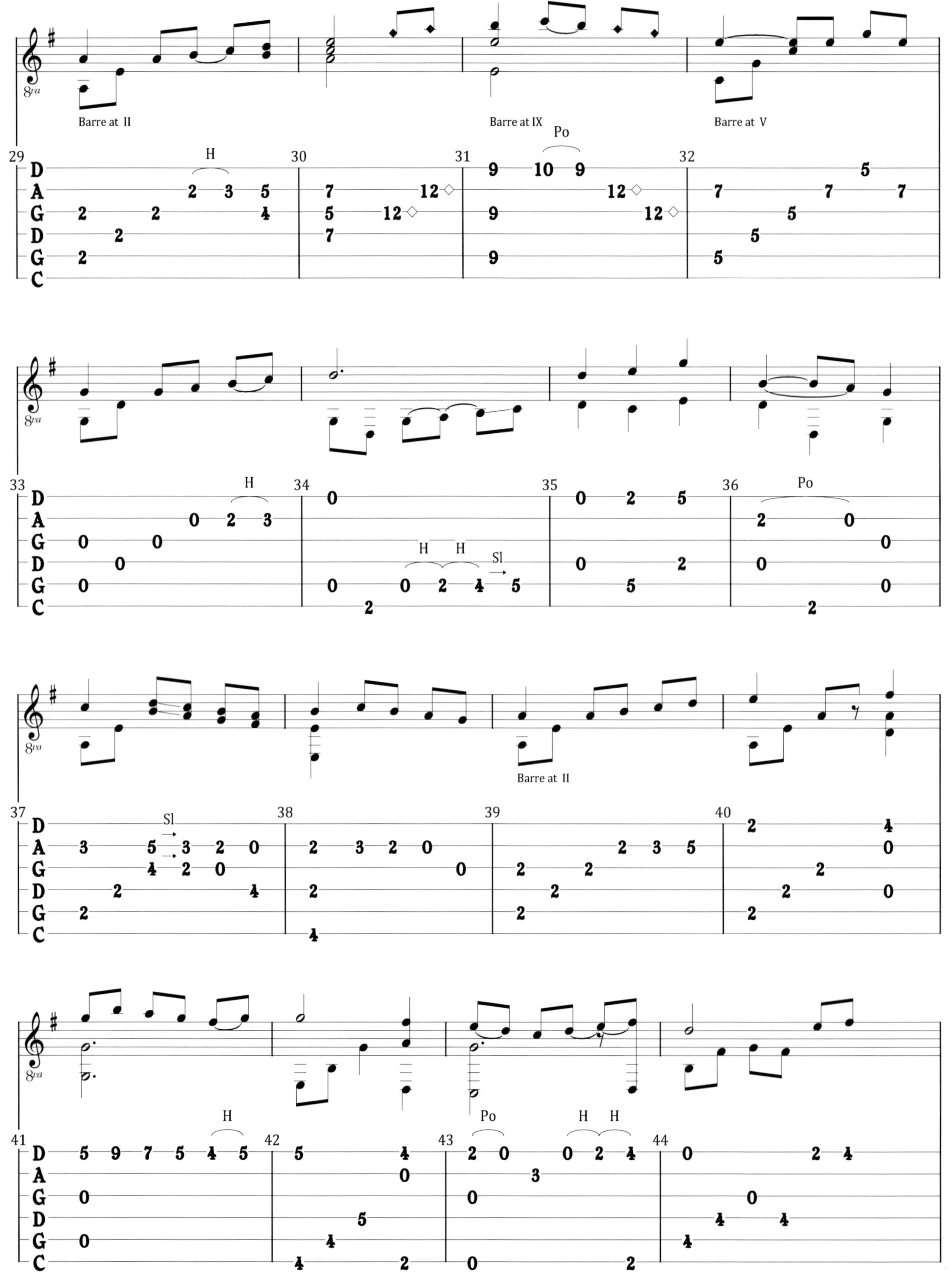
8va
Barre at II
Barre at IX
Barre at V
29
30
31
32
H
Po
D
A
G
D
G
C
33
34
35
36
H
H
H
Sl
Po
37
38
39
40
Sl
Barre at II
41
42
43
44
H
Po
H H

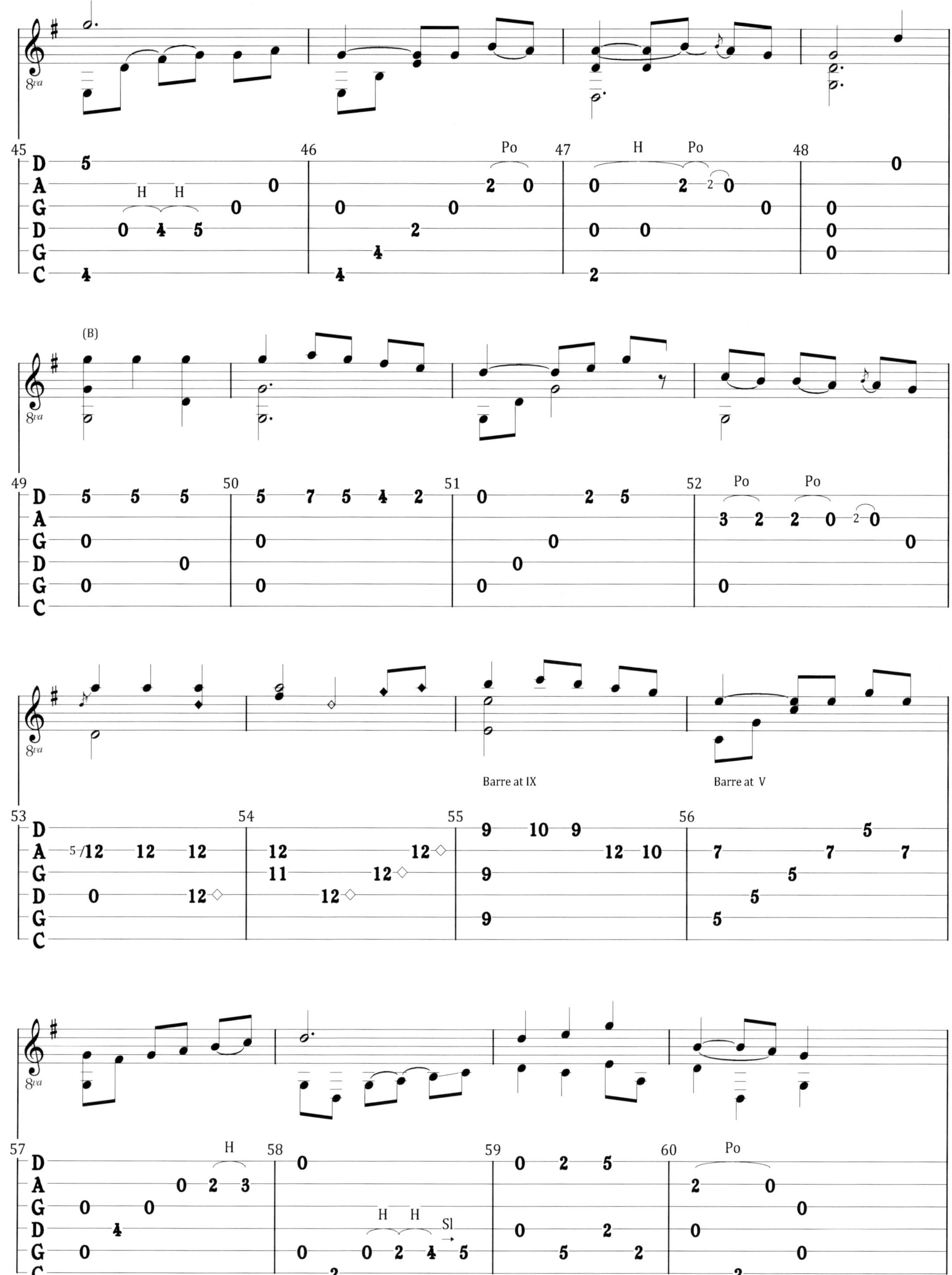
8va
(B)
Barre at IX
Barre at V
H
Po
Sl

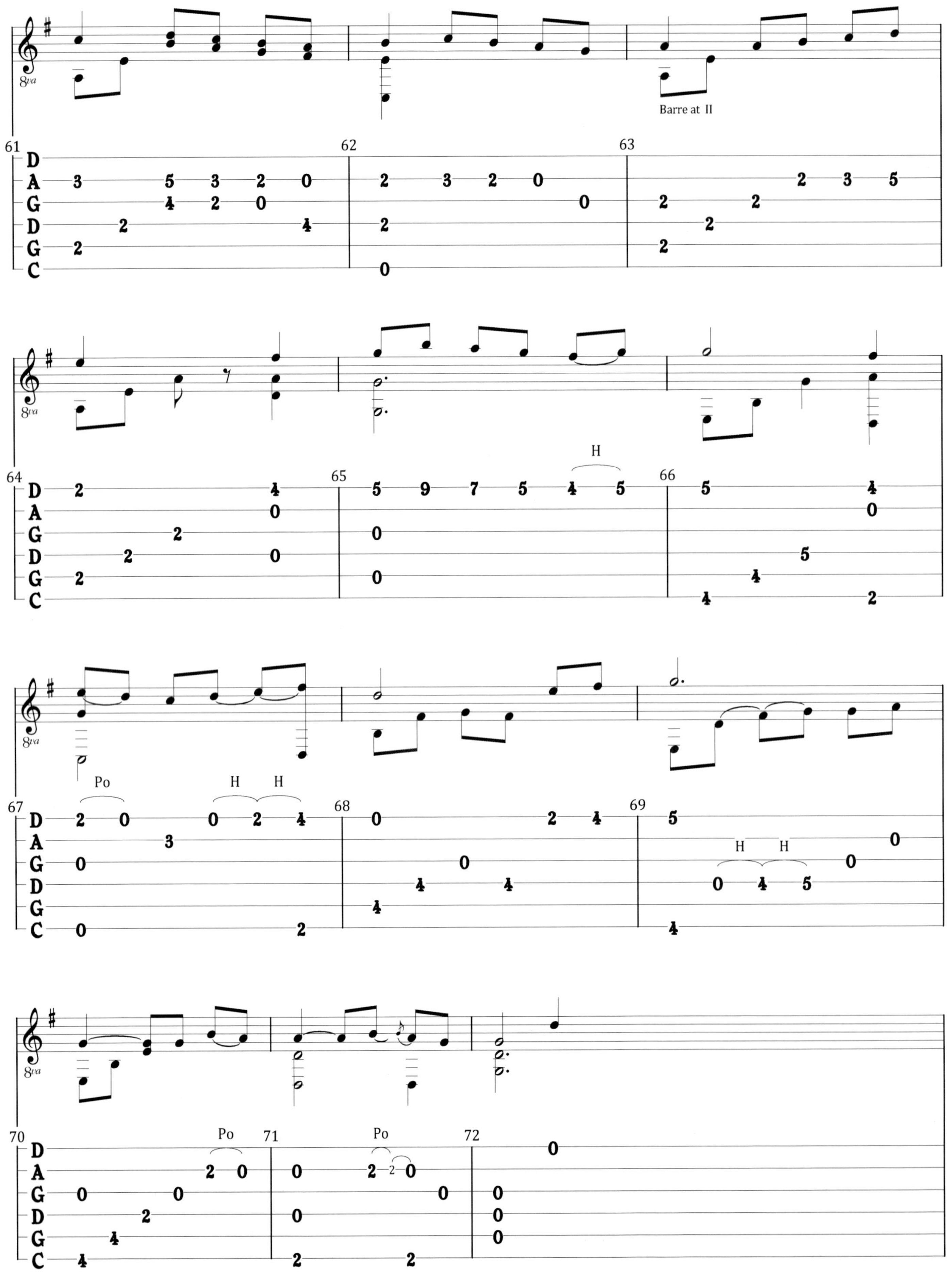
Barre at II
Po
H
Po

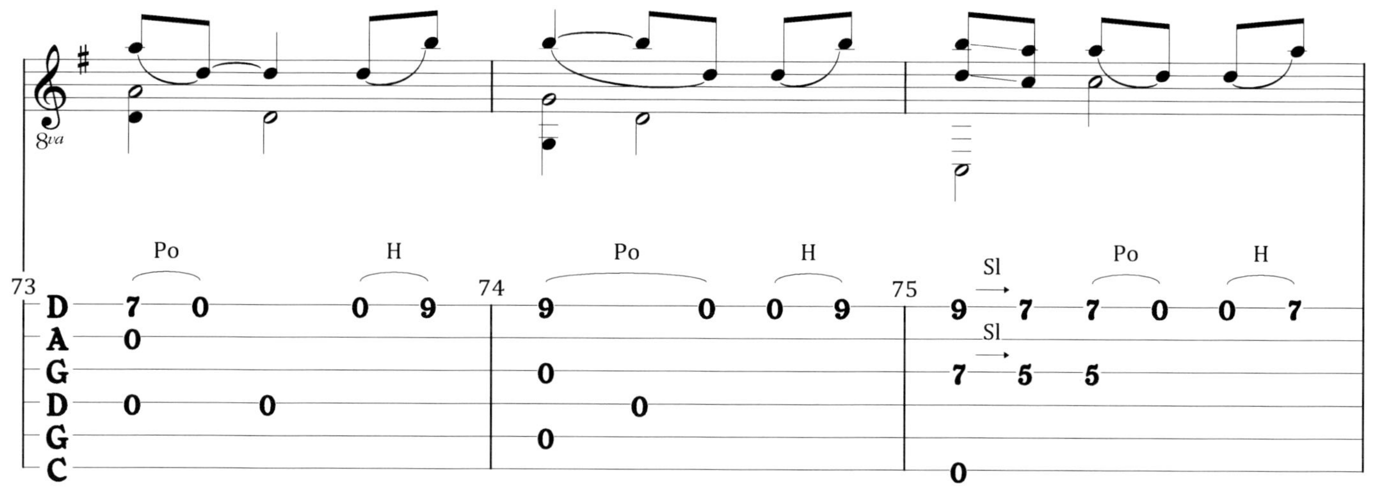
8va
Po
H
Sl
73
74
75
D
A
G
D
G
C

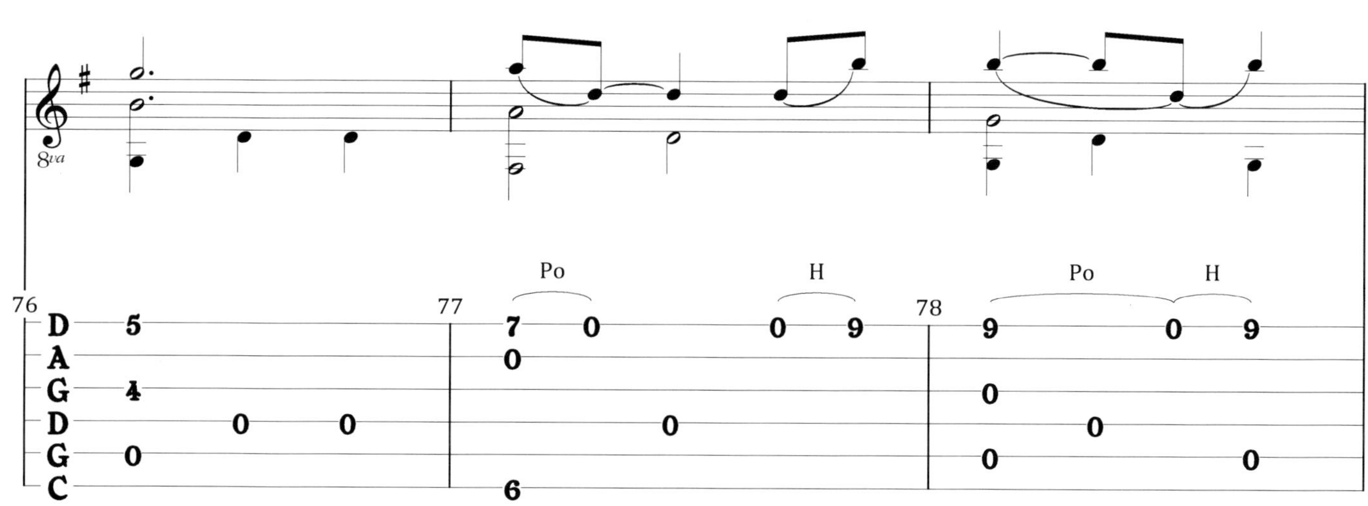
8va
Po
H
76
77
78
D
A
G
D
G
C

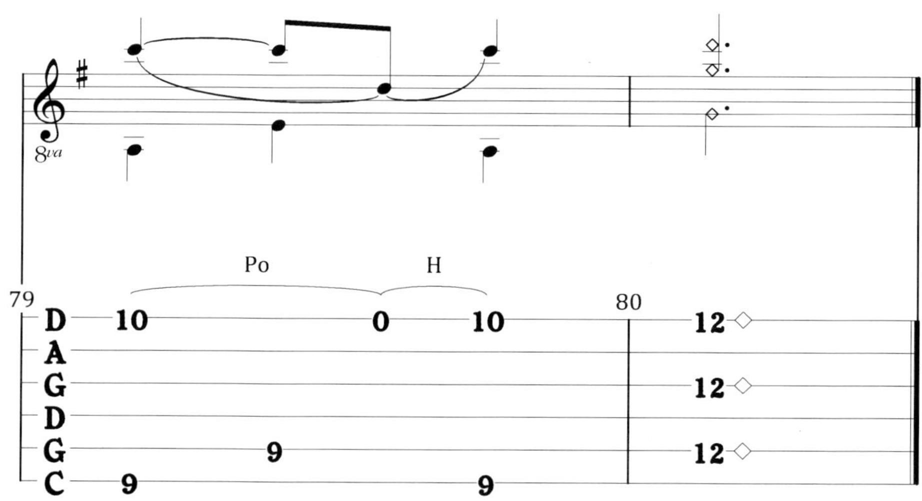
8va
Po
H
79
80
D
A
G
D
G
C

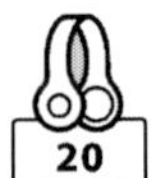

Skye Boat Song

(Traditional)

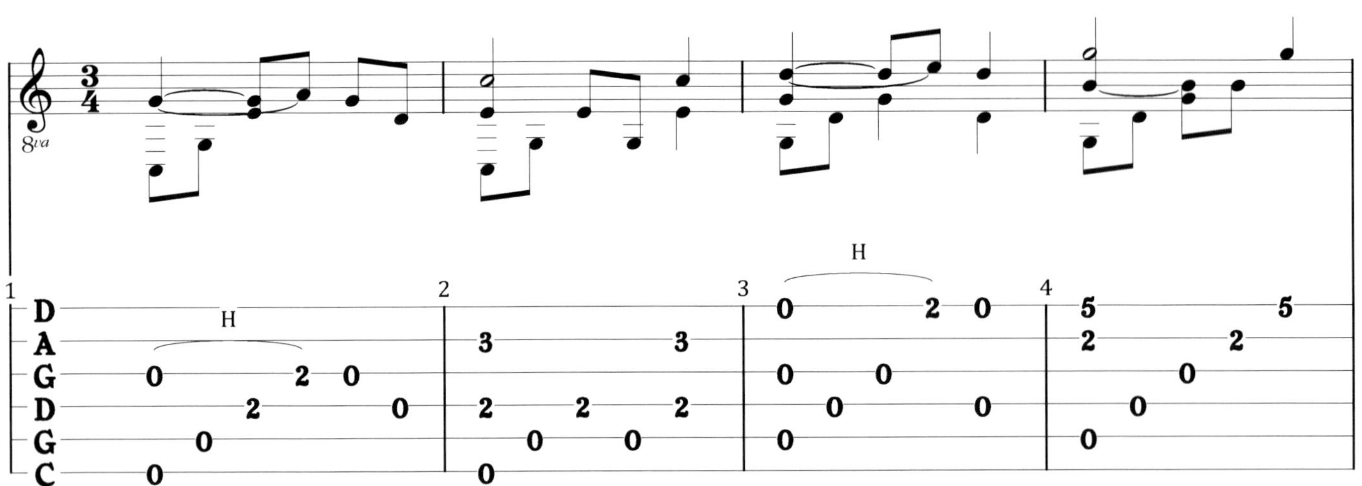

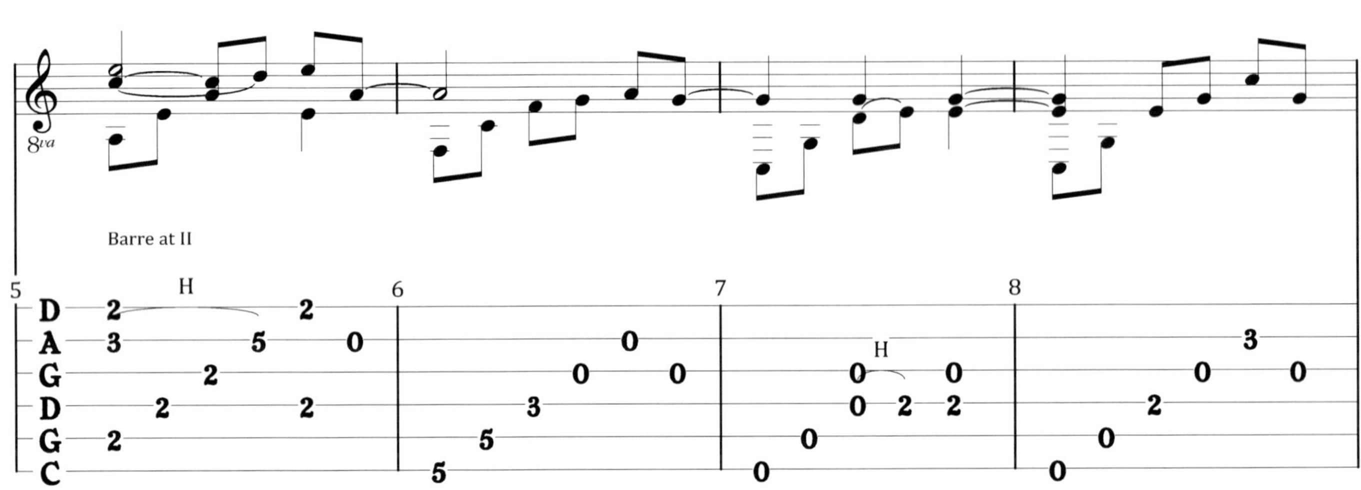

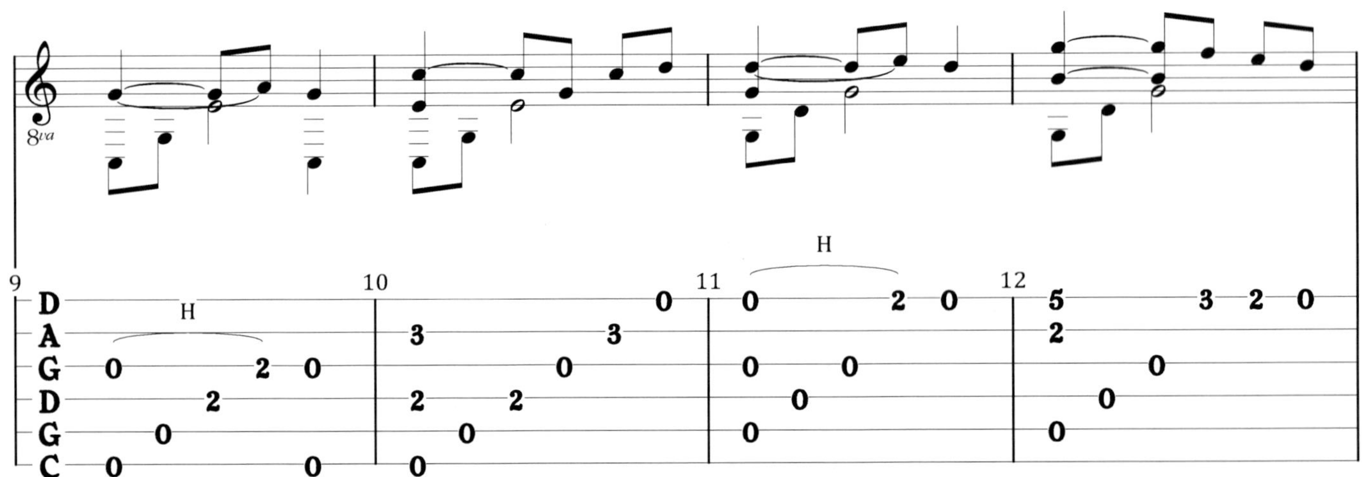

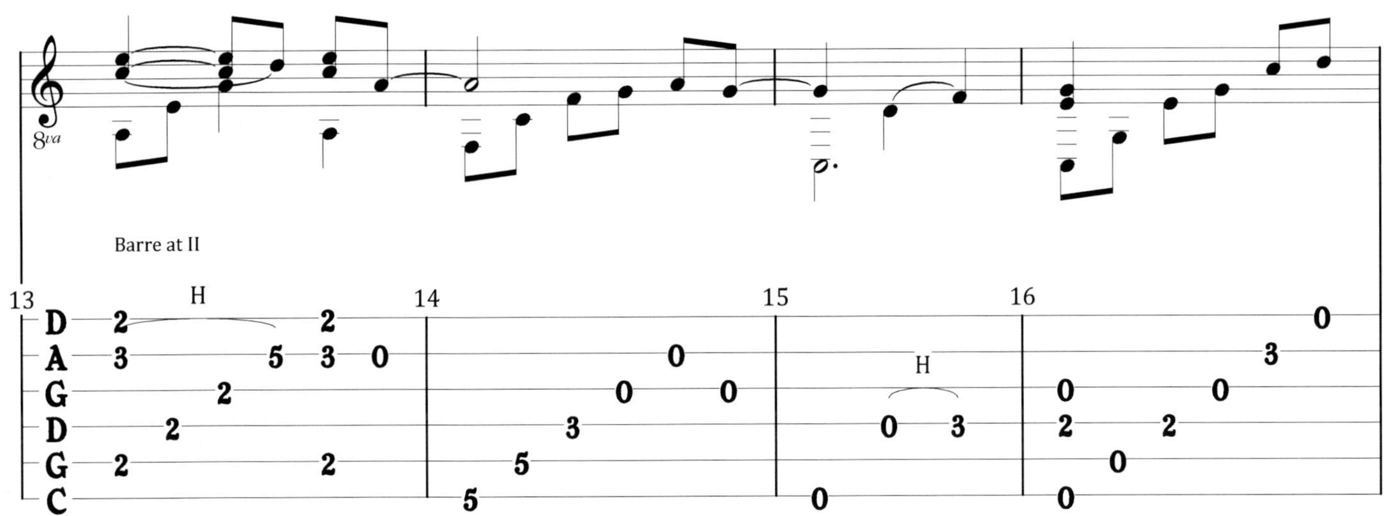
8va
Barre at II
13
H
14
15
H
16
D
A
G
D
G
C

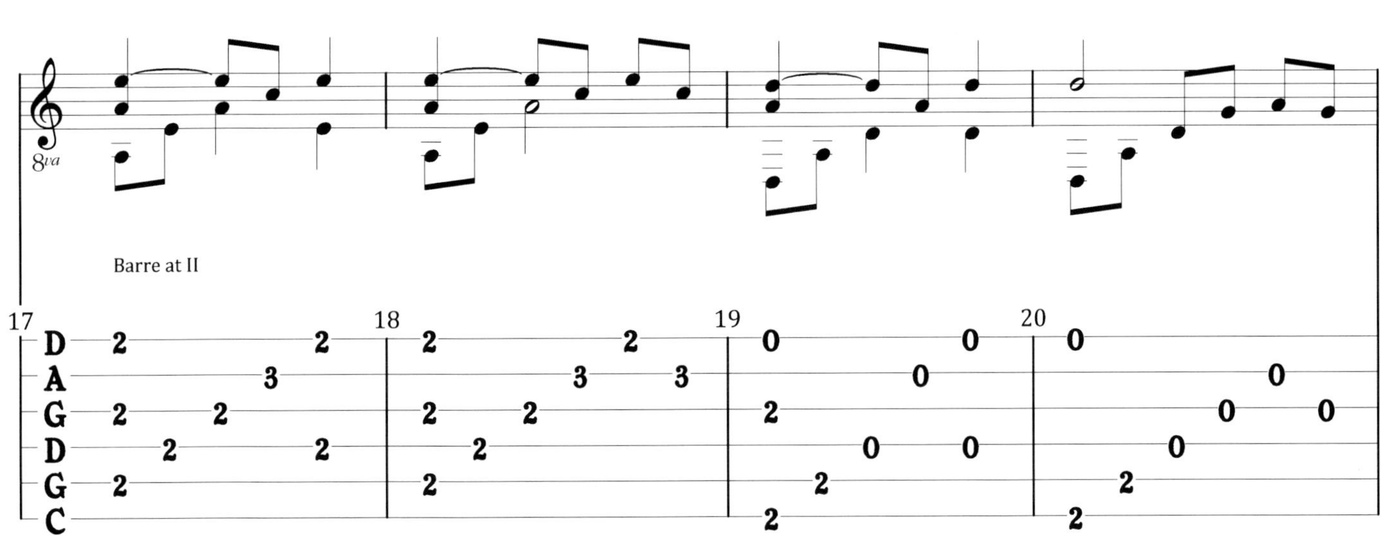
8va
Barre at II
17
18
19
20
D
A
G
D
G
C

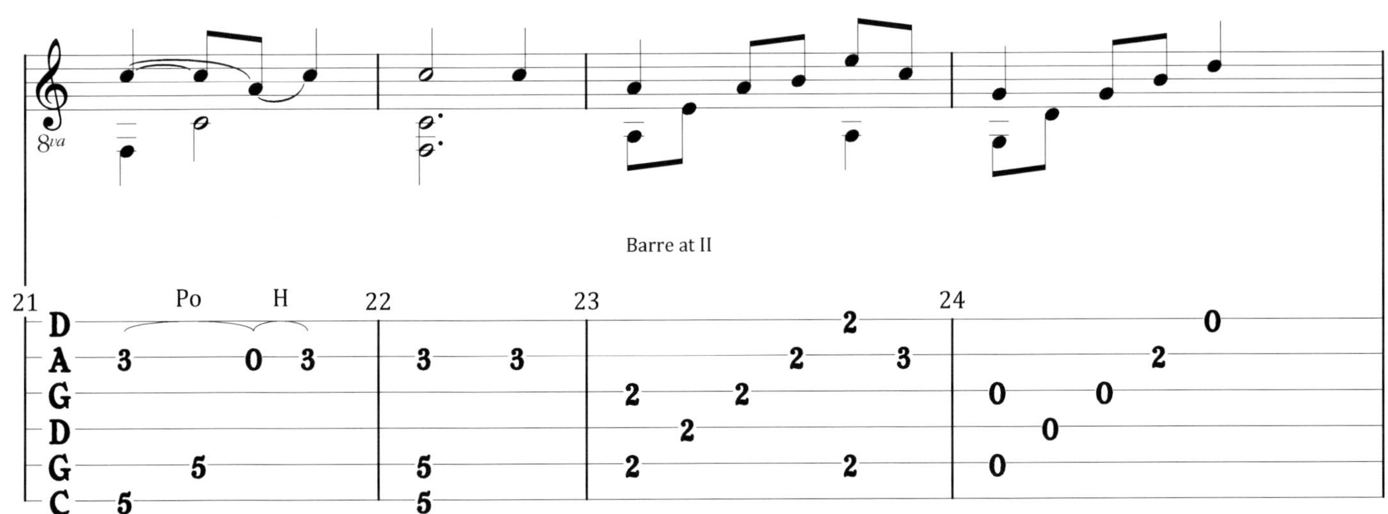
8va
Barre at II
21
Po
H
22
23
24
D
A
G
D
G
C

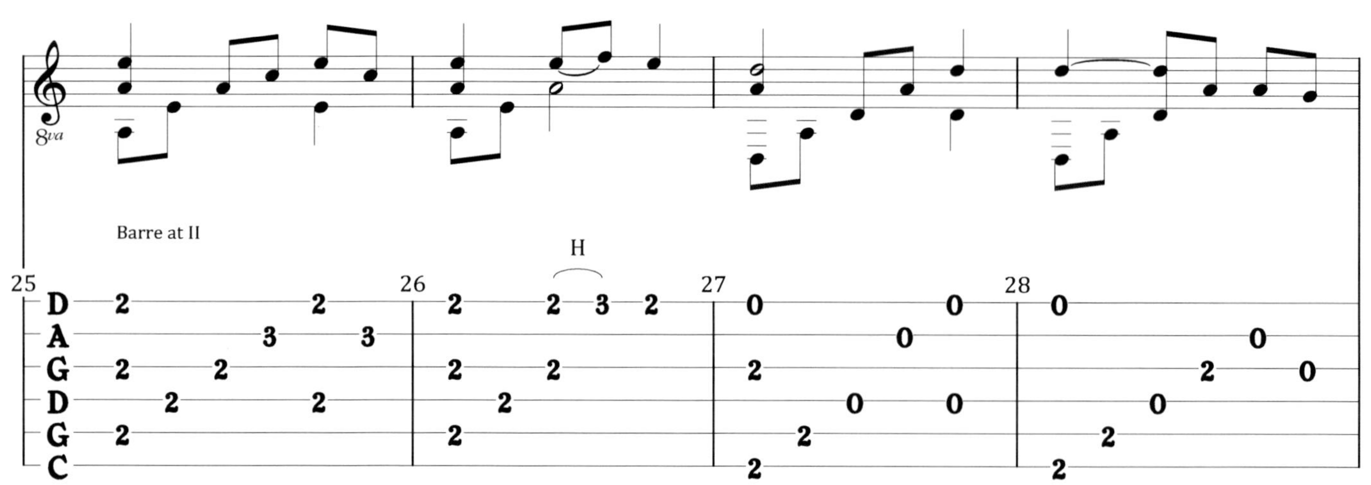
Barre at II
H
25
26
27
28
D
A
G
D
G
C

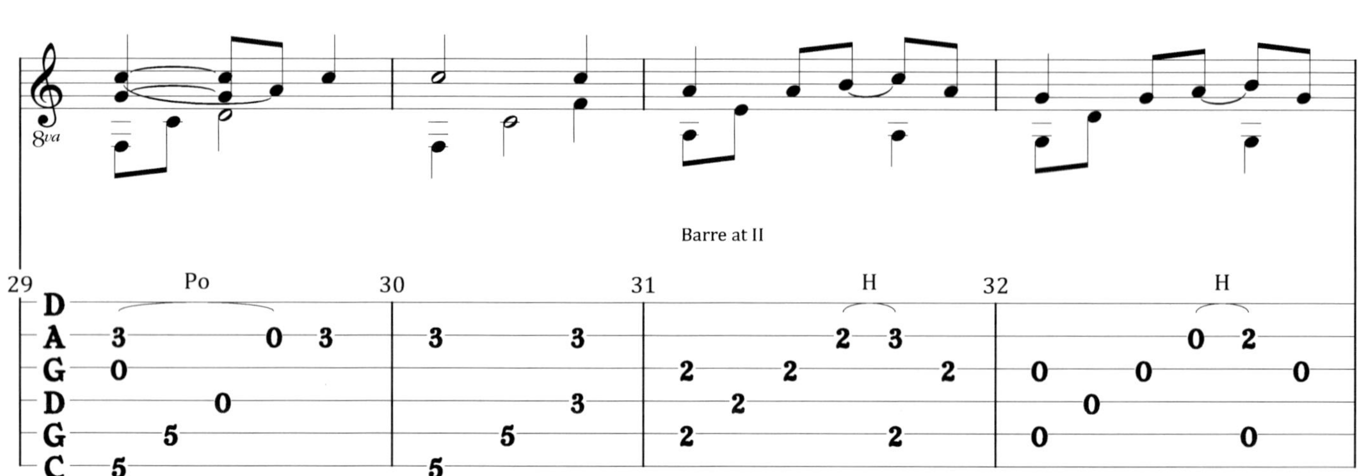
Po
Barre at II
H
H
29
30
31
32
D
A
G
D
G
C

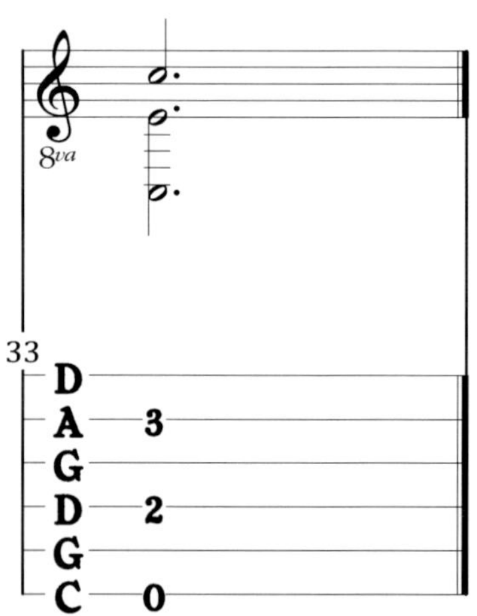
33
D
A
G
D
G
C

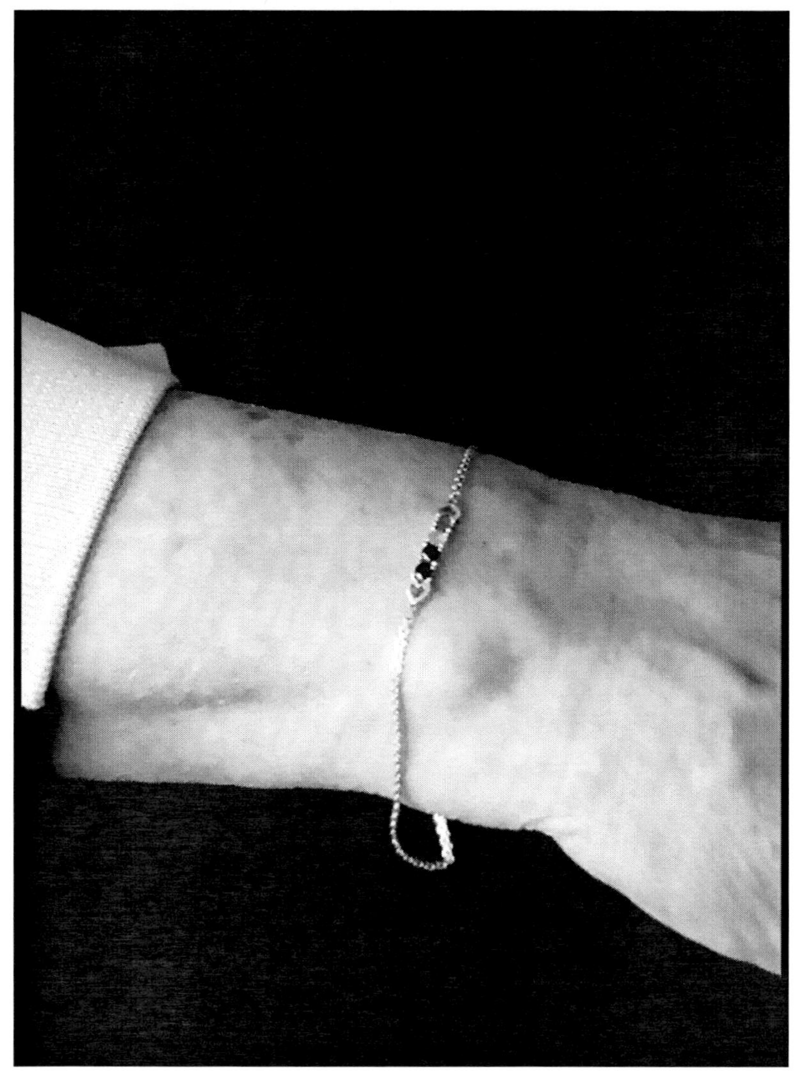

Lovely hand of El's wife Sheila

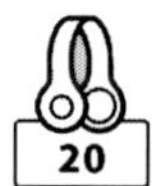

Give Me Your Hand

(Rory Dall O'Cahan)

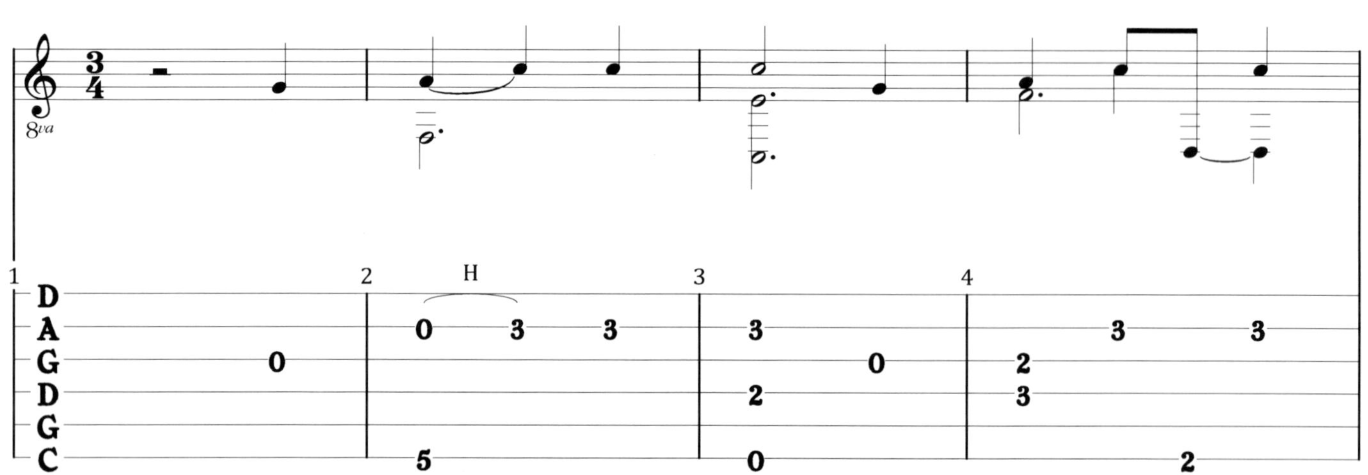

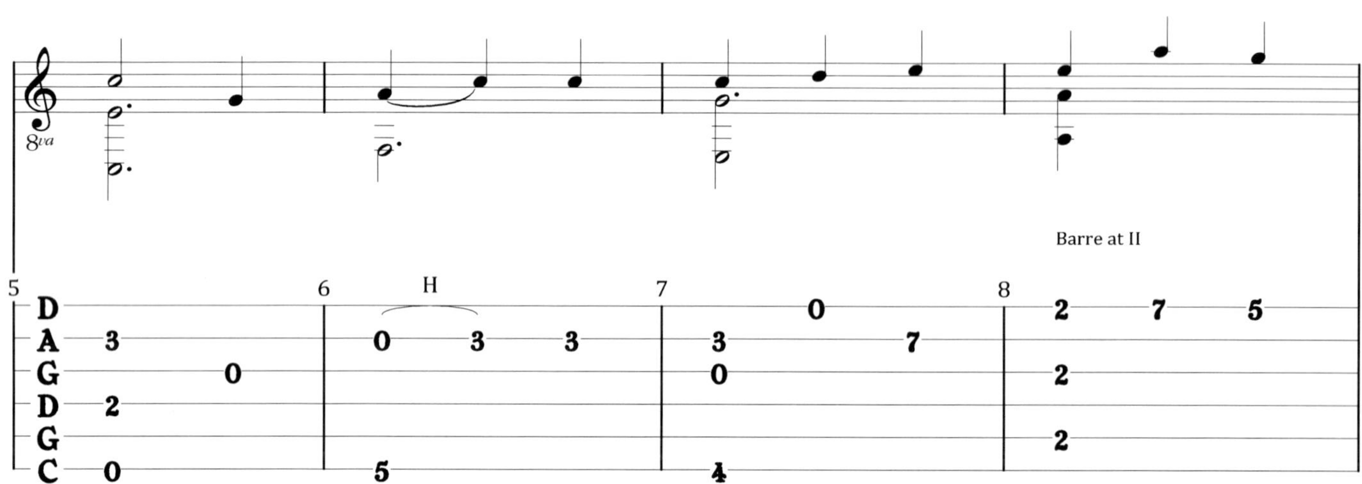

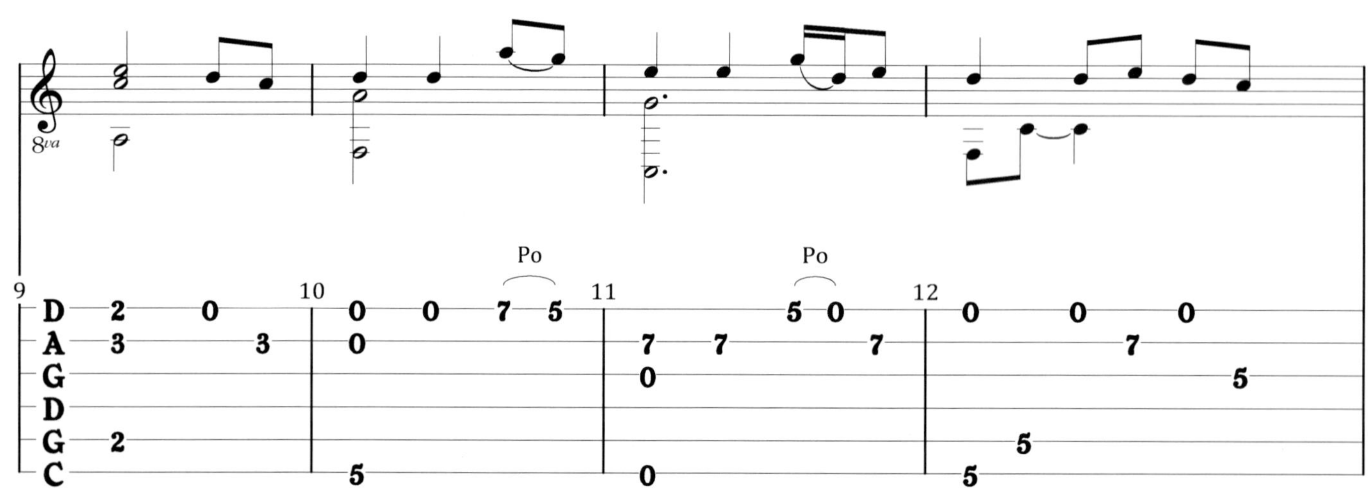

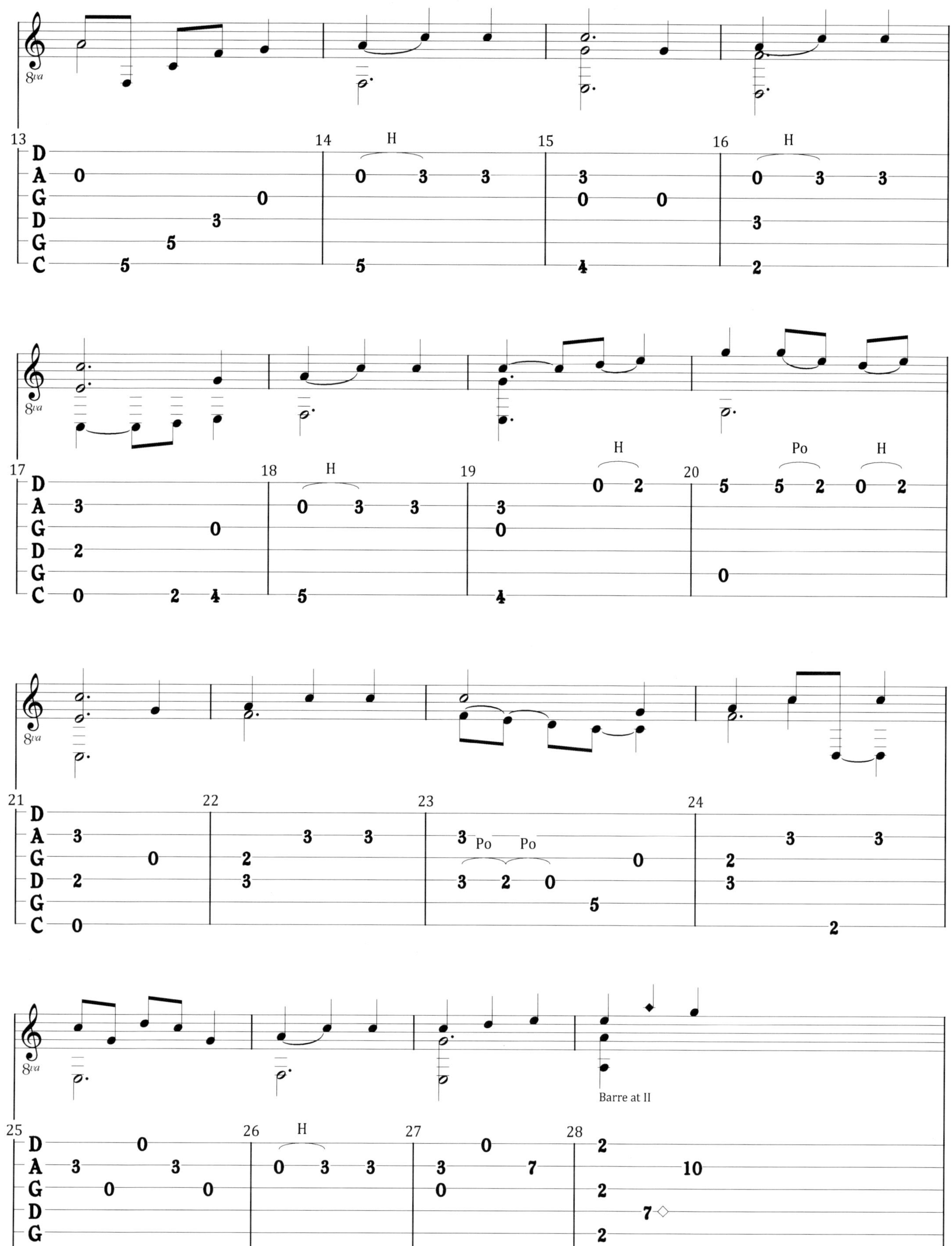
8va
13
14
H
15
16
H
D
A
G
D
G
C
17
18
H
19
H
20
Po
H
21
22
23
Po
Po
24
25
26
H
27
28
Barre at II

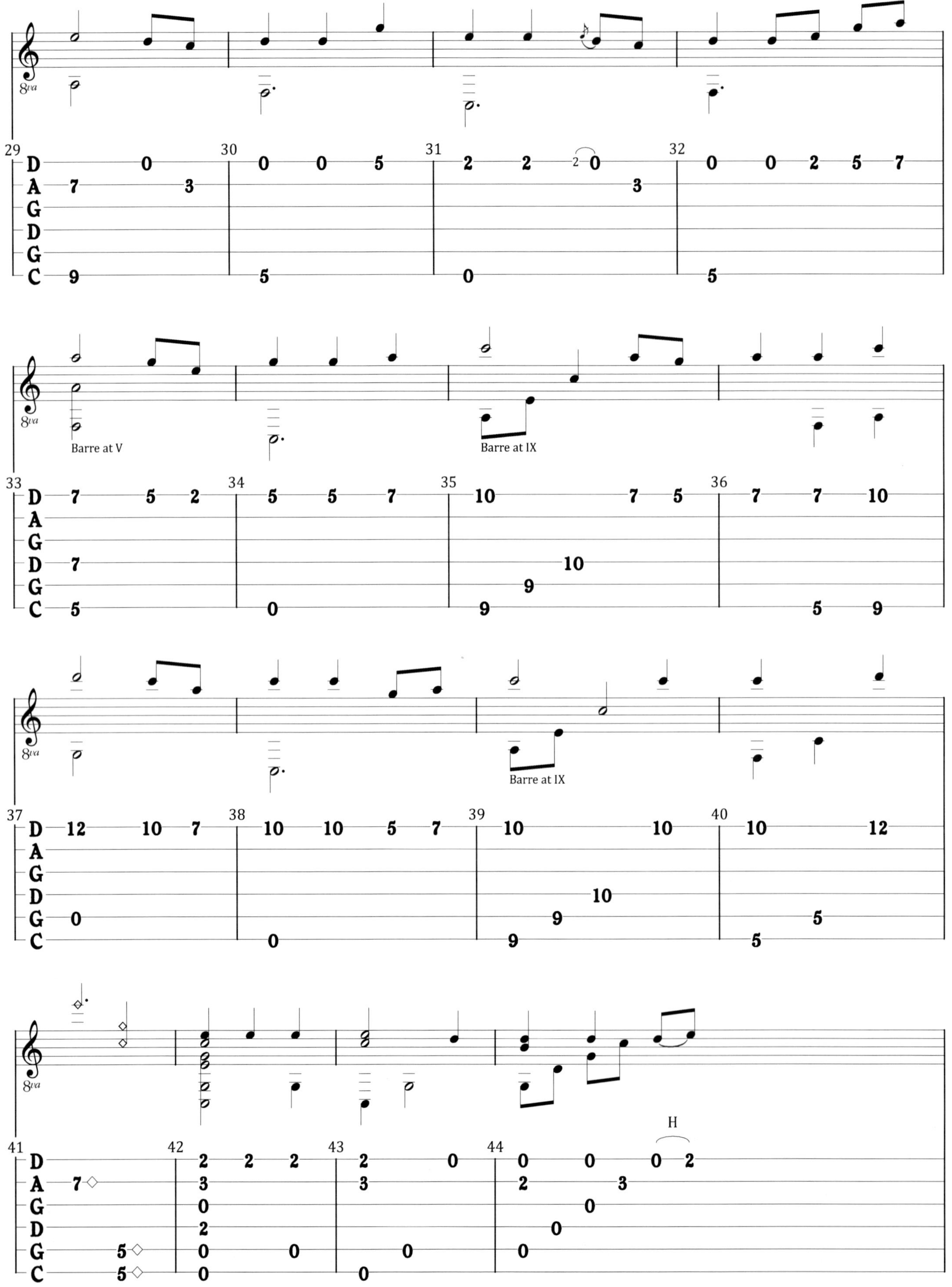
8va
Barre at V
Barre at IX
Barre at IX
H
D
A
G
D
G
C

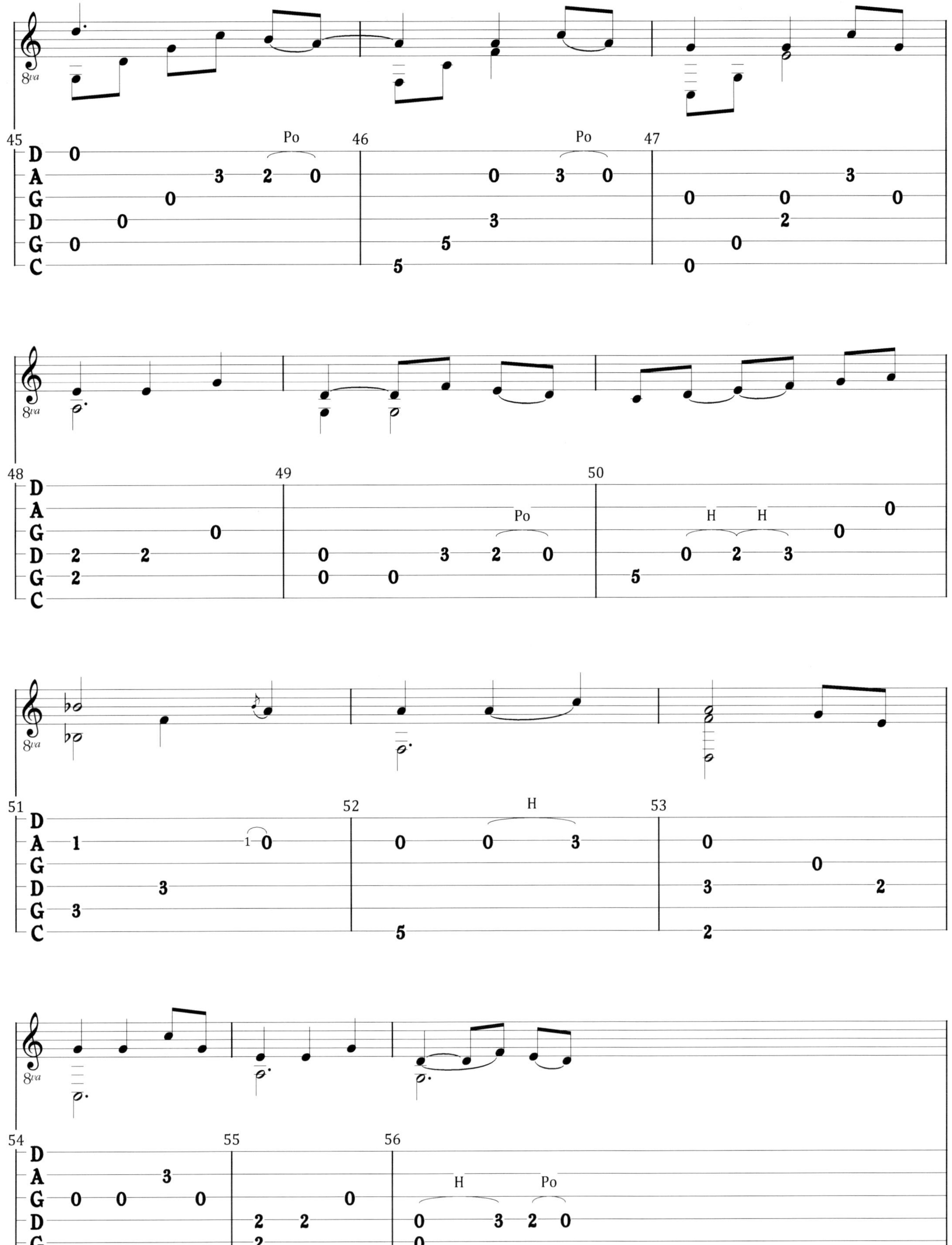
8va
45
46
47
D
A
G
D
G
C
Po
Po
48
49
50
Po
H
H
51
52
53
H
54
55
56
H
Po

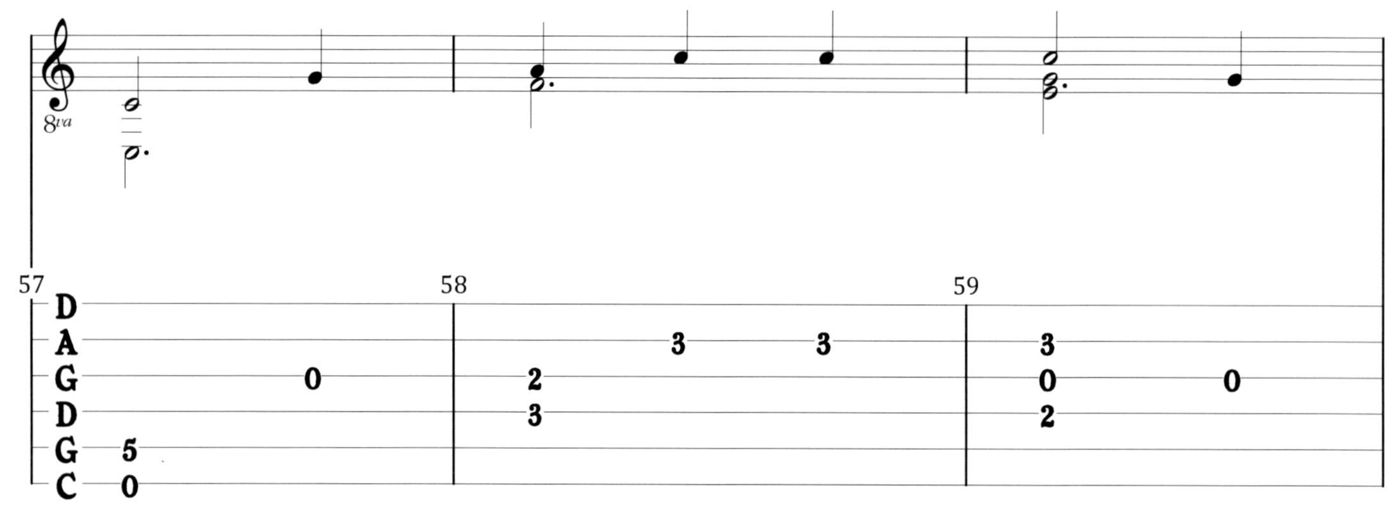
8va
57
58
59
D
A
G
D
G
C
5
0
0
2
3
3
3
3
0
2
0

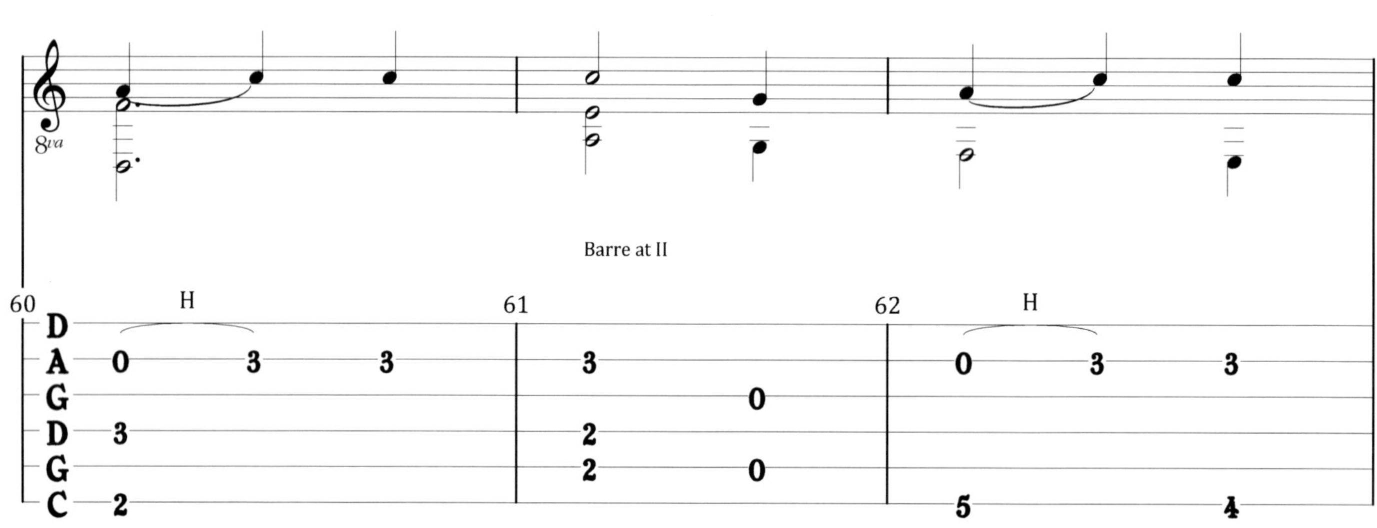
8va
Barre at II
60
H
61
62
H
D
A
G
D
G
C
0
3
3
3
2
3
2
2
0
0
0
3
3
5
4

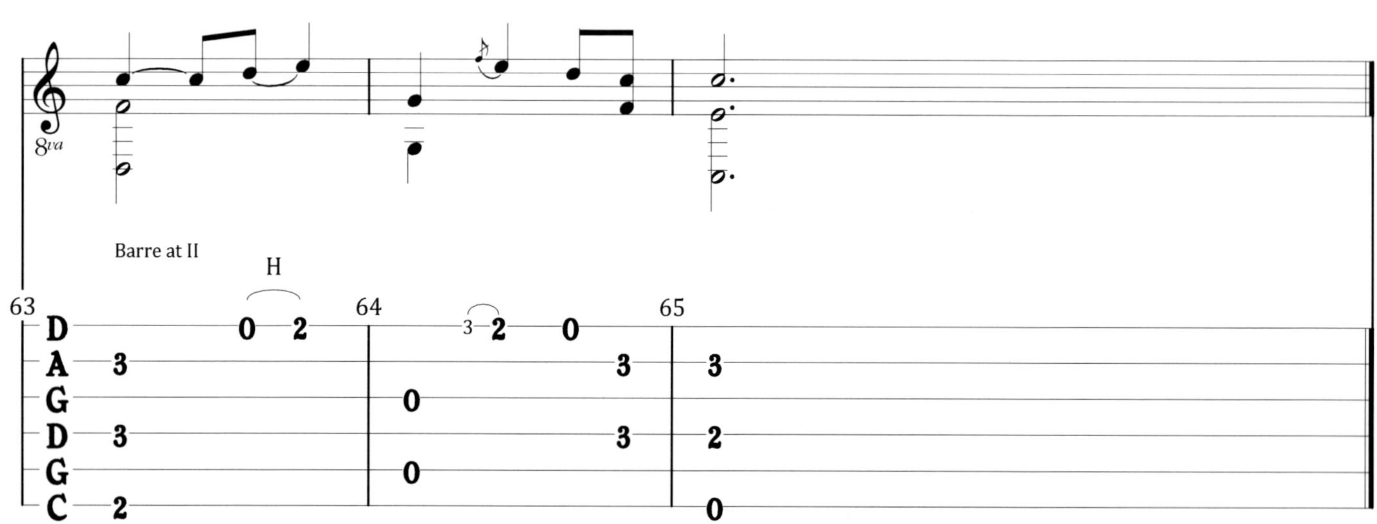
8va
Barre at II
63
H
64
65
D
A
G
D
G
C
3
3
2
0
2
0
0
3
2
0
3
3
3
2
0

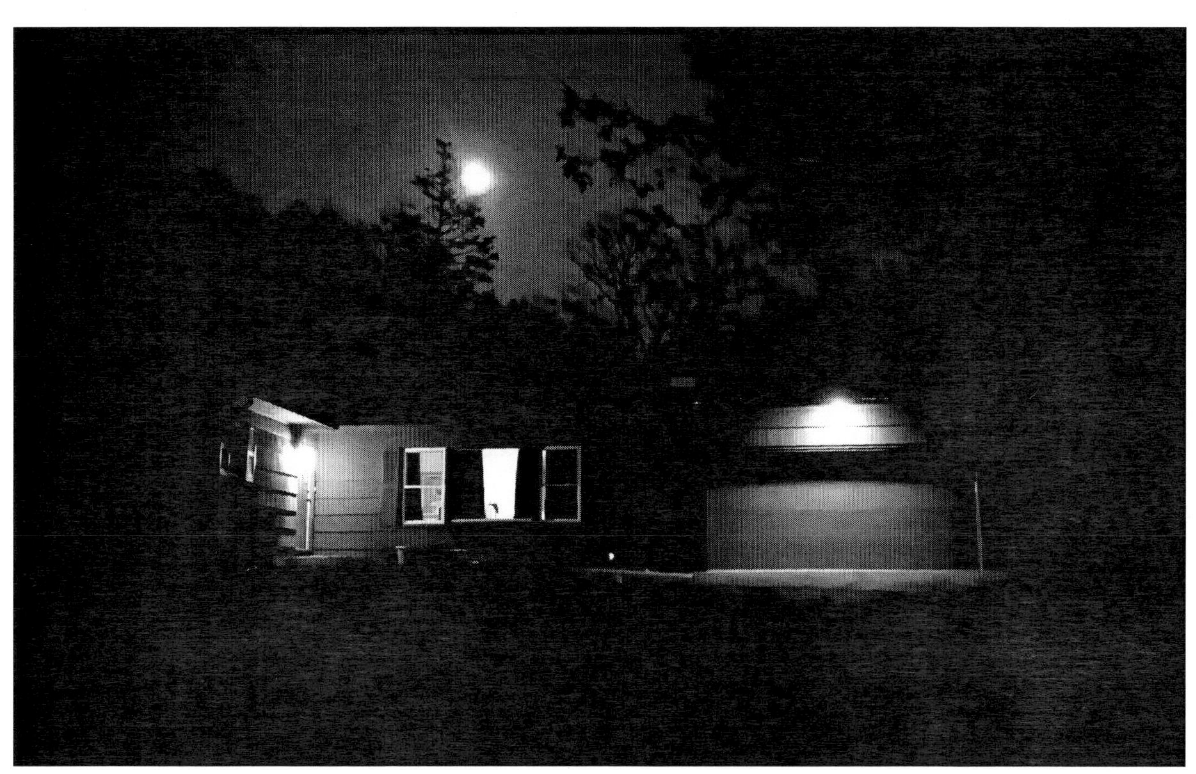

Casa El in NJ, USA

The Castle of Dromore

(Traditional Lullaby)

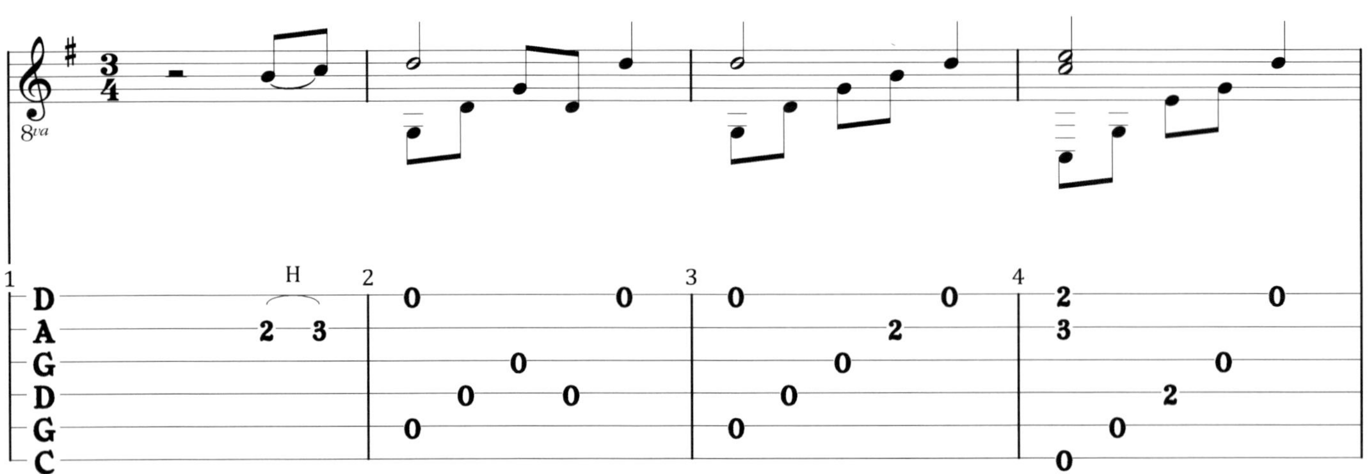

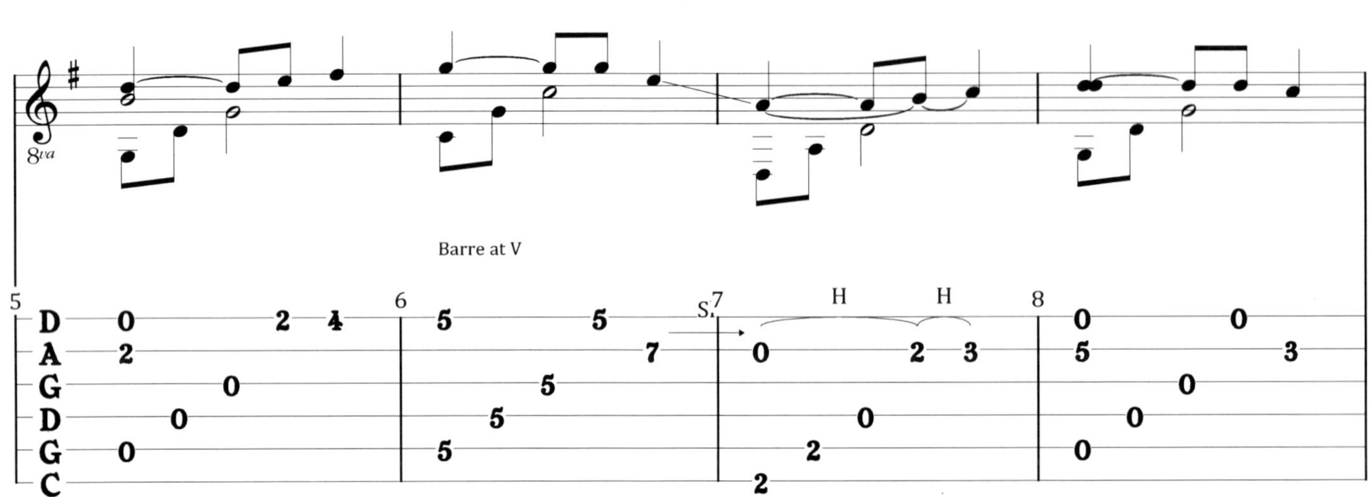

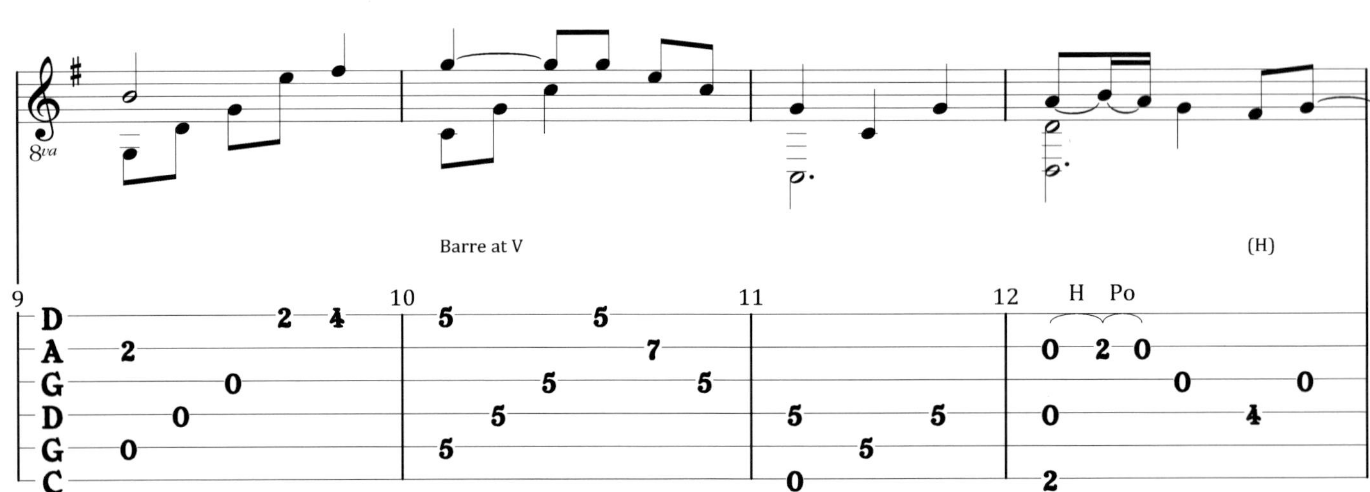

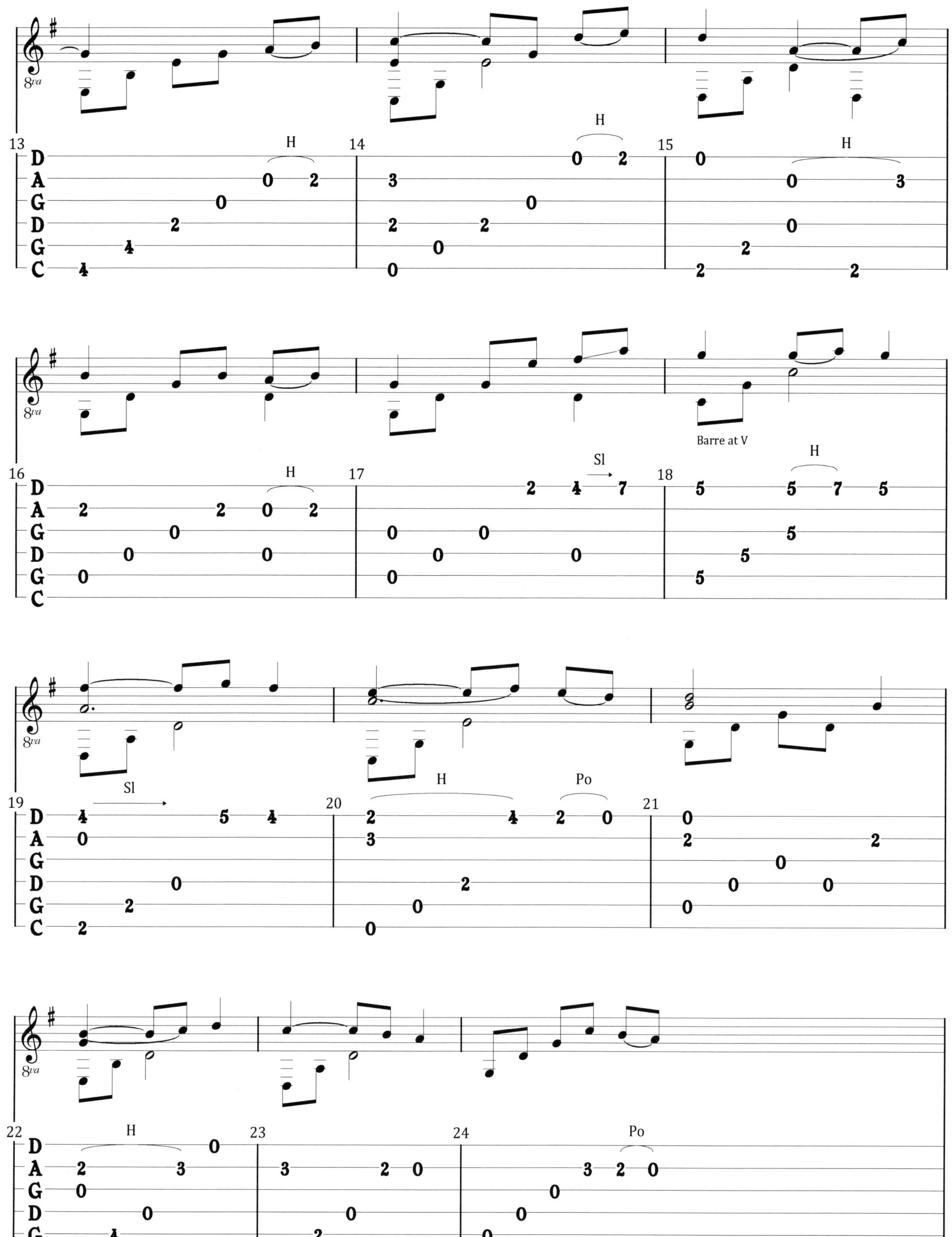
8va
D
A
G
D
G
C
H
Sl
Po
Barre at V

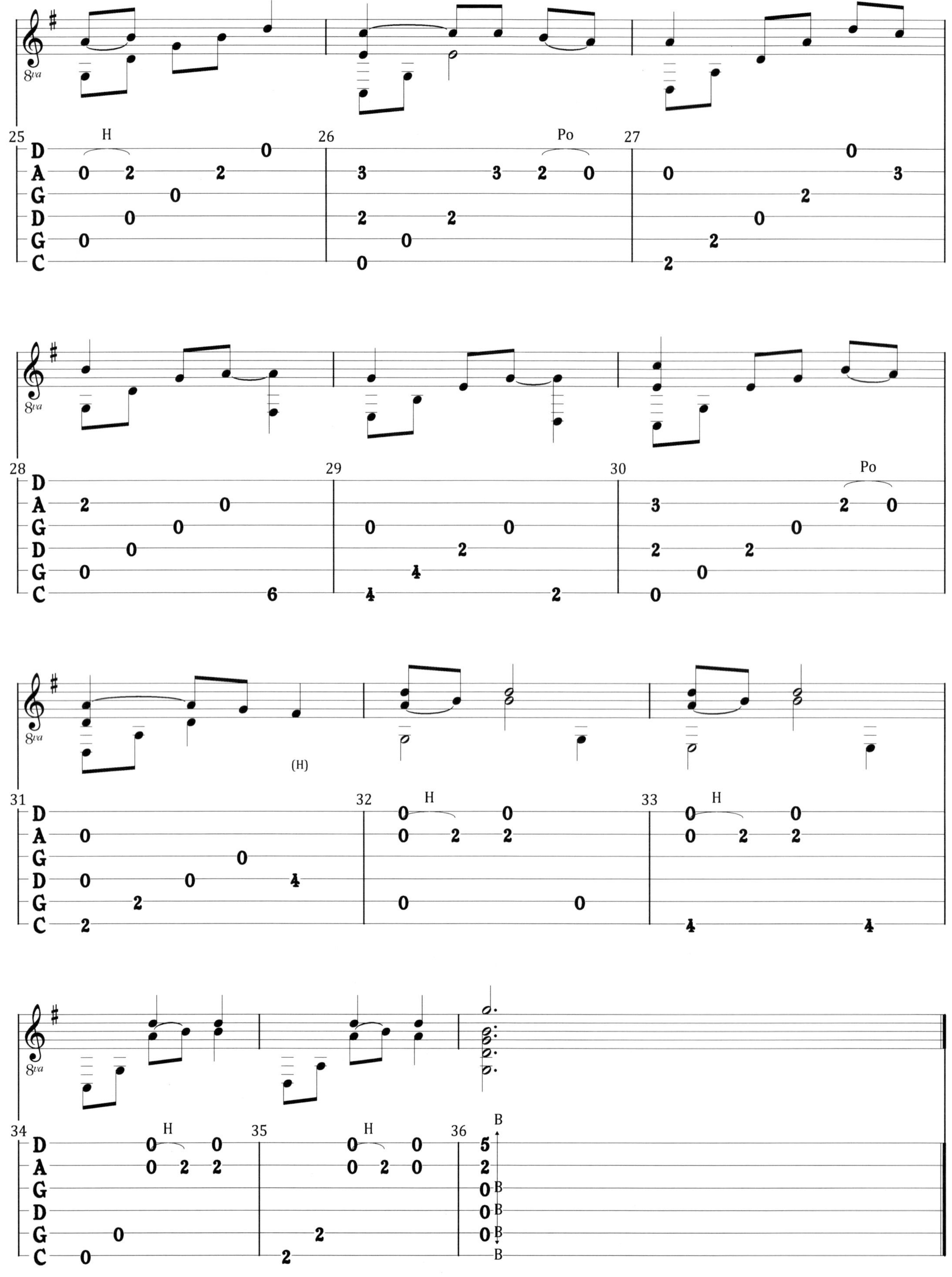
8va
H
Po
(H)
D
A
G
D
G
C
B

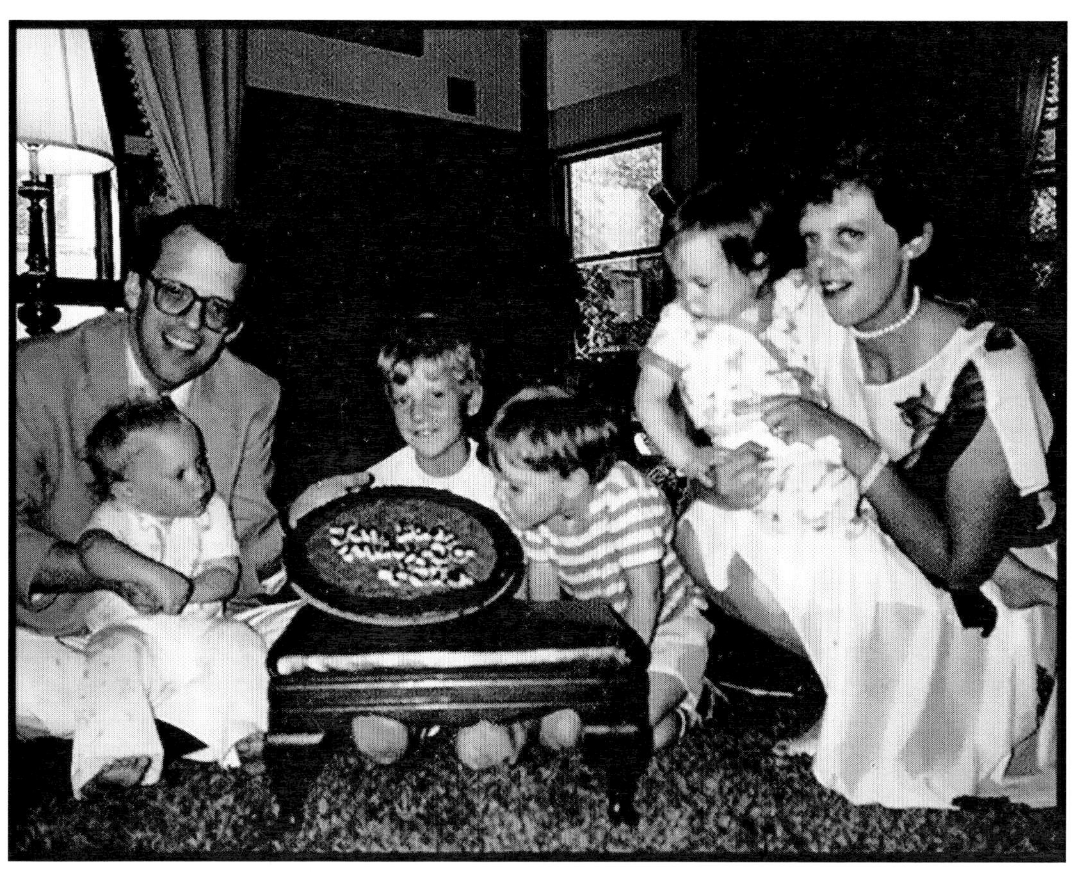

El family picture, from the 1980's, with Sheila, El, Jon, Dan, Mary and Jim McMeen, and a very large cookie

The Rights of Man

(Traditional Hornpipe)

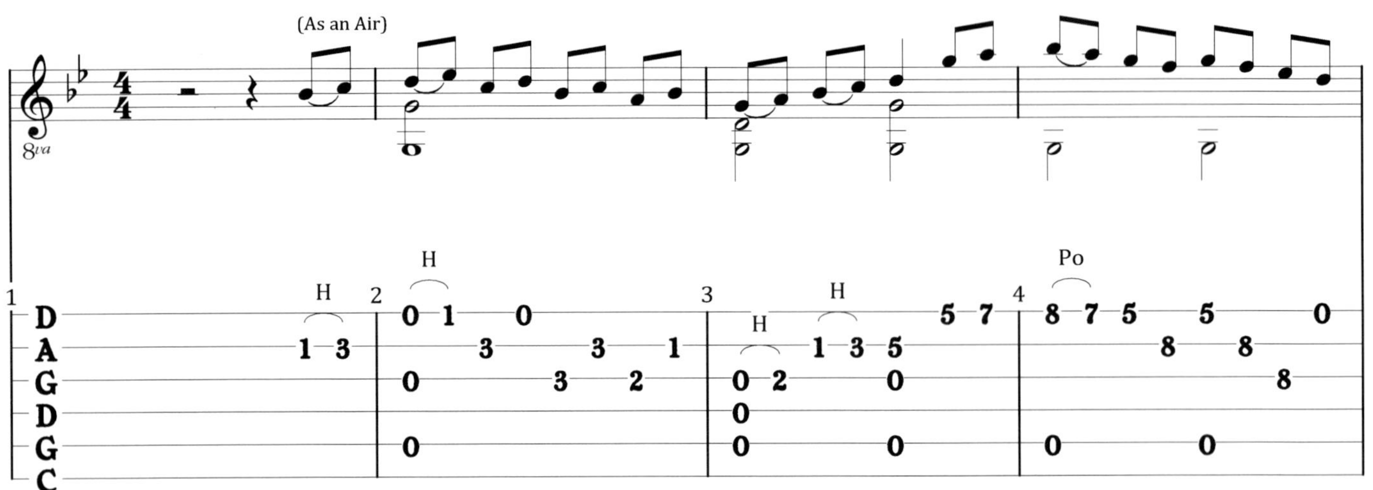

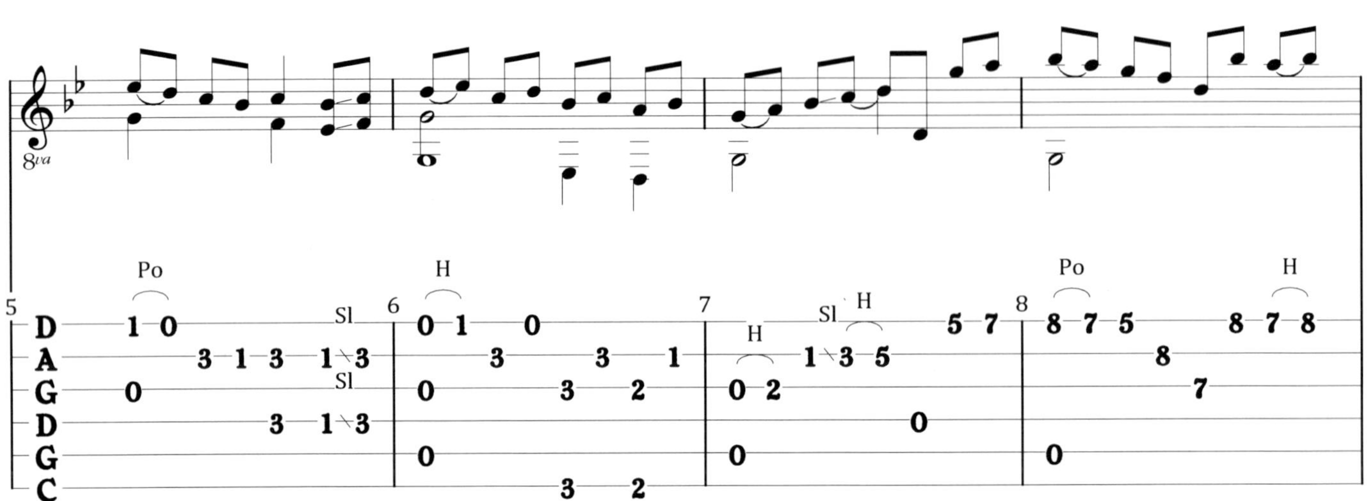

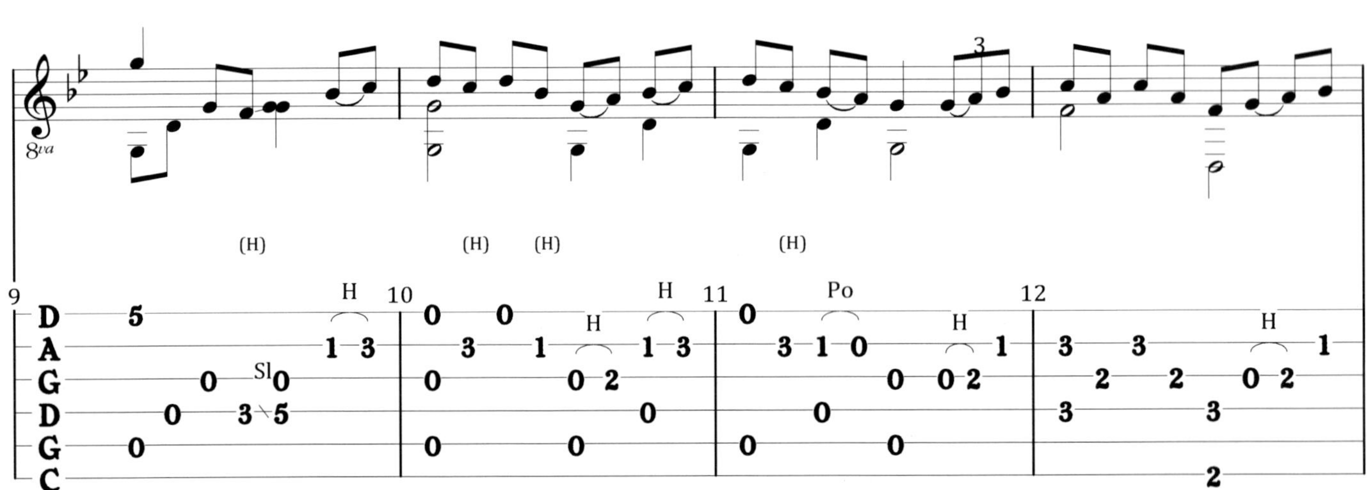

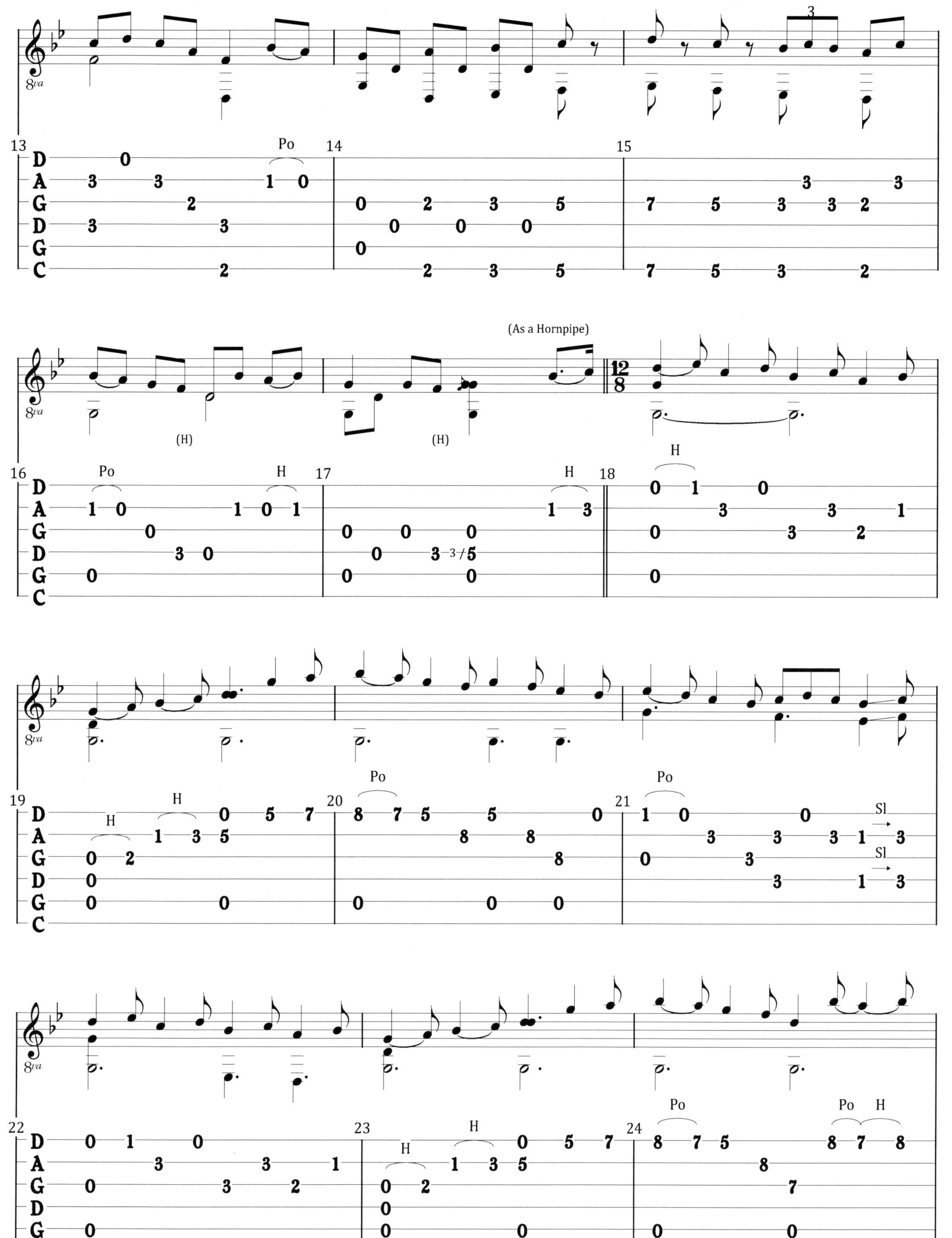
(As a Hornpipe)

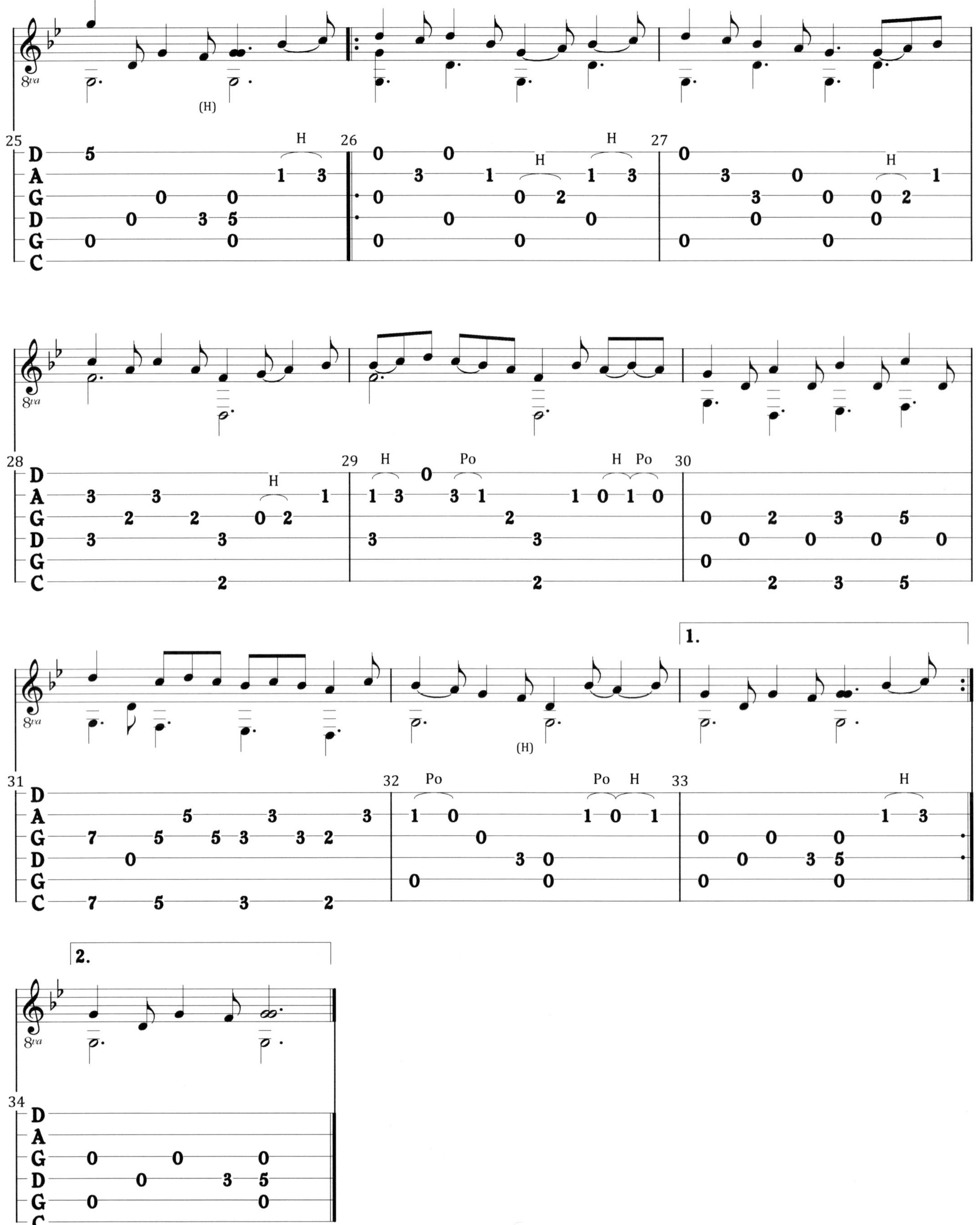
8va
(H)
25
H
26
H
H
27
H
28
H
29
H
Po
H
Po
30
31
32
Po
Po
H
(H)
33
1.
H
2.
34
D
A
G
D
G
C

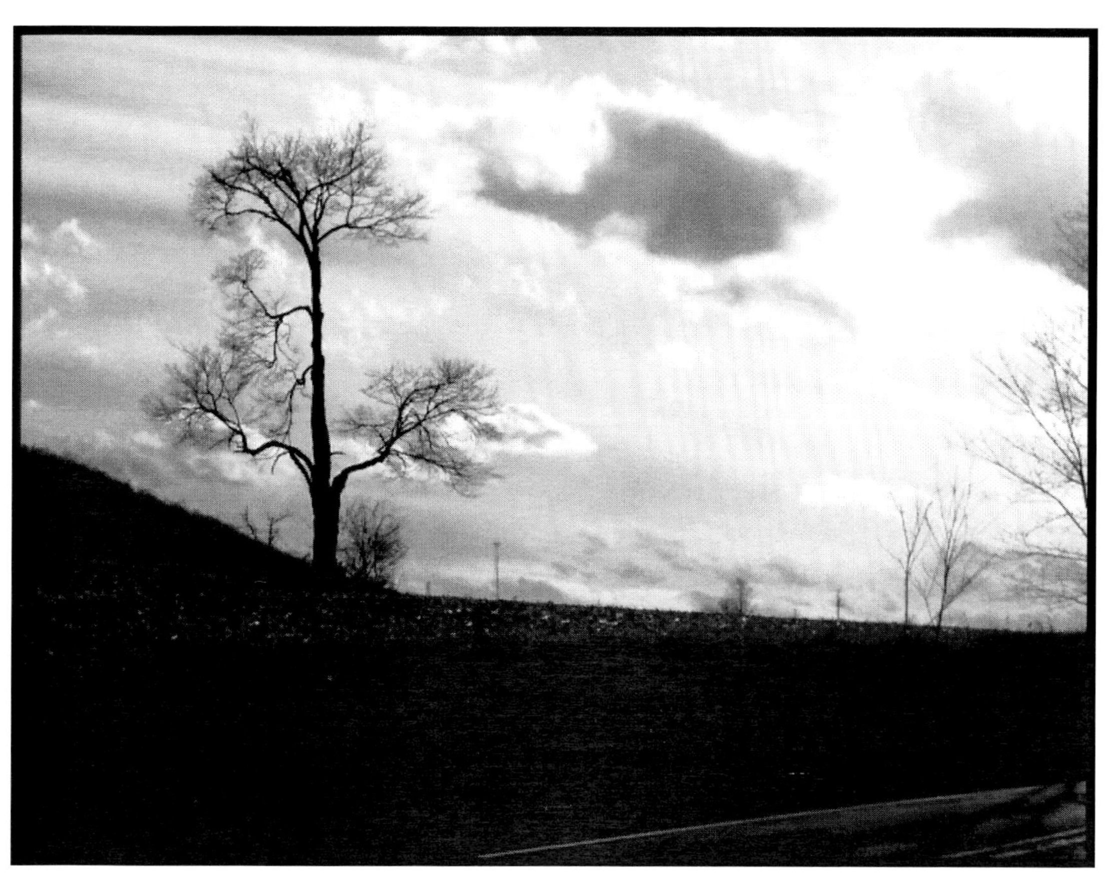

Tree and clouds outside of McConnellstown, PA, USA

Sheebeg and Sheemore

(T. O'Carolan)

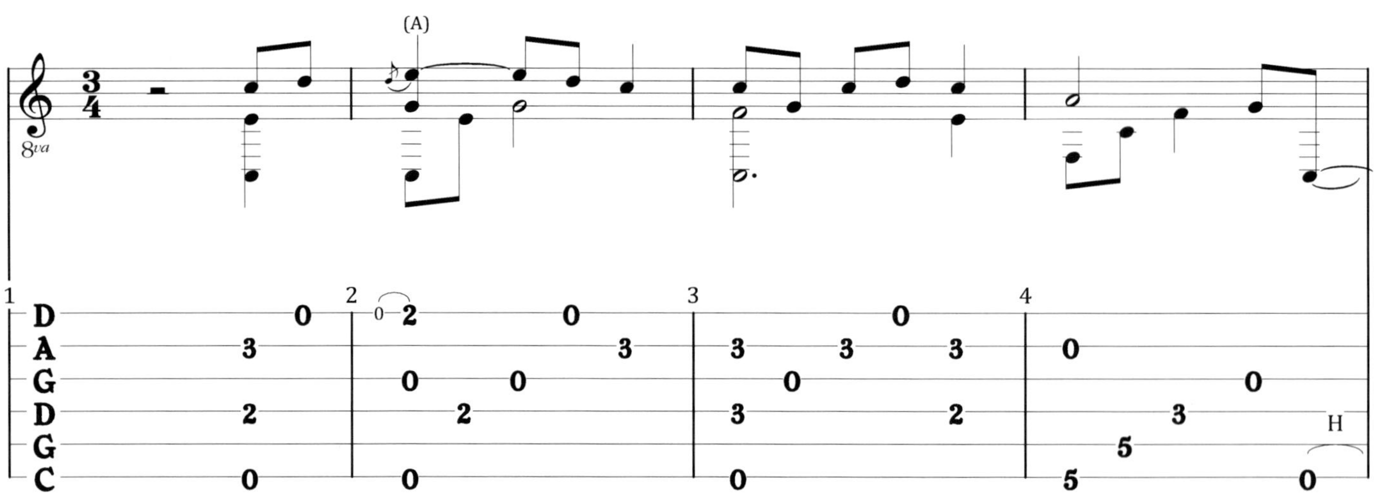

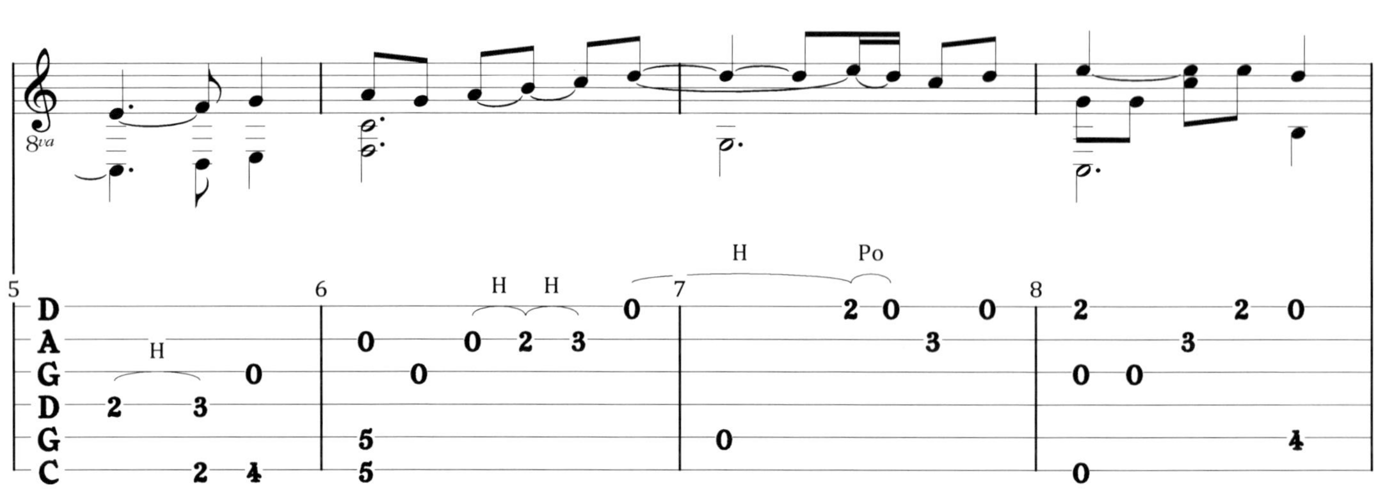

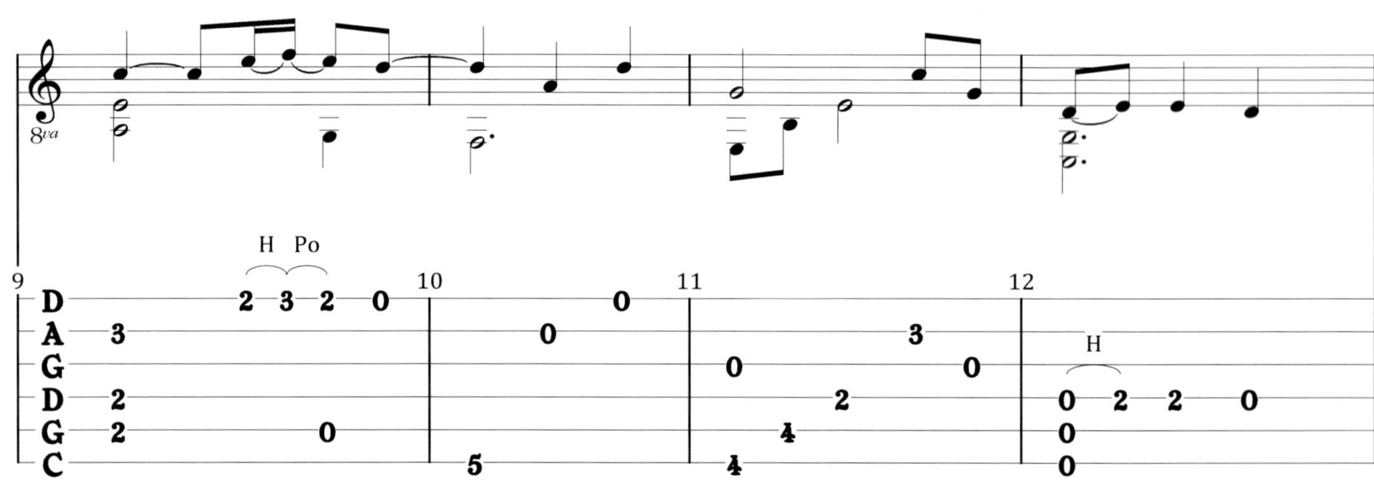

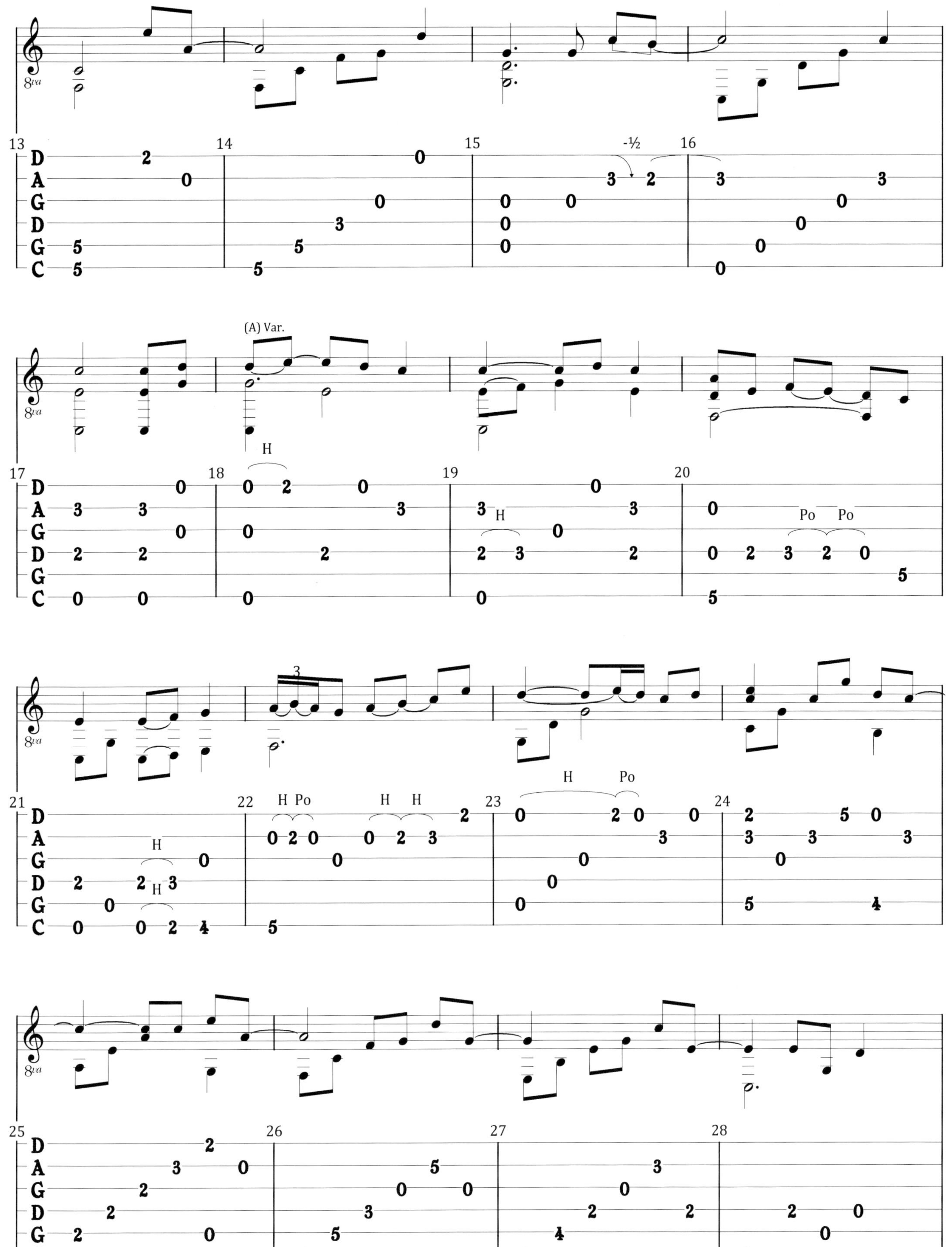
8va
(A) Var.
D
A
G
D
G
C
-½
H
Po

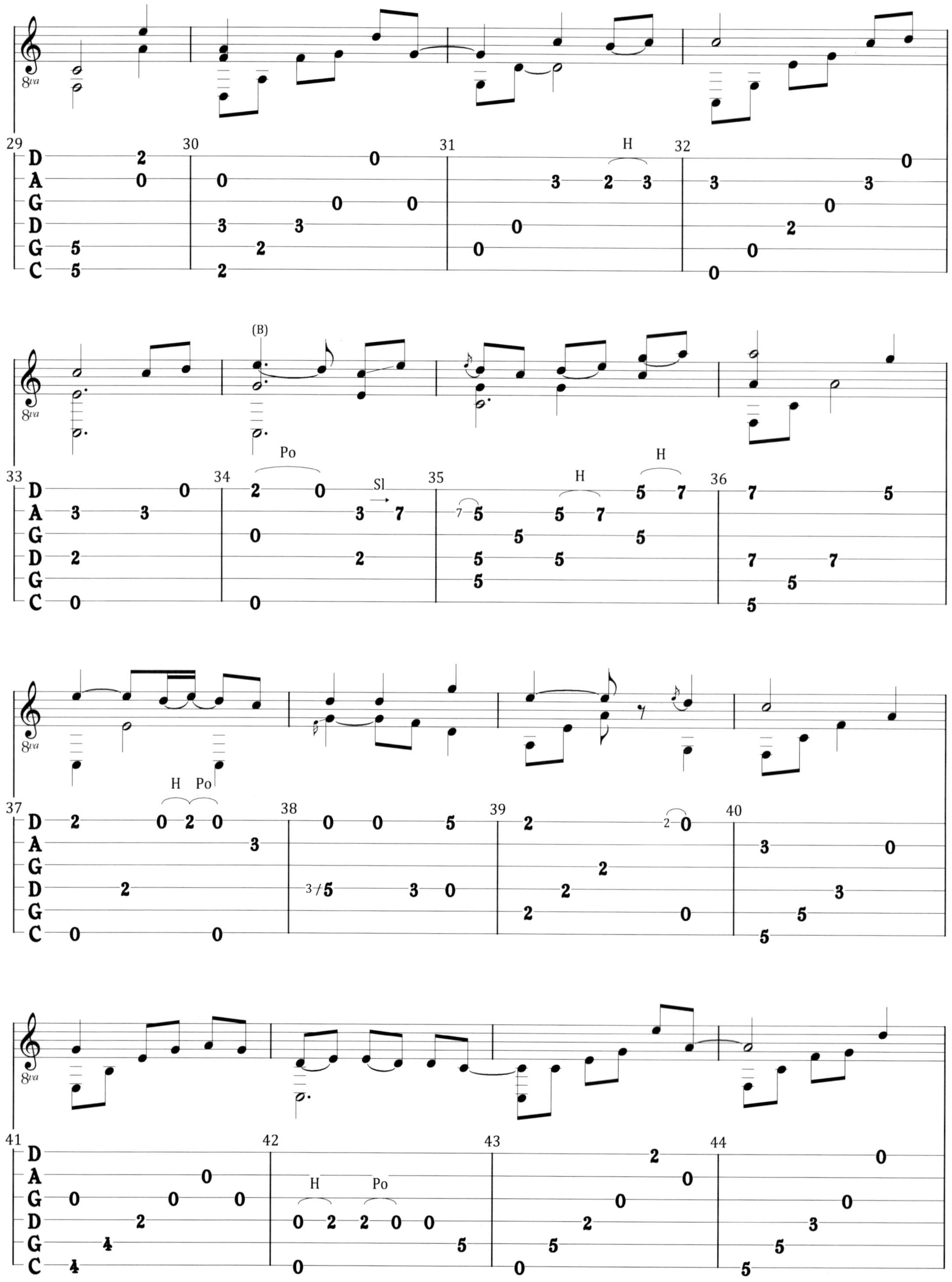
8va
D
A
G
D
G
C
29 30 31 32
H
(B)
Po
Sl
33 34 35 36
H
Po
37 38 39 40
41 42 43 44
H
Po

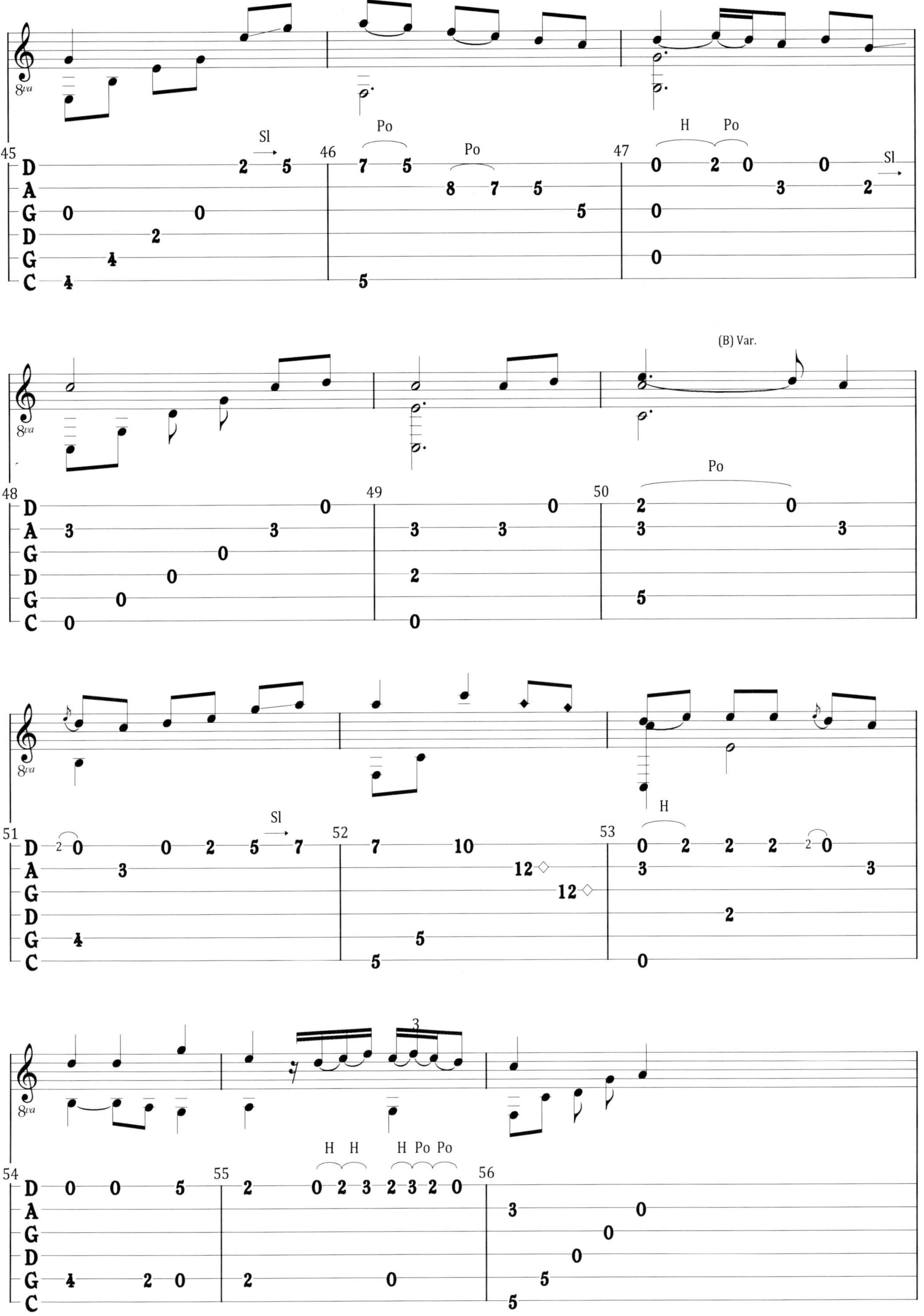
8va
Sl
Po
Po
H Po
Sl
(B) Var.
Po
Sl
H
H H
H Po Po
D
A
G
D
G
C

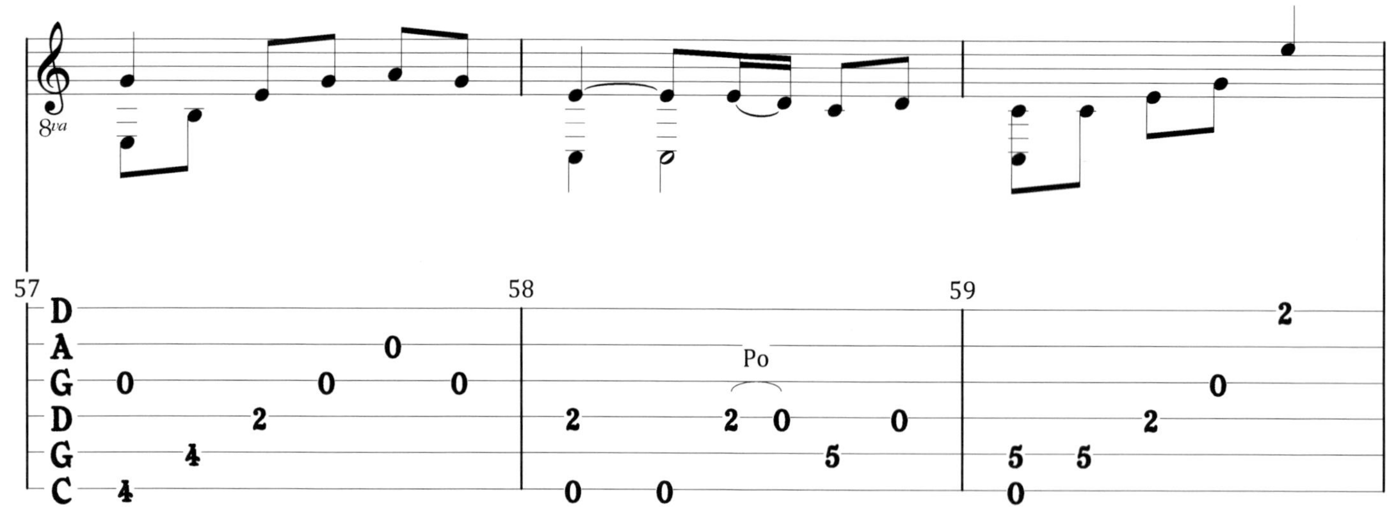
8va
57
58
59
Po
D
A
G
D
G
C

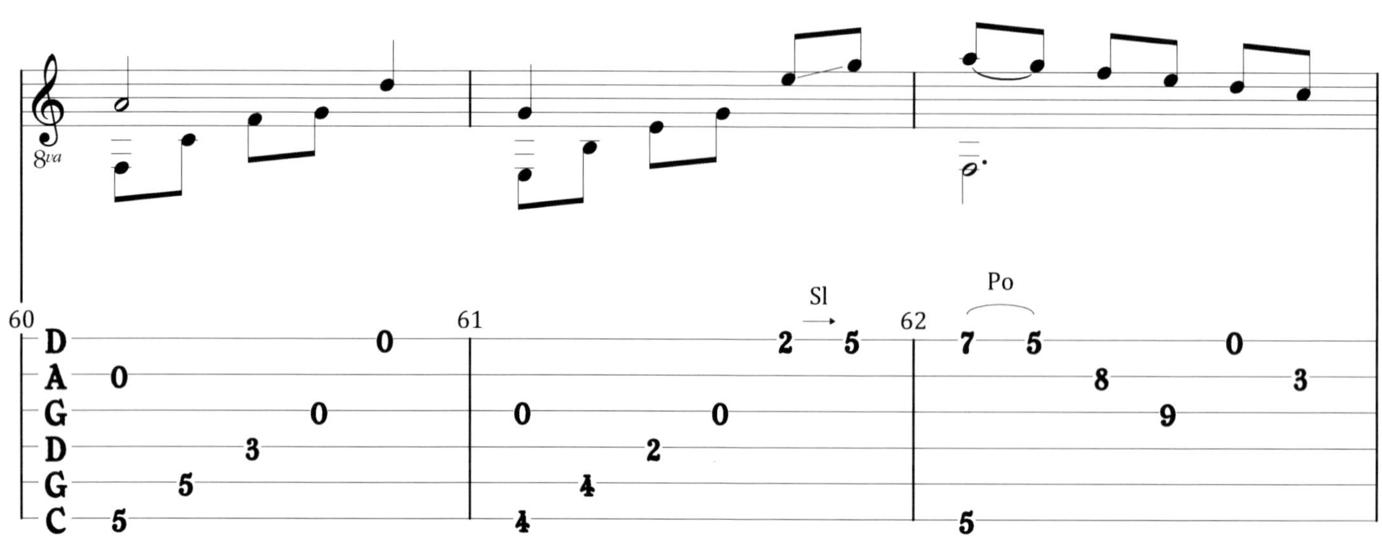
8va
60
61
62
Sl
Po
D
A
G
D
G
C

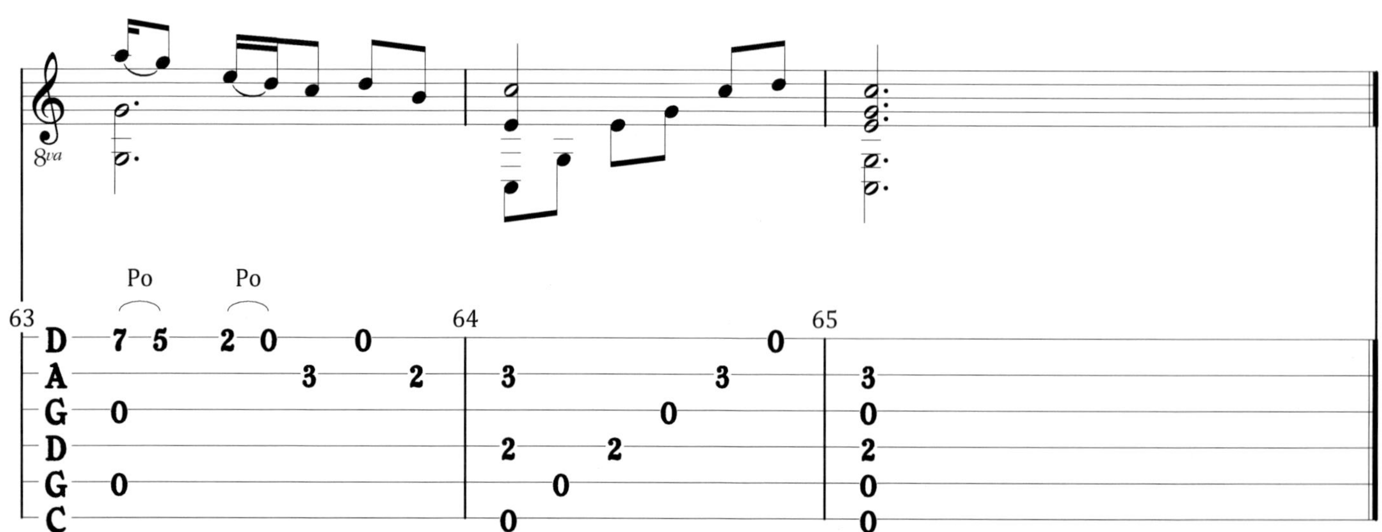
8va
63
64
65
Po
Po
D
A
G
D
G
C

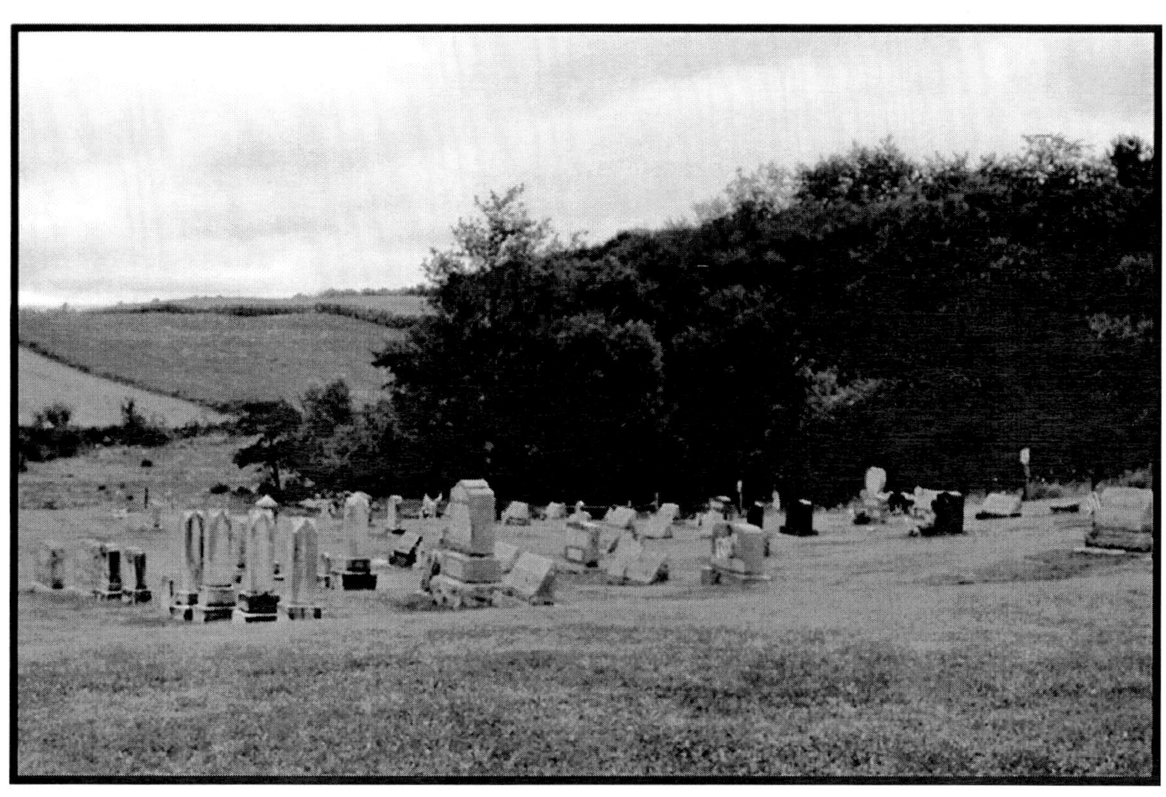

Trinity UCC graveyard, with many of El's relatives, outside of Bedford, PA, USA

Lament For Owen Roe O'Neill

(T. O'Carolan)

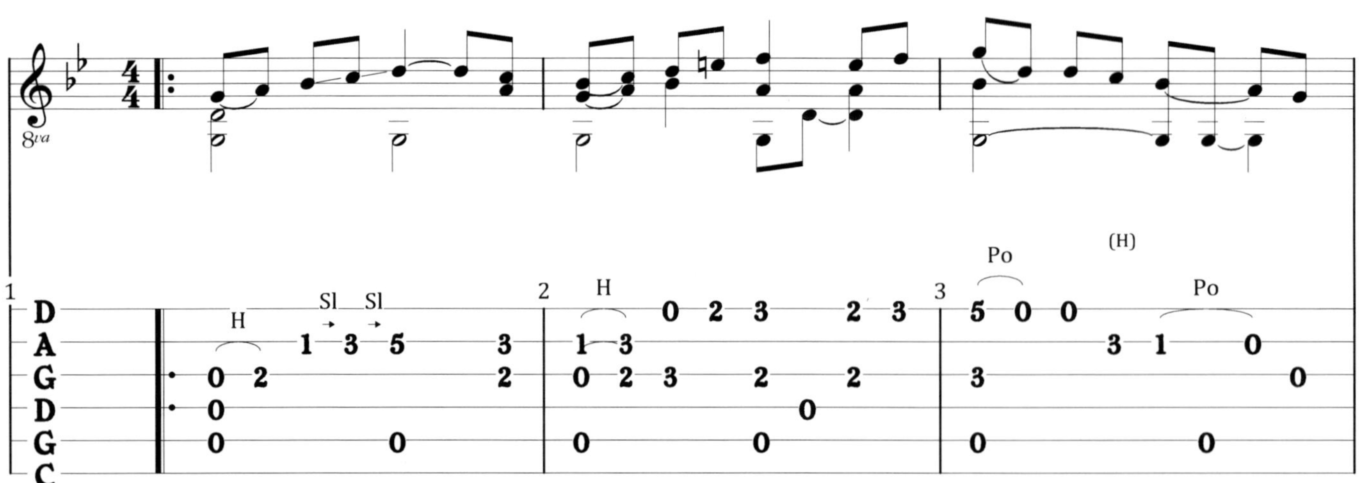

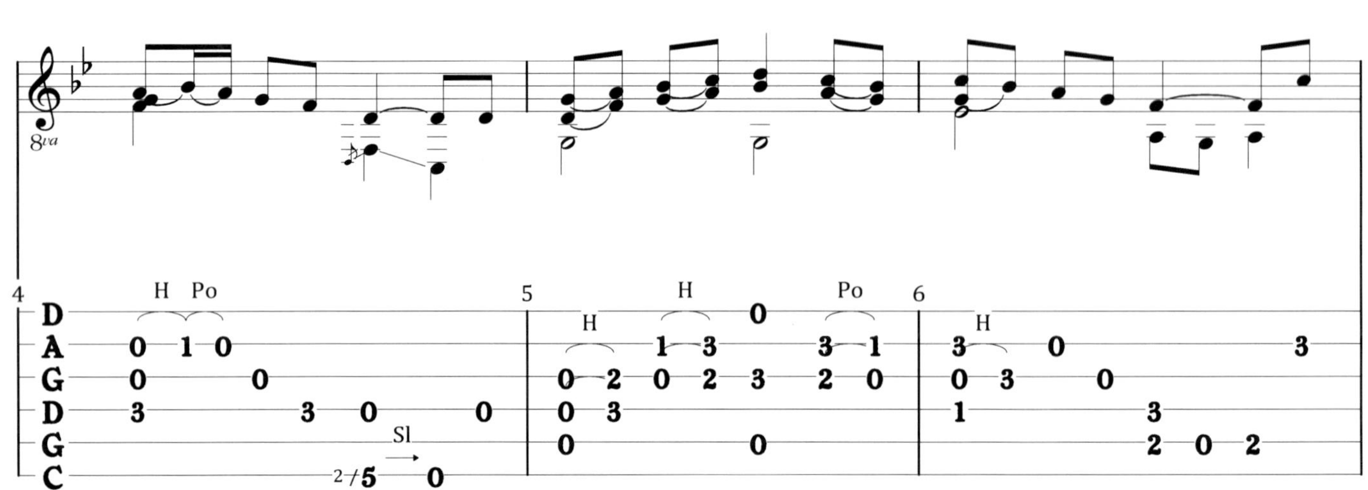

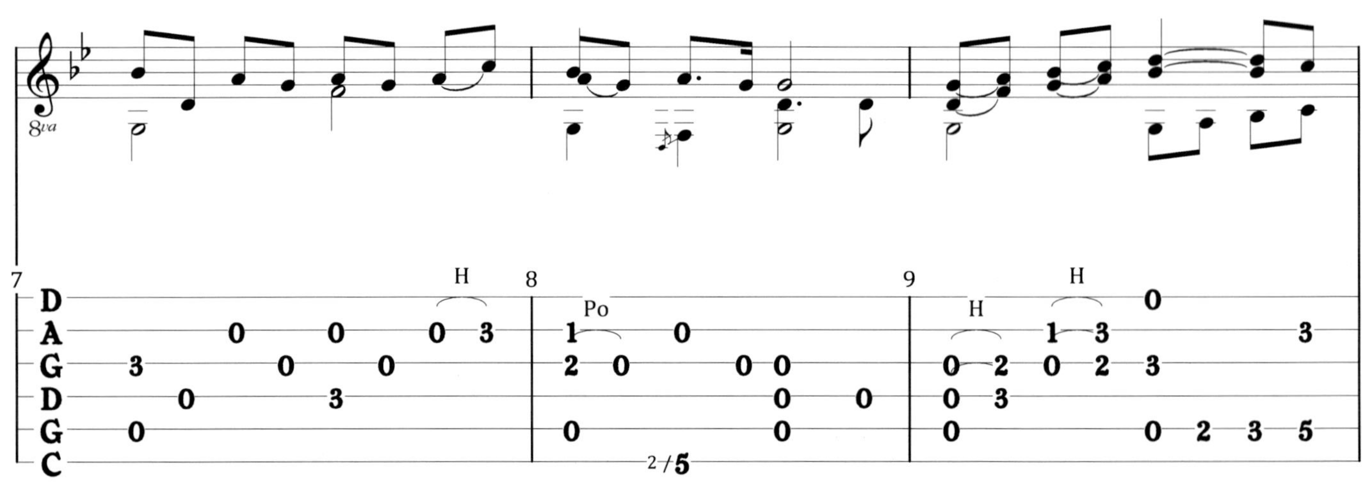

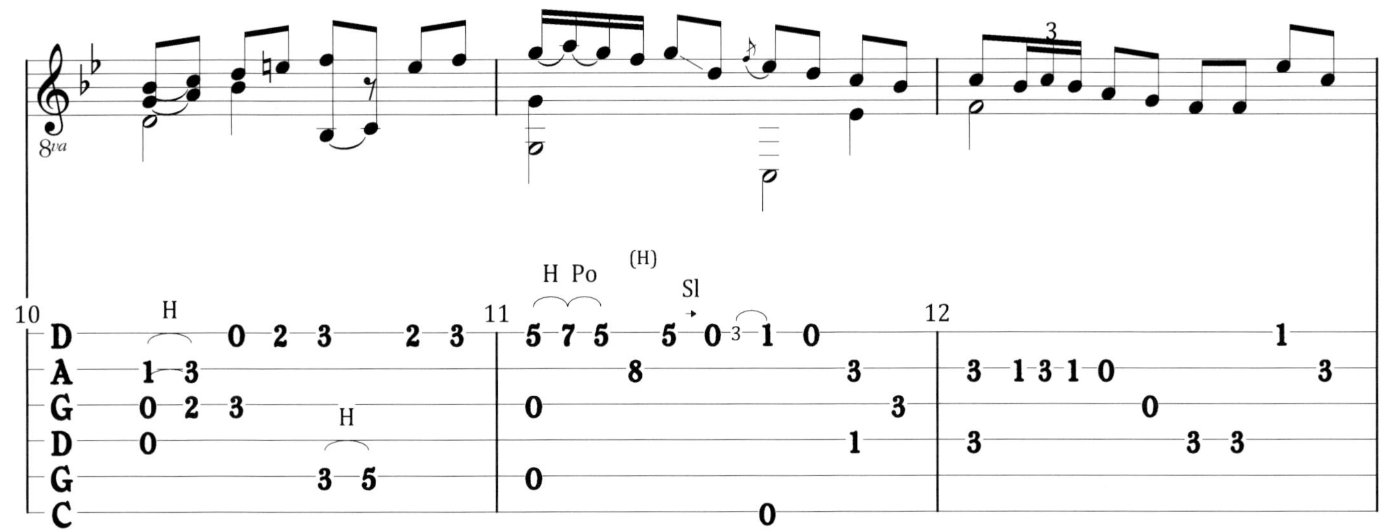

8va
10
11
12
H
H Po
(H)
Sl
D
A
G
D
G
C

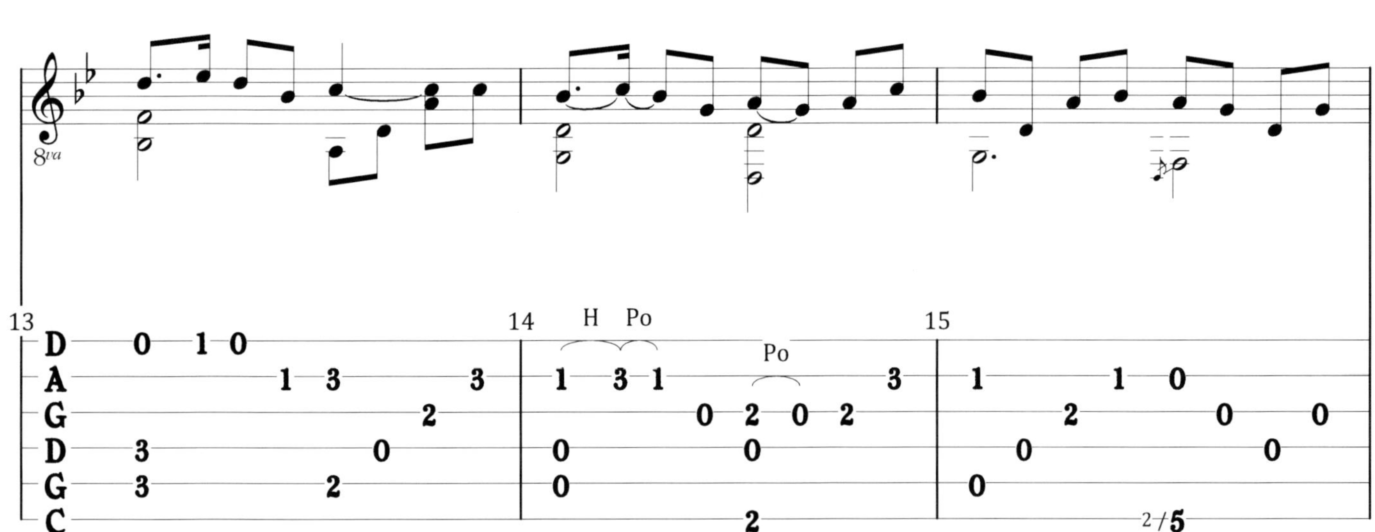

8va
13
14
15
H Po
Po
D
A
G
D
G
C

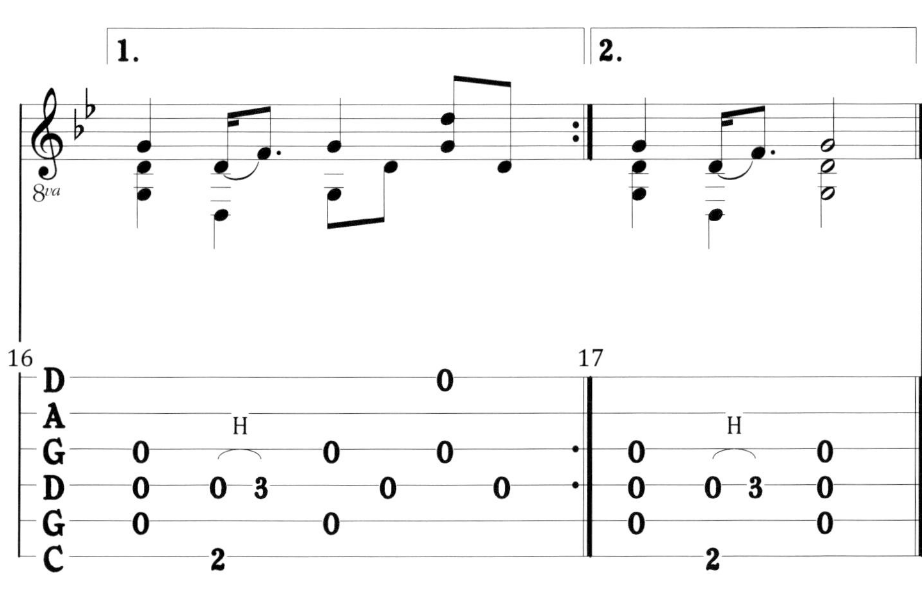

1.
2.
8va
16
17
H
H
D
A
G
D
G
C

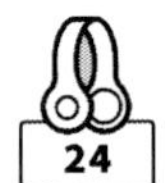

The Mist-Covered Mountains of Home

(Traditional)

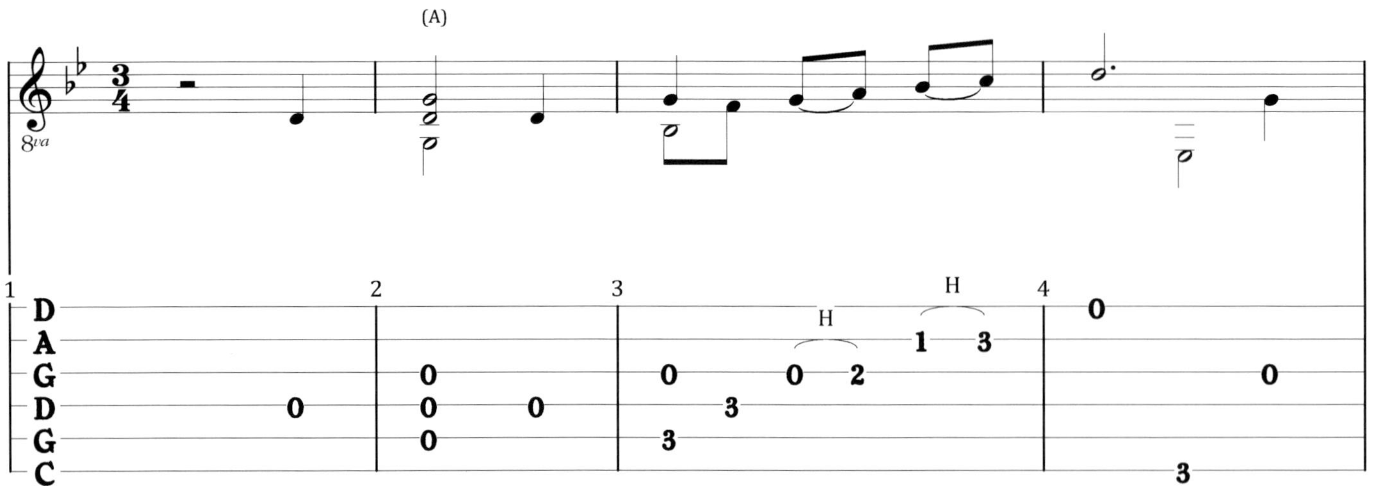

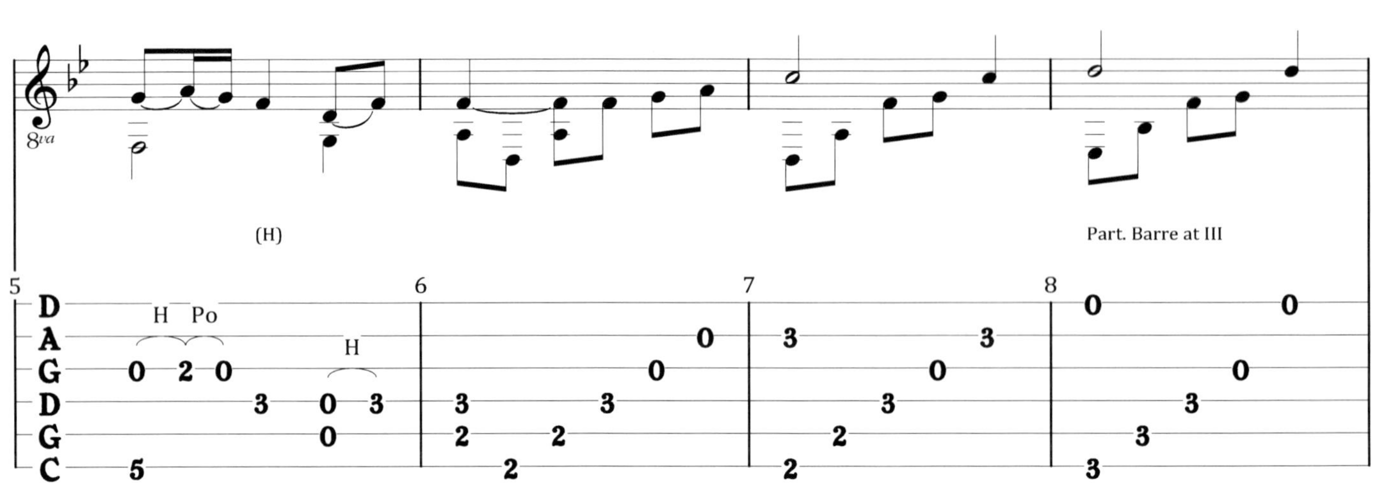

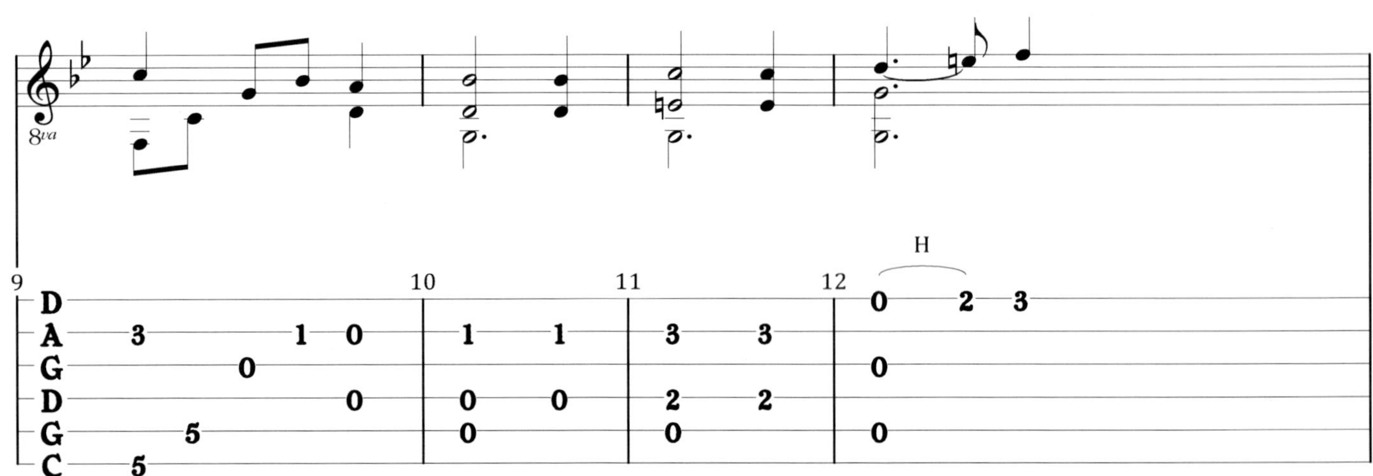

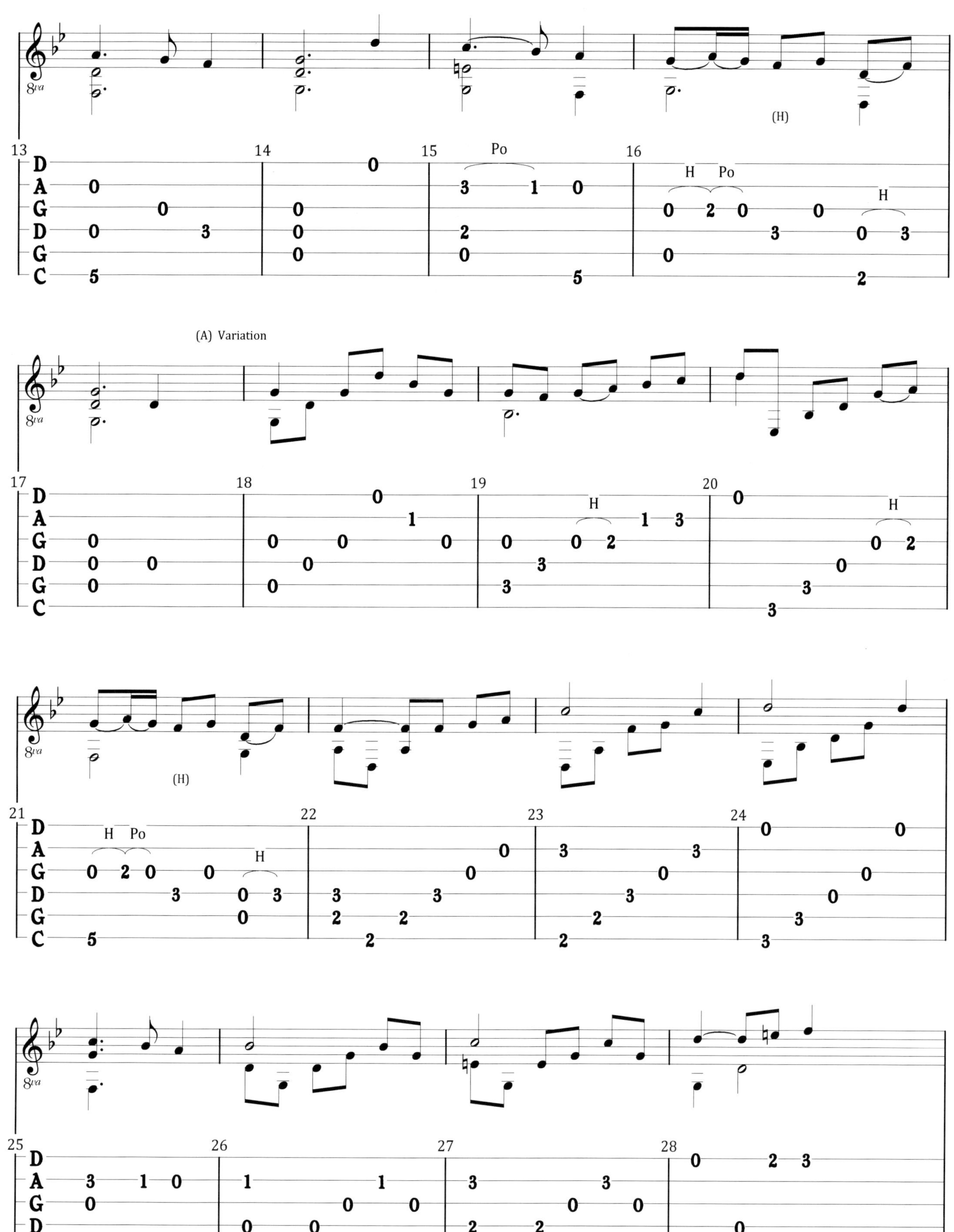
8va
(H)
13
14
15
16
Po
H
Po
H
D
A
G
D
G
C
(A) Variation
17
18
19
20
21
22
23
24
25
26
27
28

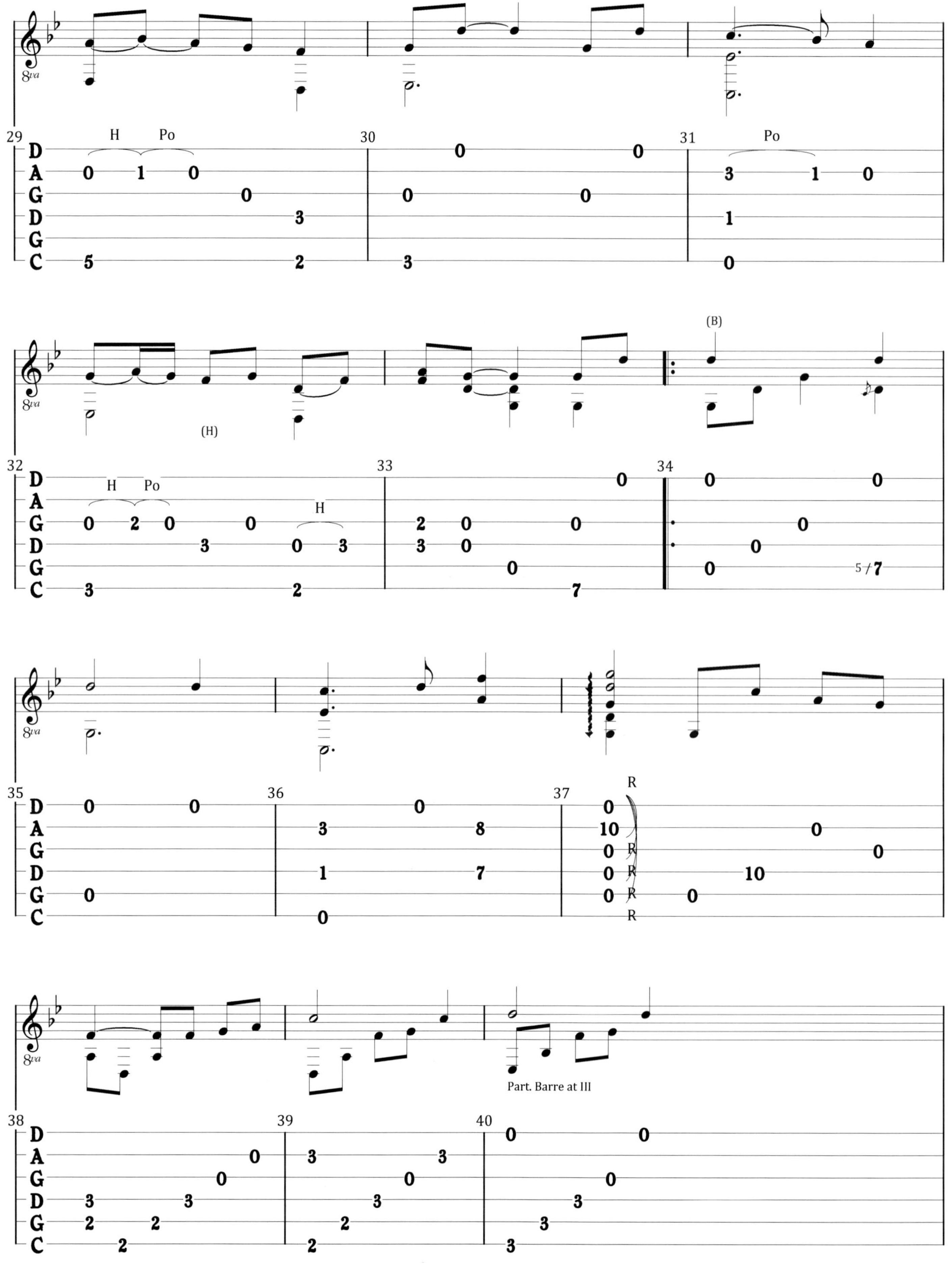
H Po
Po
H Po
H
(H)
(B)
R
Part. Barre at III

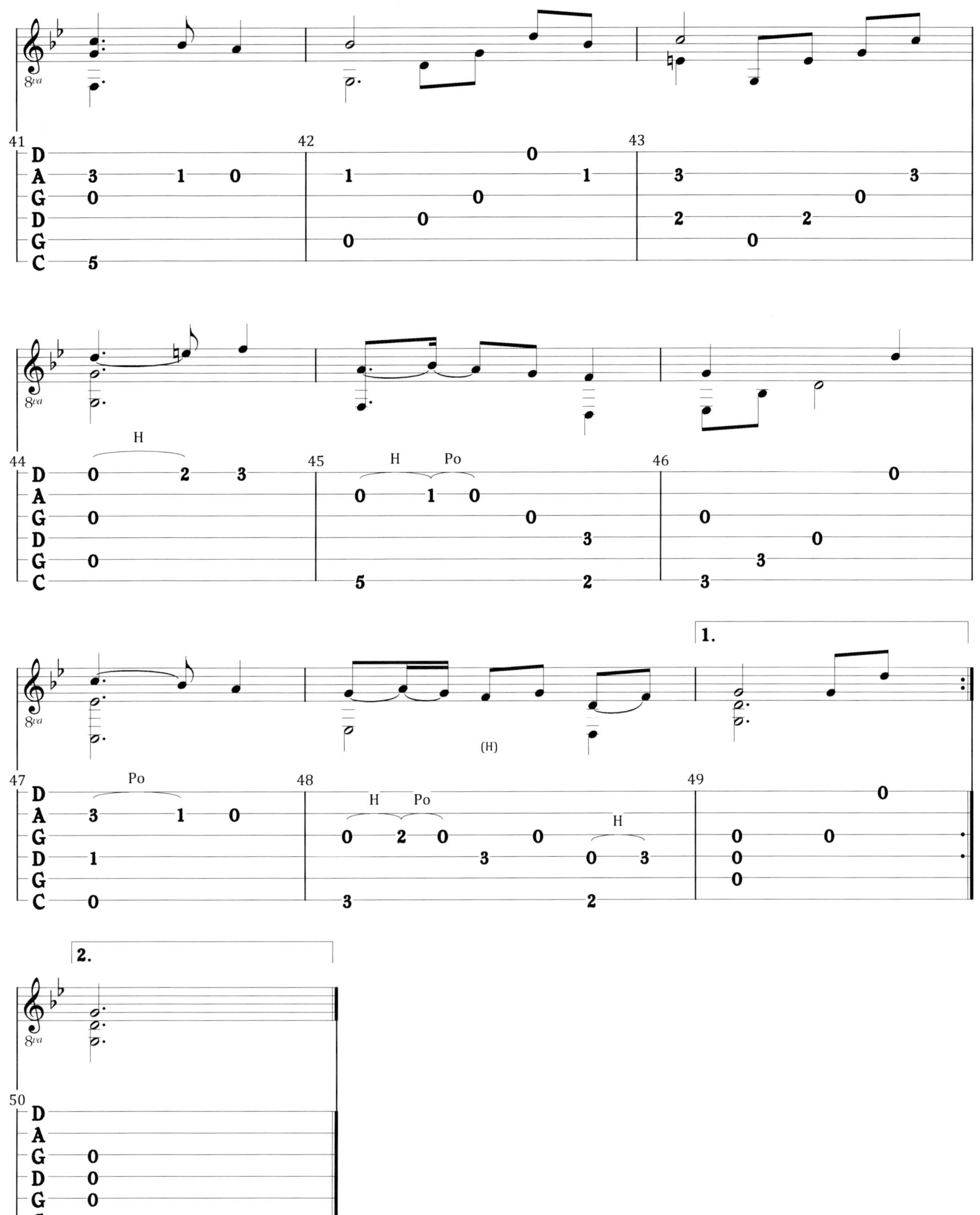
8va
41
42
43
D
A
G
D
G
C
H
Po
44
45
46
47
48
49
(H)
1.
2.
50

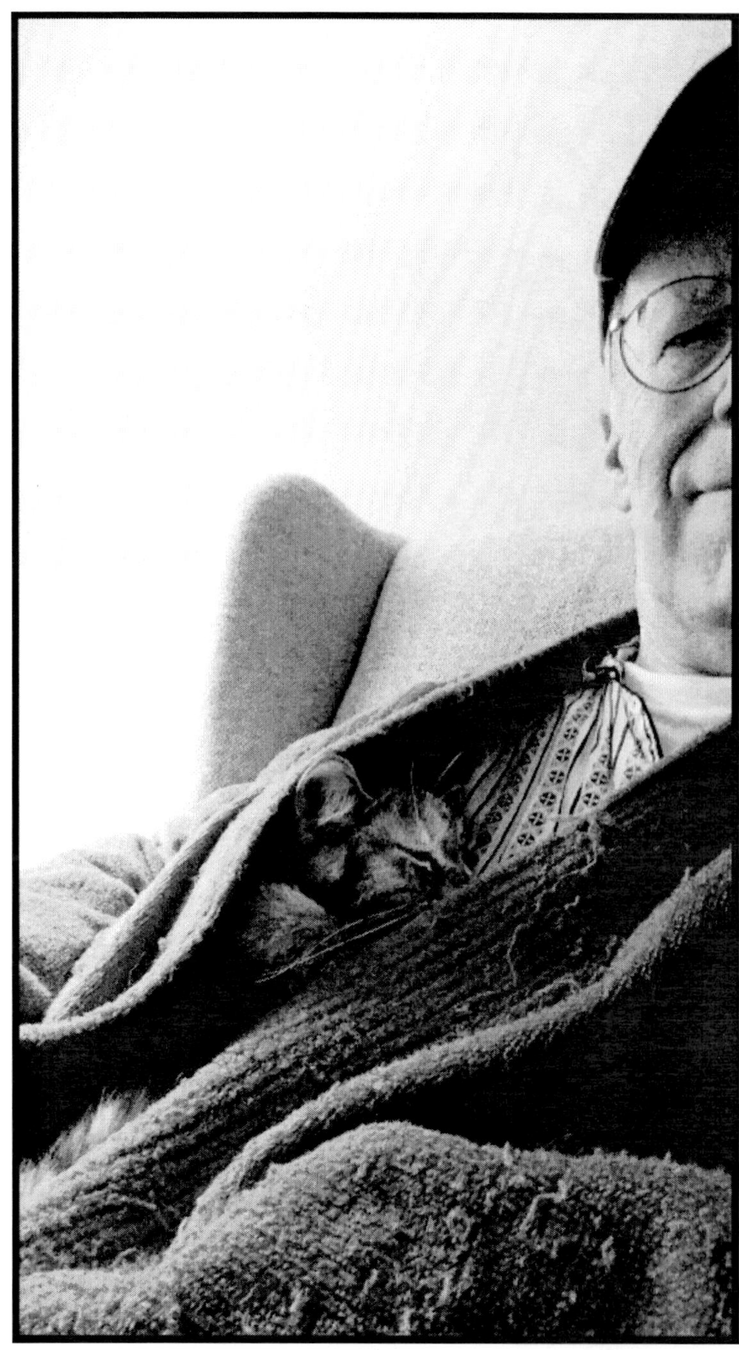

El and Millie McMeen, all warm and cozy

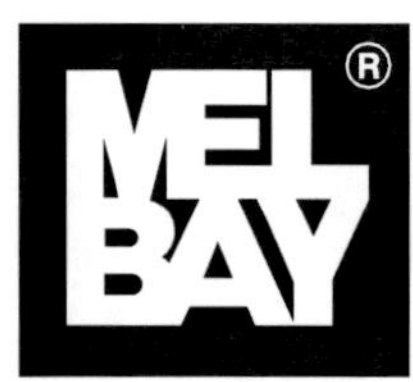